DOOM
PATTERNS

DOOM
PATTERNS

**Latinx Speculations
and the Aesthetics of Violence**   Maia Gil'Adí

Duke University Press   *Durham and London*   2025

Printed in the United States of America on acid-free paper ∞
Project Editor: Ihsan Taylor
Designed by Courtney Leigh Richardson
Typeset in Garamond Premier Pro and Flama by Westchester Publishing Services

Library of Congress Cataloging-in-Publication Data
Names: Gil'Adí, Maia, [date] author.
Title: Doom patterns : Latinx speculations and the aesthetics of violence /
Maia Gil'Adí.
Description: Durham : Duke University Press, 2025. | Includes bibliographical
references and index.
Identifiers: LCCN 2024017811 (print)
LCCN 2024017812 (ebook)
ISBN 9781478031208 (paperback)
ISBN 9781478026983 (hardcover)
ISBN 9781478060185 (ebook)
Subjects: LCSH: Speculative fiction—History and criticism. | Speculative fiction,
American—History and criticism. | American fiction—Hispanic American
authors—History and criticism. | Latin American fiction—History and criticism. |
Violence in literature. | Latin Americans—Ethnic identity. | Hispanic Americans—
Ethnic identity. | BISAC: LITERARY CRITICISM / General | SOCIAL SCIENCE /
Ethnic Studies / American / Hispanic American Studies
Classification: LCC PN3448.S64 G54 2025 (print) | LCC PN3448.S64 (ebook) |
DDC 813/.08762—dc23/eng/20240921
LC record available at https://lccn.loc.gov/2024017811
LC ebook record available at https://lccn.loc.gov/2024017812

Cover art: Ilana Savdie, *The Husband Stitch*, 2022. Oil, acrylic, and beeswax on
canvas. Photo: Lance Brewer.

Para mi familia, DANIEL, PATRICIA, YAEL.

Que afortunada soy.

After great pain, a formal feeling comes—
—Emily Dickinson, "372"

This is how one pictures the angel of history. His face is turned toward the past. Where we perceive a chain of events, he sees one single catastrophe which keeps piling wreckage and hurls it in front of his feet. The angel would like to stay, awaken the dead, and make whole what has been smashed. But a storm is blowing in from Paradise; it has got caught in his wings with such a violence that the angel can no longer close them. The storm irresistibly propels him into the future to which his back is turned, while the pile of debris before him grows skyward. This storm is what we call progress.
—Walter Benjamin, "Theses on the Philosophy of History"

Contents

Acknowledgments and *Agradecimientos*

This project emerged a decade ago as I was contending with the dissonance that happens when reading books with excessive violence—books that I find disturbing and frustrating yet at times also profoundly moving, or funny, titillating, delightfully grotesque, or aesthetically pleasing. In my graduate work at the George Washington University, I belonged to a supportive community of professors and friends, first and foremost my adviser and mentor, Antonio López. There are not enough words to express my eternal gratitude for Tony's generosity—with his time, intellect, advice. He's the type of mentor I aspire to be, and I know that I and my project are better because of his continued dedication and encouragement. I was also fortunate to have been taught and mentored by Gayle Wald, a source of inspiration and example, always kind, funny, and incisive, pushing my work in new and unexpected ways; Ricardo Ortiz, who continues to show the type of bigheartedness, enthusiasm for the profession, and influence on our changing field that I wish to emulate; and Jim Miller, who's the reason I became an English major in the first place. At GW, I also benefited from the support of Robert McRuer, Holly Dugan, Jennifer Chang, Kavita Daiya, Jennifer James, Elisabeth Anker, Manuel Cuellar, Jennifer Nash, and Jung Yun; and friends like Justin Mann, Lori Brister, Elizabeth Pittman, Molly Lewis, Nedda Mehdizedeh, Haylie Swenson, Megan Black, and Ramzi Fawaz.

At the University of Massachusetts Lowell, my first landing after graduate school, I'm thankful for the support of Jenna Vinson, Rebecca Richards, Kevin Petersen, Matthew Hurwitz, Anthony Szczesiul, Sue Kim, Maggie Dietz, Sandra Lim, Natalie Houston, and Teresa Gonzales. At Boston University, I was welcomed into a vibrant intellectual community and remarkable group of colleagues who offered their support and guidance. Thank you, Anita Patterson, Takeo Rivera, Ianna Hawkins Owen, Micah Goodrich, Amy Appleford, Joseph

Rezek, Erin Murphy, William Howell, Maurice Lee, Robert Chodat, Jack Matthews, Carrie Preston, Anna Henchman, Louis Chude-Sokei, Anita Savo, and Wade Campbell. The decision to leave this community was not an easy one, but I'm thrilled to be joining the Modern Languages and Literatures department at Johns Hopkins University and to participate in the energizing work already taking place in the Program in Latin American, Caribbean, and Latinx Studies (LACLxS). Thank you, William Egginton, Bécquer Seguín, Casey Lurtz, Christy Thornton, Angelina Cotler, Inés Valdez, Gisela Heffes, Marcelo Nogueira, Marina Bedran, Loreto Sánchez Serrano, and Dean Moyar, for making this transition a smooth one and for your warm welcome.

At Duke University Press, Courtney Berger demonstrated her commitment to this project from the start and led me through the review and revision stages expertly. Thank you to her editorial team as well as Duke's readers, whose feedback made this project better. Allison Van Deventer's work as a developmental editor was instrumental in refining this project for publication, as was the feedback from book manuscript workshop readers Catherine Sue Ramírez and Ben Olguín. Emily Maguire's mentorship through the Career Enhancement Fellowship was significant in the revision process and in helping refine my work. I'm indebted to readers who generously gave me feedback through the manuscript's various stages: David Vázquez, Ralph Rodriguez, Cristina Rodriguez, Justin Mann, Renee Hudson, Tommy Conners, Katie Lennard, and Sam Pinto. Sincerest thanks to Ilana Savdie for allowing me to feature *The Husband Stitch* on the cover, and to her studio manager and gallery for their assistance.

A famous novelist once said that getting a first draft done is "like pushing a peanut with your nose across a very dirty floor." I would not have been able to get the peanut off the floor and dusted off without a dynamic and inspiring community. In addition to the textual interlocutors cited in this book and those which animate my work, the discussions that take place within these pages also reflect formal and informal conversations with colleagues in the profoundest sense of the term. I consider myself lucky to be part of the beautiful Latinx studies community, and thankful for the opportunity to learn from a group of scholars who continue to push and influence my work: Tony López, Ricardo Ortiz, Marion Rohrleitner, Tommy Conners, Renee Hudson, Emily Maguire, Elena Machado Sáez, John Ribó, Bill Orchard, Carmen Lamas, John Alba Cutler, Ralph Rodriguez, Randy Ontiveros, Israel Reyes, Joe Miranda, David Vázquez, Jennifer Harford Vargas, Cristina Rodriguez, José Navarro, Kristy Ulibarri, Leticia Alvarado, Ariana Vigil, Ylce Irizarry, Albert Laguna, Josh Guzmán, and Cat Ramírez.

To all my friends, near and far, mil gracias. Justin Mann has read my work since grad school, and every conversation with him makes my work better; I continue to be grateful for his friendship, encouragement, collaboration, and support; a superhero through-and-through. Since meeting Renee Hudson at the Latinx Studies Association conference, I've valued coming up in the field together, learning from her, collaborating, and, most of all, gossiping and always having each other's backs. Working at my dining-room table with Tommy Conners, Katie Lennard, and Isabel Gómez was a joy and kept me going even with all the bochinche; Katie's time in Boston was too short, but I'm so grateful for all the wine-time porch hangs while she was here. The conversations, lunches, Zooms with Tommy Conners are not only fun but always energizing and heartening for me and my work; un pancito de dios. In the writing taco room, thank you to Justin Mann, Michelle Huang, Doug Ishii, Chris Eng, Cheryl Naruse, Lakshmi Padmanabhan, Keva Baui, and Francisco Robles. Saying goodbye to Washington, DC, after almost two decades was difficult, and I didn't know what to expect in Boston. Being an academic means that your people are spread all over the world, but I'm lucky to have been welcomed into communities that continue to cheerlead me along the way: Colt VanWinkle, Abby Neumayer, Cristina Rodriguez, Lelsey Offrichter, Bryan Hollingsworth, Andrea O'Meara, Jimmy Pitts, Jefferson Grau, Tara Molloy, Kristen Hoskins, Ben Shone, Jamie and Ben Wood, Sam Lyons, Isabel Gómez, Natali Diaz, Jenna Vinson, Kevin Petersen, Rebecca Richards, Dana Carlson, Elliott Wren, Michelle Geizman, Indira Mata, Sean Cavanaugh, Phillip and Amanda McLamb. I'm always grateful to Jenny Molberg, my mom and best friend, the last one standing, the one to give you the best laugh, always ready for a musical number, una flor entre las flores. Thank you to the strong and opinionated women who helped me find my own voice: Mami, Maxine Margolies, Luciana Bubola, and Miriam Otamendi.

This book is for my mom, dad, and sister. Que afortunada soy de tenerlos como familia. I owe it all to them. This book is also for Jeff. I feel infinitely lucky to have met you and am grateful for the life we've built together. I continue to be inspired by your curiosity, ambition, bounteous spirit, and capacity to grow. You've been a mainstay and reprieve these past few years of writing. Thank you for loving me so.

*   *   *

This book has benefited from the support of a six-month Career Enhancement Fellowship from the Institute for Citizens and Scholars (formerly the Woodrow Wilson Foundation), the New England Consortium of Latinx Studies (NECLS), the Mahindra Center at Harvard University, and the National Humanities Center (NHC).

INTRODUCTION

The Reading Protocols of
Latinx Speculative Fiction

The July 12, 2020, issue of the *New York Times Magazine* featured "The Decameron Project." Released during the first summer of the COVID-19 pandemic, the collection took the world-altering events as the impetus to consider the role of fiction in mediating our relationship to and understanding of the violent, traumatic, and fearful present. The project's subheading, written in chunky white letters, read, "When reality is surreal, only fiction can make sense of it." "The Decameron Project" presented reflections on the pandemic from twenty-nine writers from across the globe, concluding that fiction is not just one way but "the best way" to process grief and fear.[1]

The project's introductory essay, written by novelist Rivka Galchen, asks an old but still weighty question: "When there's a radical and true and important story happening at every moment, why turn to imagined tales?"[2] This is a question that *The Decameron* (composed between 1349 and 1353) famously poses, as it offers its readers escapist stories that take them out of the plague-stricken city of Florence but ultimately return both characters and readers to what they had attempted to flee.[3] In this book, I reframe Galchen's question in a way I think is especially salient for people of color and minoritized subjects: Why do readers continue to turn to fiction that speculatively reimagines the historical past in all its violence and trauma? To put it another way: When violence is happening at every moment, why turn to speculative fiction?

Doom Patterns: Latinx Speculations and the Aesthetics of Violence proposes that the tropes of speculative fiction—the capacious term for genres that include anything from science fiction, fantasy, cyberpunk, and utopian, dystopian, and apocalyptic fiction to horror, alternative histories, and supernatural fiction and their vast array of subgenres—offer a singular and meaningful lens through which to examine historical violence and trauma, as well as their persistent haunting of the present. Through this lens, violence and trauma appear otherworldly. Consider, for instance, Michael Zapata's *The Lost Book of Adana Moreau* (2020), which, like *The Decameron*, centers disaster, attempts to escape disaster, and disaster's inevitable return. The novel tells the story of Adana Moreau, who leaves the Dominican Republic after the island's occupation by US forces in 1916. After marrying "the Pirate," she settles in New Orleans, has a child named Maxwell, and writes a science fiction novel titled *The Lost World*. Upon falling ill, Adana destroys the manuscript of the novel's sequel, *A Model Earth*, and then dies. Decades later, in Chicago, Saul Drower is cleaning his late grandfather's apartment when he discovers this "lost" manuscript and embarks on a journey to return it to Maxwell, tracking him down in New Orleans just as Hurricane Katrina strikes the city.[4] *The Lost Book* reimagines several moments of historical trauma and cataclysm through the lens of science fiction, considering the effects of events such as the American occupation of the Dominican Republic (1916–24), the Bolshevik Revolution (1917), the Israeli-Palestinian conflict (1947–), the dictatorship of Augusto Pinochet and the thousands of "disappeared" during his regime (1973–90), Argentina's Dirty War (1976–83), and Hurricane Katrina (2005). These events are portrayed as part of a global network of unending violence with a deep influence on the present.

Before her death, Maxwell sits by Adana's bed as she describes the Dominican Republic and the islands of the Antilles, "which had been a stage setting for the Americas."[5] She also tells Maxwell that "beyond history or the mistakes of men, beyond time, which was a great and clever thief, beyond all of that, at the edge of the universe or maybe at the start and end of the universe, there was a soft murmur, a constant breath of beauty, a truth."[6] Adana presents time and history as forces in constant formation and deformation, a simultaneous creation and destruction that assembles an ungraspable record. However, she argues, beyond these elements there is a beautiful truth. We never see this truth but glimpse faint traces of it as the novel navigates its various spaces and histories of disaster. Although *The Lost Book* is not technically speculative fiction, as everything that happens in its main plot could also happen in a "realist" novel, it uses the tropes and reading protocols of the genre to contend with the paradox of finding pleasure in historical violence and trauma.[7] The science fiction book-within-the-book foregrounds a speculative orientation that reveals the otherworldly nature of Latinx histories and identity formations and, most importantly, paints a vast global network centered on the otherworldly to help us think about the formation of race, ethnicity, and national belonging beyond our entrenched notions of *latinidad*.

Decades after Adana's death, as Saul and his friend Javier look for Maxwell, they meditate on the effects of history and the possibility of encapsulating them in language. Sitting in the wreckage of New Orleans after Hurricane Katrina, the two men talk about Javier's work as an investigative journalist and his *"yearning for disaster."*[8] Disaster, Saul concludes, is the "infrastructure of the world," and it entices us to seek it out. In this reflection, he turns to writers of science fiction—"Isaac Asimov, Samuel R. Delany, Ursula K. Le Guin, William Gibson, and, now, even Adana Moreau"—as the "modern-day harbingers of disaster."[9] Saul and Javier finally point to the role of the reader in the propagation of disaster: "We are complicit in creating audiences with powerful addictions to disaster, to fear, self-righteousness, outrage, and vitriol."[10]

The juxtaposition of catastrophe with the pleasurable and fantastical worlds of science fiction is central to *Doom Patterns*. This book is about violence. Specifically, it puts the portrayal of violence in prose fiction into conversation with aesthetic pleasure as two forms of figuration that participate in the production of Latinx, multiethnic, and diasporic literature. To establish a dialogue between these two ostensibly incongruous forms, I use the methodologies of Latinx speculative fiction, which has taught me to read for elements in the text that lie hidden and to identify the excessive in what passes as mundane. The global literary networks built across the Caribbean, the American hemisphere, and beyond in *The Lost Book* point to a long history of violence that demands speculative fiction as a paradigm for reading this archive. They simultaneously signal the cyclical nature of violence in the Americas and the paradoxical readerly pleasure generated by fictional accounts of violence. The *"yearning for disaster"* and "addictions to disaster" of *The Lost Book* raise two central questions for *Doom Patterns*: How can the history of violence in the Americas be rendered in language? And how can these depictions of historical violence be paradoxically pleasurable as well?

Doom Patterns takes as its premise that speculative fiction offers an essential vector for an examination of violence in Latinx, multiethnic, and diasporic writing. Speculative fiction crystallizes the otherworldly violence that forms and informs Latinx and other minoritized subjectivities. This book asks us to consider how the reading protocols of Latinx speculative fiction can illuminate elements in a text that otherwise would be difficult to recognize. At the same time, it offers a new lens for reading speculative fiction and a speculative lens for reading violence.

Examining the connection between portrayals of violence and speculative narrative form, this book shows how destruction is unearthed through what I call *doom patterns*, textual forms and narrative strategies such as thematic repetition, nonlinear narration, character fragmentation, unresolved plots, tropes, and archetypes that, in these literatures, consistently return readers to instances of destruction. Although this study is not comprehensive, doom patterns serve as a useful hermeneutic for thinking about depictions of violence across multiethnic literatures and the use of literary tropes in this archive and beyond. The powerful appeal of such doom patterns lies in their ability to establish alternative worlds or "elsewheres" in stories of colonization, slavery, and the trauma of US migration.[11] These worlds offer more capacious understandings of "minority literature"—a literature that is often read as emphasizing upward mobility and the celebration of hybridity—by revealing how imperial, racial, and ethno-national violence continually manifests itself in the present.[12]

This book is also about pleasure—pleasure in language, in reading, and, yes, in violence. Even as these doom patterns signal horrific violence, they unexpectedly feature many forms of pleasure: humor, narrative beauty, enticing plots, *rasquachismo*, inter/intratextual references, and sexual titillation.[13] I am interested in the paradox of portraying violence and historical trauma in modes that are aesthetically pleasing for public consumption and that continue to be rewarded in the literary market, academy, and literary prize circuit. At the heart of this study is the question of how we make sense of the apparent contradiction of portraying violence, destruction, pain, and trauma in narrative modes that elicit pleasure, awe, and enjoyment.

Reading through the lens of Latinx speculative fiction showcases how the past and various forms of historical trauma are reimagined, and how these reimaginings paradoxically offer the possibility of taking pleasure in reading about the end of the world. This book examines how minoritized subjectivity is constructed through repeating forms of violence—a hemispheric network built around the cyclical remnants of historical trauma that become manifest in a text. *Doom Patterns* also develops a new way of thinking about the speculative by illustrating how excessive modes of narration reveal that ostensibly mundane violence is in fact otherworldly. Violence and speculative fiction offer an opportunity to investigate race, ethnicity, identity formations, and national belonging. The attempt to represent historical violence and trauma illustrates the impossibility of encapsulating this type of excess in language, triggering the text to break into doom patterns that cause the narrative to reproduce the violence it is trying to tell.

In this book, I approach Latinx speculative fiction as a paradigm for reading not in Latinx studies but *through* it. I read novels by Latinx authors that overtly signal *latinidad*: Cristina García's *Dreaming in Cuban* (1992) and Junot Díaz's *The Brief Wondrous Life of Oscar Wao* (2007). Although neither of these novels is typically classified as speculative fiction, I show how they exhibit the otherworldly, fantastical, and horrific through their representations of historical violence. I also analyze the Black American author Colson Whitehead's *Zone One* (2011) and the Asian American author Sesshu Foster's *Atomik Aztex* (2005). Both of these authors use tropes of genre fiction such as the zombie, time travel, and alternate histories, crystallizing matters of race and ethnicity through historical violence while also troubling the construction of literary fields based on identity. I examine the Latin American author Roberto Bolaño's *2666* (Spanish 2004, English 2008) to further destabilize definitions of *latinidad* while considering what the "hemispheric turn" in Latinx and American studies has meant for the analysis of literature that centralizes the United States in a hemispheric context.[14] Finally, I turn to the work of authors whom I read as Latinx even though they make no overt refence to *latinidad*—Carmen Maria Machado's *Her Body and Other Parties* (2017) and Hernan Diaz's *In the Distance* (2017). With this heterogeneous archive, I show not only how *latinidad* can be read within aesthetics and form but also how the reading protocols of Latinx speculative fiction illuminate global thematic literary networks around violence and the pleasure of its aesthetic representation.

My unruly archive emphasizes the forms of violence that are discursively shaped in the texts considered here and their significance in the creation of *latinidad* and multiethnic diasporic subjectivity. *Speculative fiction* is the most appropriate umbrella term for this work, one that allows me to include a wide variety of texts that might not otherwise be read together. The works in this assemblage rewrite colonial, imperial, and gendered historical violence. Most of them invoke conditions that run counter to existing epistemological possibilities (time travel, fat-ghosts, zombies) while also evoking real things that should be impossible (femicides, enslavement, dictatorship, rape). In part, *Doom Patterns* argues that when we look at these elements side by side, we can discern that distinctive forms of violence in the present are haunting continuations of other histories, which in their repetition and excess become otherworldly. In effect, *Doom Patterns* redefines Latinx speculative fiction as a literary genre that, through its presentation of excess, offers an important paradigm for reading that shows how particular types of violence are otherworldly in nature.

Each chapter in *Doom Patterns* uses the reading protocols of Latinx literature and speculative fiction to expand both categories. As each chapter progresses, an unraveling of form, ethnicity, and race takes place, asking readers to look back to what came before—in terms of the chapters themselves but also outside the book and toward the histories and literatures that they invoke. I propose that when we read these works together, newly expansive notions of the speculative, race and ethnicity, and renderings of violence in literature can emerge. Moving from individual subject positions, *Doom Patterns* turns to the collective and relational, showcasing systemic forms of violence throughout various spaces, from the United States to the Caribbean to the US-Mexico border and beyond, exposing a vast thematic literary network and expanding well-established areas within Latinx studies. Each chapter is concerned with the remnants of history that record the many forms of violence that have been enacted on the landscape, the individual subject, and the community. The chapters move between conventional genre fiction and texts that exhibit the speculative through their excessive narrative forms and descriptions of violence. Through this movement, readers will grasp how the reading protocols of Latinx speculative fiction can produce new understandings of texts usually defined as realist. By the end of *Doom Patterns*, we will have returned full circle, or full circle in another dimension, to a speculative estrangement of *latinidad*. We will revisit the individual body, this time even further removed from established notions of Latinx subjectivity—an exercise that pushes the reading protocols of Latinx speculative fiction to their limit. This conclusion once again highlights networks of exchange and connected histories in and outside literature while questioning canon formations, definitions of genre, and modes of reading. The progression of this book's chapters performs the type of inquiry that I anticipate occurring more frequently in Latinx and multiethnic literary fields: a dismantling of generic boundaries and entrenched definitions of race, ethnicity, and nationhood that allows for a capacious understanding of interrelated thematic networks and histories.

What does this new paradigm for reading mean for Latinx literature or speculative fiction? One answer is that it may help illuminate the ubiquity of violence in literature by writers who hail from different hemispheres and write in a variety of languages. The reading protocols of Latinx speculative fiction put this violence into relief by inviting us to examine the work of authors irrespective of their identities or the ways their work has been classified in the market. This methodology allows us to incorporate, for example, a writer like Bolaño within current understandings of Latinx literature by showing how his work participates in discourses of the border without belonging to the border itself, as my third chapter shows, or to see how depictions of sugar in a canonical Cuban American novel and Black American novel suggest that the violence of sugar's historical production veers dangerously close to horror, as I show in chapter 2. By reading through these lenses, we see not only the texts' doom patterns but also the significance of Latinx speculative fiction as a reading method.

Another answer can be found in the paradoxical conjunction of violence and pleasure that these texts display, which suggests critical reading practices that refuse the expectation of political remedy in Latinx and multiethnic literary studies. *Doom Patterns* is, in fact, as interested in breaking apart strict identity and field formations as it is in questioning the ethical imperative and the associated reading protocols in literary studies. Throughout this book, I ask, What happens when we do not require minoritized literature to be solely about identity formations, citizenship, exile, assimilation—in short, all the things typically ascribed to this literature? What can we learn about the formation of ethnicity, race, nationhood, and violence (and the formation of these categories *in* and *through* violence) by reading against the grain and putting books in uncomfortable juxtaposition with each other? In fact, the readers of this book should expect to be uncomfortable, not only with these pairings, but also with the violence these texts depict. Uncomfortable but also (I hope) intrigued, excited, and even pleased.

Latinx Speculative Fiction as a Reading Praxis

Latinx literary critics have begun to forge innovative and meaningful connections in Latinx literature across ethnic, national, and temporal boundaries.[15] I am motivated by the galvanizing possibility of connections among Latinx literary production, diasporic multiethnic literature, and criticism outside this field, such as Black and Caribbean studies, queer theory and disability studies, and speculative fiction studies. Accordingly, I have attempted to strengthen these links in the chapters that follow, drawing not only on Latinx studies and Latinx literary criticism but also on the work of anthropologists, geographers, political scientists, sociologists, Black studies and Asian American studies scholars, posthumanists, and queer theorists. With this extensive group of interlocutors, I have tried to expand the interdisciplinary possibilities available to literary scholars while also highlighting the networks of violence and pleasure that my archive illustrates.

A prime example is Samuel Delany's essay "Generic Protocols" (1980), which clarifies the methodology of this book. In it, Delany argues that genres are constituted through a way of reading (a protocol). This "structuration of response potential" is constructed over time by a group of texts that produce readerly responses particular to that genre—for example, how we approach poetry differently than we do a crime novel or a cookbook.[16] A protocol of reading enables us to identify one generic convention within another—the poetic within a work of prose, the dramatic within poetry—and reinterpret the text according to a set of informal codes. A genre (a protocol of reading), then, is what allows us to perceive tropes and conventions in texts outside it: "The fact that each genre is a way—a protocol—of reading (formed over a historical period, certainly, by many texts), is what allows that protocol to be applied to any number of other texts as well as what prevents a genre from being defined simply by a description of the texts themselves."[17] *Doom Patterns* shows that implementing the reading protocols of Latinx speculative fiction allows us to interpret particular phrasings, images, sentence structures, or repeating themes in such a way that "at the level of the signified, they are clearly part of SF."[18] To apply these reading protocols to texts usually not classified in this way is to approach the text with an "active desire in mind" that shapes how the text is experienced; it is to identify the narrative patterns that spill out of the text and reveal the excessive remnants of history that mark the text with doom.[19]

For scholars like Jeremy Rosen, genre is the place where "form, history, and material and institutional relations converge" to fulfill social tastes and ideals.[20] For others, like Lauren Berlant, genres "provide an affective expectation of the experience of watching something unfold" and make breakage an important part of their conventions: "the threat that *x* might *not* happen (love in a love plot, poetic justice in a thriller, death in a tragedy) allows absorbing but not shocking anxieties to be stimulated and vanquished."[21] Repeating forms of rupture are a generic convention that the protocols of Latinx speculative fiction allow us to see. *Doom Patterns*, following Rosen's definition of genre, upholds form as the place where history becomes manifest. The breakages in the literature I examine perform their role in genre by illustrating the overpowering violence of history that these texts attempt to (impossibly) narrate. In this book, I have focused on those places where texts have pronounced the haunting remnants of history and where, by using Latinx speculative fiction's protocols of reading, we can uncover these histories and the patterning effect they have not only in the text but also on the body.

In a posture of admiration for scholarship that centers systemic violence and oppression and their connection to haunting, ghosting, and silencing, throughout *Doom Patterns* I attend to the ways narrative form illuminates various configurations of violence, pleasure, and their concurrence. Inspired by Saidiya Hartman, I engage with "critical fabulation" as a "model for practice" throughout this book.[22] This model, Hartman explains, is the labor of writing against the limits of the archive while simultaneously performing the "impossibility of representing the lives of the captives precisely through the process of narration."[23] *Precisely* takes on a double meaning here, implying both the inability to be exact or accurate and the specific limitations of language and writing in representing particular forms of violence. The turn to fabulation/speculation, then, is an attempt to fill in the erasures and silences of the archive, which sets the limits on "what can be known, whose perspective matters, and who is endowed with the gravity and authority of historical actor."[24] José Esteban Muñoz similarly discusses the silencing of queerness by turning to ephemera and gesture to show how the queer can be evidenced and read.[25] Like critical fabulation, ephemera elide finitude and act as a surplus that allows us to see the "not-yet-conscious."[26] My archive, of course, is a different one. Unlike Hartman's characters, mine are mostly invented. I turn to fiction as a reflection and producer of the historical and political, and the texts in my archive illuminate repeating patterns of violence that excessively defy narration.

In many ways, the reading protocols of Latinx speculative fiction that reveal doom patterns in a text evince the ways the past continues to haunt the present—or remind us, as Kandice Chuh does, that we are within "crumpled time," which makes it impossible to contain violence within narrative form.[27] Doom patterns, in fact, enact Walter Benjamin's angel of history, which I use as an epigraph to open this book.[28] The violence and wreckages amassed via colonial, imperial, and capitalist histories pile in a critical mass while seemingly pushing us into a present and future that violently unfolds, albeit unseen. Like the angel, we cannot turn away from these violences, and our steps, like the language implemented within the texts I examine, propagate them in all their messy entanglements. The attempt to write and rewrite historical violence and its lingering trauma repeats it, unearthing violence in the text and re-creating it on the bodies of its characters.

Excess, failure, and haunting go hand in hand. Avery Gordon's trailblazing *Ghostly Matters* (1997) invokes haunting as a state in which unresolved social violence makes its presence known. Most importantly, haunting refuses the assumption that the past has been laid to rest.[29] To study haunting, to contend with its significance for the formation of social life, is to fundamentally alter our understanding of the world and knowledge formations.[30] Writing with the ghost and recognizing hauntings for Gordon is also a process of seeing and being in excess: it is a process of "inarticulate experiences, of symptoms and screen memories, of spiraling affects, of more than one story at a time, of the traffic in domains of experiences that are anything but transparent and referential."[31] Following María del Pilar Blanco's notion of "ghost watching" means recognizing haunting not simply as a metaphorical representation but as a textual phenomenon that results from a crisis of perception. This phenomenon necessitates a transformation of craft and form—"actual presences that need to be reckoned with in a narrative"—and consequently marks what is ungraspable about the present and the effect the past has on it.[32] In the concluding notes of *Dialectic of Enlightenment* (1944), Theodor Adorno and Max Horkheimer briefly offer a "Theory of Ghosts." Here they provocatively turn their attention to the way a society relates to its dead, stating, "Only the conscious horror of destruction creates the correct relationship with the dead: unity with them because we, like them, are the victims of the same condition and the same disappointed hope."[33] To underscore the formal tropes that exhume cataclysm is to contend with modernity's many violences, the complicated networks they have created, and the silences and gaps we can suppose but never know. The persistent haunting in Latinx speculative fiction exposes the "cracks" and "riggings," unearths that which was presumed to be buried, over and done with.[34] Gordon asks whether the analysis of hauntings will enable a more complex understanding of the "generative structures and moving parts of historically embedded social formations."[35] In response, I argue that writing with ghosts and illuminating the formal literary hauntings that the reading protocols of Latinx speculative fiction reveal facilitate a nuanced perception of the process by which violence sutures Latinx history and subjectivity. The doom patterns I analyze throughout this book expose the cracks and riggings, yes, but also draw us in, seduce us, and implicate us in the haunting through the aesthetic pleasure in which destruction is invoked.

Form, Violence, and Pleasure

Doom Patterns adopts a critical approach to the study of Latinx and diasporic literatures that helps us recognize and unravel the narrative dimensions of violence and trauma as constitutive forces for the construction of *latinidad* and minoritized subjectivity writ large. *Doom, (n.): fate or destiny; unavoidable ill fortune.*[36] Related to the family of words: *cataclysm, destruction, ruin, tragedy, annihilation.* The portentous suggestion of catastrophe and finality also invokes religious transformation. As narrative devices, doom patterns play within the postmodern tradition while highlighting specific violent historical events and forms of historical trauma.[37] These literary devices do not simply signal a metaphysically anarchic and chaotic universe by using parody and satire but also inscribe the novels' plots within a network of the afterlives of historical violence. Doom patterns enable readers to contend with the meaning of race, ethnicity, and the haunting of violence in the contemporary, underscoring the relationship among history, form, and performances in language. *Doom, (n.): the Last Judgement, at the end of the world.*[38] The promise of something after the end, things revealed by the apocalypse, change.[39] From the ancient Greek *apocálypsis, apocalypse* refers to the exposure of something hidden. Yet what happens when the apocalypse continues to repeat itself, when it is not a final moment of deliverance that will lead to a future filled with emancipatory possibility? What does it mean to be marked by repeating doom/s, ill-fated, wrecked, ruined, cursed, destroyed? To be more precise, what does it mean to be marked by the present progressive state of always be*ing*, being *in doom*?

Taking a neo-formalist approach, Ramón Saldívar identifies a new stage in the history of the novel, terming some of the texts I examine "speculative realism" and explaining how fiction by contemporary multiethnic authors is in dialogue with postmodern literary aesthetics, with a difference.[40] Saldívar notes that the rise of postmodernism and ethnic fiction in the postwar era must be examined through their shared "aesthetic matrix," which allows us to see how both were shaped by the same institutional histories and practices of creativity. In this dialogic context, it is no surprise that minoritized authors found postmodernism inhospitable.[41] One reason for this inhospitality is what Saldívar characterizes as the unrelentingly sardonic, cynical, and pessimistic narcissism in postmodern fiction "about the possibility of redemptive futures, progressive arcs of history, and utopian solutions to the disasters occasioned in the name of enlightenment."[42] While multiethnic writers still make use of postmodern aesthetics, Saldívar argues, they turn to a variety of genres to consider the meaning of race, ethnicity, and social justice today.

The authors I analyze in *Doom Patterns* push postmodern aesthetics to their limits and extend their work beyond this mode through their attention to and reimagination of the historical past. Theorists of postmodernism and its attendant aesthetic forms, most notably Fredric Jameson, have argued that postmodern play evacuates violence and its legacies from literature and culture, creating a depthlessness that discourages a hermeneutic relation to the object and thus forecloses a reader's connection to historical and political interpretation.[43] But the turn to surface and the decorative with which Jameson is concerned in fact does not exorcise history from the object; rather, it transfers its manifestation onto narrative form. More recent valuations of surface by scholars like Stephen Best, Heather Love, Sharon Marcus, Uri McMillan, José Esteban Muñoz, Anne Anlin Cheng, and Amber Jamilla Musser provide useful interdisciplinary interpretive strategies for reading texts.[44] Surface, as McMillan posits, conceals nothing and insists on being seen. Foremost for our purposes, surface produces excessive meaning; narrative form thus excessively circulates violence in the aesthetic. This emphasis on surface illustrates the relationship among form, reading, affect, and the body, acknowledging "perception as a bodily experience as much as an intellectual one."[45] As Linda Hutcheon, Cheng, and Musser argue, surface troubles the ideas of transparency, authenticity, and objectivity, further confounding distinctions between decorative surplus and what is "proper" to the thing.[46] Jameson's concern about surface reading and ahistorical inclinations that postmodern texts invite is countered by scholars like Hutcheon, who suggests that the postmodern novel, or what she calls "historiographic metafiction," captures the postmodern experience and its relationship to the past by emulating this experience through a text's formal choices. The reflexivity about the construction of knowledge, Hutcheon goes on to argue, shows postmodern fiction to be "resolutely historical, and inescapably political," precisely because of its intertextuality—the "presence of the past"—as well as its demarginalization and destabilization of the literary through its confrontation with the historical.[47]

The texts I examine illustrate how postmodern metafictional play is tinged with the violence of history for racialized and minoritized peoples. Fragmentation, nonlinear narration, multivocal perspectives, and narrative approximations all lead readers again and again to violence, destruction, and death. These literary modes, moreover, illustrate a textual excess that spills over onto itself: each work attempts to narrate violence, yet, unable to encapsulate it, is forced to break—the violence it struggles to describe is so extreme, excessive, and repeating that it creates textual eruptions that return readers again and again to moments of destruction. Narrative excess, the too-muchness I identify, maintains a close association with abjection, failure, and what can be seen as messy and dirty. Bucking literary conventions, the texts in my archive characterize a disobedient surplus that reimagines and rewrites stories of violence, and offer new ways of seeing formations such as race, gender, citizenship, and nationhood.[48]

Excess is understood throughout this book as a register in the texts that comes to define violence and historical trauma. Colonial, imperial, ethno-racial, and gendered violence lies at the center of my archive. Because these violences cannot be contained within traditional narrative forms, the authors turn to excessive narration in an (impossible) attempt to tell a story that struggles to be conveyed in language. In this impossibility, postmodern aesthetics also falls short as a literary mode for telling these stories of violence, and the authors I examine, among others, draw on various traditions, including postmodernism, magical realism, and social realism, to reimagine the past. Extending Saldívar's investigation of this new stage in the history of the novel, I show how texts engage in what Berlant calls "genre flailing": a "mode of crisis management that arises after an object, or object world, becomes disturbed in a way that intrudes on one's confidence about how to move in it."[49] Flailing is not failing, of course, but it signals how violence pushes narrative toward a variety of structures, forms, traditions, and tropes that will always be in surplus. Unlike Saldívar, however, I focus on how the historical violence the narratives are attempting to tell drives the formal breakages in a text. Instead of signaling political remedy, the else-wheres these texts propose reveal the haunting remnants of violence and its repetition in form.

I focus on prose fiction, primarily in the form of the novel. The novel, even in the postmodern moment, is considered a work that displays complexity, chronicling sequential and usually interrelated events and deploying in-depth characterization. These elements allow us to see how thematic trends develop in a protracted fashion, how narratives attempt to represent historical violence yet break, and, ultimately, how novels use their world-building to actively engage and implicate the reader in the paradoxical interplay of violence and aesthetic pleasure.

My theorization cannot fully express the magnitude of the violence these texts attempt to describe. The word *violence* is inevitably an intellectualization that takes us away from the sadism, destruction, cruelty, pain, and carnage the narrative describes and performs. Yet what other word can be used to illustrate the extreme and excessive forces behind colonization, slavery, dictatorship, exile? I follow Elaine Scarry's work on the impossibility of expression in the face of trauma and pain, but I focus on violence and its aftermath in both individual and communal terms as they are manifested in narrative form.[50] Grappling with the elsewheres revealed through Latinx speculative fiction's reading protocols is not only about reimagining the historical past and possible futures. It is also about imagining alternative historiographies and undoing the common ethico-political implications that underwrite reading practices within Latinx studies.

To identify doom patterns, then, is to recognize the many ways violence blueprints itself on the text, as a discursive scaffold that is also bound to its construction as an aesthetic object, with all that implies—the beautiful, decorative, appealing, and pleasurable. *Pattern, (n.): a model, example, or copy.*[51] That which is repeated, a prototype, blueprint, archetype. *Pattern, (v.): to order or arrange; to design or organize for a specific purpose.*[52] To pattern, to shape, to arrange, to decorate or design. Speech patterns, fashion templates, architectural patterns, tessellations, fractals, spatiotemporal patterns. To pattern, to shape, to model is to construct imaginative worlds. To pattern doom intimates its continued repetition as a model to be followed—the action of arranging and the arrangement itself. Doom's finality cannot describe the continued horror and violence in the Latinx past and present. Aesthetics, defined broadly as the artistic rendition of the world and the judgment of this composition according to notions (among other things) of the beautiful, ugly, and humorous, is a crucial site for understanding historical violence and its haunting traces. Aesthetic practices shape how we perceive the world, understand history, and handle social relations and culture.[53] As Michel-Rolph Trouillot has shown, literature and culture are apertures for grasping nationhood and citizenship, acting as their constant referents.[54] Yogita Goyal similarly argues that "history repeats itself as form" to dispute assumptions about the opposition between form and history, form and politics, and form and identity.[55]

Latinx speculative fiction interweaves histories and geographies in an effort to construct an archive with cataclysmic violence at its center, which constitutes the foundation for the close readings and historical materialist contextualizations I offer in this book. The incomplete and deformed—the ghostly, haunted, monstrous, excessive—breaks and deforms form. My readings center narrative form, showing how formal devices and tropes unpack the remnants of violence and their repeating histories into the present. I focus on the formal elements of fiction to excavate the methods through which they conceptualize historical violence and its afterlives. I am particularly interested in the form of violence and the violence of form, following Jennifer Harford Vargas's analysis of the dictatorship novel in Latinx literature.[56] My socioformal analysis that uses Latinx speculative fiction as a reading praxis for texts outside this canon treats the "ideology of form" as world-building within the novel itself but also as imparting meaning in our world. For the purposes of this book, I also understand this ideology to be writing grammars of repeating dooms that pattern themselves throughout the text and return readers again and again to moments of cataclysm.[57] My position throughout this book—a stance that others have taken before me—is that literature is both an object and a mode of inquiry and, as such, presents a unique way to understand and represent violence, through which we can demand a more nuanced approach to its investigation.

My study of narrative form recognizes the significance of this category, which developed in the Enlightenment and was assigned a distinct value and place in culture as a special object of analysis. When I speak of aesthetics, I am not making a claim about universality, and I am cognizant of the white supremacist forces through which notions of aesthetics emerged and through which the hierarchization of ideas and modes of representation is established and maintained.[58] Yet, like Chuh, Goyal, Vargas, and others, I believe that turning to form and genre offers an important entry point for examining how the aesthetic is entrenched in the history of modern thought and the contradictions of modernity. Aesthetics indicates the relationship between the senses and the formation of structures of value that reflect political ideologies, relations of power, and forms of knowledge.[59] This field, then, can be understood as integral to the production of difference, as Chuh argues, and one of this book's tasks is to highlight and investigate the subjugated forms and ways of knowing that have persisted as fundamental to current estimations of aesthetics.[60]

This development in aesthetic inquiry is essential in *Doom Patterns* for three reasons. First, it recognizes the significance of the text as a discrete creation that can be read, examined, and appraised—in other words, it underscores the literariness of literature. Second, it explains why work by minoritized people has often been studied through the lens of the political and not credited with the artistry intrinsically ascribed to Anglo-American texts, a move that calls attention to the art object and its position in the literary market. Lastly, to examine minoritized literature for its literariness—as an aesthetic object—necessarily calls attention to its formal qualities as opposed to those of other forms of documentation (social sciences, public policy and gray papers, anthropology) that might treat similar subject matter but use other generic conventions to circulate knowledge. I focus on aesthetics because I am primarily interested in the difficulty of pinning a definition down, and so this focus constitutes a point of departure rather than a conclusion. The ambiguity of the term also evokes the diverse forms of affect usually attributed to aesthetics: disgust, pain, horror, fear.

The aesthetics of violence—seen in the various doom patterns examined in this book—signals this mode of analyzing the formal elements of the text through the lens of Latinx speculative fiction. The fictions in my study focus on how narrative form attempts to reimagine and fictionalize histories of systemic violence, their material repercussions for individuals and their communities, and the ideologies that accompany these types of oppression. By this

I mean that literary portrayals expose distinctive yet intersecting histories of violence and trauma (conquest and settler colonialism, expansionism and imperialism, dictatorship and exile, slavery), the effects of this history on the body (gendered and sexual violence, physical violence, racism, addiction to sugar and sex, Indigenous genocide), and their conceptual justification (misogyny, ableism, homophobia, heterosexism, upward mobility, eugenics). This list of forms of violence is not comprehensive, and as *Doom Patterns* reminds us in every chapter, the violence inflicted on minoritized peoples in the Americas has always been excessive and cannot be encapsulated in narrative form or even cataloged into distinct categories. The types of violence I examine are extreme and messy and become even more complicated when imbricated with aesthetic pleasure. Throughout, I address calamities that are long-lasting, though they are sometimes perceived to have dissipated. They vary from the sensationally visible to the kind of violence Rob Nixon designates as "slow": "a violence that is neither spectacular nor instantaneous, but rather incremental and accretive."[61] What is most important, for both Nixon and me, is the way these calamities and their repercussions play out across diverse temporal scales. While Nixon's investigation of slow violence highlights solely those forms that happen faintly over time and space, I am concerned with the haunting reminders and remainders of historical forms of spectacular violence that accrue over time, lingering in a protracted manner into the present. Doom patterns facilitate a new understanding of violence as that which overflows boundaries—geographic, temporal, and narratological—by unearthing the ongoing repercussions of spectacular historical events.

The many forms of ongoing historical violence also reflect the uneven configurations they can take as they are organized through and around heteropatriarchal ideologies foundational to the nation-state. The texts that comprise *Doom Patterns* indicate this discrepancy, focusing on violence—systemic, physical, psychological—that is performed on women and their bodies. One only need look to film and television—not only fictional—for confirmation of the many ways women continue to experience too many forms of violence, from the most miniscule to larger kinds of systemic oppression that attempt to regulate and subjugate their bodies. And yet the texts I examine are not about resistance to violence or about political repair as a response to violence. The tendency in the field has been to read Latinx literature using what Eve Kosofsky Sedgwick calls a "reparative reading" that moves away from a "hermeneutics of suspicion" and the privileging of paranoia to expose systemic oppression.[62] Effectively, Latinx literary and cultural studies has been organized around oppositional and overt drives for political amelioration, stemming in part from moments of disruption and revolt.[63] *Doom Patterns* shows, however, that representations of violence and pleasure go hand in hand and, in fact, that pleasure is not achieved in spite of or after violence but often through it. This reading practice offers an alternative to using literature as a tool for political remedy and reveals how texts reproduce violence even as they attempt to depict historical trauma.

In these texts, the fictionalization of pain and destruction paradoxically foregrounds the pleasure in humor, narrative beauty, and the grotesque that can be found in reading about cataclysm and destruction. As a paradigm for reading, then, Latinx speculative fiction illustrates the fundamental role of violence both within and outside Latinx literature, a paradigm that concomitantly shows how *latinidad* has been constructed through and around violence. The aestheticization of violence translates violence from the real, perhaps providing another form of pleasure for readers who can see themselves at a remove from the acts being described. Doom patterns and the elsewheres they create highlight not only the foundational role of violence in the histories of minoritized peoples in the Americas but the central role violence plays in narrating their stories.

Violence in this estimation is a ludic and nonteleological formation that invites us to read for something other than amelioration, remedy, and resistance. Consider a canonical text in Latinx letters, Gloria Anzaldúa's *Borderlands/La Frontera* (1987), in which Anzaldúa describes the border as *"una herida abierta"* (an open wound), "where the Third World grates against the first and bleeds. And before a scab forms it hemorrhages again, the lifeblood of two worlds merging to form a third country—a border culture."[64] Her description of this space can, of course, be taken metaphorically, yet treating Latinx speculative fiction (a genre in which Anzaldúa also wrote) as a paradigm for reading allows us to see the otherworldly in this description as well: the violence of the border past and present creates such rifts that it anthropomorphizes the land in an unending cycle of pain and fashions a science-fictional landscape and a new type of alien species in border culture. A more recent example can be found in Justin Torres's *We the Animals* (2011), a bildungsroman about three young brothers of white and Puerto Rican parentage as they navigate their life in rural upstate New York, and the nameless protagonist's exploration of his queerness and breaking away from his family. At the novel's culmination, the protagonist's family finds his journals, in which is written "a catalog of imagined perversions, a violent pornography with myself at the center, with myself obliterated."[65] These writings indeed undo the self: the protagonist, sent to a psychiatric hospital, describes himself as fully animal, sleeping with peacocks and lions, dreaming of the day when he can walk upright.[66] Like Anzaldúa's depiction of the border, Torres's text can be read metaphorically: he feels *like* an animal but has not actually transformed into one. But what if he has? The trauma *We the Animals'* protagonist experiences is so extreme—a violence that cannot be extricated from race, colonization, diaspora, poverty, and their intersection with his queerness—that it translates in the text into a loss of human subjectivity.

Doom patterns signal the interruption of violence within the text but always in the interest, as Robert Appelbaum maintains, "of something which is non-fictional in origin."[67] Much as violence is ubiquitous in Latinx literature, violence underlies constructions of *latinidad*. As B. V. Olguín's *Violentologies* (2021) shows, Latinx studies and *latinidad* have a presumed counterhegemonic position.[68] The reification of this mode of resistance obfuscates the "salience of violence in Latina/o theories of being and knowing."[69] *Salience* is crucial to Olguín's methodology and to my implementation of Latinx speculative fiction's reading protocols. The term denotes standing out, protruding, and being conspicuous, but as Mark Jerng argues, salience also changes our sense of the world through the noticing and pointing out of what might not be visible but nevertheless is taking place.[70] Olguín's inquiry into the fundamental nature of violence for the proliferation of *latinidades* expands on voices such as Nelson Maldonado Torres, Edmundo O'Gorman, Walter Mignolo, and Aníbal Quijano and Immanuel Wallerstein, all of whom in one way or another position the "invention" of the Americas as happening through violence.[71] Most fundamental for the argument of my book is Olguín's demonstration of the ways Latinx history *is* violence and as such is central to our understanding of Latinx identity past and present.[72] In a similar vein, but with more geographic specificity, Nicole Guidotti-Hernández considers violence as constitutive of the American borderlands.[73] Her work, of course, follows Anzaldúa's *Borderlands/ La Frontera*, and as I show in chapter 3, this region continues to be marked by the haunting effects of colonial, imperial, and necropolitical violence. Guidotti-Hernández surveys what she calls "quotidian and yet spectacular" violence, a designation that invokes the physical scope and reach of violence while intimating the affective and psychic response it engenders.[74] The mundanity of violence juxtaposed with its "spectacular" nature also suggests that which is stunning, extravagant, and dramatic in its execution—with all the connections to performance and ornamentation this word calls forth. It is a violence *so* extreme, *so* repeated, and *so* commonplace and expected that it must be described as spectacular. Paradoxically, the commonplace nature of violence does not soften its spectacular and extreme nature. *Doom Patterns* underscores this paradox by showing how violence is deceivingly mundane in its cyclical repetition and haunting nature, which effectively underscores the power and enormous reach of violence. *Spectacular* and *speculative*, of course, have the same etymological root—*spectāre* (to watch), from *specere* (to look at)—which showcases the relationship between that which is re/imagined and its dramatic, aestheticized renderings. *Doom Patterns* sustains the correlation among the otherworldly, the excessive, the violent, and the aesthetic that these rooted words suggest, offering a reading practice that is an alternative to those that uphold depictions of violence as tools for political and other remedies.

The texts I examine, however, do not callously portray or celebrate violence, even as they perform the pleasure derived from its aestheticization. *Doom Patterns* recognizes violence as an ever-present and integral force for Latinx literature, speculative fiction, and minoritized subjectivity. I show that violence is fundamental to our understanding of history and minoritized subjectivity and that violence acts as an animating force for the field's genesis and growth. By reading through the lens of Latinx speculative fiction, I question the presupposition that literature promotes empathy, altruism, and social justice.[75] Complicating the conjecture of the "use of history as rescue," I attempt to show how in the reimagination of the past, Latinx literature and the doom patterns and elsewheres it formulates continue to underscore the "excessive recursiveness" of violence, to use Guidotti-Hernández's terminology, and the pleasure in reading about violence and destruction.[76] Along these lines, I hope this book will encourage work that looks outside binary models into the messy spaces that emerge in discussions of violence, historical trauma in the Americas, race, ethnicity, gender, diaspora, migration/emigration/immigration, nationhood, and genre. This is not to say that *Doom Patterns* offers a prescriptive mode of reading; instead, it asks whether and how our reading practices participate in the reproduction of very particular forms of interpreting *latinidad*, speculative fiction, and Latinx and multiethnic literature, and in the reception of this literature in the market.

Doom Patterns demonstrates how the tropes of Latinx speculative fiction can reveal important dimensions of race, ethnicity, and nationhood that tend to be obscured in analyses of realist fiction. Naturalism and realism, as Muñoz argues, "falter in their attempt to depict or describe the brownness of the world," because their attempts at mimetic representation will always be incomplete but do not acknowledge their incompleteness.[77] Placing *latinidad* at the center of discussions about speculative fiction enhances our understanding of the genre. Yet, contrary to the long-standing tendency to read a utopian spirit within Latinx speculative fiction, I argue that the salient violence on the level of content is performed and repeated on the level of form. To pattern is to speculate. *Speculate, (v.i.): to meditate or ponder.*[78] From the Latin *specere*, to see, look, behold what is before oneself. To see what has already taken place and what might happen in the future. *Speculate, (v.t.): to wonder, to theorize.*[79] To visualize, envision, invent, imagine, but also to reckon with and expect. The speculative fashions repeating narrative patterns of destruction, which I stitch together here. The aestheticization in Latinx speculative fiction repeats violence as it attempts to narrate it, creating breakages in the text that return us to apocalypse.

Central to this analysis is the understanding that apocalypses have already happened, continue to happen, and have real effects for Latinx and other minoritized populations. The apocalypse in this context relates to its biblical meaning of the end of the world and to the meaning of the ancient Greek term *apocálypsis*, which refers to the exposure of something hidden. As a reading protocol, Latinx speculative fiction reveals the cataclysmic effects of, among other things, colonialism, enslavement, imperialism, dictatorship, and exile, and the cyclical haunting of eschaton into the present. Cataclysm's disruption would seem to provide the opportunity to do away with the old world and create what Slavoj Žižek calls "emancipatory subjectivity."[80] Žižek's four horsemen imbue the apocalypse with redemptive potential, a teleological narrative that culminates in liberation. James Berger similarly describes the apocalyptic event as that which must clarify and illuminate "the true nature of what has been brought to end."[81] However, as he explains, the apocalypse in its most radical form has not occurred—we would have no means of recognizing it or recording it if it had. Similarly, Edward Said invokes "beginnings" as a formal organizing principle that gives a sense of order and continuity (teleology), albeit falsely. Beginnings function as historical architecture that "compensates us for the tumbling disorder of brute reality that will not settle down" and, in fact, always implies the end.[82] The apocalypse in my estimation occurs in the form of transformative and cataclysmic events—1492 and the modern/colonial divide, the Spanish conquest of the Aztec empire, for example—and their symbolic representation. In this sense, the apocalypse creates a new understanding of the world and the cyclical nature of violence. Yet, as Berger explains, postapocalyptic discourse attempts to represent the unrepresentable: "Post-apocalyptic representation . . . often takes place at a site of conjunction between [what *cannot* be said] and [what *must not* be said]—a site where language stops, both for reasons of internal logic and of social prohibition."[83]

While the text re-creates the many forms of violence it is narrating, it also produces many pleasures, which I group into three types: the paratextual, textual, and metatextual. My analysis shows how excessive violence is interlinked with unwieldy pleasure in reading about destruction and in tapping into literary worlds outside the text. This pleasure is experienced by characters within the text and, I hope, by the readers of *Doom Patterns*. In writing this book, I have allowed myself at times to emulate the unruly and extensive violence and pleasures of the works I analyze. This choice illustrates—like the many types of violence these texts expose and investigate—that pleasure is excessive, slippery, and disruptive. Pleasure can be found paratextually, for example, in a work's intertextuality, heteroglossia, lyrical prose or "writerliness," humor, or enticing and seductive plotlines; textually, in characters who enjoy having sex, eating, working, killing zombies, cheating, hitting a cabbie; and metatextually, through the pride a reader takes in finishing an epic novel like *2666*, understanding the plot of a difficult book like *Atomik Aztex*, reading about "authentic" Latinxs in *Oscar Wao*, or even enjoying the visibility and representation that *Oscar Wao* or García's novel seem to offer within the market and the academy. Pleasure, of course, can also be experienced in the horrific and grotesque; the frustration of reading multilingual, metareferential, labyrinthian texts; the voyeurism and titillation of reading depictions of sexual violence; and the stimulation of reading about worlds and times outside the realm of possibility in this one.

As consumers of literature, we must consider why and how particular histories of violence become entertainment. For example, why are stories of women's experiences of physical, emotional, and sexual abuse so predominant in literature, television, and film? One answer might be that women experience an inordinate amount of violence in the world. But we know this fact already. As readers and viewers, why do we continue to seek out these forms of entertainment, and what does it mean for us that we find enjoyment in these forms? How do we come to terms with the aestheticization of horrific events that take place in our world? Production and consumption are always interrelated, and pleasure in the aesthetics of violence considers the fundamental relationship between the text and its reader. Reading is a meaning-making "event" that occurs between the reader and the text.[84] Literature as "event" depends on the close attention to structure, form, syntax, and other linguistic and literary qualities in the text that transform a sentence from an object into "something that *happens* to, and with the participation of the reader."[85] Instead of asking what a sentence means, we might more usefully ask what the structure and form of the sentence *do*.[86]

Any pleasure derived from these texts is, of course, subjective. Not all readers will receive the many forms of violence reimagined in these texts in the same way, and some will even believe that no pleasure can be found in them.

Certain moments in this book will duplicate narrative violence that is difficult to read, while also showing how this violence is depicted in language that is beautiful or entertaining or enjoyable or thrilling. This endeavor is problematic at best. There are no easy solutions to the violence these speculative fictions reveal, and my reproduction of specific passages gets to the heart of my argument by showing that any attempt to represent violence in language ends up on some level replicating it. The pleasure I identify in Latinx speculative fiction's portrayals of violence highlights the beauty found in the art object that unsettlingly transforms violence into aesthetically pleasing texts for the enjoyment and consumption of the public. The market success, response from the award circuit, and position within the academy of many of the books examined here underscore this enjoyment. Pleasure works differently across spaces, structures, institutions, and individuals, and my position throughout *Doom Patterns* is that the texts analyzed herein act as representative case studies for how violence happens concomitantly with the humorous, with expert writing or beautiful prose, or with an entertaining plot.

Speculative Imaginaries, Violent Futures

In "*Sleep Dealer* and the Promise of Latino Futurity," Lázaro Lima argues that Latinx literature lacks a science fiction tradition, unlike the Black or Asian American traditions, which have notable figures like Octavia Butler, Samuel Delany, S. P. Somtows, and Laurence Yep at the helm. (A more updated version of this list would include figures like Colson Whitehead, N. K. Jemisin, Nalo Hopkinson, Rivers Solomon, Charles Yu, Ling Ma, and Ken Liu). Lima contends that this tradition is absent in part because Latinx literature is primarily concerned with history and the past. This argument assumes that science fiction is mainly oriented to the future. Scholars of the genre, however, remind us that it is as much about restructuring our experience of the past and present as it is about imagining possible futures.[87] Lima's concern about the lack of a Latinx science fiction tradition can be extended to the more comprehensive category of speculative fiction. The capacious quality of this last term frees and complicates it, much as *latinidad* is complicated by its own sweeping range.

Speculative fiction and speculative fiction studies, stereotypically male and white-dominated fields, have traditionally elided work by writers of color. Latinx literary studies has also typically overlooked speculative fiction in favor of work that seems to represent the Latinx experience more accurately in stories of immigration, assimilation, resistance, and so on. That said, these areas have seen dramatic shifts, unexpected expansions, and exciting developments in recent years. I build on the work of scholars like andré carrington, Mark Jerng, Isiah Lavender III, Catherine Sue Ramírez, Lysa Rivera, Darieck Scott, and Sami Schalk, among others, who have demonstrated the essential role of race in the study of genre and genre fiction.[88] Their work has enabled more nuanced readings of the racial implications of literary texts and shown how attention to race and ethnicity can unearth ideologies and histories of violence within a text. For example, as I argue in chapter 2, the birthday cake and portrayals of sugar consumption in *Zone One* crystallize the violent history of transatlantic slavery, addiction, and monstrosity within the novel. In this book, therefore, an analysis of violence illuminates issues of race, ethnicity, and historical trauma that might otherwise be obscured at the same time that it demonstrates how speculative tropes can be read through this excess.

Doom Patterns uses Latinx speculative fiction as a reading protocol for analyzing literature by writers from diverse backgrounds because of its ability to unveil the ethno-racial, historical, and speculative where they might otherwise go unnoticed. The question of what constitutes Latinx speculative fiction has guided scholarship in the past decade, most of which focuses on science fiction, as the field has attempted to establish itself within Latinx studies.[89] Matthew David Goodwin proposes that Latinx science fiction is still in the "recovery period," "meaning that at least for the present time, there needs to be a focused attention on the group to bring to light works that have not received critical analysis."[90] Latinx studies scholarship that focuses on Latinx speculative fiction, including my own, agrees with Goodwin's point that we "need the category to see what has been missed."[91] Yet we can see in novels like *Dreaming in Cuban* and *Oscar Wao* that the historical violence and trauma at the center of these works reveal speculative elements. That is, the historical violence and trauma in their plots force the texts into excessive formal elements that allow us to redefine them as speculative fiction. In this way, recovery work involves mining the texts at the heart of what we call the Latinx literary canon for speculative elements that have been overlooked. If Latinx speculative fiction, as scholars of the genre maintain, is about reckoning with the past, and texts within the canon that are not considered speculative fiction are also concerned with the remnants of history, then we can use Latinx speculative fiction's reading protocols to discover elements of the genre within these texts as well.[92]

Latinx speculative fiction operates in three distinct but at times intersecting ways. First, it uses all the literary devices we typically associate with genre fiction—ghosts, monsters, time travel, alternative worlds and histories, intergalactic travel. Second, it invokes the historical past by revealing the otherworldly nature of this history and of the formation of Latinx subjectivity. This second Latinx speculative fiction modality exposes unearthly dimensions within texts that are usually read as realist. Lastly, contemporary Latinx texts expose the speculative nature of *latinidad* and of the term itself. Ultimately, all three capacities of Latinx speculative fiction show Latinx subjectivity to be a speculative endeavor that necessitates the language of horror, fantasy, science fiction, and utopian and dystopian fiction—in short, the language of the speculative—to describe it. Catherine Sue Ramírez's examination of "Chicanafuturism" has begun this work and prompted scholars to reclaim texts that are not conventionally included within the generic parameters of speculative fiction. Ramírez theorizes that speculative fiction can be defined through its aesthetics of disrecognition and estrangement, making the histories of "many communities of color in the United States, and of the colonized and diasporic peoples of the (aptly called) 'New World'" something akin to science fiction plots.[93] Ernest Hogan similarly describes being Chicano as a "science fiction state of being," and in her analysis of "Latinofuturism," Cathryn Merla-Watson shows that horror fiction is a particularly salient genre for Latinx storytelling that, as in Ramírez's argument, illuminates how "horror and terror have been endemic to and have textured Latina/o lived experience"—graphic violence both banal and apocalyptic that is the stuff of horror.[94]

Speculative fiction, therefore, is a significant place to look for the haunting remnants of colonial, imperial, and ethno-racial violence. Genre fiction enables new modes of thinking and seeing the world and, for the purposes of my study, is particularly important for the ways we see and talk about the construction of race, gender, ethnicity, and nationhood. Scholars such as Aimee Bahng, Jerng, Dorinne Kondo, Merla-Watson and Olguín, and Joy Sanchez-Taylor, among others, have shown that race and ethnicity are central to the speculative. Equally important, they argue, is recognizing the centrality of the speculative for race-making.[95] Indeed, a significant branch of academic criticism published on speculative fiction, especially speculative fiction by people of color, focuses on questions of emancipation, resistance, and political repair. Recent work in the field has made arguments like Saldívar's, wherein he positions the "post-race novel" and "speculative realism" as establishing a "new imaginary" that foregrounds an ethico-moral imperative for disrupting social hierarchies and enabling a different orientation to our current conditions.[96] The groundbreaking anthology *Altermundos* (2017), edited by Merla-Watson and Olguín, expanded speculative fiction scholarship by focusing on the contribution of Latinx authors and thinkers to genre fiction and speculative fiction studies. Preceded by two important dossiers in *Aztlán*, also edited by Merla-Watson and Olguín, that focused on speculative fiction, *Altermundos* continues the editors' project of correcting the representational aporia in speculative fiction, an imperative I take seriously throughout these pages.[97] The work highlighted in these dossiers and in *Altermundos* challenges the misconception that Latinx speculative fiction does not exist while expanding and remapping generic boundaries to allow for a more nuanced understanding of speculative fiction, *latinidad*, and Latinx letters within genre fiction.[98]

Yet recall that part of this book's claim is that it is impossible to think of Latinx identity and *latinidad* without turning to the speculative and that being Latinx is itself a fantastical form of being—a speculative incarnation that is prompted by many forms of historical violence that continue into the present. Mariachis on Mars, Hogan explains, come naturally to him, as do the zombies, Aztex time travelers, and fat-ghosts that populate this book. Hogan associates perceptions of *latinidad* with that which transforms the "natural" into the fantastic: "Even when I try to write mainstream, or even nonfiction, it's seen as fantastic."[99] Self-perception and reception of Latinx identity are translated as otherworldly. Anzaldúa's *Borderlands/La Frontera* similarly turns to the "alien" to describe the subjectivity generated on the US-Mexico border, a space of exchange, struggle, ambiguity, violence, and complexity. Alien consciousness, indeed, is part of the aftermath of the history of struggle on the borderlands.[100] While all the texts examined throughout *Doom Patterns* might not be recognized as traditional speculative fiction, I show that through narrative excess and literary tropes, they harbor the speculative, revealing the otherworldliness of Latinx subjectivity as well as the cyclical repetition of violence. Depictions of violence in speculative modes invite readers to question the ideologies undergirding race, ethnicity, gender, and citizenship and the historical events and traumas that have formed them. What brought me to speculative fiction is an intriguing trend in Latinx literature that centers the excessive and violent. In this book, I show how Latinx speculative fiction represents violence as intrinsic to *latinidad*—it is at once so fundamental and abundant in Latinx history and identity formations that it is also mundane, while its excess defines and translates it as otherworldly. Something that is essential to this trend is the reproduction of violence through aesthetic forms that are pleasurable. The texts I have gathered here act as primary interlocutors in the project of showing the many facets of doom patterns and the violent histories they invoke, interlocutors that offer avenues for further exploration of pleasure, narrative patterns, and modes of reading.

The Otherworldliness of *Latinidad*: Notes on Terminology

This book is about excess that extends beyond the content of the text. To speak of Latinx literature or *latinidad* is to confront a definitional surplus that exceeds categorization. In *On Latinidad* (2007), for example, Marta Caminero-Santangelo reviews the complexity of defining a pan-Latinx identity or a *latinidad* that bridges transethnic, transracial, transnational, and transclass identities. Many Latinx scholars, like Caminero-Santangelo, have investigated the usefulness of the term *latinidad* in spite of, or because of, its excessive impossibility, while others have called for its cancellation.[101] I use the terms *Latinx* and *latinidad* in this book because of their impossibility and speculative enterprise, while acknowledging that they allow for a potentially whitewashing shorthand. In using these terms, I also gesture to the intersecting and bifurcating histories that formed and continue to form Latinx and diasporic literature. Carmen Lamas's *The Latino Continuum and the Nineteenth-Century Americas* (2021) proposes a different deployment of the term *Latino*, arguing for it as a continuum established in and beyond space and time. She suggests that "Latino" identity is neither wholly Latin American nor US American, nor is it simply transnational. Instead, Lamas argues that *latinidad* is a "sort of identity that simultaneously occupies multiple spatialities while inhabiting and crossing diverse temporal moments."[102] This excess and this speculation are central to *Doom Patterns'* investigation. As a reading praxis, Latinx speculative fiction offers a way to bypass national identifications in order to encounter intra-Latinx and intra-ethno-racial networks that enable alternative scales for reading the larger systems of oppression in the present and across time—systems that might seem phantasmal but have real, haunting effects on people's lives.[103]

Debates over the term—*Latino* and its iterations, *Latino/a*, *Latin@*, *Latinx*, and now more and more *Latine*—highlight its political utility as a "strategic coalitional orientation," even as the term's obfuscation of difference has been underscored.[104] In particular, the substitution of the *x* for the *o*, *a/o*, and *@* in recent years has caused a great deal of debate both within and outside academia. Online articles with titles such as "Why I Chose to Not Be Latinx," "Why I Embrace the Term Latinx," and "What's the Right Way to Pronounce Latinx?" demonstrate the anxiety and confusion the *x* brings with it.[105] Yet the uneasiness and difficulty the term presents are precisely why I have incorporated it into this project as a praxis for reading speculative fiction. As Renee Hudson argues, *latinidad* is speculative in nature: it encourages us to "turn to shared histories, affinities, and dreams while also creating a future for a *latini-*

dad that does not yet exist."[106] I propose that this theorization of *latinidad* as a speculative endeavor for the not-yet-here is expanded in Latinx speculative fiction, which underscores how the histories that form Latinx subjectivity seem taken out of science fiction, fantasy, and horror.

The continued speculation about the possibilities and complications presented by the *x* offers an important aperture for this project on the reading protocols of Latinx speculative fiction. Claudia Milian, for instance, regards the *x* as that which is lost in translation, presents difficulty for pronunciation and pluralization, and is always unstable: the *x* is "restive and hard to pin down and pushes against those things we thought we knew and understood."[107] The *x* offers the possibility of redefining the self, through such gestures as a return to the Indigenous or the underscoring of that which has been eternally lost—precisely the work of critical fabulation that frames this project. In the use of *Latinx* throughout this book, I recognize the term's disruption of gender binaries and heteronormative definitions, even in those texts that precede the use of the term or those that do not necessarily highlight what are commonly thought of as "queer topics." *Doom Patterns* points to the excessiveness and the speculative in being Latino/a/@/x. The *x* acts as a consistent reminder and remainder of the histories of violence that are exposed through narrative doom patterns in Latinx fiction. The incongruency ascribed to *Latinx* is precisely why the term is so useful for describing what it means to originate from and reside with the histories of colonial, imperial, racial, and gendered violence, and at their intersection. Antonio Viego, for example, ties the use of the *x* to violence and trauma, stating that the letter "cannot be made to make sense and it dissembles attempts at fixed meaning; it is the trauma that cannot be delivered in speech."[108] The *x* makes visible that which "we must bear" but which "cannot be borne," signaling violent histories that exceed understanding and narrative interpretation.[109]

As the mathematical symbol for the unknown variable—that which must be solved—the *x* in *Latinx* describes a condition of being more than, unknown, extreme. Adding the *x* also provocatively gives the term the look and sound of the inhuman, posthuman, and robotic. Attending to the complications in pronunciation and the impossible labeling task the term has been assigned, I situate the *x* within larger narratives of violence that remain unsayable, recursive, and intimately tied in the Latinx imaginary to the speculative language of the otherworldly. *X* demarcates the attempt to capture violence through language that always falls short of doing so. The texts examined in *Doom Patterns*, like the *x* in *Latinx*, turn "toward a void, an unknown, a wrestling with plurality, vectors of multi-intentionality."[110] *Latinx* provides an entry into the histories of violence I investigate. Far from a transparent, objective description for a knowable identity, the term acts as a mediator among notions of race, ethnicity, and nationhood and bodies within the United States and the American hemisphere.

The Chapters

This book examines works published since the beginning of the 1990s—the decade during which what we now call *Latinx literature* gained larger market recognition and solidified as an academic field. The 1990s was a foundational decade for literature by this heterogeneous minoritized ethno-racial group. The decade saw an explosion of publications by Latinx authors, especially women, including García's *Dreaming in Cuban*, Julia Alvarez's *How the García Girls Lost Their Accents* (1991) and *In the Time of the Butterflies* (1994), Ana Castillo's *So Far from God* (1993), Sandra Cisneros's *Woman Hollering Creek* (1991), and Helena María Viramontes's *Under the Feet of Jesus* (1995). It was also during the 1990s that the Latinx canon emerged and that this literature began to be anthologized.[111] While this decade is fundamental to contemporary understandings of the field, I recognize the long history of Latinx letters within what is now the United States and the continued shifts in definition within literary and ethnic categories. The 1990s is noteworthy for symbolic reasons as well, if we consider that the year in which García's first novel was published marked the five-hundred-year anniversary of Christopher Columbus's arrival in the Americas and the cataclysmic event that established what Mignolo calls the "modern/colonial" world system.[112] The colonial period is important for the foundation of *latinidad* and its haunting history that continues into the present, in literature's thematics and elsewhere. In fact, the books I examine in *Doom Patterns* manifest a sense of belatedness, or a participation in slow violence that addresses specific historical moments that took place years, decades, and sometimes centuries in the past: Bolaño's posthumously published *2666* considers the violent ripple effects of the 1994 signing of the North American Free Trade Agreement (NAFTA); Whitehead's *Zone One* (published in 2011) focuses on the world-changing effects of 9/11 and the magnitude of terrorism in the American zeitgeist, considering this threat against the backdrop of Barack Obama's presidency and the "postracial" society it promised to inaugurate; and although Machado's 2017 collection, *Her Body and Other Parties*, does not directly address the election of Donald Trump in 2016, it is difficult to read the text without thinking of the cruelty of "grab them by the pussy" and the increased violence against women that attended the rise of Trump.

In all this, *Doom Patterns* tracks how Latinx literature and Latinx studies be-comes a field that represented a recognizable demographic in the 1990s while exploring how this legibility seems to be dissolving from within. One of the key issues that propelled the writing of this book is the perception that the field tends to imagine a unified *latinidad*. In response, this book offers alternative avenues of relation. The texts in my study, spanning 1992–2020, are organized around the thematic juxtaposition of doom patterns such as sugar, archival and textual silences, blood, and the corpse. What better model for reading juxtapo-sition than speculative fiction, which inherently relies on this method to tell stories about alternate histories or fantastical worlds that resonate because of their contrast with our own?

Doom Patterns opens with a central but controversial figure within Latinx letters, Junot Díaz. One of the most renowned Latinx authors of our con-temporary moment and the recipient of numerous prestigious awards, Díaz epitomizes literary excellence, fiction's ethico-political imperatives, and the "authentic" depiction of Afro-Latinx life in the United States. His fiction navigates the unstable line between the worlds of "high art" and popular mass-market fiction and focuses on immigration and the legacies of colonialism and dictatorship as it affects the Dominican diaspora. In chapter 1, "Doom Pattern-ing the Postcolony and the New Caribbean Mythology," I argue that the no-tion of "fukú americanus" that opens *The Brief Wondrous Life of Oscar Wao* de-fines the Caribbean as a postapocalyptic space created through anathema that produces otherworldly bodies. Generated by Columbus's arrival in the "New World," this curse organizes Díaz's oeuvre, and the narrative strategies of his primary narrator, Yunior, define apocalyptic violence as ongoing from 1492 to the present in colonial, postcolonial, dictatorial, and diasporic forms. Expand-ing common readings of fukú, I show that the curse is a tangible narrative en-tity that animates chronic hauntings in the Americas while also eliciting many forms of pleasure. In this chapter, I also examine how Díaz's essay "The Silence" (2018)—a nonfiction account of sexual abuse and its long-lasting effects in his life and fiction—and the sexual misconduct allegations that followed compli-cate common readings of his work as decolonial fiction.

Doom Patterns remains in the Caribbean for a moment longer, moving from the Dominican Republic and its diaspora to Cuba and Cuban America. Chap-ter 2 juxtaposes the enjoyment in the monstrous with the violence inflicted on the individual body while showing how the tropes of speculative fiction reveal the ethno-racial. In "Sweet Apocalypse: Sugar and Monstrosity at the End of the World," I offer a comparative analysis of depictions of sugar production and con-sumption that show how sugar is both sweet and violent. Consuming it gives pleasure, but it also makes bodies grotesque and calls up colonial and dictatorial pasts. Reading Cristina García's *Dreaming in Cuban* alongside Colson Whitehead's *Zone One*, I show how sugar activates apocalyptic destruction: its consumption creates zombies, monsters always coated in the history of sugar production, transatlantic slavery, and the fear of the colonial masters' return. This chapter's comparative analysis of Latinx and African American novels reveals an otherwise unexplored thematic relationship between García's post–Cold War novel, on the threshold of a derelict Cuba after the collapse of the Soviet Union, and Whitehead's post-9/11 novel, invested in the wreckage of New York City after the fall of the Twin Towers. Depictions of sugar paint a picture of violence in the Caribbean as excessive and otherworldly, allowing us to read *Dreaming in Cuban* as a work of speculative fiction. This reading also makes it possible to read *Zone One* as Afro-Caribbean and to use the tropes within Whitehead's novel to illuminate the horrific elements in *Dreaming in Cuban*. Finally, reading these books together illustrates the importance of reading across ethno-racial fields and shows how the speculative can begin to disentangle portrayals of minoritized identity in literature.

Considered one of the most influential Latin American writers of his generation, Chilean-born Roberto Bolaño exemplifies celebrity status in English-language "world literature," even as he derided the literary mainstream while his works became canonical. My third chapter, "Approximation, Horror, and the Grotesque on the US-Mexico Border," turns to fragmentation, interrupted similes, and women's dead bodies to show how they reveal the otherworldly horror of the US-Mexico border and the ongoing nature of imperial, colonial, and gendered violence in this space. Focusing on Bolaño's posthumous novel, *2666*, I show how the conventions of genre fiction such as horror and the crime novel expose the otherworldliness of a particular historical destruction: the sexual assault and murder of hundreds of women in Ciudad Juárez, Mexico. Bolaño's novel instrumentalizes the figure of women's corpses to produce grotesque excitement in repeated sexual violence, voyeuristic pleasure in reading about this violence from a safe distance, and satisfaction in the accomplishment of finishing this massive tome of labyrinthian stories. In tension with the redemptive politics of Chicanx border studies and Chicana feminism, the novel imagines this subject through literary fragmentation—the repeated use of similes, for example—to underscore its desire but inability to describe the horror of the corpse or the borderlands that produce it.

My attention shifts toward "Greater Mexico"—the idea that Mexican nations have always continued to exist in the US territorial space—in chapter 4,

"Rekonkista: Brownface, Time Travel, and Cyberfascism in 'Greater Mexico.'" I discuss how Sesshu Foster's novel *Atomik Aztex* reimagines the historical cataclysm of the Spanish conquest of Mexico by resorting to the tropes of science fiction—particularly time travel—and in so doing exhibits what I call a "Latinxface" performance that revises both minstrelsy traditions and our expectations for justice-imagining works of art. I show how this Asian American novel unsettles key Chicanx concepts like Indigenous identity, ancestry, and nationhood to reveal that Los Angeles never stopped being Mexico. Collapsing the Chicano Movement's employment of a pre-Columbian homeland (Aztlán), *Atomik Aztex* advances my book's overarching argument by showcasing the cyclical repetition of violence and the pleasure in reading about it, in this case in the frustration the text produces alongside its humor and reinvention of Latinx history. Bolaño's and Foster's complicated and unstable relationships to Latinx narrative and *latinidad* signal the messy and slippery position they occupy while allowing me to expand the boundaries of the field and their genres.

Doom Patterns culminates with an investigation of the singular that reflects on the individual body and the effects of history on it. Chapter 5, "Her Body, Our Horror: Self-Abnegation; or, On Silence, Refusal, and Becoming the Un/Self," examines short stories from Carmen Maria Machado's collection *Her Body and Other Parties* (2017) to argue that the female body is presented as a speculative arena through which self-abnegation and refusal are explored in relation to hunger and desire. I use the place of Machado in Latinx literature to consider my own position in the field—as a woman, as someone who has battled with what it means to be fat in Western culture, as someone who has experienced sexual violence, as an immigrant, as Latinx. Latinx scholars have shown an affective attachment to reading Machado as a Latinx author, although her work evinces no overt signs of race and ethnicity, either Latinx or white. Imagining Machado's work as Latinx positions *latinidad* as a speculative endeavor that is outside the reach of language—unsayable and unknowable—even as it is happening through language. My examination of the speculative female body in Machado's work unearths unexpected narrative strategies, literary patterns, and networks. These networks are particularly significant in our contemporary moment, in which difficult conversations about sexual abuse and its intersection with race, ethnicity, and financial and institutional power dominate the zeitgeist.

In my coda, "Thinking from the Hole: *Latinidad* on the Edge," *Doom Patterns* returns to the dissipation of ethno-racial markers in Latinx literature. I consider Hernan Diaz's novel *In the Distance* (2017) as a Latinx novel in disguise. Telling the story of a young Swedish immigrant who attempts to make his way to New York from California in the mid-nineteenth century, Diaz's novel presents the American landscape as marked by otherworldly possibility and danger. Invested in reinvestigating notions of "foreign/ness," "citizenship," and "nation," *In the Distance* is imbued with proto-Latinxness yet is even further removed from an ascription to brownness than Machado is. By "unbinding literature" from the parameters that govern the field, Diaz's novel confirms *latinidad* as a speculative generic mode.[113]

DOOM PATTERNING
THE POSTCOLONY AND THE
NEW CARIBBEAN MYTHOLOGY

As soon as you start thinking about the beginning, it's the end.
—Junot Díaz, "The Sun, the Moon, the Stars"

The opening short story of Junot Díaz's collection *This Is How You Lose Her* (2012), "The Sun, the Moon, the Stars," centers the breakup between Yunior de las Casas and his girlfriend, Magdalena. After Magdalena discovers Yunior's various infidelities, they take a vacation to the Dominican Republic, the country of his birth, in an attempt to reconcile. There, Yunior meets two men at the hotel bar who take him to the Cave of Jagua, which they label "the birthplace of our nation."[1] The cave—really a hole in the ground—activates a memory of meeting Magdalena for the first time, a memory that predicts the dissolution of their relationship. Being inside the cave overwhelms Yunior, and he imagines it as a space to "become somebody better."[2] Instead of a redemptive experience, however, the cave instigates apocalyptic thinking, writing, and narration. Inside the hole, Yunior remembers the pleasure of the beginning of their relationship and states, "And that's when I know it's over. As soon as you start thinking about the beginning, it's the end."[3] His statement is filled with grammatical ambiguity that allows his insight to be read as happening within the present action of the cave ("that's" read as "that is") or as projected into the past memory of his first encounter with Magdalena ("that's" read as "that was"). This conflation in tenses is followed by a shift from first- to second-person point of view, which confuses the "I" and turns what should be read as Yunior's realization into a generalization that exceeds his relationship or relationships writ large. This present progressive statement is conditional in nature, and the "as soon" that qualifies it inflicts the same outcome on all thinkers of beginnings and insists on the impossibility of invoking any creation without also inciting its destruction.

This chapter considers the mythical, speculative world invoked by the "birthplace" in Díaz's story. Central to Yunior's thought is the critical aporia between writing, narration, and repair that the cave reveals. When he is lowered into the hole, Yunior enters a mythic and metaphorical space that connects the birthplace to histories of colonial conquest, genocide, and dictatorial power and the ominous destruction of worlds. Yunior's present progressive statement also suggests incipient action, which marks this space as persistently "discovered," conquered, created, and destroyed. Dominican birthplaces and origins, therefore, are repeatedly apocalyptic in nature.[4] Yunior's experience in the cave is a mythological experience that exhumes personal and national trauma, indicating the impossibility of breaking the cycles of violence in their personal and communal forms. His apocalyptic phrasing reproduces emotional violence that undercuts the restorative potential of communal longing to return to a beginning before birth, before time and history, before the construction of myths.

The confluences of temporal markers as Yunior imagines past, present, and future evoke a desire to undo the significations that make time, history, and the birthplace readable. His experience inside the cave, which could mitigate the trauma of diaspora and undo the histories the space signals, is foreclosed. As a product of the New World, a place of continuous, violent displacements, the Afro-Dominican subject always evokes the "fateful/fatal encounter" that was staged between Africa and the West.[5] As Stuart Hall suggests, the experience of displacement that constructed the "New World" as a place also "gives rise so profoundly to a certain imaginary plenitude, recreating the endless desire to return to 'lost origins,' to be one again with the mother, to go back to the beginning."[6] The Dominican Republic is thus the unreachable mother-object that instigates apocalyptic thinking and apocalyptic violence, which Yunior narrates within the birthplace. Afro-Dominican people are always displaced, and the impossibility of return becomes the foundation of representation, "the infinitely renewable source of desire, memory, myth, search, discovery."[7]

Doom patterns—the textual forms and narrative strategies I analyze in this book—return readers again and again to moments of cataclysmic destruction. In Díaz's fiction, the dominant doom pattern is the depiction of "fukú"—the curse of the New World—and the cyclical violence it unleashes in his novel, *The Brief Wondrous Life of Oscar Wao* (2007). As the central protagonist and narrator in Díaz's fiction, Yunior reproduces the violence of the curse in the description of excessive and otherworldly bodies, the detailing of gendered violence, and textual silences and fragments. In this chapter, I show how Díaz's fiction writes a new Caribbean mythology through its rendition of fukú and how fukú can serve as a lens through which to read Díaz's oeuvre. In Yunior's many interpolations throughout Díaz's fiction, the desire to tell stories of colonial, diasporic, dictatorial, and racial violence creates a series of narrative doom patterns that revisit the apocalyptic violence of the modern/colonial divide. Fragmentation is central to Díaz's portrayal of the history of the Dominican Republic and its diaspora, a portrayal that reveals the haunting effects of colonial, racial, and ethno-national violence. The mobilization of the curse suggests that narrating the Caribbean will always lead to fragmentation—of the text, the self, and the world. This traumatic historical violence remains as a physical presence that haunts the present throughout Díaz's fiction, narrating a world system with the curse of colonialism and its violence at its center. I expand a common reading of fukú to suggest that this world-building project establishes the "discovery" of the "New World" as an apocalyptic event that foments the Dominican Republic and the rest of the Americas as a postapocalyptic space created through anathema that reproduces colonial violence on the bodies of Afro-Caribbean subjects, a composition that is reiterated throughout Díaz's fiction.[8]

Considering violence and its many vestiges, in this chapter I reflect on the limitations of language when it comes to depicting historical trauma and its aftermath, and on the impossibility of the repair that narration in all its interpolations—as accounting/recounting/reaccounting, testimony, witnessing, recording—seems to promise.[9] Yet Yunior clings to language's transformative potential. Returning to Magdalena after his experience in the hole, he tells her, "All we have to do is try."[10] These words are emblematic of Yunior's narrative practice: he attempts to use writing and narration as exorcizing tools. His memory, however, reveals that the possibility of repair is undercut by imminent injury, and in fact suggests that narration can perpetuate violence.[11] Writing the past, retelling, reconstructing the historical archive—these are impossible tasks, especially because they are circumscribed by the paradoxical aesthetic pleasures found within narrative "failures" such as fragmentation and "páginas en blanco" (blank pages), the brutalization of gendered and racialized bodies, and the use of pop culture and nerdery. The moral reckoning that narration seems to promise is replaced by the pleasure found in the impossible attempt to describe the long history of violence in the Antilles and the rest of the Americas.

My analysis of fukú asks how our reading is affected by taking the curse at face value, by which I mean: How does reading fukú not as a symbolic device but as a textual creation with real effects within the plot alter our understanding of the story and its characters? To answer this requires reading Oscar's question, "Who more sci-fi than us?" not as rhetorical but as an expression of real embodiment that redefines the novel as a work of science fiction.[12] While violence is banally of this world and undergirds many Latinx subjectivities, Yunior's worldmaking project shows how, in its mundanity, violence repeats itself to the point that it appears excessive and otherworldly.[13] The characters of Díaz's oeuvre, then, are produced through this violence and embody the supernatural. This reading, in other words, is contingent on Yunior's narrative practices.

The doom patterns of Díaz's work are an essential element in the construction of a new Caribbean mythology that holds anathema at its center. Díaz's fiction is organized around repeated failures, byproducts of colonial and postcolonial violence, that are stylistically modeled within the structure of the plot.[14] Fragmentation, multivocal and multilingual prose, metafictional style, and paratextual sources illustrate the inability to contain violence within traditional narrative forms and the many types of pleasure that are also found in the text. Form and content operate as interlocking dual forces that compel readers to unremittingly navigate between a plot that centers violence and a narrative structure that accentuates it. Doom patterns are and perform the present time of the narrative and enable, among other things, a remythologizing of the official archives of the Americas that holds fukú as foundational. Fukú is also a reminder and remainder of conquest and discovery that patterns itself throughout Yunior's narrative strategies, creating a system that contains the curse of colonialism and the violence of colonial modernity.

When I refer to Caribbean histories and Afro-Caribbean embodiment in this chapter, I do not intend to imply a monolithic view of this heterogeneous region or a conflation of the particularities of the Dominican Republic and its diaspora. However, Yunior's new Caribbean mythology with fukú at its core offers a reading of the Antilles and the rest of the Americas as networked through the cataclysmic event of the New World's "discovery." Hispaniola—contemporary Haiti and the Dominican Republic—is the site of the first European settlement in the Americas and therefore the birthplace of the "New World," and the invention of Latin America depends on this narrative of discovery. The literary depiction of fukú defines the Caribbean as originating from cataclysm, which structures the novel and foregrounds this space of death as the creator of excessive forms of embodiment.

Speculative aesthetics illustrates the legacy of violence in the Caribbean by yoking Antillean history, identity, and the trauma of diasporic migration to the otherworldly, and it enables a rethinking of the Caribbean as postapocalyptic. The experience of cognitive estrangement that speculative fiction creates, which allows us to glimpse unfamiliar worlds and to interrogate the one we know, also allows us to see the Antilles of the novel as science fictional.[15] Fukú's "strange newness" ("novum") imagines a science-fictional Caribbean that is haunted by the past's historical anathema.[16] Through excessive description and speculative representation, Díaz takes us to another world where extreme violence is pervasive. The language of cognitive estrangement is what makes it possible for Yunior to be an unreliably seductive, hyperacademic, and apparently knowledgeable narrator even without having immediate access to the events he describes. More importantly, the aesthetic pleasures found in the text—beautiful description, seductive narration, enticing plot, humor, nerdery—affect our reading of violence through their synchronous occurrence and, in fact, subsume it.

Writing in Díaz is both an effect of apocalyptic violence and affects the production and repetition of apocalyptic imaginaries. The linguistic and literary heterogeneity of the novel forces readers to engage with various forms of knowledge (or the lack thereof), to contextualize the narrative's information by performing as archivists and researchers, and to actively participate in the construction of the text. Discursive heterogeneity makes it impossible to achieve any encompassing understanding of a subject as violent and difficult as the post/apocalypse. Writing the post/apocalypse underscores the difficulty of representing the violent history of the Caribbean and depicting the Afro-Caribbean body. Fragmentation, beginnings that re-begin, endings that re-end, and proliferating voices, perspectives, and languages evince textual anxiety about the task of retelling the Caribbean's post/apocalyptic science-fictional condition. In the face of this anxiety, the narrative produces a textual failure that re-creates violence with each rereading.

In this chapter, I first show how Yunior writes a new Caribbean mythology that ossifies the curse as foundational for the construction of the Americas and defines the Caribbean as post/apocalyptic. I then explore how Yunior's mythology re-inflicts violence on Afro-Caribbean bodies, defining them as science fictional, excessive, and otherworldly. My analysis of Yunior's chronicle of Oscar's monstrously feminized body and Belicia's brutalization clarifies one of the major concerns of *Doom Patterns*: that while violence in the Americas is generally excessive, it is inflicted on women's bodies in exorbitant ways. In the chapter's third section, I illustrate how the curse generates textual failures that lead to the fragmentation of the text and the self, even as Yunior's writerly desires seem to promise amelioration and repair. I turn to "The Silence"—Díaz's nonfiction essay about his experience of childhood sexual abuse—in the final moments of this chapter. I have published on this essay before, but I return to it here to show how Díaz's fiction and nonfiction reproduce violence in a way that scholarship about his work has often overlooked.[17] Any consideration of Díaz's work, I argue, needs to be reframed through the publication of this essay and the sexual misconduct allegations that followed. "The Silence" and discussions surrounding the controversy raised important questions about the recognition and promotion of Díaz's work by leading institutions of the art and publishing world, which have placed him at the apex of Latinx and Anglo-American canonicity.

Writing the New Caribbean Mythology

The Brief Wondrous Life of Oscar Wao tells the multigenerational story of Oscar de León and his family in the Dominican Republic and their New Jersey diaspora. The story focuses on Oscar's "nerdish-ness" and inability to get a girlfriend—an inability that precludes him from "authentic" Dominicanness—and is told by a seemingly omniscient narrator who eventually reveals himself to be Yunior, Oscar's college roommate and a "closeted nerd" but notorious "player." By the end of the novel, Oscar does find a girlfriend, which leads to his murder, an act that allows Yunior to become our narrator. Yet the story Yunior tells is also the history of violence in the Dominican Republic, beginning with Christopher Columbus and the introduction of fukú, moving back and forth in time to account for the mid-twentieth-century dictatorship of Rafael Trujillo, who ruled the country from 1930 to 1961, Oscar and Yunior's life in the mid-1990s, and gesturing to an unspecified future. The novel also contains a seemingly first-person narrative from the perspective of Oscar's sister, Lola; details the upbringing of his mother, Belicia, and her near-death experience in the Dominican Republic; and recounts the murder of his grandfather, Abelard, at the hands of Trujillo's armed forces.[18]

Before the narrative of Oscar's life begins, Yunior gives an exposition on the meaning of fukú and its origin and impact on the Americas. This formulation organizes the novel's plot around the "Curse and the Doom of the New World," a doom pattern that continually returns readers to the creation of the Antilles and the rest of the Americas through the apocalyptic.[19] Yunior's portrayal of the Antilles participates in a larger archipelagic rhetoric of the cataclysmic. Antonio Benítez-Rojo's *The Repeating Island* (1992) similarly evokes a violently birthed Caribbean: a "geographical accident" that is the site of repeating histories that continually wash onto the shores of the present.[20] The Caribbean Benítez-Rojo describes is also apocalyptic, a "big bang" that "throughout modern history threw out billions and billions of cultural fragments in all directions."[21] A site of endless creative production, the Caribbean is home to the "New World apocalyptic site," the plantation, from which the "new" in the New World emerges.[22] The power of imperial violence is rendered through the graphic "rhetoric of birth-through-conquest" that analogizes this space to a female body without subjectivity but accessible for others to use—a trope that appears in Díaz's fiction, as I show below.

The apocalyptic origin of the Antilles correlates the creation of the modern/colonial encounter with the De León and Cabral family's Afro-Caribbean diasporic condition:

> They say it came first from Africa, carried in the screams of the enslaved; that it was the death bane of the Tainos, uttered just as one world perished and another began; that it was a demon drawn into Creation through the nightmare door that was cracked open in the Antilles. *Fukú americanus*, or more colloquially, fukú—generally a curse or a doom of some kind; specifically the Curse and the Doom of the New World. Also called the fukú of the Admiral because the Admiral was both its midwife and one of its great European victims; despite "discovering" the New World the Admiral died miserable and syphilitic, hearing (dique) divine voices. In Santo Domingo, the Land He Loved Best (what Oscar, at the end, would call the Ground Zero of the New World), the Admiral's very name has become synonymous with both kinds of fukú, little and large; to say his name aloud or even to hear it is to invite calamity on the heads of you and yours.[23]

Oscar Wao's opening synchronously binds the histories of the transatlantic slave trade, Indigeneity and Indigenous genocide, and the European presence in the Americas. Their merger takes place through the violent seizure and transportation of Africans to the Antilles and the genocide of Indigenous populations that instigates the end of the world and the creation of the postapocalyptic modern/colonial moment. Fukú thus encompasses syncretic religiosity and racial miscegenation and signifies a geosocially specific Antillean condition of postapocalyptic embodiment and belief. In this way, the novel treats the construction of race as a curse with tangible and material consequences, particularly in the form of physical violence in the colonial period, but also in the form of the embodiments suffered by the novel's characters in the postcolonial era.[24]

Yunior creates a new Caribbean mythology that defines the Columbian encounter as foundational and traumatic, 1492 as an apocalyptic year that marks the colonial and postcolonial eras as postapocalyptic, and Afro-Caribbean people as otherworldly beings. The novel writes the Caribbean as created through anathema, Afro-Latinxs as reproductions and reproducers of apocalypse, and history as a haunting presence that forms the body and persists as a physical marker. By continually writing and rewriting itself as a form of self-correction and addendum, the opening, like the novel's three endings and many subsections, points to the narrator's inability to encapsulate the horror, humor, and science-fictional strangeness that is the history of the Americas. This fragmentation and textual excess are thus the byproducts instantiated by the Caribbean's postapocalyptic condition, itself organized around fukú and the Columbian encounter.

Yunior's world-building project rewrites a Eurocentrist mythology with race and racism at its center.[25] As the site of the original Columbian encounter, the Caribbean is the nexus of the "coloniality of power," defined by Aníbal Quijano as that "specific basic element of the new pattern of world power that was based on the idea of 'race' and in the 'racial' social classification of world population," whose "most significant historical implication is the emergence of a Eurocentered capitalist colonial/modern world power that is still with us."[26] Race and racism, Quijano notes, "have been the most visible expressions of the coloniality of power during the last 500 years."[27] The coloniality of power organized a series of worldviews and institutions according to Eurocentric epistemologies that transformed "differences into values."[28]

Using myth as an analytical framework shows how ideologies are ossified into enduring truths. Myths "evoke the sentiments out of which society is actively constructed" by telling stories derived from their expression "of paradigmatic truth."[29] In other words, myths establish, verify, and entrench stories that express and explain beliefs in a common origin and future. The distortion and erasure of historical specificity of subaltern knowledges of diverse populations and their experience of colonial domination and its aftermath are the foundation of the modern/colonial divide. The coloniality of power is further constituted through the cleaving of the pre-Columbian Americas by Europe into a depoliticized discourse of progress. The "discovery" of the Americas becomes a vessel through which to naturalize and render opaque the many and diverging violent histories that include genocide, environmental exploitation, European and American expansionism and imperialism, racism and racial violence, and the upholding of Eurocentric knowledges.[30] Thus, the historically specific classification of populations through the idea of race reinforces a racist and Eurocentrist lens of history and knowledge and deforms them into seemingly eternal and natural formations. Central to this world system is Columbus, a figure who in the nineteenth century was co-opted by an emerging Anglo-American empire by severing the Columbian myth from Europe and used to forge a rhetoric centered on the United States as a "civilizing" force.[31] Therefore, the Columbian encounter and the Eurocentrist capitalist/modern world power it established are foundational to the creation of discourses of "discovery" and the classification of populations along racial lines.[32]

If mythmaking is about the expression of seemingly timeless, communal beliefs that explain relationships as fixed and collective identities as absolute, Yunior's new Caribbean mythology makes cataclysm the origin of Dominican identity. Yunior's narrative strategies in *Oscar Wao* make it impossible to dissociate the Caribbean from the message of fukú. Fukú is the meaning of the Caribbean—the sign of the "discovery" of the Americas by Europe and the colonial and postcolonial bodies that this "discovery" created. The novel's mythology defines the Caribbean, and the rest of the Americas, through fukú, foregrounding the violence of encounter, colonialism, and its aftermath in all its valences. The use of fukú unearths how the coloniality of power suppresses and erases non-Western forms of knowledge.

This new Caribbean mythology, however, defines the Antilles and Antilleans as existing within an always already dead postapocalyptic environment, implying that cataclysmic violence is foundational to the hemisphere while reproducing this violence in the text. The terrorist act that established the modern/colonial divide in the Antilles reverberates in the rest of the Americas and creates a repeating doom pattern of conquest throughout the continent. Through his narration, Yunior establishes a network of violence that stretches from Santo Domingo to Paterson, New Jersey, linking events like the Vietnam War, John F. Kennedy's assassination, the 1960s American invasion of the Dominican Republic, and the two Gulf Wars. The novel thus defines fukú as a constant spectral presence that creates bodies—those who live in the Caribbean and its diasporic communities—that are the result of what Yunior and Oscar term sci-fi living conditions. In fact, Yunior designates the novel a "fukú story," which presages fukú's effects on the novel's characters: Oscar "was a hardcore sci-fi and fantasy man, believed that that was the kind of story we were all living in. He'd ask: What more sci-fi than the Santo Domingo? What more fantasy than the Antilles?"[33] To these questions, Yunior offers his own revision: "But now that I know how it all turns out, I have to ask, in turn: What more fukú?"[34] His revision stitches Oscar's love for genre fiction to the curse, making the novel and the lives of its characters inextricable from fukú's history and impact. Yunior's revision also connects the speculative to this doom pattern instead of treating the speculative as a form of repair. Drawing these connections defines the Americas; race; colonial, postcolonial, and dictatorial violence; and diaspora as byproducts of the apocalypse and as elements of genre fiction.

Yunior's narration, of course, is the vector of analysis for the history being written in *Oscar Wao*. Yunior sees himself as the story's "Watcher," equating himself with the extraterrestrial, all-powerful beings who watch over but are forbidden to interact with other characters in the *Fantastic Four* (1961–)—a rule they break on several occasions.[35] His "Watcher" duties are what makes it possible for the violence of fukú to reach our page and affect the characters he is narrating. His surveillance of fukú does not impede its spread but rather records it. Yunior's "intentions" might be "pure" (no one is laughing, I promise), but they do not enact repair.[36] Scholars like Jennifer Harford Vargas, Elena Machado Sáez, and Monica Hanna have illustrated how Yunior centralizes writing and narration, foregrounding his active participation and editorial hand in the De León and Cabral narrative and the history that accompanies it.[37] Writing himself as an objective observer through the use of academic footnotes, for example, Yunior shows the impossibility of encapsulating the violent history of the Caribbean without defaulting to unreliability, silences, and multiplicity. Even though he does not reveal his name until more than halfway through the novel, he repeatedly uses the narrative "I" to contextualize Oscar's story, even as he questions the historical archive and his own reliability. We can only read the violence that is narrated to us, and Yunior is the most seductive of narrators. This does not mean that he is accurate or comprehensive but rather that the violence that does reach the page comes through his mediating hand. The violence that Yunior describes is happening everywhere and, read paratextually, showcases his capacious knowledge of hemispheric American history, canonical literature, fantasy and science fiction, popular culture, and nerdery, as well as his command of the story.

The novel attempts to construct a fuller and more accurate archive of Caribbean history by evaluating its fantastical qualities and recurrently citing this history alongside works of science fiction and fantasy. Yunior's worldbuilding project places science fiction and the apocalyptic imagination at the center of global politics, Caribbean history, and his own writing. For him, science fiction and fantasy are a crucial lens through which to imagine the Antilles and its history within a hemispheric network outside the "official" archive. Yunior uses fukú to express a humorous disdain for US foreign policy that foregrounds the importance of exposing and analyzing its consequences. Much as he describes Columbus and the curse itself, Yunior narrates Trujillo's centrality in world politics as a haunting, supernatural burden. Trujillo is a consequence of fukú but also its custodian, and Yunior compares the dictator to supervillains and fantastic creatures like Sauron, Arawn, and Darkseid. The constant return to genre presents readers with a world system where violence haunts the Caribbean and its diaspora.

In speaking about Trujillo's "tight" relationship with fukú, for example, Yunior states that if "you even thought a bad thing about Trujillo, *fuá*, a hurricane would sweep your family out to sea, *fuá*, a boulder would fall out of the clear sky and squash you."[38] Fuá accents the string of fukúisms and emphasizes how doom is patterned in the novel's plot and the Dominican Republic more generally. Fuá marks the results of fukú's swiftness and allows it to be enacted in the text before the reader has a chance to question its authenticity. The onomatopoeia acts like the acute accent in the word, marking the text with its powerful inflection. Of course, fuá can also produce pleasure—in the word's sound, in its mocking of its own superstitious belief, and in its violence. Its rhythmic play creates a dizzying soundscape that confuses readers while making it difficult to question the existence of fukú. Fuá marks doom in the text and positions the Dominican Republic as central to global politics and networks of violence; it expresses a haunting curse that since the fifteenth century has been reproducing its apocalyptic violence through a pattern of conquest in the Americas. Fuá also showcases the excessive nature of the curse and the violence it has unleashed, making the act of writing and narrating fukú an impossible performance. Writing and narrating necessitate multiplicity and excess—of languages, histories, genres, archives, and time periods—that parallel the characters within the text, as much as they reveal the interplay between violence and aesthetic pleasure.

Such narrative pleasures are fundamental devices for the staging of speculative fiction. The irony and humor found throughout *Oscar Wao* underscore its violence, as can be seen in the curse's name. For Machado Sáez, fukú can be read as "a thinly disguised obscenity" that launches its narrative in a cycle of "'fucking' (with) the reader."[39] This "'fucking' (with)" highlights the inability to access "Truth," and it alludes to Yunior's habit of playing with, distorting, and withholding information. In fact, he expands the etymology of "fucú" by substituting a *c* for a *k*, which mocks the act of naming even while it maps the term's lineage and effect on the Americas.[40] The interplay between serious violence and sardonic humor is intensified in the curse's binomial nomenclature—*fukú americanus*—and its mockery of Western epistemology. If we extend Machado Sáez's analysis of the curse's aural qualities, "americanus" makes the curse an inextricable function of the hemisphere's geography while also mocking its own name: fukú not only "fucks (with) the reader" but ass-fucks America(anus) as well. By extension, Yunior makes sexual violence a foundational element of Caribbean anathema but in a tongue-in-cheek way that grants him distance from the reader, seemingly hides his "suppressed romance with Oscar," and displaces sexual abuse onto the reader.[41]

Yet, while the novel challenges its own apocalyptic origin story through a science-fictional lens, scientific naming, and a tone that toggles between the lighthearted and the sardonic, it maintains the curse's centrality and veracity (as belief and material experience) as the haunting afterlife of the modern/colonial divide. After introducing the effects of fukú while synchronously using ironic humor that challenges the curse's legitimacy, the novel's opening concludes that belief in the curse is irrelevant because "no matter what you believe, fukú believes in you."[42] The text returns to the conventions of science fiction by imprinting the curse with otherworldly omniscience and power. In fact, *Oscar Wao* equates fukú's supremacy with that of comic book and science-fictional villains; "it" (fukú), like science-fictional villains, "always—and I mean always—gets its man."[43] The repetition of "always" makes fukú a timeless entity, a force that is always operating regardless of belief in its power.

Writing the Curse onto the Body

Oration and narration, writing and retelling, bear enormous weight in *Oscar Wao* and in Díaz's work generally. I use *weight* intentionally here to indicate how writing and narrating create monstrous bodies as byproducts of fukú—bodies on which colonial violence is performed. Although Yunior poses writing and narration as potential exorcising actions, these narrative practices are mechanisms through which apocalyptic violence is recorded and reproduced. In a continuation of the rhetoric surrounding fukú, Yunior offers his narrative as a "zafa"—fukú's "counterspell"—in response to fukú's "many heads," its infinite capacity for propagating violence, and the potential to expel the curse on personal and continental scales. Yet the multitude of references and sources fail to summarize the violence and underscore the pleasure of this miscellany. As fukú, fuá, and zafa show, Yunior's literary performances reenact the apocalyptic destruction that recreates colonial and dictatorial violence on the bodies of Oscar and his mother.

Oscar's introduction in the novel is also his initiation into the curse. What begins with the "blessed days of his youth" when Oscar is "(still) a 'normal' Dominican boy" quickly becomes a metamorphosis into monstrosity and rejection from his diasporic community.[44] Yunior posits this shift through the lens of heterosexual inadequacy that marks Oscar's nonnormative practices as failures to enact authentic Dominican maleness and heterosexuality. He also presents Oscar's excessive embodiment as an inexorable byproduct of fukú, his Afro-Caribbean heirloom. The Cabral and De León family history is organized through the "Great American Doom" that shapes not only the lives and deaths of the novel's characters but also Yunior's narrative practices, which themselves mirror the despotic violence of the Trujillato.[45] Through the description of fat and monstrosity, the novel reenacts the violence of colonialism, models the new Caribbean mythology with fukú at its center, and demonstrates the impossibility of overcoming the curse.

Oscar's body is the terrestrial landscape on which colonial violence is confirmed: "The fat! The miles of stretch marks! The tumescent horribleness of his proportions!"[46] The high volume and exaggeration that the exclamation points lend to each statement mark his body with excess and melodrama. The humorous tone of Yunior's description likens Oscar's physical form to bodies in comic books, an association that makes fat embodiment that much more extreme. The use of a metaphor that equates stretch marks with distance and length returns readers to the origin of fukú—which defines Santo Domingo as the "Ground Zero of the New World" and "fukú's Kilometer Zero"—and makes Oscar's body the space onto which the novel maps and replicates the curse.

Fat is excess, a disruption of normative imperatives and stable categories. As a branch of fat studies has established, fatness disobeys chrononormative commands, which Elizabeth Freeman defines as "the use of time to organize individual human bodies toward maximum productivity."[47] Lives are only legible, therefore, through a timeline of progress and maturation, and those that fall within a "queer time" are pathologized.[48] Fat subjects are queer/ed because fat transgresses "normative standards of gender and sexuality, health and morality."[49] Yunior queers Oscar and pathologizes him, defining his body as wholly outside Dominican normativity. Elena Levy-Navarro has also shown that fat is a form of historical haunting. Using Carla Freccero's notion of haunting (which reminds us that the "past and the present are neither discrete nor sequential" and that the "borderline between then and now wavers, wobbles, and does not hold still"), Levy-Navarro shows that the "fat are history itself—that is, they are the past that must be dispensed with as we move toward our seemingly inevitable future progress."[50] Fat, then, is a constantly interrupting presence in the novel that marks the Afro-Caribbean body as the reproducer of fukú.

Oscar's weight, however, is actually immaterial. It is Yunior's representation of his proportions that makes him monstrous, describing his body as defying the human through its unquantified substance. In *Fearing the Black Body*

(2019), Sabrina Strings shows how contemporary ideologies around fat and fat phobia emerged alongside anti-Blackness and the policing of Black bodies.[51] In this vein, Yunior's monstrification of Oscar makes the former complicit in the reproduction of colonial domination, with its hyperawareness of and attention to racialized bodies. Like fat, Oscar's physicality becomes both a signifier for fukú and its byproduct, which exceeds the flesh and spills over onto all aspects of his life, becoming the medium through which his national allegiance and *Dominicanidad* are called into question. Oscar has "no knack for music or business or dance, no hustle, no rap, no G"; he has "no looks," which is highlighted by "his semi-kink hair in a Puerto Rican afro," "unappealing trace of a mustache," "close-set eyes that made him look somewhat retarded," and "enormous Section 8 glasses," which his friends call "anti-pussy devices."[52] The novel thus describes Oscar with a series of individual characteristics, collating physical unattractiveness with elements of hipness and cool, national identity, poverty, disability, and heteronormativity that, when amassed on a single body, turn it excessive and monstrous. But part of Oscar's monstrosity for Yunior is his fleshiness, which associates him with femininity—an authorial fixation that raises the question of how Yunior knows so much about Oscar's stretch marks.

Fatness, in any case, interrupts the expectations of the "fly bachatero" and replaces it with an excessive body that plangently reiterates his ethnic identity.[53] Oscar's body and death are byproducts of fukú, but the novel's unrelenting violence creates a space in which to examine the aesthetic pleasures of reading about this violence without the expectation of political remedy or repair. Pleasures are juxtaposed here as well with the disgust Yunior seemingly feels toward Oscar's body, a denial of the potential enjoyment he would find in it. *Oscar Wao*, therefore, is a world-building project in which violence and pleasure are pervasively interlinked.

Monstrosity and excessiveness are foundational elements in the Caribbean and its diaspora and a legacy of fukú and its generational circulation. The novel marks the inevitable reproduction of fukú through Oscar's mother, Belicia Cabral, writing her body, femininity, rage, and even desire to dance as excessive. Much like Oscar's body, Belicia's is a landscape that mirrors the violence of the curse, which is perpetually enacted on feminized bodies, including Oscar's. Her trajectory from the daughter of a reputable doctor to working as a "criada, a restavek," is also excessively violent.[54] As an orphaned child (the result of the Trujillato vis-à-vis the curse), Belicia is turned over to distant relatives who sell her to a family in Azua. There she works as an indentured servant and is burned with hot oil by the family's patriarch. La Inca, a cousin of Belicia's father and her adoptive mother, finds her after these events. Describing her burned back,

Yunior overindulgently extends his portrayal of her body, mirroring the cruelty of the act and juxtaposing it with the playful language of role-playing games: "(One hundred and ten hit points minimum.) A monsterglove of festering ruination extending from the back of her neck to the base of her spine."[55] The act of burning a girl is horrific—an act the text cannot fully describe—and I am claiming that because this moment is introduced through references to Trujillo and the Trujillato, burning is a manifestation of a systemic project of violence. Furthermore, mentioning Belicia's burning alongside the dictatorship, its violence, and rural poverty makes it symptomatic of not only dictatorial violence but also fukú's aftermath. Finding the mathematical parenthetical insufficient to encompass the violence of the burn, the text resorts to metaphorical comparisons through the language of disease and decayed landscapes. Belicia's scars are so monstrous that Yunior invents a new word in the attempt to visually represent her back ("monsterglove"). He equates her scars with a "bomb crater, a world-scar" that resembles "those of a hibakusha," comparing them to mutilated terrestrial spaces and disease.[56] *Hibakusha*, translated as "bombed person" (*hi*, "suffer"; *baku*, "bomb, explode"; and *sha*, "person"), is a grotesque term, denoting to "burst open." Like Oscar's stretch marks, Belicia's back is the geography on which the text stages a global network of atomic violence that reestablishes the curse as central to the Americas.

The text pathologically returns to Belicia's body, foregrounding it as the site in which to exercise violence. The family's "Fallout" results in her Black-skinned birth; the "first sign" of the family's downfall is her being "born black. And not just any kind of black. But *black* black—kongoblack, shangoblack, kaliblack, zapoteblack, rekhablack," her complexion "an ill omen."[57] Belicia's extreme Blackness—one that necessitates its italicized repetition and the creation of portmanteaus that allocate Blackness geographically and culturally—returns us to the Cave of Jagua and the creation of Blackness as a curse intrinsic to the Caribbean and its creation as a byproduct of fukú and otherworldly violence. Inside the cave, Yunior yokes its mythic origin and deep Blackness to his body. The hole's fantastic elements in association with Blackness positions race as an unstable and fluctuating theoretical construction that is produced through the effects of history and colonial modernity. Blackness here is also, and perhaps more importantly, a foundational and communal form of lived experience that is both the result of its historical construction and a reminder of its own forging.[58] Blackness in Díaz is an extra-ordinary element of the Antillean condition.

Yunior's narration of Belicia's body makes her experience of violence analogous to her Dominican lineage, inherent to Antillean history and one of the many byproducts of fukú. Yet the violence she suffers (as many of the female characters in *Oscar Wao* do) is part of a larger project in Díaz's oeuvre. By this I mean that women's bodies are presented as the arenas in which male characters explore their desires, their sociopolitical positions, and the role of national power in global politics, often at the expense of women's feelings and physical well-being. Yunior writes Belicia as a telluric space imbued with continental history and the violent landscape on which it is mapped. In this way, Díaz's fiction undercuts any attempt at a decolonial and anti-misogynistic politics by consistently using women's bodies to display world-ending violence and violence that is the medium for male self-exploration. Belicia's presence in the text belies repair: Yunior needs Belicia and her assault for his "fukú story" because she is part of the system he is trying to write his way out of—much as Díaz attempts to extricate himself in "The Silence" and to occlude his own experience of sexual abuse.[59]

The physical assault Belicia experiences continues the novel's apocalyptic world-building and underscores how women's bodies are used as mediums for male self-reflection in Díaz's oeuvre. Belicia is taken to the cane field, a space of violence that Oscar, too, will visit and where he will ultimately die—a textual representation of the cyclical nature of the curse. In the cane field, Belicia is "plunged 180 years" into the colonial past.[60] The experience of violence is delayed by the lush description of the natural world outside the car, a strategy that exacerbates violence once it arrives: "The moon, it has been reported, was full, and the light that rained down cast the leaves of the eucalyptuses into spectral coin. The world outside so beautiful, but inside the car . . ."[61] The lyric beauty of Yunior's language, preceding Belicia's brutalization, highlights the violence, as does the brief silence of the ellipsis, which hints at the inability of language to encapsulate the horrors of the assault. The initial silence of the ellipsis demonstrates pain's unsharability and resistance to language. Pain does not "simply resist language but actively destroys it, bringing about an immediate reversion to a state anterior to language, to the sounds and cries a human being makes before language is learned."[62] As a result, resistance to language is not simply a derivative of pain but an essential part of pain itself.

Saidiya Hartman's question in *Scenes of Subjection* (1997)—"What does the exposure of the violated body yield?"—is crucial for considering Díaz's work.[63] Writing about the afterlives of slavery, Hartman argues that the frequent reproduction of "ravaged" bodies "immure[s] us to pain by virtue of their familiarity" and that depictions through "theatrical language . . . reinforce the spectacular character of black suffering."[64] She asks whether, in spite of the unsharability of pain, the repeated depiction of Black suffering gives the violated body a form of expression and corroborates the veracity of violence. Or does the repeated depiction of Black suffering reveal our own titillation and voyeurism, as we use the suffering body as a narcissistic medium of self-reflection? What is implied in Hartman's work is the burden placed on the suffering body to be exposed and used as an evidentiary didactic tool. Fred Moten argues that Hartman's omission of Aunt Hester's scream is "illusory" and that, moreover, the omission of the shriek in fact reproduces it by its reference and rejection.[65] What Hartman considers the naissance of the enslaved person—violence—is also a site of consumable and reproducible pleasure.[66] The trace of enjoyment for Hartman, as Moten argues, the "specter of enjoyment," is reason enough for her to omit the encounter.[67] As Moten goes on to claim, Hartman's work offers the aperture of skepticism that challenges the "opposition between the mundane and quotidian, on the one hand, and the shocking and spectacular, on the other."[68] The displacement of violence defines it as pervasive and its reproduction as inescapable. Díaz's fiction brings to light the repercussions of slavery as they intersect with colonialism and dictatorship in the Dominican Republic. But unlike Hartman, Yunior details both the beating and its aftermath and returns frequently to women's damaged bodies. This tendency to dwell on ravaged women can be read as a desire to expose and utter the unsharable and unspeakable, especially as they relate to the byproducts of violence caused by coloniality, dictatorship, and exile. In its return to the violence performed on Belicia's body, however, the novel proves the incommunicability of pain and relishes, with bombastic language and exacting detail, in the re-creation of violence.

The affected language and detail with which Yunior describes the damage done to Belicia's body point to the writerly-ness of the text: the scopophilic extravagance derived from presenting a woman's damaged body.[69] The respite the ellipsis provides is brief, and what follows is a graphic description of her assault, which I exclude because I do not want to replicate its violence on the page. My decision to omit the description of Belicia's assault falls in line with Hartman's refusal, even while I acknowledge the inevitability of reproducing it through its reference. Part of the argument of this chapter, and this book generally, is that violence is so excessive that it can never be fully excluded and that, moreover, violence is reproduced in language. The choice to exclude Yunior's description stems in part from a recognition of the uncomfortable pleasure such depictions can arouse (with all the erotic implications of that verb). Violence to women's bodies in the novel provokes the "terror of the mundane" that Hartman describes, seen not only in overt depictions of sexual and physical violence but also in the ordinariness that makes this world. What, Moten asks, are the politics of reproducing the unavoidably reproducible? The refusal to cite this physical assault derives from the meditation on the significance of lingering on scenes and descriptions of violence, reproducing it not only for myself but also for the reader. As *Doom Patterns* shows, violence in the Latinx canon is constitutive of *latinidad*: excessive, otherworldly, and unavoidable. In Díaz's case, however, the preponderance of violence is held within the narrator's grammar and the aesthetic pleasure it generates.

The description of Belicia's assault begins with "They'd been," which positions her in a progressive state of being punched. The repeated asides and moments of self-referential introspection such as "Her fierceness astounds me" not only stand in stark contrast to Yunior's unwillingness to let Belicia speak for herself but also define pain through narcissistic moments of self-reflection and edification.[70] What is more, the text stages Belicia's reaction to the beating—"Beli offered hers up"—as an act of defiance that invites more violence.[71] Yunior also reverts to external referential points in order to illuminate Belicia's beaten body—"About 167 points of damage in total"[72]—instead of describing the pain of the body itself. And while the text's enumeration of injuries in medical terminology attempts to encapsulate the violence done to her, it also transforms her affective experience into a formal and detached analysis. Here, too, Yunior resorts to the numerical and nerdy language of role-playing games. With this language, despite providing a detailed account of the assault's physical effects, he manages to give little information about Belicia's emotional response while also placing this event within the realm of fantasy and pleasure. Thus, Belicia's body is used through "analogical substantiation" to lend the human body the "aura of 'realness'" that upholds Yunior's power as the narrator and his espousal of narrative veracity and authority.[73] The comprehensive description of Belicia's assault makes her pain wholly unknowable and even re-creates the violence perpetrated on her body. If, as Elaine Scarry stipulates, pain is "incontestably and unnegotiably present" for the sufferer and therefore the "most vibrant example of what it is to 'have certainty,'" then Belicia exists in the novel only as a body defined by violence and the pleasure found in its aesthetic representation.[74]

(Impossible) Narration = Fragmentation

In the previous sections, I showed how Yunior's writing produces an apocalyptic Caribbean that he continually manifests on the Afro-Caribbean body. Here, I shift to how his narration repeatedly collides against "páginas en blanco," the silences and missing texts that are the extension of colonial and dictatorial violence. The novel continually underscores the impossibility of re-creating Caribbean history—individual, national, or diasporic—in writing and suggests that any attempt to narrate this history will lead to fragmentation and failure. The cyclical violence of the curse is exhibited in the novel's form, illustrating that there can be no conclusion when narrating the legacies of historical trauma. As *Oscar Wao* attempts to expose how the Americas were established through cataclysmic violence and its reverberation throughout the centuries, the text is forced to turn to fragmentation, silences, and paratextual references that expose the limitations of writing and narration in the face of this trauma.

The Brief Wondrous Life of Oscar Wao never ends. Chapter 8, "The End of the Story," is not an end at all. Containing five subsections, this "final" chapter epitomizes the unfinishedness of *Oscar Wao*'s project: the narrative (and its author) does not seem to know when to end, starting and stopping repeatedly to (impossibly) depict its violence. Each subsection rewrites the one that preceded it, acting as a corrective addition, and the untitled section that follows reveals the "End" to have been a penultimate attempt to conclude, and fukú as a force that obligates the continuation of violence and the attempt to (impossibly) answer the silences introduced by the novel. Trying to conclude its plot, the text again resorts to the language of estrangement and implies that unending violence lies at the heart of the Caribbean. Paging through Oscar's copy of Alan Moore's *Watchmen* (1986–87), Yunior turns to the book's only circled panel, in which Dr. Manhattan tells Adrian Veidt: "In the end? Nothing ends, Adrian. Nothing ever ends."[75] This final line underscores the eternal reverberations of violence, especially that perpetuated in the name of repair and progress. The metafictional use of the comic in the context of Oscar's death and the possibility of writing a counterspell against fukú maintains the impossibility of ending violence's aftershocks. Indeed, this last section, which begins with "It's almost done. Almost over," concludes with Dr. Manhattan's words insisting on the impossibility of an end or even of "justice."[76]

Eight months after Oscar's death, a package arrives in New Jersey with two manuscripts, one comprising more chapters from his science fiction novel, the other a letter to his sister, Lola. In "The Final Letter," Oscar asks her to look out for a second package that will contain a book about his investigations of the Dominican Republic with the promised "cure to what ails us."[77] Yet the book never arrives. Instead, the letter that "concludes" the novel ends with another fragment that calls forth not only the literary canon but also the history of colonization and racism: "The beauty! The beauty!" Oscar writes about finally having sex with Ybón.[78] Echoing the last statement in Joseph Conrad's colonial narrative, *Heart of Darkness* (1899), Díaz rewrites the seriousness of "The horror! The horror!" and undercuts it by equating the vagina with a space of colonial exploration. The turn to this paratextual reference also exposes the violence the novel is unable to enclose in its pages, and the horror of Oscar's death. The "end" in *Oscar Wao* is a brief repose that through the white space on the page that follows "The beauty!" signals that the narrative must continue its doom patterning of cataclysmic violence.

The reader's knowledge of the missing book is possible only because of Oscar's death, which the text analogizes to Oscar's body missing from the text and the unfinished story he was writing before his murder. This lack of completion also allows Yunior to become our narrator and the interlocutor of this event. As Michel-Rolph Trouillot reminds us, there are silences "inherent in history because any single event enters history with some of its constituting parts missing," even as there is also an active silencing caused by "uneven power in the production of sources, archives, and narratives."[79] The active silencing Trouillot recognizes in the archive is taken up by Hartman in her work on "critical fabulation," which entails "straining against the limits of the archive" to underscore the impossibility of representing the lives lost in the slave trade through the process of narration.[80] *Oscar Wao* strains against the archive, showcasing the impossibility of representing colonial violence while exploring the ludic experience that fiction can offer.

The attempt to represent the violence that caused the breakages in the first place requires a turn to the speculative. The novel's fragmentation, multiplicity of voices, and metafictional references establish pastiche as the natural form in which to narrate the Caribbean. Díaz's use of postmodern aesthetics does not simply signal a metaphysically unfounded and chaotic universe but leads us back to fukú. Fragmentation is doom, destruction, and death. The use of pastiche and fragmentation thus re-creates violence, silence, and the impossibility of ascertaining truth. As this chapter and those that follow show, narrative fragmentation is a crucial device for approximating the portrayal of violence and the legacies of historical trauma that continue to haunt Latinx spaces.

This approximation, riddled with fragments and unknowns, paradoxically involves many forms of pleasure, such as pleasure in the mix of popular culture, nerdery, and "high" art that rewrites official historiographies. It is also what comprises the formal excesses and "spilling over" of the text: unable to hold the story, the text overflows into footnotes, narratorial asides, and trips through private histories and public (counter)annals both major and minor. The novel's multiplicity of starts, the literary and cultural references, and even the blank spaces (those found within the plot's "páginas en blanco" and on the physical blank page) enact the excessiveness of the story it is trying to narrate.

In the end, however, fukú acts as an impediment to narration. When Yunior writes Oscar's death in the cane field, he does so in a frustrated attempt to fill in one of the silences in the narrative, finally admitting that "if you're looking for a full story, I don't have it."[81] Narrating, then, is fastened to fukú: it is what leads to the family's "Fall," and Abelard's rumored-to-be-disappeared book is paralleled with Oscar's lost one. The repetition of history is analogous to fukú's atomic fallout and the impossibility of encompassing its violence in writing. In fact, what Yunior exposes is the repetition of apocalyptic violence initiated by fukú. Repeatedly colliding with silences that signal the unreliability of the written record (official or counternarrative), fukú becomes consonant to the blank page, making all silences in the novel a signifier for the original anathema of the Columbian encounter, and all attempts to reconstruct or rewrite Dominican history (individual, national, diasporic) a return to writing the original apocalypse.

In this situation, the language of rumor is paradoxically the only reliable language to turn to. Rumor in the opening description of fukú and throughout the novel acts as a doom pattern that conscripts violence into the history of the Americas even while it inscribes it with the pleasure of *chisme* (gossip). The gossipy and ambiguous "They say" that introduces the curse sets the tone for the rest of the novel, defining everything that is written after the first line as slippery, undetermined, and questionable.[82] Statements of supposed fact are interrupted by the parenthetical "(dique)" (apparently/supposedly), which challenges the account itself. From the Spanish *dizque* (a form of *dice que*), the parenthetical reaffirms the opening's "They say" and makes a seemingly historical statement into an unconfirmed rumor.[83] The opening pages are littered with rumor-like intimations, placing equivocality within the present and the past and projecting it into the future.

Oscar's death and his missing book allow Yunior to become our narrator and simultaneously remind us of his writerly shortcomings. After his death, Yunior keeps all of Oscar's things—books, games, manuscripts, comic books, papers—in "four refrigerators," "the best proof against fire, against earthquake, against almost anything."[84] These refrigerators act as makeshift archives for the reconstruction of the family's, the nation's, and the diaspora's history. Yet the missing book is crucial. The archive—the refrigerator—cannot safeguard text, body of work, physical body, or nation against the cyclical violence of history, the "almost" that creeps through. Besides acting as makeshift archive, the fridge is a coffin that signals Oscar's death, his absence from the text. The contents of the fridge, which Yunior preserves (like a corpse) with nerd-like care, are rumor itself, an amalgam that approximates but cannot be made complete, cannot reconstitute what has been lost—the missing book, Oscar. In Frankenstein's-monster fashion, the four refrigerator-coffins continue the depiction of the postapocalyptic Caribbean condition. Faced with the silences of the archive, Yunior's historical counternarrative will by definition be incomplete. Trying to manage these silences, he writes and rewrites beginnings and endings as self-correction and addendum. In a final note of hope, Yunior imagines Lola's daughter, Isis, coming to mine the refrigerator-coffins for "the answer to what ails us" (dique).

These final pages are heavy with Oscar's ghost, which not even Yunior's ventriloquizing can exorcise. Like his mother, Oscar is taken to the cane fields, this time not once but twice. The first time, like Belicia, Oscar is severely beaten; the second, he is killed. This return is an unavoidable repetition of history and textual symmetry as the inevitable outcome of fukú. His death yokes the history of sugar production and the violence it engendered to the consumption of the commodity. Sugar, as is explored in more detail in chapter 2, is metaphorized as a colonial tool that, in the novel's present, develops into the postcolonial violence of the nation-state and its constant infliction of pain on the body. Oscar's two encounters in the cane field and his death in it are a repetition of familial history and American kismet. The uncanny sensation he experiences, "strangely familiar" to him, returns us to his mother's assault and the establishment of colonial power on the island.[85] His first experience in the field convinces Oscar of the inevitable repetition of the curse. In the hospital, Oscar rolls "fukú" "experimentally in his mouth" but because of his injuries translates it into "fuck you," finally having to write it for Yunior.[86] The humor that accompanies the curse's name is erased in the face of violence, and what begins as an assessment in sound (and feeling?) becomes materially explicit in writing. This act cements fukú in the text and on the body. Yet communication is fashioned as that which happens between physical experience, oral mis/pronunciation of the word, and its presentation in writing, all of which approximate the curse without being able to fully circumscribe it.

Perhaps this is why Oscar's second encounter in the field is a tearless one (dique), but one no less filled with violence. The cane patterns apocalyptic violence in the novel, forcing Oscar once again into this space as one of the final enactments of cataclysm. Oscar's soliloquy on love in the field (dique) is another moment of normalizing violence in the novel, textual instability, and fantasy, where Yunior discloses his editorial hand in the fabrication of the family saga. The cruelty of the joke through which he is killed, by translating "fuego" (fire), forces Oscar to participate in his own execution, even as he "laughed a little too through his broken mouth."[87] The symbolic weight of the broken mouth defines oration, narration, and pleasure as self-annihilating. As a metaphor, it can be extended to the writing of the novel itself: by translating "fuego," the mouth is made analogous to the gun—a colonial technology of violence. Breaking Oscar's mouth turns what was the experimental mouthfeel of the curse into a reality and re-silences its protagonist. It is also a précis on attempting to narrate the history of the Caribbean: writing, oration, narration reproduce the violence they attempt to describe. Writing Oscar's death also ends his presence on the page, an act that forces the text to revert to silence, epitomized in Yunior's inability to write or speak: "Oscar—"[88] The courageous speech Yunior imagines for us against the injustice of the state is betrayed by the image of the broken mouth. The return of the em dash leads to a series of fragments caused by the violence it attempts to represent. Such silence is illustrative of the impossibility of repair and, in more general terms, of the apocalyptic narration that is *Oscar Wao* itself.

Junot Díaz after "The Silence"

Since his first short story, "Drown," was published in the *New Yorker*, Díaz's writing has been widely circulated. In the eleven years between the publication of *Drown* (1996) and *Oscar Wao*, Díaz received, among other awards, a Guggenheim Foundation Fellowship, a PEN/Malamud Award, a Radcliffe Institute Fellowship, and a MacArthur Fellowship (colloquially known as the "Genius Grant"). *Oscar Wao* received praise from the highest echelons of literary reviewers and won the most significant prizes in fiction such as the National Book Critics Circle Award and the Pulitzer Prize for Fiction, and it was selected by multiple important publications (the *New York Times*, *New York Magazine*, *Publishers Weekly*) as the best novel of 2007.[89] In short, Díaz and his work enjoy success and centrality within Latinx letters and Anglo-American literature and culture. Chosen by arbiters of "high art" and literary taste, his work has been included in various anthologies that in many ways determine which literature appears in the university classroom and thus sets readership patterns. In this way, Díaz's work has set the tone for how readers think of fiction by and about Latinxs. His use of popular culture, intermixed with nerdery, science fiction, sexually charged language, and hipness and cool, became a phenomenon in the literary market that has made him a celebrity writer. Silvio Torres-Saillant, for example, states that "a consequence of his inhabiting the republic of letters as a prominent artistic voice in American fiction and as a spokesperson for the national community in the public sphere is that Díaz has reached the point of commanding the discursive power necessary to alter the literary tradition from which he writes."[90] Here, Torres-Saillant highlights the centrality of Díaz's fiction and its transformational power within the Latinx canon.

Díaz's oeuvre portrays a Caribbean founded through the anathema of conquest, which produces postapocalyptic, otherworldly bodies in both the Dominican Republic and its diaspora. The desire to tell stories of colonial, dictatorial, and racial violence creates a series of narrative doom patterns that return readers to the apocalypse of the modern/colonial divide. This cyclical repetition outlines the limitations of language when it comes to conveying violence, which leads to various silences and silencing, and ultimately to the fragmentation of the text and the self. This trend is continued in Díaz's nonfiction essay "The Silence." In this essay, Díaz maintains the yearning we see in Yunior's desire for mastery through language while being unable to prevent language's ultimate failure. "The Silence," moreover, develops and augments the tendency in Díaz's fiction to mobilize women's bodies as the repositories of violence through which doom patterns are performed.

Díaz published "The Silence" in the April 16, 2018, issue of the *New Yorker*. This nonfiction account describes the author's experience of sexual abuse as a child and the lingering effects of that trauma on his life and fiction. "The Silence" raises important questions about literary canonicity and misogynistic representations in Díaz's work. This essay and the sexual misconduct allegations that arose after its publication have important implications for understanding his oeuvre. Díaz's work has generally been read as supportive of reformist political positions, a view that is epitomized in the edited volume *Junot Díaz and the Decolonial Imagination* (2016), which argues in part that Díaz has transformed American letters by giving Latinx writing unprecedented visibility and that his work is actively engaged in an aesthetic project that is deeply rooted in progressive and liberating politics.[91] This scholarship assumes the transformative power of Díaz's fiction—a position endorsed by the author himself.[92]

I discuss "The Silence" here because it brings together the questions at the heart of this chapter. As in his fiction, Díaz turns to fantastical language to describe his experience of sexual abuse. Rendering trauma as excessive and mythological, "The Silence" defines it as that which shatters the self and is world-shattering: "Trauma is a time traveller, an ouroboros that reaches back and devours everything that came before. Only fragments remain."[93] Like an ouroboros, trauma destroys all that came before it and is a cyclical form that necessitates the repetition of violence: beginning and ending (mouth and tail) become indistinguishable from each other. Invoking this mythological creature stresses that the speaking of trauma—speaking against silence—is an act that also concretizes violence: writing (speaking) trauma is a creative act that will not lead to repair but is simultaneously destructive, a destruction that in Díaz's work is both individual and hemispheric. As a symbol, the ouroboros is emblematic of Díaz's fiction. It acts as a doom pattern in "The Silence" and throughout his texts, a textual eruption that marks the attempt of language to convey trauma and also its failure. The snake opens its mouth in an attempt to speak but paradoxically swallows its own tail, accenting the difficulty in narrating and writing stories of violence and their traumatic legacies. Speaking trauma defines violence as an infinite and forceful consumption of the self: the ouroboros's circularity makes violence a continual presence that speaking and writing cannot undo, a presence that returns violence to the body. In fact, the mythology that both author and narrator create holds apocalyptic violence at its center, a violence that undercuts the mastery that Díaz seeks and Yunior pantomimes.

"The Silence" begins with an address to an unknown woman who approached him at a book signing to ask about the sexual abuse "alluded to" in this fiction. Told in epistolary form, the essay details various romantic relationships and explains how Díaz's rape at eight years old compulsively led him to mistreat these women. Díaz also explores how his experience of abuse marked his writing, his creation of Yunior, and his literary success. The essay was read widely. The responses began with celebrity writers, actors, and figures in popular culture tweeting their support and admiration for the essay, and a number of scholars joined in. Not all responses to "The Silence" were favorable, however. Notably, Zinzi Clemmons tweeted, "As a grad student, I invited Junot Diaz to speak to a workshop on issues of representation in literature. I was an unknown wide-eyed 26 yo, and he used it as an opportunity to corner and forcibly kiss me. I'm far from the only one he's done this 2, I refuse to be silent anymore."[94]

What has become clear is that while attempting to evade violence, Díaz has reproduced it on women's bodies, much as Yunior writes it onto women and feminized male bodies. "The Silence," like Díaz's fiction, asks us to consider the legacies of racial and gendered violence that manifest even in "decolonial" literature, and to reflect on whether decoloniality is in fact possible. As Tiffany Lethabo King's nuanced analysis of *Oscar Wao* shows, to consider how Díaz's sexual misconduct manifests in his fiction is to think about it "structurally and as a legacy of conquest."[95] The legacies of trauma in his fiction and nonfiction are intimately tied to their manifestation in cultural production, writing and narrating, and the literary marketplace. The "grammars of conquest" that King identifies in Díaz's novel bind historical trauma to the trauma of abuse, explaining, without excusing, his behavior as the legacy of coloniality. "The Silence" continues Díaz's association of sexual violence and the legacies of trauma with histories of conquest, juxtaposing the fear of speaking out with a land formation that evokes the map of the Americas, separated from the "Old World" by the Atlantic Ocean: "But I was afraid. I'm still afraid—my fear like continents and the ocean between."[96] Díaz invokes the histories of conquest and colonization that make him always already sexually abused and abject.[97]

But decolonial repair is unattainable, as the historical violence the narrative attempts to describe is simply too exorbitant to encapsulate. Yunior seems to promise a form of mastery over the story he is telling through the substantial number of references and hyperacademic notes, as well as his direct addresses to the reader, which create a sense of intimacy and position him as the authoritative voice of the text.[98] His forays into the second-person point of view assume that the reader can empathize with the story being told, and the shifts between the narrative "I" and appeals to the reader ("you") create the illusion of accessible knowledge while maintaining distance between reader and narrator through the withholding of information and the unavoidable "páginas en blanco." Amid these references and narrative strategies, Yunior consistently meets with textual failure, and the only thing that remains is the pleasure of consuming the narrative's aesthetic rendition. The intimacy signaled by the turn to "you" (us) strains against the information Yunior actively withholds, and his authorial mastery is marred by the things he does not have access to and cannot know. As a result, the narrative creates an unbridgeable gap that showcases the limitations of communicating through writing, muddies the relationship between reader and narrator, and forecloses the possibility of empathy and repair in the novel. As a writer of color, Yunior (and by extension Díaz) is put in a fraught position as cultural spokesperson and "native informant," and his possibilities for self-expression are limited by the act of narrating selfhood to mainstream audiences.[99] A similar authorial intimacy and attempt at control are seen in "The Silence." As Ruth McHugh-Dillon argues, its publication invited audiences to read Díaz's own biography in his fiction and conversely to question his desire to "confess" during the time of #MeToo.[100]

As he does in his fiction, Díaz uses grammar to hide women's pain behind his own in "The Silence." Referring to each woman by her initial followed by an em dash, Díaz treats each citation as a vehicle for his own therapeutic remediation. The women's pain is extraneous to his story of redemption, and the initials function, as Shreerekha Subramanian argues, as "props and footnotes in the stories of powerful men."[101] While his disclosure of childhood sexual abuse is important, Díaz still strategically obfuscates the "hurt [he] caused" and reduces each woman to a thing that functions only for its use value as an empty medium for self-reflection: "I think about you, X— . . . I think about silence; I think about shame, I think about loneliness. I think about the hurt I caused. I think of all the years and all the life I lost to the hiding and to the fear and to the pain."[102] If Belicia's pain is a vehicle for the reader's understanding of (and admiration for?) Yunior, women in "The Silence" function as instruments for Díaz's anticipatory presentation of himself as a person in pain and a redeemed wrongdoer.

The elision of first names and the genre of the memoir makes "The Silence" a work of speculative fiction. The essay makes it clear that all writing is derived from trauma and re-creates trauma aesthetically.[103] Like Trujillo, Díaz is both fukú's servant and its master—his experience of sexual abuse is fukú's aftermath, and his victimization of others its inevitable repercussion.[104] Díaz is an author whose protagonist persistently writes about the process of the male self-pardon, contending that his confessions act as exonerations, "a man reckoning with himself."[105] However, as Carmen Maria Machado asks, how can recording one's transgressions while continuing to transgress add up to making amends?[106] As I have shown throughout this chapter, the language Díaz uses throughout his oeuvre reproduces gendered violence. By consistently returning to the trope of the male self-pardon, Díaz's fiction limits its ability to encourage redemption and forgiveness.

Yunior's experience in the Cave of Jagua, which began this chapter, is another evocation of a futile attempt at repairing the damage that has been done. The imperative to "try," which he invokes as the ultimate impetus of accomplishment ("all we have to do"), underscores the endurance of retribution and the cyclical repetition of violence, as well as the impossibility of forgiveness. Díaz's oeuvre shows, and "The Silence" exemplifies, that language is overburdened with the weight of coloniality and its haunting effects on the body. The worlds Díaz and Yunior create hold mythologies of violence and silencing, such as fukú and the ouroboros, at their center, where the histories of colonial conquest, expansion, dictatorial violence, and imperialism collide. Their desire to "become somebody better," to write the story of "what ails us," is undercut by the silences of the archive and the inability to articulate violence's totality. Most tragically, their oeuvre defines the Caribbean and its diaspora as cyclically haunted by these histories of violence, showing how their attempt at decolonial writing fails because of their instrumentalization of women as vessels for this violence.

SWEET APOCALYPSE

Sugar and Monstrosity at
the End of the World

¡Azúcar!
—Celia Cruz

In the summer of 2014, the artist Kara Walker exhibited *A Subtlety, or the Marvelous Sugar Baby* in the Domino Sugar factory in Williamsburg, Brooklyn. This site-specific and temporary installation was composed of a monumental sphinx measuring over thirty-five feet in height, built out of polystyrene foam and coated in sugar bleached to a monochromatic white. Naked save for a handkerchief knotted over her head, the sphinx framed her breasts between her crouching forearms, and her exposed buttocks and genitalia were outlined by her rounded feet (figures 2.1–2.3). Measuring over seventy-five feet in length, the mammy-*cum*-sphinx was surrounded by a "procession of black boys" made from sugar byproducts who slowly melted around her in the summer heat.[1]

A Subtlety launched the history of sugar production and consumption into the lived environment. Exposing the continued importance of the commodity, Walker's installation represents the vestiges of plantation economies, marked by and marking the sweet and violent pleasures of eating sugar. The Sugar Baby

FIGURES 2.1 AND 2.2. Kara Walker's *A Subtlety*. Photographs by Jason Wyche, 2014.

FIGURE 2.3. Kara Walker's *A Subtlety*. Photograph by Jason Wyche, 2014.

portrays the violent histories of plantation slavery and sugar production, the effects of this history on the body—particularly Black women's bodies—and the lingering effects of this history on the present. Walker distills the history of sugar production in the Americas into a human figure, albeit one that is extreme and otherworldly. The construction of the sphinx within the refinery poignantly registers in the sculpture's body the long and complicated history of the construction of wealth and empire through the consumption of sugar and the Black bodies that produced it, the pleasure of sweetness and the euphoria and addiction it creates, the racialization and enslavement of the bodies needed to produce the commodity, and the fetishization of Black women's bodies.

I begin with Walker's sphinx to introduce the embodied monstrosity that is revealed through portrayals of sugar production and consumption in Colson Whitehead's *Zone One* (2011) and Cristina García's *Dreaming in Cuban* (1992). Whitehead's novel focuses on the attempt to rebuild New York City after a zombie apocalypse and is invested in questions of security and terrorism, reimagining the anathema of September 11, 2001, through the zombie, as well as signaling the mephitic danger of colorblind racism within its form. García's novel tells a multigenerational story on and off the island of Cuba, moving back and forth in time from the years before the Cuban Revolution to the mid-1990s. *Dreaming in Cuban* is an exemplar of post–Cold War Cuban American fiction, and it circulates exile nostalgia for a lost homeland that sits on the threshold of dereliction after the collapse of the Soviet Union.[2] *A Subtlety* is another evocation of the sugar contagion that the zombie carries on its body and the colonial disease that characters in García's novel spread through the dissemination of the commodity. A sculpture that signals the ruins of apocalyptic Caribbean sugar production and the brutal legacies of colonialism, the Sugar Baby evinces the pleasures of seeing these violent histories rendered in the art object.

In this chapter, I show how the zombie in Whitehead's novel and the fat, festering, and yearning Cuban body in García's illustrate historical trauma and act as mediums through which to explore the violent history of the Caribbean—an implacable force that cyclically returns to haunt the present. The narrative doom patterns I explore throughout this book coalesce in depictions of sugar production and consumption, where the violence of conquest, colonialism, enslavement, and dictatorship creates nonnormative bodies and troubling textual pleasures. These pleasures are enjoyed textually, metatextually, and paratextually: characters eat sugar and partake in its sweet addiction, as well as share in the violent history of wealth and taste it elicits; characters refuse to participate in upwardly mobile narratives of redemption; readers watch bodies become grotesque through consumption of the commodity; and readers of this book explore these two novels together. All this is performed through sugar: its ingestion instigates the zombie apocalypse in *Zone One* and produces fat, otherworldly, diasporic, decomposing Cuban bodies and extreme transnational longing in *Dreaming in Cuban*. Sugar triggers the re-creation of unregenerative imperial, racial, and ethno-national violence, challenging traditional expectations of minority literature and hegemonic cultures of remedy in all their liberal and radical guises.

The production and consumption of sugar in *Zone One* and *Dreaming in Cuban* illuminate a sweet addiction that sticks to the body and suggests the monstrous. These portrayals reveal the world-ending capacities of sugar. In particular, *Dreaming in Cuban* and *Zone One* expose the violent foundation hidden underneath sugar's sweet facade, a foundation that exceeds "normal" forms of representation and necessitates extreme and fantastic expressions, such as fat female bodies and the zombie. In fact, the overt tropes of speculative fiction mobilized in *Zone One* invite us to see *Dreaming in Cuban* in a fresh way. Turning from Whitehead's zombie novel to García's Cuban American text shows the former's investment in the tropes of genre fiction through portrayals of sugar that provide an aperture for returning to the latter with an eye for the otherworldly. Examining García's canonical Latinx novel through the reading protocols of speculative fiction, I highlight how depictions of excess, such as those that accompany the production and ingestion of sugar and sugary foodstuffs, the nostalgic longing for a "lost" homeland, and the desire for the triumph of transnational communism—excesses that the novel mediates through shifts in time, points of view, and formal variations—continually evoke historical forms of violence that veer toward the unearthly.

The attention to the hermeneutic of the archipelago in American and Latinx studies offers an opportunity to consider the invocations of sugar in depictions of Cuba, the Cuban diaspora, and the island of Manhattan. As Brian Russell Roberts and Michelle Ann Stephens, among others, explain, the archipelagic turn in American studies calls for a "decontinentalizion" of the way the United States, and the Americas more generally, is discussed and translated in scholarship, involving a recognition that the continent is "a set of spaces that has been persistently intertwined with, constituted by, and grounded in the archipelagic."[3] The connective tissue and multiplicities fashioned through various mobilizations evoke a palimpsest of historical and physical crossings that encompasses countless relations in difference. Archipelagic ontologies, moreover, accentuate the "power of cross-currents and connections" between islands that stress movements of relation.[4] Archipelagic thinking, in the work of Édouard Glissant, Rebeca Hey-Colón, Katherine McKittrick, Yomaira Figueroa-Vásquez, and Marisel Moreno, among others past and present, underscores a fluid set of assemblages, networks, and filaments that generate discursive spaces of textual production.[5]

In this way, archipelagic thinking is a provocative method for exploring island-island connections. As Hey-Colón reminds us, New York City is an island that in the context of Latinx studies must be read through the ocean that laps against its shores. The "protean sea has the capacity to surpass physical boundaries, promoting the fashioning of a regional identity rather than a national one," contends Hey-Colón, proposing a reading of Manhattan as a diasporic extension of the Caribbean archipelago.[6] *Doom Patterns* argues for the significance of exploring the US-Mexico border alongside the Caribbean, another cardinal geopolitical space within Latinx studies, while calling attention to both regions' specificities. Following scholars such as Hey-Colón, Moreno, Lorgia García-Peña, and Maria Cristina Fumagalli, I assert the need for comparative, transnational, and transregional research about borders and borderlands that moves us away from US-centric models.[7] My comparative analysis of Whitehead and García contributes to such research by incorporating a text that is ostensibly outside the field. By engaging Whitehead, an important author in the Black American literary tradition, this chapter illustrates the flow of people, goods, trade, culture, and affects, and the global forces that instigated these movements. In addition, an examination of the points of contact and networks of exchange between the Caribbean and the United States lays bare the knotted filaments in the racist ideologies and practices that are constitutive of the Americas but tend to be occluded by the compartmentalization within literary studies.

Reading through the lens of the archipelagic reveals subtle changes in material and cultural processes, as well the lapping return of history that washes up on islands' shores and connects the archipelago. This hermeneutic illuminates how sugar functions as a physical agent of sweetness and destruction in both novels: as a unifying literary trope, it metaphorically uncovers the violent histories of exchange between the Caribbean and the United States, highlighting how the commodity enabled the construction of an American empire, its capitalist system, and the monstrous bodies depicted in both. The new Caribbean mythology that chapter 1 identified in Junot Díaz's oeuvre, which depicts the cataclysmic ramifications of the Columbian encounter and the modern/colonial divide, is evident here as well. My analysis of *Zone One* alongside *Dreaming in Cuban* shows how portrayals of sugar render the Caribbean as geographically and symbolically adjacent to Manhattan, allowing us to read *Zone One* as not only a Black American text but also an Afro-Caribbean one. The inauguration of the zombie apocalypse through the consumption of sugar in *Zone One* evinces the text's investment in the Caribbean's colonial plantation economy past. The fat body in García's novel and the zombie in Whitehead's doggedly remind readers of the violence demanded by the production of sugar and the violence that is exhumed in its consumption. The examination of sugar imaginaries unearths interrelated narrative strategies, literary patterns, and networks that foreground fantasies of violence without concern for regenerative progress or optimism. Instead, these novels exhibit the unrelenting violence of Caribbean cataclysms and the pleasure of excessive consumption, violence, and addiction.

Zone One is not a work of Latinx literature, and *Dreaming in Cuban* is not typically read as a work of speculative fiction. Yet the depictions of sugar production and consumption constitute an important thematic network that spans the two novels and illustrates relational historical imaginaries. The reading protocols of Latinx speculative fiction redefine the speculative to include narrative forms that on the surface appear traditional but in their portrayals of extreme violence reveal other worlds. Sugar enacts what I term *end-time rhetorics* in García's and Whitehead's texts by acting as a trope that gives rise to the annihilation of worlds. The zombie in Whitehead's novel explicitly shows what is hidden within García's sugar end-times logic. Spaces of death—cultural, sociopolitical, and psychic—where the production and consumption of sugar point to historical violence also reveal how capitalist modes of production mark the body as monstrous and subject to violence.

Sugar is the product of cataclysmic violence, and any invocation of the commodity must recall its apocalyptic history. By *apocalyptic history*, I mean the destruction of worlds that are narratively unearthed through depictions of sugar production and consumption. Sidney Mintz's formative study *Sweetness and Power* (1985) investigated the essential role sugar played in the establishment of a capitalist system fashioned by slave labor that was crucial in the development of European and American empires.[8] What began as a luxury of the wealthy became a mass necessity by the mid-nineteenth century.[9] This shift toward the substantial consumption of sugar not only necessitated a large number of enslaved laborers but also mirrored the commercially oriented expansionist desires of Europe that led to the active construction of capitalist markets in the seventeenth and eighteenth centuries, which transformed the world.[10] At the core of sugar's sweet and ubiquitous presence lie the violent histories of transatlantic slavery, colonialism, and neocolonialism and the concomitant formation of Blackness as a category. Sugar discourses, to use Antonio Benítez-Rojo's phrase, play a central role in the formation of national and cultural identities.[11] Through depictions of sugar's world-destroying capacities, *Zone One* and *Dreaming in Cuban* show the transformative power of sugar in the history of the Americas.

To assert that sugar production and consumption are speculative and science-fictional might seem like an overstatement. Yet it is true that sugar slavery in the New World changed everything, making the foodstuff akin to an apocalyptic catalyst: Indigenous genocide, the enslavement of millions, and the environmental decimation that fueled the construction of European and American empires were processes of such extreme violence that, arguably, only the tropes of speculative fiction can come close to conveying them, even as these tropes also show the mundanity of the institution of slavery and the construction of empire and their haunting presence in the present.[12] In the novels, stories of colonization, slavery, and migration generate breakages in the text that instigate their end-time rhetorics. In turn, evocations of the otherworldly allude to colonial, imperial, and ethno-racial violence. *Dreaming in Cuban* explicitly overwrites its sugar-addicted "horrors" with the themes of national identity, Cuban American hybridity, and female kinship, while *Zone One*'s determinedly "literary" prose is strained by spectral racial meanings it does not overtly foreground. These grotesque forms remind us of the supernatural brutality in the production of sugar and the violence shown in its consumption.

In the section that follows, I argue that Whitehead's reimagination of this quintessential Caribbean monster not only tethers Manhattan to the Caribbean but also shows how the history of sugar production and consumption that the zombie carries on its grotesque body exhumes this past. Displaying the essential function of sugar in the construction of settler colonial and racial capitalism, *Zone One* paradoxically mobilizes pleasure in eating, in killing, in the use of sardonic humor, and in the liminal white space of irresolution at the novel's conclusion. Whitehead's evocation of the zombie directs our attention to the excess on the level of plot and form in García's text, which indicates the recurring and haunting violence of the Caribbean that is manifested as otherworldly. Sugar instigates apocalyptic reckonings in *Dreaming in Cuban* that also evince various kinds of pleasure, from the eating of sugar to the interlinked, multivoiced narratives, and the possibility of reconciliation that the novel forecloses.

In both novels, sugar activates apocalyptic violence that spawns monstrous bodies that compulsively ingest sugar, becoming even more grotesque. Sugar production and consumption thus act together as a driving metaphor and doom pattern, revealing the loss of kinship and the monstrosity and death that takes its place. In unearthing the excessive violence of the Caribbean through nontraditional forms, *Zone One* and *Dreaming in Cuban* portray New York and the Caribbean as connected postapocalyptic spaces that produce material and metaphorical death through their long histories of exchange in the form of the transatlantic slave trade, the production of sugar, and imperial expansion. *Doom Patterns* began with an examination of an author, Junot Díaz, who until recently was the exemplary model of *latinidad* in literature. In this chapter, I challenge the practice of reading for representation, loosening the criteria by which we recognize *latinidad* and the speculative in a text. If García's characters are clearly marked as Cuban and Cuban diasporic and Whitehead's protagonist seems to be unmarked by race, sugar facilitates an intersecting racial reading of both that further elucidates *latinidad*'s historical-material construction.

Birthday Cake and the Walking Dead

Zone One's postapocalyptic Manhattan is a ravaged wasteland. An unidentified plague has separated the population into the undead and the living. It is unclear how the plague began or how many years have passed since it decimated the world. The Zone, a blockaded strip of Lower Manhattan between Canal

Street and Battery Park, is considered by the new government, the American Phoenix, to be a model for the rest of the nation. The novel's protagonist, known only by his postplague moniker, "Mark Spitz," is one of the three members of the Omega Unit, a sweeper team whose job is to clear the Zone of remaining zombies. Over the course of a weekend, Spitz and the rest of his team sweep the city for "stragglers," the anomalous one percent of zombies who return to specific landscapes and remain apparently frozen. The other type of zombie introduced by the novel, the "skel," is the typical flesh-eating monster, believed by the characters to exist completely outside the Zone. Spitz's name is a parody of achievement, referencing both the Olympic champion and former world record holder in multiple swimming events and the racist stereotype that Black people cannot swim. His postapocalyptic name comes into play at the novel's culmination. In these final pages, Gary, one of Spitz's teammates, is bitten by a straggler-turned-skel, and to distract him from his impending death, Spitz recounts the origin story of his ironic nickname and reveals to the reader that he is Black. Almost immediately, the barricades that have structured the novel as well as the Zone begin to collapse as the zombies overtake the city, and Spitz walks into the horde.

In this section, I argue that portrayals of sugar in *Zone One*, and specifically the cutting of a birthday cake, enact apocalyptic violence in the novel, exhuming the undead and the violent histories they carry on their bodies. The zombie's presence, moreover, scripts New York City's influence within these histories as a devouring force analogous to the zombie's mouth. This scripting, in turn, exposes the central role that sugar, the Caribbean, and the transatlantic slave trade played in the construction of US empire. The novel's closing moments emphasize the precariousness of inhabiting a racialized body and the inability to escape racial models, even in the postapocalypse.

Some reviewers of *Zone One* condescendingly referred to the novel's genre by implying that Whitehead was "slumming it" by turning to the zombie. As one critic put it, "A literary novelist writing a genre novel is like an intellectual dating a porn star."[13] The patronizing tone of these reviewers is indicative of the general low regard for genre fiction in the academy and among the gatekeepers of the literary market.[14] The anxiety about the novel's investment in pulp dismisses genre as a form for "serious" consideration in "high art" and says nothing about what Whitehead is doing with the horror genre, and specifically the zombie, in *Zone One*. Scholarship on the novel highlights its mordant view of futurity: while the reconstruction of the nation is an optimistic act of survival, the postapocalypse is not a tabula rasa but rather a revival and continuation of the racist past that ultimately leads to the collapse of the Zone's barricades.

Such readings of *Zone One* separate the novel's use of genre from its treatment of race and present the zombie apocalypse as a tool with which to address the Anthropocene, "postracial" America, futurity, biopower, and securitization.[15] Yet the zombie is much more than a tool; it is central to the novel's Caribbean origins, poetics, and exploration of Blackness.

As the embodiment of the histories of plantation slavery and sugar production in the Caribbean, the zombie's presence in Manhattan outlines the city's influence within this history. During his sweeper duties, Spitz imagines his team leader, Kaitlyn, as the instigator of the end of the world. In his estimation, the plague and the postapocalyptic world it created did not begin in the conventional fashion—brewed in a government laboratory or activated through the bite of an African monkey—but rather emerged from a "perfect" middle-class birthday party and, more importantly, a birthday cake:

> Mark Spitz sees it clearly: Kaitlyn's implacable march through a series of imaginative and considered birthday parties . . . each birthday party transcending the last and approaching a kind of birthday-party perfection that once accomplished would usher in an exquisite new age of bourgeois utopia. . . . Maybe, he thought one night, . . . it was Kaitlyn herself who had summoned the plague: as she cut into the first slice of cake at her final, perfect birthday party, history had come to an end. She had blown out the candles on the old era, blotted out the dinosaurs' heavens, sent the great ice age sheet scraping forth, the blood counts zooming up into madness.[16]

Spitz's birthday cake fantasy is the only explanation given for the zombie apocalypse, a conceptual explication that places sugar at the center of the novel's world-building, where it functions as the catalyst of apocalyptic violence that actuates the zombie. Indeed, the birthday cake is the quintessential object of the zombie apocalypse, and its innocent sweetness is ironically juxtaposed with the destruction of the world. The zombies that originate in the cake, bearing the saccharine residue of the cane field and the sugar mill, act out a revenge fantasy on the colonizer and the system of racial capitalism that engendered them.[17]

While sugar hypothetically enhances the celebratory aspects of birthdays and weddings, *Zone One* reveals the wounding essence of sugar and the indelible saturation of the commodity in the violent histories of colonization, transatlantic slavery, imperialism, and dictatorship. As scholars like Elisabeth Anker have demonstrated, the sugar plantation established the development of racial slavery, Indigenous dispossession, and modern liberal freedom, and as Eric Williams and others have argued, the sugar plantation specifically served as the foundation for modern capitalism.[18] Sugar's centrality in the slave trade and the plantation economies of the Caribbean has informed the depiction of Black people as monstrous and the emergence of the zombie in popular culture. Haiti and the Caribbean were associated with the figure of the cannibal in the sixteenth century and came to be seen in the Western imagination as spaces of eternal slavery as the threat of the cannibal was replaced by that of the mindless zombie.[19]

The zombie, which originated in Saint-Domingue as a spirit that could possess a human body, came to signify a person who had lost consciousness and could be forced into slave labor through a voodoo spell.[20] Although the source and date are debated, various scholars point to William Seabrook's 1929 travelogue, *The Magic Island*, as the official introduction of the monster to US audiences.[21] Narratives about zombies predate Seabrook's; they arose as Haiti gained its independence in 1804—stories of voodoo and cannibalism that underscored the country's primitivism and savagery.[22] The belief that Haiti's self-destruction would spill over to the rest of the Americas was prominent in the nineteenth century. Haiti, therefore, was a country to be saved and, through its salvation, contained.[23] Early depictions of the zombie portray for US consumers a Caribbean dead space replete with undead Black bodies that are at the service of transatlantic corporations that traffic in sugar. These bodies threaten the United States with racial infection carried by the sugar they produce. The folkloric zombie of Seabrook's travelogue has been transformed multiple times in the hemispheric American cultural imaginary of the twentieth and twenty-first centuries.[24] Born in the cane fields and the sugar mills of the Caribbean and mobilized through the rhetoric of slave labor, the zombie symbolically embodies these histories. It also personifies the fear of the return of the colonial master, offering a critique of slavery and the Black body in capitalist labor while simultaneously enabling the reenactment of empire and its power structures.

The zombie, then, is always coated in the violence of sugar production, which fuses together Caribbean and US geographies. In *Zone One*, New York plays a central role in this extended space. New Amsterdam was the terrain where European imperial ambitions continuously manifested themselves and where sugar and exchange with the Caribbean played vital roles in the city's expansion and monetary gains.[25] The acquisition of New Netherland was an imperialist decision made with the intention of exploiting the potential wealth of the sugar market.[26] In *Zone One* and *Dreaming in Cuban*, the city, with its ties to the plantation economies of the Caribbean, implicates the rest of the nation in its bloody history.

The mouth is the site through which Whitehead examines the political implications of the zombie in New York City. Political beliefs cleave to the mouth, making it the space where the progress of the nation and futurity are measured. In the postapocalypse, survivors are recognized as adherents to the ideology of reconstruction through their consumption—the use of corporate-sponsored clothing and accessories or government-grown and subsidized corn indicates their support for the government's reconstruction efforts. If the mouth of the pheenie—that is, of a survivor who believes in the reconstruction mission of the American Phoenix—represents a virtuous and restorative consumption, then only anxiety and desire are projected onto the mouth of the zombie, and its fearsome bite poses a threat to national identity.[27] The mouth, as Kyla Wazana Tompkins points out, is the place where food "as mediated experience imperfectly bonds with the political to form the fictions that are too often understood within everyday life as racial truths."[28] Arguing that "eating culture" produces political subjects and is the medium through which racial formations and racist ideologies are consolidated in the body politic, Tompkins shows that the mouth is a space for political reflection where the human and post/human are differentiated. The same is true in Whitehead's novel: the zombie's mouth and its imprint are the loci through which the readers access the history of violence and colonialism in the Caribbean, the history of sugar production and consumption, and the impossibility of reconstruction in *Zone One*/Zone One.

Zone One also personifies the city as monstrous, making it contiguous to the zombie's presence—the city and the zombie are textual foils that work in tandem to thwart reconstruction efforts. A description of the zombie's chomp on a straggler's neck, for example, where "exposed meat resembled torn-up pavement tinted crimson," coalesces the bite with the urban space inhabited by the zombies.[29] The zombie's flesh in this description, which occurs at the novel's culmination, returns readers to the novel's earlier performances of New York, staging monster and city as mirror images of each other. The zombie's wound is a "scabbed hollow of gaping gristle, tubes, and pipes: the city's skin ripped back," creating a dizzying effect in which both bite and wound refer back and forth from city to zombie and reveal the postapocalypse as an inescapable, chronic force.[30] The zombie's chomp becomes a textual marker for the impossibility of reconstruction: the "torn-up" flesh invokes New York's violent composition, rendering its foundational structure as marked by the violence that has always hidden beneath the surface. In a series of Janus-like literary elements, the zombie's mouth exposes the city's bloody infrastructure. Following the colon, "the city's skin ripped back" carries grammatical and visual import, the "scabbed hollow" reveals the "crimson" sinews of New York and presents the postapocalyptic restoration efforts as equivalent to the scab, a thin ornamental endeavor. The scab cannot heal the diseased history signified by the zombie's body, which the monster's maw implacably protests. Together, the literary representations of the city as a consuming landscape and the zombie's mouth show how the violent history that the zombie embodies constantly returns to enact its vengeance. The end of the world reveals New York City as a dangerously sibylline place, a truer mirror image of itself.

As a model for the rest of the nation, the city implicates the country in this violence, exposing the central role that sugar and the transatlantic slave trade played in empire building. The zombie and the city act as excessive textual forces that mirror the novel's style—a claustrophobic coiling of the past—and show that postapocalyptic violence and the history it has unearthed are inescapable. Although the narration is third-person-limited, the novel follows Spitz's movements and thoughts so closely that at times it can be mistaken for a first-person narration, a device that creates a sense of claustrophobia, tension, and urgency and forces readers to occupy the narrative's point of view. These elements are sharpened by the intercalated use of the past and past perfect tenses, a technique that dizzyingly accentuates the overpowering force of the apocalypse within the text. Most of the novel takes place through memory, both in the years before the apocalypse and in those after the end of the world, a choice that suggests that violence cannot be contained in a linear fictional mode. The novel breaks form by telling this story from the future, in the postapocalypse, which ironically relocates the reader in the past, which is also technically post, and illustrates a constant cycle between "posts" mired in violence.

Zone One's metropolis is portrayed through the zombie's presence as a pinnacle of mindless consumerism, and thus as the archetypal space in which to confront its monster double. The zombie's unrelenting threat and ultimate invasion of the city trusses its history with that of the sugar-producing Caribbean, underscoring how the Dutch colony's success in the seventeenth century—like that of the British colony that followed—was due to the slave trade and the colony's mercantile investments. The zombie apocalypse and the monsters it exhumes also draw attention to national and transnational economic institutions within the Zone, whose origins are found in the European colonization of the hemisphere, and to the establishment of the United States as a capitalist empire. In short, the city is central to *Zone One*: a key character in the plot, Manhattan rivals Spitz for space and attention. The novel is as much about the city—a symbol of progress and empire—as about Spitz's camouflaged Blackness, or the zombie's embodiment of sugar and plantation economies. From the novel's outset, the city forewarns us of the dismembering nature of the plague and evinces within its architecture the zombie's devouring power. Effectively, *Zone One*'s depiction of the city superimposes the preapocalyptic past onto a postapocalyptic present, revealing its unchanging nature. The metropolis is built on an unbridled accumulation—"bigger, better"; "story by glorious story"; "idea by unlikely idea"—that prepares it to be occupied not by the unwashed masses or the "millions" of the past but by the zombie swarm.[31] Even visions of the city's future residents in the postreconstruction era make them edible and disposable. In Spitz's future-vision, the new residents of the island become concomitant with the city's earlier waves of immigrants: "When the sweepers finished their mission, who would be the new residents of the island, bellies up to the boat rail, gaping as expectantly as those other immigrants who had come to the harbor, that first fodder?"[32] Immigrants are consumable goods that undermine this seemingly hopeful image: the city's past and future are ferocious spaces of ingestion that call forth the novel's present devouring force, the zombies. The future is not an achievable end point in *Zone One* but a cyclical return to the past, where new arrivals are the foodstuff that fuels the city's hungry expansion. Textual associations of past and future immigrants with food expose the city's landscape as a postapocalyptic consumer of flesh with origins in the colonial past. New York City is an environment one must survive, suggesting that its new immigrants—members of the American Phoenix—will inevitably become "fodder" themselves. Spitz's question is both a textual flashback and a foreshadowing that reminds us of the city's recurring violence: the city has always maimed its citizens, will become (has always been) post/apocalyptic, and will rip (has already ripped) its citizens to pieces.

The process of reconstruction in *Zone One* is a symbolic act of optimism that harkens back to the period following the US Civil War and the failure of this era. While geographically specific, the process of clearing the Zone is also national and speculative in scope. Manhattan, imagined as "the biggest version of everywhere," is an emblem of hope for the rest of the country, an element satirized by the novel.[33] By the end of *Zone One*, Spitz comes to ridicule the American Phoenix's investment in the city as a vessel of optimism, foreshadowing his understanding that all postapocalyptic survivors will repeatedly become the city's "first fodder." Immediately following the revelation of Spitz's race, skels outside the Zone breach the barricades and overtake the city. The fortifications erected to create the Zone, like the conceptual barricades created in the postworld, are fallible objects that cannot withstand the zombie's force or the history it embodies. The facade of normalcy that the barricades provide is their downfall: the archaic technologies of the preapocalypse are replicated in the postworld, underscoring the inanity of reconstruction. The novel's closing moments, where the zombies overtake the Zone and Spitz walks into the horde, foreground the pleasure experienced in the production and reproduction of destruction and demonstrate the impossibility of suppressing this violent history or the nation's involvement in it.

Optimism and violence—sweetness and destruction—synchronically circulate throughout *Zone One*. Reconstruction, in this context, requires the erection of barricades, the definition of the zombies as "monsters," and the physical eradication of the monsters from the Zone. This reconstruction, which is envisioned through structures of exclusion, is aimed at reestablishing the social and biopolitical boundaries of the past. It is contingent on removing the visible markers of the zombies and the history their bodies signal, to "erase the stains."[34] This nostalgic look back to a utopian American past defines home and country through security and exclusion.[35] Yet the novel departs from conventional apocalyptic narratives, in which humanity tends to emerge "triumphant or chastened," by showing that the nation-state has always been formed through futile efforts at containment that expose the weakness of national sovereignty and foreshadow the reconstruction's failure.[36] Remembering why he volunteered as a sweeper for the Zone, Spitz reflects that the reconstruction effort will "force a resemblance" to what the city once was with "new lights seeping through the black veil like beads of blood pushing through gauze until it was suffused."[37] The desire to reinstate a lost time is overshadowed by violent language that contaminates the grammar of renewal. Although the plague seems to invoke the erasure of history through the destruction of the known world, the violent history of the Americas cannot be contained, and the present time of the text is doom-patterned with the violence that depictions of sugar unleash. Even the name of the reconstruction effort, the American Phoenix, euphemistically creates a barricade against the terrifying reality of the zombie plague, parodying the buoyant image it invokes: the cleansing and destructive force of fire connotes optimism and violence while simultaneously corporatizing the future. The similarity to American political campaigns and governmental measures invites readers to pleasurably mock their participation in any version of a nation-building project. *Zone One*, in fact, offers the nation as an oozing wound, its formation and reconstitution as a bloody endeavor.

The birthday cake and other allusions to sugar inscribe the text with end-time rhetorics. The stragglers inhabit a time and space where the past of sugar plantation slavery crashes against the postapocalyptic present and reveals a haunted dimension. Upending conventional depictions of the zombie, *Zone One* also challenges definitions of humanity, memory, and citizenship. The introduction of the stragglers defies the genre's conventions: as a zombified posthuman subject that attaches itself to a particular location and remains in it, the straggler does not move, attack, or feed, and therefore this "aberrant one percent" is unreadable to the reconstruction effort. Despite carrying the visible markers of zombification, the straggler does not perform what should be its cannibalistic role. Conversely, the skel is all mouth and seemingly mindless ingestion. The anxiety that surrounds the zombie's presence is associated with eating; the zombie's mouth holds the threat of racial infection and the deadly spread of the histories of slavery and production of sugar. Furthermore, the straggler's attachment to specific places implies an argument about exhumed histories. The straggler haunts the landscape of the novel, and as María del Pilar Blanco reminds us, haunting illuminates "*simultaneous landscapes and simultaneous others* living within unseen, diverse spaces in the progressively complicated and cultural network of hemispheric modernization."[38] Haunting, then, is a "*stylization of space*" that presents the disconcerting experience of perceiving the "collision of temporalities and spaces."[39] The spatiotemporal coordinates that merge to produce haunting manifest in the straggler as a narrative phenomenon that threatens the text and its characters: the straggler's apparent passivity is transformed at the end of the novel when a straggler becomes a skel, which in turn upends the narrative and the reader's understanding of its protagonist.

Spitz moves through most of the novel as a racially unmarked character. At a key moment of the novel's culmination, as mentioned earlier, he reveals to the reader that he is Black. The revelation of Spitz's "race" at the novel's culmination is yet another impediment to reconstruction. Much as the straggler's transformation upends the conventional definition of the zombie, Spitz's Blackness upends common conceptions of racialization in literature. Both are vehicles through which to examine the re-destruction of the world. If the reconstruction effort is contingent on the plague's apparent expunging of the markers of history—which the novel sardonically derides as a critique of Barack Obama–era colorblind racism and postraciality—while attempting to bring back the past, then the exposure of Spitz's race, which is revealed through the straggler's transformation and a significant plot twist that revolutionizes the novel, cements his position as a threat parallel to that posed by the zombies. That is, once Spitz discloses to the reader he is Black, he embodies even more strikingly that which the American Phoenix is attempting to erase. By withholding Spitz's race until this point, the novel upends the reader's assumptions: Spitz is strategically camouflaged through this omission until the explicit articulation exposes him as Black.[40] As I show in chapter 5 when discussing Carmen Maria Machado's *Her Body and Other Parties* (2017), the obfuscation of ethno-racial markers not only challenges readerly assumptions but also forces the ethno-racial onto the level of form. Spitz's name, known from the outset to be a parody of ambition and success, is revealed to have been assigned through a stereotype, which racially marks him with "the black-people-can't-swim thing," as he describes it.[41] His race is a device with which to explore the haunting of the past, a tool through which the text expresses the past's engulfing of the present. As a product of narrative, Spitz's Blackness is an effect of the text, much like its speculative tropes, and the revelation of his race causes the novel to unravel. Spitz's postapocalyptic moniker inscribes him as an elusive and subversive presence, much as the straggler's transformation is a source of confusion and textual disruption. Because we are never told Spitz's "real" name, we are forced to read him through the stereotype. In this respect, Spitz embodies Glissant's "right to opacity": his nickname and the obfuscation of his race amount to refusals of legibility.[42]

The revelation of Spitz's race executes a narrative unraveling that saturates the final pages of *Zone One* with the histories of the Middle Passage and plantation slavery. Here the zombies infiltrate the Zone like a flood, an inundation that "bubbled and frothed" down the avenue.[43] Water imagery and oceanic metaphors, Paul Gilroy reminds us, refer to the Middle Passage and the "half-remembered micro-politics of the slave trade and its relationship to both industrialisation and modernisation."[44] Carrying this history onto the streets of Manhattan, the zombie-ocean threatens to flood the American landscape with Blackness. The "first fodder" enacts a revenge fantasy and forces the histories the zombies carry on their bodies onto the city. Oceanic rhetorics have long served as animating forces in Black artistic production, theory, and criticism, what Tiffany Lethabo King calls an "arterial through line" that defies Eurocentric discourse and normative thought.[45] This oceanic horde, like the city, is an embedded narrative whose language Spitz learns to decipher, a textual message that acts as a final corrective. In this sea, Spitz sees the "inhuman scroll as an argument, 'I was here, I am here now, I have existed, I exist still. This is our town.'"[46] Against the grammar of renewal, the zombies' language articulates an insistence on unearthing the history of violence that the architects of the reconstruction wanted to expunge. The repetition of "I am" and "I have" demands that the presence of the zombies now and in the past be acknowledged. This demand maps the violence inflicted on Black and brown people in the service of sugar production onto the US landscape.

Narrative futurity is foreclosed for Spitz once his race is revealed and he learns to read the zombies' grammar. The "dead-bound subject," as Abdul Jan-Mohamed argues, is defined by the constant threat of death and "produced as a subject by the process of 'unbinding.'"[47] The Black subject, then, is outlined by the violence enacted on their body. Spitz's Blackness scripts him as a target of violence that serves as the "vestibule for the Democracy that is to come": his suffering is necessary for the achievement of the American promise of progress and equality.[48] In a similar vein, Anker shows how key practices of race-making in the United States originated in the sugar plantations of Barbados, practices that go hand in hand with American frameworks for understanding freedom and democracy.[49]

Since Spitz's death is a necessary byproduct of the nation-building project, he walks into the zombie horde and into the white space of the book, where language stops. This white space is what Christina Sharpe describes as the "no-space," which "the law is not bound to respect."[50] Spitz's disappearance illustrates how the erasure of Black pain is constitutive of American life. As Sharpe argues, Black suffering cannot be apprehended by mainstream forms of representation, and the Black body is routinely ejected by a system that "reimagines and reconstitutes itself" through this ejection.[51] Black exclusion and death are normative and necessary for nation-building projects, and thus Spitz must be killed, erased, or eaten.

The collapsing barricades, however, index the insolvency of nation-state sovereignty, even as for Spitz they signal the exclusion of the Black subject from American reconstruction efforts.[52] Spitz's final thought, "Fuck it," rejects the reconstruction as well as notions of futurity and progress.[53] This is a moment of pleasure and humor as well. As I explored in chapter 1 with Díaz's use of "fukú"—the doom of the New World—Spitz's curse is marked with sardonic humor. Fukú and "Fuck it" reproduce the violence of colonial hemispheric formations and enslavement while humorously mocking Western epistemology. These terms also mock the reader with wordplay, obscenity, and the withholding of crucial information.

Spitz walking into the sea-horde and out of the narrative demands that we contend with the white space that follows. In Sharpe's words, it is "in the wake" that Black being is constituted "through and by continued vulnerability."[54] Sharpe's phrase "in the wake" evokes Saidiya Hartman's "position of the un-thought," which describes the possibility of action on the part of the enslaved that centers a "radical refusal of the terms of the social order or these acts that are sometimes called suicide or self-destruction, but which are really an embrace of death."[55] While Spitz's death is not described, the narrative follows his perspective alone, making it clear that he is speaking to us from the dead, or from a space of no-death, a space beyond the common understanding of life and death. From that vantage point, his actions are decisive, and his renunciation clear. "What would it be, deeper still, what is it, to think from no standpoint; to think outside the desire for a standpoint?" Fred Moten asks.[56] Moten describes this "no standpoint" as having the potential to end the world. We can read *Zone One* as an attempt to answer his question through Spitz's final action. Walking into the horde is world-ending: after Spitz walks into the throng, the novel ends, leaving the reader with no language outside violence, the zombie's mouth, or the vengeance the zombies embody.

Spitz's disappearance into this portentous horde returns us to the novel's opening pages and Spitz's invocation of the city's past and future "fodder," where its inhabitants are turned into consumable goods and pieces of obsolete technology on which the city subsists. Visualizing his consumption, Spitz displays an ironic pleasure in being part of the city's mechanism. Within this fantasy, he can enact violence on his own body, preempting the violence that will be performed by the city and zombie in the postapocalypse. Indeed, his body's consumption is posited as a form of pleasure—for readers and the protagonist—and as an accomplishment, even as it is also an argument about Spitz's racial expendability. His tumbling in the novel's opening is transformed in the conclusion into an act of disavowal. These moments of ingestion (both in the imagined past and in the textual present time) are staged as cyclical inevitabilities that confirm Spitz's anti-identitarian opting out. The white space that follows Spitz's final action destroys any remaining political hope by serving as a continuation of the past, which defined Black suffering as a necessary condition for national progress. Spitz's Blackness, then, is a marker for his walking-deadness, excluding Spitz from the fantasy of political "life." *Zone One* finally shows us that the *post* of the postapocalypse is a categorical fiction: apocalyptic terror continues to destroy Black being.

Fat, Sugar, and the Otherworldly Body

Dreaming in Cuban tells the story of Celia del Pino; her daughters, Lourdes and Felicia; and her granddaughter, Pilar, following Lourdes's immigration to the United States with her husband, Rufino Puente. Lourdes eventually pays a return visit to the island with her daughter, Pilar.[57] Moving between Cuba and the United States, the novel shifts not only in space but also between points of view, time periods, and narrative forms. Nominated for a National Book Award, included in many anthologies, and thus almost immediately canonized, *Dreaming in Cuban* has attracted a great deal of scholarly attention, most of which focuses on the novel's identity politics, Latinx hybridity, exile, ethnic nostalgia, and depictions of female kinship.[58] Discussions surrounding *Dream-*

ing in Cuban most commonly rely on feminist and postcolonial readings that highlight the novel's investment in questions of Cuban and Cuban American history, nationality, and citizenship. It is often pointed out that portrayals of exile and migration, especially through the character of Pilar, illustrate what Gustavo Pérez Firmat terms "life on the hyphen."[59] Firmat's gentle interpretation of being culturally in-between and dual is read in the novel as a recuperation of cultural authenticity and *Cubanidad* that enables fluid forms of communication across geographic lines and generations.

In my reading of *Dreaming in Cuban*, I highlight how the many forms of excess within the novel depict the Latina as monstrous and the Caribbean as an atemporal postapocalyptic space: the three generations of del Pino women monstrously embody the overwhelming, recurring, and haunting violence of Cuba and its diaspora. *Dreaming in Cuban* portrays a ruined Cuba and its haunted US exiles, creating a distinctly apocalyptic scenario that is framed by depictions of sugar production and consumption on and off the island. Although the novel is not considered a work of genre fiction, revisiting *Dreaming in Cuban* through the lens of Latinx speculative fiction and following an exploration of *Zone One* reveals that the two works belong to the same literary archipelago, subject to the same currents and winds. By analyzing them side by side, we can see how their mutual literary trope—sugar—exhumes shared histories of violence that verge on the fantastic. In particular, *Zone One*'s association of sugar with zombies helps us recognize that the excessive embodiment and affective longing in *Dreaming in Cuban* harbor the speculative and horrific.

Through portrayals of sugar, García constructs *Dreaming in Cuban* around impossible returns. Instead of depicting celebratory homecomings, the novel exhibits the unrelenting violence of Cuban histories and the pleasure of sweet ingestion and destruction. Invocations of sugar and its consumption return us to apocalypse in the text, New World rhetorics of recurring and seemingly unending unearthly destruction that define the Caribbean as a space of cyclical chaos. In this way, the portrayals of sugar are windows onto the speculative aspects of the novel that invite us to see it as something other than a work of magical realism or traditional Latinx literature.

The narrative shifts between time and space, past and present, moving from Cuba to New York, all the while staging Cuba as temporally isolated from American imperial modernity and geographically detached from the rest of the hemisphere. Visiting Cuba with her mother, Pilar says she feels "like we're back in time, in a kind of Cuban version of an earlier America."[60] Cuba is described as an "island-colony" that has been relegated to the past; it can be reached in a "thirty-minute charter flight from Miami, yet never reach[ed]" at all.[61] The

Cuban Revolution occasions the geographic and geopolitical irrelevancy of Cuba in the novel, producing postcolonial subjects inscribed by violence. Lourdes, for example, is metaphorically created through geographic and temporal shifts that make human speech and time unutterable: "The continents strain to unloose themselves, to drift reckless and heavy in the seas. Explosions tear and scar the land, spitting out black oaks and coal mines, street lamps and scorpions. Men lose the power of speech. The clocks stop. Lourdes Puente awakens."[62] The violent shifts in time and space that bring Lourdes's body and the land into being also mark her textual introduction. This accelerated and transtemporal depiction of modernity imagines an otherworldly space where language and time are insufficient to describe a Cuban woman in the diaspora.

The novel textually scripts Lourdes's coming-into-being through violence and absence, marking her body as excessive and unruly. This violent creation underscores the essential role that ingestion plays in the creation of excessive bodies, establishing the centrality of the unearthly: "The flesh amassed rapidly on her hips and buttocks, muting the angles of her bones. It collected on her thighs, fusing them above the knees. It hung from her arms like hammocks. She dreamt continually of bread, of grainy ryes and pumpernickels, whole wheat and challah in woven straw baskets. They multiplied prodigiously, hung abundantly from the trees, crowded the skies until they were redolent of yeast."[63] Her food fantasies are so voracious they plague both her consciousness and unconsciousness, becoming associated with disease. Lourdes's ingestion and weight gain are yoked to disability, as her body's internal framework and even her skeleton are altered by the flesh's softening. Her physical changes cast Lourdes's unruly hunger and body as symptoms of the violent histories of colonialism, slavery, and the Cuban Revolution. The novel thus inscribes Lourdes's postrevolution exile within a space that provides her access to limitless quantities (and fantasies) of food while depicting this space as burdensome.

Lourdes, the owner of a bakery in Brooklyn, is defined by her hunger and excessive "flesh," whose amassment is an inactive process outside her control and serves to counter the rhetoric of scarcity associated with postrevolution Cuba. She is excessive in more ways than one; she has an insatiable appetite not just for food but also for sex. When Lourdes eats uncontrollably, her sexual desire is also insatiable, and, conversely, when she stops eating, she stops reaching for her husband. Her corporeality and appetite are mirrored by an extreme experience of trauma and loss: she lost land in Cuba and through it a connection to the nation. Most significantly, she was raped and miscarried her second child. This trauma is a catalyst for her emigration to the United States, and it plagues Lourdes throughout the novel, physically and psychically.

In the abundance of food fantasies and her participation in American capitalism, Lourdes can distance herself physically, psychically, and ideologically from her mother and motherland, since her mother, Celia, chooses to remain in Cuba. US emigration, accompanied by a vision of ethnic difference and upward mobility vis-à-vis sugar, enables Lourdes to re-create post/colonial violence. At the behest of her father's ghost, Lourdes plans to open a second bakery, which the ghost claims will demonstrate "what we Cubans are up to, that we're not all Puerto Ricans."[64] The ghost's denigrating comment and Lourdes's sugar visions effect a divisionary Latinx position and a reenactment of colonial violence both toward the Latinx-self and toward the Anglo-US other. As Antonio López explains, various US state-sponsored programs have enabled the Cuban exile experience to be defined as "different," particularly in relation to that of the Puerto Rican.[65] The disassociation from Puerto Ricanness, accomplished by owning and naming private property, becomes a mechanism through which Lourdes can separate herself from ethnicized racialization and Blackness and thereby avoid the "menacing possibility of a 'blackening' in the Anglo-U.S. gaze."[66] Indeed, Lourdes relishes the possibility of participating in an American nation-building project by encouraging patriotism.

These desires are mediated by the consumption and dissemination of sugar and products made from it. Through her ownership of a bakery and her peddling of sweet baked goods, Lourdes repositions herself as an off/white landowner who reproduces the violent histories of the plantation economy on the streets of Brooklyn and beyond. Her patriotic fantasy is steeped in Americana:[67]

> Lourdes ordered custom-made signs for her bakeries in red, white, and blue with her name printed at the bottom right-hand corner: LOURDES PUENTE, PROPRIETOR. She particularly liked the sound of the last word, the way the "r"'s rolled in her mouth, the explosion of "p"'s. Lourdes felt a spiritual link to American moguls, to the immortality of men like Irénée du Pont, whose Varadero Beach mansion on the north of the coast of Cuba she had once visited. She envisioned a chain of Yankee Doodle bakeries stretching across America to St. Louis, Dallas, Los Angeles, her apple pies and cupcakes on main streets and in suburban shopping malls everywhere.
>
> Each store would bear her name, her legacy: LOURDES PUENTE, PROPRIETOR.[68]

The text performs American colonial conquest in both form and content and mobilizes apocalyptic violence through Lourdes's fantasy of Yankee Doodle bakeries overtaking the United States. Likening herself to business magnates such as du Pont allows Lourdes to indulge in a colonialist fantasy where she can enjoy the tropical beauty of her homeland that simultaneously defines her as an exploitative outsider. The leisure of tourism is mixed with the expansionist desire for conquest as the narration moves from Cuba through New York and to the Midwest, Southwest, and western United States. The bakery is thus transformed into a symbol of apocalyptic violence where Lourdes can imagine overtaking the American landscape to re-create imperial conquest. The spread of sugar from coast to coast maps the history of enslavement and the otherworldly violence in the production of sugar onto Brooklyn and, through Lourdes's fantasy, the rest of the nation. The history of plantation slavery is carried into the United States through her bakeries that spread west in an archetypal American movement associated with progress and nourishment. Her legacy, however, is no longer in Cuba, and the nation she is building and feeding is the one where she is an exile.

Sugar in the novel is a driving metaphor for the impossibility of physical and metaphorical return to the island. The Yankee Doodle bakery becomes a space where Cuban exiles gather to conspire and discuss potential anti–Fidel Castro actions that might allow for their eventual return. However, Lourdes's insistent remembering of an inaccessible Cuban past—one in which she and her husband are still the owners of the Puente estate—prohibits this return and ensures that her eventual visit with Pilar will be merely transitory. The bakery is the vehicle through which Lourdes can express an ethnic, politically tinged yearning for Cuba while asserting her patriotic affiliation with the US nation-building project. Through "tricolor cupcakes and Uncle Sam marzipan," Lourdes believes that "she can fight communism from behind her bakery counter."[69] The sugary treats of her bakery are thus encoded as symbols of American nationalism: through her capitalist endeavors, they disseminate addiction and infection, blanketing the landscape in the sugary frosting of the commodity's violent history.

Sugar also functions as a metaphor for Lourdes's ambivalent relationship to her *Cubanidad* and investment in her adopted home. Through the commodification and circulation of sugar, Lourdes performs a self-disruption of her Latina identity, associating herself with those "American moguls" who consumed the Caribbean as a space of leisure. The quintessentially Anglo-American treats she imagines baking, "apple pies" and "cupcakes"—instead of the Cuban *pastelitos de guayaba* (guava pastries) or flan—become agents of addiction in Anglo-US spaces such as main streets and shopping malls. Lourdes's vision asserts her power over the landscape and allows her to author herself as a Latina within an Anglo-American narrative. In conjuring a destiny of capitalist conquest, she conjoins her Cuban and American identities in a revenge fantasy that appropriates symbols of Anglo-American patriotism to spread colonial disease—sugar addiction—among the American population from coast to coast.

These saccharine visions allow Lourdes to pursue American upward mobility. As a property owner specializing in sugar products, she repudiates the nationalization of private property in Cuba and her mother's leftist politics. By owning property and disseminating sugar, Lourdes establishes not only her capitalist tastes but also her defiant cravings for an inaccessible Cuban past. Ricardo Ortiz, in his critique of the classic Cuban exile, calls this nostalgic desire for return a "chronic and aporetic addiction" that reveals a "stubborn, compulsive refusal to surrender their claim to lost property and lost capital."[70] Lourdes's pathological consumption and production of sugar products informs her "fantasies of return, reunification, and restitution," incongruent as they might be.[71]

Unlike Lourdes, Celia del Pino, the novel's matriarch, remains in Cuba after the revolution and is deeply invested in the nation's post-1959 communist project. Her narrative bookends the novel and in doing so not only sets its tone but also defines the possibilities for all the characters on and off the island. From her coastal home she guards the nation, superimposing the island's colonial history onto it as she names the fishing boats in the distance: "the *Niña*, the *Pinta*, and the *Santa María*."[72] This gesture and the novel's constant return to Celia's letters to her lost Spanish lover—epistolary interruptions that drive the narrative forward while anchoring it to the past—reveal the del Pino family history and the island itself to have been formed through this colonial encounter, forcing them (and it) to endure its eternal return.

Sugarcane is also presented as a fundamental commodity within the island's present.[73] Celia's focus on the "rumors" that "*yanquis*" will drop "germ bombs to wither the sugarcane fields" underscores the centrality of sugar as a literary trope while conveying her fear of global violence and catastrophe.[74] Through symbols of the island's colonial past, the novel's opening pages collapse past and present, creating a friction in the text that is exacerbated by the various movements between narrative perspectives, points of view, and temporal standpoints. The temporal collapse also alludes to Cuba's history of slavery, and particularly its reliance on sugar production since the eighteenth century and the restrictions suffered after the revolution.

The production of sugar in postrevolutionary Cuba is posed as ideologically corrupt and violent, an image at odds with the depiction of the opportunities it provides Lourdes in the United States. Through the physical labor required for sugar's cultivation, Celia becomes the perfect *compañera* (comrade) for the revolution. Celia submits to the physical toil of cutting sugarcane: she "consigns her body" to it, submitting herself to a nation-building project in opposition to

Lourdes's.[75] Through her association with the crop, Celia becomes temporarily racialized. The fear that abolitionists and sugar boycotters of the nineteenth century felt is incarnated in a movement of the machete when a *machetero* (cane cutter) slashes a volunteer, whose blood mingles with the stalks. *Dreaming in Cuban* thus defines the cane field as a space of racial tension and physical violence that exposes the nation's colonial past. The volunteer's injury embeds the 1970s Cuban cane field in the history of slavery and the history of American and European dependence on the commodity.

The cane field also underscores Celia's class privilege while allowing her to fantasize about a transnational communist network. It is one of the only moments of the novel where race and class difference are specified, identifying the *machetero* in opposition to the volunteer. In reaction to the volunteer's injury, a Creole woman "spits out" a curse, "Celia does not know to whom," establishing a moment of ambiguity and misrecognition that displaces her.[76] Yet the fantasy of communism's global success, in which communism promotes economic growth, national participation in geopolitical exchange, and global relevance, is marred by the violence in the field. Celia imagines sugarcane traveling in "three-hundred-pound sacks of refined white sugar deep in the hulls of ships," reaching people "in Mexico and Russia and Poland."[77] But as international communities "spoon out her sugar for coffee, or to bake in their birthday cakes," the *machetero*'s bloodshed perverts the commodity's sweetness, flavoring it once again with violence, as the slave trade did a century before.[78] The machete that cuts the sugarcane also historicizes the apocalypse and its aftermath by representing them as effects of the Cuban Revolution. The machete, the Creole's scream, and Celia's global sugar visions place the blade within a Latin American agricultural context, defining Cuba's dystopian conditions as byproducts of communism and of continued colonial violence in the Americas.

Celia's national project, which is diametrically opposed to Lourdes's vision in the Yankee Doodle bakery, demonstrates how the trope of sugar links Cuba and the United States even as it incongruously impedes transnational communication. Sugar not only evokes the long history of exchange between the two countries but also reveals the obstacles that hindered political, ideological, or physical trade between the two nations after the revolution.[79] Sugar thus enacts in literary terms the political and economic tensions between both countries, nationally and individually. Each photograph Lourdes sends Celia of a "glistening éclair" and "strawberry shortcake" becomes a "grenade aimed at Celia's political beliefs" and a "reminder of the ongoing shortages" on the island.[80] The language of war and violence confirms sugar's destructive power. In this instance, as in many others, *Dreaming in Cuban* mobilizes the production and consumption of sugar to signal national alliances and geopolitical status, much as the zombie's mouth marks the progress of the reconstruction in the postapocalypse of *Zone One*. The confectionary evidence that Lourdes sends her mother testifies to the aftermath of the Cuban Revolution, reminding Celia of the island's colonial past and current scarcity under Castro. Further, these pictures enable Lourdes to re-create colonial and ethno-racial violence: the explosive and atomic possibilities ascribed to sugarcane enact the fantasy of violence promised by mutually assured destruction, and so Lourdes in effect threatens Cuba and her mother with nuclear annihilation while also consolidating sugar's position as a symbol of anticommunist ideology. In this way, the trade in sugar buttresses a trans-American female community defined through annihilation that precludes familial reconciliation.

Celia's demand that Pilar "remember everything" is usually read as a gesture toward recuperative hybridity. Her Cuban American identity is understood as a gentle portrayal of being culturally in-between with a fluid communication across geographic and cultural lines, a position from which she can reclaim and repair her *Cubanidad* without having to forgo US-American belonging.[81] In my reading, Celia's imperative is yet another marker of the excessive in *Dreaming in Cuban*. Pilar's lack of access to "authentic" Cuban history results in what Elena Machado Sáez defines as a form of nostalgia exemplified by her consumption of products in the global marketplace.[82] Unable to access *Cubanidad* outside commercialization, Pilar situates Cuba in an archaic past. In a record store at St. Mark's Place, she remarks of the legendary singer Celia Cruz that "she hasn't changed a hair or a vocal note in forty years. She's been fiftyish, it seems, since the Spanish-American War."[83] Machado Sáez argues that in this moment Pilar participates in the commodification of Cuban culture and also ascribes to Cruz—who shares a first name with her grandmother—a "certain timelessness" and "authenticity" that "defy any and all historical changes brought about by colonialism as well as the Cuban Revolution."[84] Expanding this reading of Pilar's relation to Cuban cultural productions and to Cuba itself, especially in relation to Cruz and the idea of a regenerative achievement of identity and a cultural past, I interpret Pilar's relationship with Cuba and her Cuban past as an example of the otherworldly.

A comfortable hybridity is usually read in Pilar's statement that "sooner or later I'd have to return to New York. I know now it's where I belong—not *instead* of here, but *more* than here."[85] I read this statement, however, as expressing a psychic excess rooted in Cuba's colonial past and communist present that positions her "more than-ness" as the product of exile that cannot be contained in singular definitions of national belonging or the self. In light of the association between excess and sugar throughout the novel, it is unsurprising that Pilar's entrapment of Celia Cruz within the past is mediated by sugar: Cruz's trademark phrase "¡Azúcar!" ("Sugar!") has become metonymic of her Afro-Cuban body through its repetition. As Frances Aparicio states, the word *azúcar* "carries within it the history of Cuba's plantation culture and the economics of slavery," and it "reaffirms the role of Celia Cruz's voice and body as an icon of Cuba's African-based heritage and *mestizaje*."[86] In committing Cruz to the island's colonial past, Pilar transforms Cruz into an Afro-Cuban object through which she can explore her Cuban heritage and experience nostalgia for an unrecoverable past. Pilar's comments about Cruz not only locate the singer in a "timeless" space but also, through the singer's permanent association with *azúcar*, zombify her as well. The excessive violence of sugar's production and consumption, as well as its close link to the zombie, relegates Cruz's body to a colonial past where progress is impossible. With these comments, Pilar turns Cruz's body into something that can be repeatedly exploited for national identification and celebration. With the same gesture, she renders the island as a space where time has stopped and where *azúcar* is endlessly produced. This budding tradition of "zombie Celia Cruz" is an example of Latinx speculative fiction's reproduction of monstrosity across genres and time periods.[87]

Dreaming in Cuban characterizes physical and psychic excess through images of mercantile exchange that confirm how the text replicates the violence of Cuban American exile and the histories it signals. From her home in Brooklyn, Pilar can hear the whistles of ships as they sail "past Ellis Island and the Statue of Liberty" toward the Atlantic.[88] Although she "want[s] to go with them," the narrator does not name their destination.[89] The Atlantic is described only as a mirror of the "cement plot" of Pilar's Brooklyn home near the East River, and Pilar can only imagine the ships in association with place-names near her shores: "Bayonne, New Jersey, and the Bay Ridge Channel."[90] Unable to follow the ships to Cuba—the object of her desire—Pilar finds herself entombed, as the Atlantic echoes the city back to itself, magnifying the coldness of her lived environment.

Sugar scripts the start of the family's life in the Cuban diaspora but also the beginning of the end—a death reminiscent of apocalypse. Upon their arrival in New York, Pilar comments that the city seems "optimistic as a wedding cake," a remark that calls forth the millions of immigrants who crossed through Ellis Island, the maritime journey undertaken by exiles to the diaspora, and the mercantile routes that traded sugar for Black bodies and Black bodies for sugar.[91] Although Pilar at first reads the city through the sweetness of confection and the reproductive possibilities that weddings connote, the optimism Pilar reads into the city is undercut by the excessive destruction that sugar always signals.

Pilar notes of Brooklyn that it is "the living that die here."[92] Cake, the sweet symbol of the passage of time and marker of special occasions, heralds destruction. Behind Manhattan's sugary facade lie the histories that enabled the creation of US empire through the pathological consumption of sugar, the enslavement of Black people, and the ruined Cuban nation. Pilar's association of the city with cake also calls forth Celia's vision of global communism achieved through the consumption of sugar, coating the optimism of Manhattan with disease, death, and failure.

It is not a coincidence, then, that when Pilar remembers the start of her new life in the United States, it is through an evocation of sugar that simultaneously implies death. The family's arrival is grounded in the capitalist sugar system and the disease and addiction it circulates. Pilar and her parents become the city's victims who will fall prey to the zombie's bite in *Zone One*. In this way, *Dreaming in Cuban* evokes the excessive body that is addicted to sugar—physically and ideologically—and the nation in ruin. Pilar's association of New York City with sugar asks readers to consider the history of the Caribbean, a history that requires that the novel be narrated with speculative tropes that illuminate the extreme violence disseminated within this space.

The Visual Afterlives of Sugar

I return to Walker's *A Subtlety* because of its insistence on the haunting reminders of the history of sugar production and consumption. The Sugar Baby, like the zombie in Whitehead and the fat and yearning body in García, illustrates the enveloped histories, movements, and filiations that emerge in depictions of sugar. Her breasts, buttocks, and vulva are meant to shock viewers into reckoning with their dependence on the Black female body as a source of labor and pleasure on the plantation, in the domestic space, and in the cultural imaginary. Although silent, the sphinx is imposing: she is larger than life, overwhelming; her nakedness is defiant, forcing viewers to recognize that Black women's bodies have been created as a site of desire, objectification, lust, and exoticization. The sphinx's colossal size allows us to consider the spectacle of "civilization" and the slavery used in its construction. The choice to house the Sugar Baby within the Domino refinery—which by 1870 was one of the largest in the world and produced over half the sugar consumed in the United States—exposes the extended footprint of settler colonial projects and the legacies of slavery. The Fanjul brothers, who owned the refinery, for example, profited by closing it and selling the land for condominium developments as part of New York's gentrification. Substituting one construction for another would seem to abrogate the violence that is still occurring in this space. As Amber Jamilla Musser argues, Walker's sphinx is "a memorial to exploitation" that implicates spectators in the history of sugar production and consumption past and present.[93] In fact, the Sugar Baby indicts the built environment in which she is housed and those who come to observe her.[94]

In the factory lies apocalyptic potential. The silent presence of the sphinx is challenging and aggressive. Behind her stoic expression, viewers can glimpse the zombie's maw. That she is covered in the sweetness of sugar is as ironic as the title's description of her body and the history that encompasses it. Here we are reminded of Pilar's use of Cruz as a point of entry into Cuban culture. Cruz's song "Azúcar Negra" ("Black Sugar") emulates the contradictory modes of defiance and objectification that characterize the sphinx. The song's opening lines affix the sweetness of sugar and the Afro-Cuban rhythm to the body:

Soy dulce como el melao'
Alegre como el tambor
Llevo el rítmico tumbao.[95]

Melao (molasses), a viscous byproduct of sugar, becomes associated with Afro-Cuban femininity. In the song, as in the sphinx, the association of Black womanhood with sugar is an objectifying gesture, but it is also one that articulates joy and challenges objectification:

Mi sangre es azúcar negra
Es amor y es música
Azúcar negra
Hay cuanto me gusta y me alegra.[96]

Making sugar a part of the body's life source places the commodity as a central element of the Black body but simultaneously makes it a source of exultation and through it an exaltation of the Black female form. Like the molasses of Cruz's lyrics, *A Subtlety* does not lack agency. The Black body of the sphinx and Cruz's song "stick in the throat of the (white) body politic, refusing to be consumed as part of the capitalistic logic of racism and slavery as well as the cultural and literary matter that they produced."[97]

A Subtlety is grounded in the history of sugar production and consumption and of slavery in the Americas. The sculpture, "grotesque," "fantastic and overbearing," is overwhelming and resists description in language.[98] *A Subtlety*'s subtitle, *or the Marvelous Sugar Baby, an Homage to the unpaid and overworked Artisans who have refined our Sweet tastes from the cane fields to the Kitchens of the New World on the Occasion of the demolition of the Domino Sugar Refining Plant*, for example—which points to the sentimental novel and slave narrative of the eighteenth and nineteenth centuries—also speaks to its excess and indescribability. Indeed, much of Walker's work forces viewers to recognize the limits of any form of representation that attempts to describe the violence of slavery. Theorizing the possibilities of pleasure during slavery, Treva Lindsey and Jessica Johnson describe the Sugar Baby as compelling the viewer to understand the Black female body as "subject and object . . . visible but illegible; as mysterious, unknowable but knowing; as ambivalent and as powerful. The virility of the Sugar Sphinx is palpable, but her desires and intimate longings remain mysterious, though not unknowable or unspeakable."[99] These paradoxes are at the heart of *A Subtlety*, which brings out the viewer's hunger to know her secrets, the hankering for the sugar coating her body. As Musser argues, Walker's installation shows the importance of thinking about appetite as the "manifestation of one's location within multiple circuits of power."[100] Craving, hunger, taste, and addiction are at the heart of not only sugar production and the consumption of Black bodies but also the colonial project and the wealth it produced.

Ultimately, the visual afterlives of sugar resist any attempts to decipher them. The Sugar Baby's embodiment of the histories of slavery and sugar production and consumption, although fleeting, haunts us with its reminder of apocalyptic violence. As this chapter has shown, depictions of sugar activate all sorts of monstrous bodies, from the zombie in a Caribbean novel by a Black American author to the fat-embodied and sugar-addicted Latina who challenges upward mobility and ethnic hybridity in Latinx literature. The impending decay that haunts *A Subtlety* is also evident in the attendants dispersed throughout the factory, who slowly melted throughout the summer of 2014. Modeled after figurines Walker found online, the Black boys are in a state of suspended labor. Carrying bananas and baskets, they toe the line between compelling cuteness and racist minstrel iconography, but like the stragglers of *Zone One*, they also resist incorporation into exploitative capitalist labor practices of consumption. Even so, as Musser argues, the melting boys signal the history of wealth accumulation through conquest and the "colonial consumption of black servant bodies."[101] Like the refinery walls coated in molasses, the melting boys saturate the "gallery," are inhaled by viewers, and thus are physically incorporated. The "acrid smell" of the factory produced by the melting boys is an unavoidable result of the exhibit's construction; it ensnares us in a communal fantasy of conquest, empire, consumption, and pleasure. While offering "an escape from the totalizing grasp of consumption," the boys' melting is a pleasurable reminder of racialized renunciation.[102]

APPROXIMATION, HORROR, AND THE GROTESQUE ON THE US-MEXICO BORDER

La historia, que es una puta sencilla, no tiene momentos
determinantes sino que es una proliferación de instantes,
de brevedades que compiten entre sí en monstruosidad.
—Roberto Bolaño, *2666*

The Part about the Argument

In an interview a year before his death, Carmen Boullosa asked the Chilean-born writer Roberto Bolaño whether he considered his fiction "realist" or "fantastic." Boullosa frames her question around Bolaño's geographic trajectory along Latin America's edges—Chile and Mexico. "Hallowed tradition," Boullosa states, teaches us that the southern part of Latin America is "home to the fantastic," while the northern part is "the center of realism." Responding to this question and her assertion that the English-speaking North pigeonholes Latin American literature within singular traditions, Bolaño emphasizes that the compartmentalization of literature should never be taken seriously. In his answer, Bolaño hitches the creation of speculative fiction and the fantastic to the Global North, whereas in Latin America "economic underdevelopment" prevents these genres from evolving, and he problematically connects wealth to the possibilities of the imagination. "I'd like to be a writer of the fantastic, like Philip K. Dick," Bolaño says, "although as time passes and I get older, Dick seems more and more realist to me. Deep down . . . the question doesn't lie in the distinction of realist/fantastic but in language and structures, in ways of seeing."[1]

Yet Bolaño's work, and particularly his posthumous novel 2666 (Spanish 2004, English 2008), rejects these generic demarcations along geographic lines and shows how a variety of literary tropes and genres can be incorporated into one novel. The importance of Bolaño's reference to Dick's fiction cannot be overstated. The author of central texts in the speculative fiction canon, Dick is not technically a writer of the fantastic but rather an author of realist science fiction. Although Bolaño's description of Dick as an author of the fantastic is a misnomer, it illustrates how Bolaño's literary training informs concepts such as "realist," "fantasy," and "genre." His invocation of Dick points to the limitations of describing the "language and structures" required to write about the US-Mexico border, and his desire to write "like Philip K. Dick" states an approximation, an appeal to figures of speech and representational language that circle around an object without being able to represent the object itself. Bolaño's answer indicates not only that language cannot describe certain subjects, like the violence of the border, but also that what appears fantastic to some is the lived reality of others.

Approximation, especially the simile, is the central literary device in this chapter, which analyzes Bolaño's 2666. Together with women's corpses, the simile acts as a narrative doom pattern that enacts apocalyptic violence and textual excess in the novel. By examining how the novel uses similes to make this violence legible, I explore how 2666 attempts but ultimately fails to represent the horror of violence on the border and the horror of the border itself.

2666 comprises five labyrinthian and Borgesian sections that are linked by varying degrees of concern for the unsolved murders of hundreds of women in the fictional border town of Santa Teresa, a city based on Ciudad Juárez, Mexico. This center of the export processing zone acts as a connecting landscape for all five sections. The novel opens with "The Part about the Critics," in which a group of scholars search for an elusive German author, leading them to Santa Teresa. There they meet Óscar Amalfitano, the protagonist of section 2, "The Part about Amalfitano," which focuses on his obsession with a geometric treatise and a nightmarish voice that causes his mental health to decay. What follows is "The Part about Fate," which centers on a Black journalist sent soon after the death of his mother to cover a boxing match in Santa Teresa, where he focuses on the femicides instead. The novel's fourth and most notorious section, "The Part about the Crimes," has no linear plot but moves between 1993 and

1997 through the gruesome description of women's corpses found throughout the city and its surrounding areas. The novel "concludes" with "The Part about Archimboldi," which acts as a bookend to *2666*'s first section and explores the life of the mysterious author so eagerly sought by the critics.

In this chapter, I argue that *2666* continually resorts to the language of approximation and the grotesque, using the tropes of horror and detective fiction to reconstruct the excessive violence and monstrous bodies on the US-Mexico border in the form of the semi-publicized femicides that began in the early 1990s.[2] Women and their bodies are treated in *2666* as fleshy mirrors that incarnate the border's violence. In this way, the bodies, like the simile, function as a doom pattern that reveals a global network of violence that converges on the border and exposes the border as the exemplary space in which to investigate this network. Although the novel persistently returns readers in form and content to the violent history of the US-Mexico border, from settler colonialism to contemporary neocolonial enterprises and the effects of this history on postcolonial subjects, the world-destroying excess in the novel encompasses many cataclysms across nation-states and time periods. In doing all this, the novel aestheticizes horror and the grotesque, mobilizing the simile and women's bodies as speculative tools that illustrate the extreme and unnatural violence of this geopolitical space. Simultaneously, Bolaño uses speculative tropes drawn from horror, crime, and apocalyptic fiction—the worldly destruction seen in apocalyptic and dystopian fiction, the shocking disgust and terror of horror, and the mysterious clues and grit of pulp and detective fiction—to expose the pleasure of re/producing ethno-national and colonial violence.

I begin this chapter with the understanding that the type of violence *2666* describes makes it a work of speculative fiction. Drawing on the tropes of various genre fictions like horror and the crime novel, *2666* exemplifies a textual excess that attempts unsuccessfully to capture the violence of the US-Mexico border. The attempt to portray the violence of the border causes breakages in the text: it is impossible to convey such excess in language, which triggers the text to break into doom patterns that reproduce the violence it is attempting to tell. As Bolaño's invocation of Dick and the fantastic suggests, to write the border requires "ways of seeing" and the "language and structures" of the fantastic: science fiction, horror, and the speculative. The novel's use of the simile shows *2666* to be an approximation itself, participating in the discourses of the border while not being of the border itself—a productive simulation that offers a new avenue for defining what we now call *Latinx literature*. Bolaño's statement also echoes Gabriel García Márquez's depiction of Latin America's "realidad desaforada," an "outsized reality" that requires the tropes of the fantastic.[3] Latin American reality, according to García Márquez, cannot be faithfully depicted through the historical archive or "realist" fiction. The "ways of seeing" that reimagine literary structures are evident in *2666*, and in this chapter, I show how the novel depicts the "realidad desaforada" of the border by turning to the tropes of apocalyptic horror and the crime novel to represent this monstrous space and its bodies.

Bolaño's literary eminence was heralded by the translation of *Los detectives salvajes* (published in Spanish in 1998, in English in 2007 as *The Savage Detectives*), *2666*, and *Los sinsabores del verdadero policía* (published in Spanish in 2011, in English in 2012 as *Woes of the True Policeman*), and his success has become a reference point for the reestablishment of Latin American literature in the global literary market.[4] His position parallels Junot Díaz's celebrity status and has drawn the attention of scholars, literary critics, national media, and fans of popular culture, especially after his untimely death in 2003. Bolaño's literary "genius" and his captivating biography, which includes personal experience of the Augusto Pinochet coup and his death from liver failure rumored to be caused by heroin use, manufacture a "Bolaño" who is ripe for US consumption.[5] Yet much like those of the Boom generation before him, Bolaño "foments a (pre)conception of alterity that satisfies the fantasies and collective imagination of U.S. cultural consumers."[6] As scholars of Latin/x literature have shown, reductive depictions of Latin America appeal to US readers because they provide the illusion of translatability and familiarity and thus foster readers' pride in their cultural competence, even as they add spatial and temporal distance between the two regions of the hemisphere—"*That* cannot happen *here*." This cultural transaction is an ethnicized commodity that allows Westerners to explore foreign soil from a safe distance.[7] *Translatability* here does not refer simply to linguistic transference but to a sociopolitical act that reads texts in the periphery (in this case, the Southern Cone) from the center (the United States and Europe), actively forging and circulating easily digestible properties that can be ascribed to the traditions from which these works emerge.[8] As others have argued before me, Bolaño's fiction, while often called postnationalist, does not fit comfortably within the Latin American canon or the matrix of "world literature."[9] Oswaldo Zavala, for example, argues that his work reveals the limitations of the world literature paradigm as a "system that reproduces the silences and exclusions of the dominant English-language global editorial market," which erases literary fields outside European and Anglo-American coordinates.[10] While Bolaño's works have been analyzed as global novels within a Latin American template, I read *2666* through the protocols of Latinx speculative fiction, as a work invested in the porosity of the US-Mexico border and the violence in this space as the vestiges of the two nations' long history of exchange.

This chapter shifts our attention from the Caribbean and its diaspora, which were the focus of the first two chapters of *Doom Patterns*, to the US-Mexico border. Building on the analysis in chapters 1 and 2, which defined the Caribbean as a postapocalyptic space, this chapter focuses on the violent histories particular to the border that mark it as postapocalyptic as well—histories that include Spanish colonial domination, imperial expansionism, American annexation, and the advent of globalization, export processing, and governmental policies that continue to affect this region. This geographic shift in *Doom Patterns* underscores the networks of violence that reach across territories and ethno-national demarcations and highlight literary patterns and leitmotifs that appear across the Latinx texts in this book. Through examinations of literary production from and about Caribbean, US, and Latin American spaces, *Doom Patterns* participates in a growing and important tendency in Latinx literary and cultural studies to read intra-ethnically, transnationally, and across ethno-racial demarcations. It also shows that placing texts in uncomfortable juxtapositions throws into relief previously overlooked narrative strategies, literary patterns, and networks. My choice to use the reading protocols of Latinx speculative fiction to examine *2666* intentionally destabilizes the terms *Latinx* and *speculative* by, on the one hand, pointing to the unstable construction of each category and, on the other, illustrating the otherworldliness of this construction.

In this chapter, the history of US-Mexican entanglements, which have always been marked by violence, is particularly significant.[11] As Nicole Guidotti-Hernández argues, the United States and Mexico "need to be defined and historicized in relation to each other."[12] The movement of people, ideas, and capital between the United States and Mexico established the long history of violent association and exchange that makes it impossible to read one place without the other. My reading stresses how *2666* explores this history through speculative tropes. The corpse, both seen and unseen, functions as a monstrous symbol of illegality that continually threatens the border, signaling its porosity and the fabricated nature of concepts such as national sovereignty, citizenship, and legality/illegality. In fact, the novel reduces Mexico to an atemporal state of death, a hellish landscape of post-NAFTA factories littered with the bodies of women who are as easily replaceable as they are disposable. The apocalyptic violence enacted in the novel, therefore, persistently reminds us that the economic configuration of the borderlands affects the body—particularly women's bodies—and creates a psychic space of death that is replicated on the body and the border.

Throughout its 1,126 pages (almost 900 in its English translation), *2666* expresses a textual anxiety about its inability to enclose the gruesome violence performed on the gendered and racialized body or the violence of the export processing system on the US-Mexico border within its pages. Its fragmented structure, labyrinthine and nested stories, multiplicity of protagonists, metafictional literary devices, paratextual references, and unanswered questions formally demonstrate this narrative fretfulness—a "failure" that reproduces borderland violence in form and content. The novel's length is another expression of textual anxiety and paradoxical pleasure: unable to capture the violence of the border, the narrative is forced to continue (would the novel have ended without Bolaño's death?). Its length creates a certain violence among its readers as well. Rigorous and unforgiving, *2666* forces readers to become dedicated students of violence. The commitment it takes to read a novel of this size and difficulty gives the reader a stake in what Carol Clover calls the "sadistic, voyeuristic side of horror—the pleasure he may take in watching, from some safe vantage or other, women screaming, crying, fleeting, cringing, and dying, or indeed the pleasure he may take in the thought of himself as the cause of their torment."[13] Invested in the aesthetics of the grotesque, *2666* establishes an opening where the reader becomes a voyeuristic participant in the reproduction of ethno-racial and colonial violence. By *aesthetics of the grotesque*, I mean that Bolaño's novel artistically renders the mundanity of sexual assault and murder, putting this violence into an aesthetic category that highlights its excessiveness and grotesquerie. The grotesque is a mode that makes use of the monstrous, deformed, and excessive and has been noted for its unpredictability and lack of fixity. The grotesque's ability to trouble boundaries also contributes to its irresolution, its depiction of contradictory and opposite forces (high and low; the vulgar and refined) together. In this way, the aesthetics of the grotesque exemplifies a form of artistic pleasure that underscores the mixture of beauty with disgust, of the pleasurable with the humorous.[14]

In what follows, I first show how *2666* stages the US-Mexico border through cataclysmic language that defines this space as postapocalyptic. I examine how the text depicts women's corpses through forensic documentation and excessive repetition, moving readers away from subjective *testimonio* and political remedy to a death fugue without end. I argue that in its attempt to depict these horrors, the novel resorts to approximation—and in particular the simile—in a way that not only illustrates the impossibility of encapsulating violence but also replicates it. I then explore how women's violation and death are presented in the novel as "natural" byproducts of the export processing zone. In the third section of this chapter, I turn to a part of the novel that is usually elided in criticism, "The Part about Fate," to show how the novel mobilizes depictions of Blackness on the border. Focusing on how Black memory and mourning are juxtaposed with women's violated bodies, I argue that Fate's race is magnified on the border, forcing him to constantly consider the unstable position he inhabits, and specifically his precarity within the United States. Read alongside the descriptions of violated women's bodies, the character of Fate acts as a lens through which to inspect the corpse. My analysis highlights that the text's participation in "US Black discourse" is another formal approximation: pointing to many enactments of violence, the novel relies on formal and narrative tools as well as geographies and characters in its attempt to expose the object of violence and enclose the entirety of the horror that would make the border legible. Indeed, *2666* as an art object exemplifies a kind of narrative approximation as it attempts to tap into Chicanx studies, border rhetorics, and Latinx literary traditions while continually revealing that it is always at odds with its border object.

In the final section of this chapter, I consider how reading *2666* through the tropes of Latinx speculative fiction not only demonstrates connections to the Latinx literary past and present but illustrates how the novel's investment in the discourses of the border participates in the Latinx literary tradition while allowing for its expansion. Throughout the chapter, I show that Bolaño's world-building articulates a planetary logic constructed through global war, where everyone—character, critic, reader—is implicated within practices of violence.[15] This world-building forecloses any notion of an innocent position through which to read the text. The novel's enactment of horror within the space of the border and its effects on the critic/reader present a cyclical and inescapable history that enables the replication of ethno-racial and imperial violence toward the self and the other.

The Part about Approximation and Women's Corpses

In the novel's fourth section, "The Part about the Crimes," FBI agent Kessler is taxied through Santa Teresa, where he sees a landscape "fragmented or in the constant process of fragmentation, like a puzzle assembled and disassembled every second."[16] Turning down a desolate street, Kessler notes:

> Even the brush was covered in a thick layer of dust, as if nearby an atomic bomb had dropped without anyone noticing, except for the victims . . . but they didn't count because they'd lost their minds or were dead, even though they walked and stared . . . gazes of people living in another dimension and whose stare no longer touches us, we notice them but they don't touch us, they don't adhere to our skin, they pass though us.[17]

The novel thus organizes the landscape and the people within it in a perpetually unfinished process of being ripped apart, violently defining them as walking-dead subjects, haunts that exist within a space they cannot touch or affect. The US-Mexico border is also defined as created through a cataclysmic event, which establishes the city and its inhabitants in an unending state of formation that is never accomplished.[18] This cruel and all-encompassing "fragmentación constante" (constant fragmentation) suffered by people and the land is reproduced by the novel's form and style: told in multiple fragments, ranging in length from one short paragraph to a few pages, the novel attempts unsuccessfully to convey the violence of the border and the femicides. The repetition, revision, and return to the same spaces in the text never find the killer/s or the coveted author but instead force readers to simultaneously be consumed by and consume the novel, the corpse, and the apocalyptic landscape. As the readers observe the assembly and disassembly "every second," they enact the making and destruction of the text and, within it, the landscape and its people.

The text does not specify exactly when or where this cataclysmic event took place and therefore defines it with the language of approximation ("as if"/"como si") and inexactitude ("nearby"/"por aquellos lugares"). The inability to locate these "facts" illustrates a narrative wavering that requires further fragmentation, assembly, and disassembly to reach the puzzle's completion. The ambiguity lends the cataclysmic event, mired in the language of war and transnational nuclear annihilation, an atemporal narratological weight. Like the usage of "fukú"—the curse of the New World—in Díaz's *The Brief Wondrous Life of Oscar Wao* (2007), which defines the Caribbean as created through anathema, the atomic bomb in *2666* defines this space as formed through destruction and violence. Unlike *Oscar Wao*, in which apocalypse occurs in the specific time and place of the modern/colonial encounter, *2666* uses unfixed language surrounding the bomb that implies a perpetual apocalypse. The text therefore characterizes the US-Mexico border as a space in a never-ending stage of destruction, where even its re/formation is predicated on its ruin.

The landscape's fragmentation—mirrored in the text's form—exposes its effects on the human body and defines these effects as monstrous. The novel engenders an alternate creation myth in which the falling of the atomic bomb, unnoticed by those outside the fallout zone, creates "another dimension" that is replete with monstrous subjects. The hundreds of women who emanate from the ground in "another dimension" are thus produced through the narrative conventions of apocalyptic horror and grotesquerie. This description has real effects in the novel that alter the plot, its character, and the landscape and make it reasonable to read *2666* as a work of speculative fiction.

Kessler's observation of Santa Teresa, which is presented through a simile, underscores the centrality of figurative language in describing this space. Unable to portray its horror, the text relies on "as if" to approximate the violence Kessler sees without defining the thing itself and highlights the violence of the city by comparing it to something otherworldly. Like Bolaño's use of the simile to describe his writing and his wish to write "like Philip K. Dick," the use of "as if" expresses a desire to capture the violence of the border through description. Faced with the impossibility of realizing this desire, the text resorts to figures of speech, the grotesque, and the excessive to approximate this violence.

The atomic "as-ifness" of the border is tethered to the body. Chicanx authors and other cultural producers have long associated the body, especially women's bodies, with landscapes. A landscape is not simply scenery, as Mary Pat Brady argues, but a cultural and social formation created through articulation, narrative technique, and grammatical structures.[19] In the preface to the groundbreaking and foundational *Borderlands/La Frontera* (1987), Gloria Anzaldúa states that the border is "not a comfortable territory to live in, this place of contradictions. Hatred, anger, and exploitation are the prominent features of this landscape."[20] The violence Anzaldúa describes has a physical effect on the body, to which she constantly returns to describe the terrestrial, a narrative strategy that defines women's bodies on the border as the byproduct of violence:

> 1,950 mile-long open wound
> dividing a *pueblo*, a culture,
> running down the length of my body,
> staking fence rods in my flesh,
> splits me   splits me
> *me raja   me raja.*[21]

The unhealable wound Anzaldúa describes "hemorrhages again" before a scab can form over it, defining the border and the bodies within it as instantiated through recurring violence.[22] Land and body continuously signal each other and, as in Kessler's observation, require narrative forms that exceed the traditional. Like *2666*, *Borderlands/La Frontera* replicates the violence of this landscape on the body. The bilingual text used to underscore the border's violence becomes a form of repetition that magnifies the effect of the "fence rod" staked in her "flesh." Reiteration in Spanish and English augments the violence performed on the body as well. The line breaks and irregular formatting expose a textual incapacity to express the condition of being a borderlands woman, with silences and re-beginnings, enunciation and re-enunciation. Anzaldúa's depiction of space requires the excessive and horrific, declaring a textual anxiety about the inability to showcase the effects of the border on the body. The repetition of "splits me   splits me / *me raja   me raja*" performs a textual stutter that demands not only repetition in a single line, translation into English, and a line break between the two but also an extra pause within each line. This pause—a silence, a breath—textually stresses the weight of violence splitting (*rajando*) the body. Yet the translation of *raja*, to split, proves inadequate to clarify the violence being performed; *splitting* connotes the breaking apart of an object, yet *raja/rajar* denotes a messier and bloodier act, such as gashing or slitting. Taken together, all these textual elements create an overwhelming and inescapable effect of violence.

Like Anzaldúa's description of the border, *2666* translates this space through violence performed on women's bodies while simultaneously exhibiting narrative anxiety about its own inability to capture this violence, an anxiety that is expressed through approximation and horror. The novel, in fact, marks the passage of time and change in the landscape through the murder and discovery of women's bodies. The novel thus showcases women's corpses as an effect of apocalyptic violence, as an oozing byproduct of the landscape. While not all sections focus exclusively on the victims of femicide, they all hold the killings and the atomic violence of the border at their center.

"The Part about the Crimes" begins with the line "The dead woman [girl] appeared in a small vacant lot in colonia Las Flores."[23] This opening portrays Santa Teresa and the desert that surrounds it as a space of death where women's corpses suddenly appear.[24] While marking the passage of the years through the dead women, the section's opening pinpoints the first victim of femicide in an official capacity but then quickly rescinds its authority through ambiguity, showing the futility of attempting to fully capture the horror performed on women's bodies, especially through "facts" or the historical archive: "This happened in 1993. January 1993. From then on [A partir de esta muerta], the killings of women began to be counted. But it's likely there were others before [que antes hubiera otras]."[25] *2666* textually scripts the first female corpse found in Santa Teresa, placing a temporal marker for readers (as it does throughout the section) while also rejecting the certainty of the corpse's "firstness." The uncertainty of the record defines the border as an unstructured space of death and points to the failure to locate or translate its violence. While "la muerta" succinctly signifies a gendered corpse for readers of Spanish, English does not allow for the gendered language of death needed to portray the violence of the border in this section of the novel. The tone describing the femicide victims is forensically cold, but the English-language version of the novel alters the detachment and repetition of gendered violence that occurs throughout this section. For example, a translation into English of "A partir de esta muerta" as "From then on" removes not only all gendered markers from the text but also the corpse itself.

The repetition of "esta muerta" and variations thereof, such as "otra muerta" (another dead woman [girl]) and "mujeres muertas" (dead women [girls]), has a numbing effect on the reader. Specifically, even as the repetition of these phrases accentuates the pointedly gendered violence of this space, the repetition becomes constitutive of the text and implicit in it—this repetition, much like a refrain in poetry, drives the narrative forward as well as forces readers into reading about dead women and complicitly consuming their bodies. The 110 names that appear throughout this section similarly invoke individual murdered women, a humanizing force that attempts to provide some type of biographical information or ancestry for each woman. Yet the repeated fragmentation of the text forecloses the possibility of dwelling with each victim as the reader quickly proceeds to the next dead body. The effect of this narrative strategy is not to emphasize the individuality of the dead women but to perpetuate the violence done to the corpses by gathering them all into an overwhelming textual mass, effectively producing what Sianne Ngai calls "stuplimity." With stuplimity, Ngai extends the idea of the Kantian sublime to account for this new phenomenon wherein boredom combines with shock and awe: numbness and astonishment in the face of the overwhelming comprise the stuplimitous.[26] In this way, "The Part about the Crimes" underlines the specifically gendered violence of the US-Mexico border while showing the overwhelming nature of this violence. "She had been vaginally and anally raped" is repeated approximately forty times throughout this section, as are similar phrases. The reiteration of this refrain foregrounds the violence done to women's bodies, with continual variations and additions—"and strangled," "raped and beaten," and "raped innumerable times."[27] The repetition, much like the multiplicity of victims' names, is at once overwhelming and paradoxically allaying. Creating a catalog of almost indistinguishable products rendered in the cold terminology of an autopsy desensitizes readers to the violence and makes it difficult, if not impossible, to remember individual cases—the technical jargon amasses the femicide victims and makes singular crimes lose their meaning. The novel's cold description of the corpses effectively keeps readers at a safe distance from the act itself, a reading practice that reifies the language of the autopsy and dehumanizes the victim.

With each new victim, "The Part about the Crimes" corrects and amends itself, resorting to excessive description that aestheticizes horror and re-creates violence on women's bodies. For example, within a four-page narrative fragment that narrates the bodies of Aurora Muñoz Álvarez, Emilia Escalante Sanjúan, Estrella Ruiz Sandoval, two unidentified women, and Jacqueline Ríos is the brutal description of Mónica Posadas's body. I do not cite this and other passages from *2666* in a morbid attempt to shock or casually participate in the novel's aestheticization of horror. Instead, I replicate them because of their excessive quantity and quality, which determines the novel's investment in the violence enacted on women's bodies through which the novel considers the border.

According to the medical examiner, Mónica had been anally and vaginally raped, although traces of semen were also found in her throat, which led to talk in police circles of a "three-way" rape [violación <<por los tres conductos>>]. There was a cop, however, who said that a full rape was one done to all five orifices. Asked what the other two were, he answered the ears. Another cop said he had heard of a guy from Sinaloa who raped seven orifices. That is to say, the five known orifices plus the eyes.

And another cop said that he had heard of a guy from Mexico City who raped through eight orifices, which were the seven already mentioned, plus the navel, where the guy from Mexico City made a small incision with his knife, not very big, and then put his cock in [le metía allí su verga]. . . . In the case of Mónica Posadas, the victim had not only been raped "through three orifices" but also had been strangled. The body, which was found half hidden behind some cardboard boxes, was naked from the waist down. The legs were stained with blood. So much blood that if seen from a distance, or seen from a certain height, a stranger (or an angel, since there were no buildings from where to observe her) would have said she was wearing red tights. The vagina was torn [desgarrada]. The vulva and groin showed clear signs of bites and tears, as if a street dog had tried to eat her.[28]

The violence performed on the body becomes a tool through which characters and readers alike can reproduce gendered and ethno-racial violence on the other that, in turn, reproduces the history of neo/colonial rule. The novel scripts Mónica's corpse through the expected refrain "anally and vaginally raped," yet it extends the violence to other parts of her body and uses her as a tool for the anecdotes of policemen. While the passage begins in typical forensic fashion by describing her rape, the text digresses into "locker-room talk" in which the policemen "best" each other's stories. Presented through the language of a rumor—an approximation in itself—the policemen's anecdotes are a means through which they, and through them the readers, can fantasize, from three to five to seven to eight, about other cruelties and orifices through which to perform them. The aesthetics of the grotesque exemplified above becomes almost Rabelaisian, and the female corpse is turned into an outlandish spectacle. The many addendums that appear throughout Mónica's description modify and magnify what came before, deforming her body into an otherworldly site. These textual additions extend the violence done to the corpse. While comparing the amount of blood on her legs to an article of clothing might seem to conceal the violence performed on her body, the text amends itself again by describing the extreme distortion of Mónica's genitals. The text homes in further to revise and extend its description, turning to a simile that pushes the narrative's violence outside the human realm and into the bestial. The simile builds on the description of Mónica's vagina in the original Spanish, using *desgarrar*, which denotes the act of ripping or breaking with animal claws. This narrative tool interprets the agent of violence as an animal, but it creates a mysterious space of speculation in which animal and human are intimately linked through the carnage enacted on a specifically female sex organ.

As the passage about Mónica's corpse showcases, femicide violence is depicted by *2666* as a national phenomenon that inculpates all sectors of society, both inside and outside the text, even as this particular violence is depicted as occurring in Santa Teresa. The border is imagined as a postapocalyptic nightmare that radiates horror from its center and extends its reproduction of violence beyond the text. The policemen's anecdotes underline how the violence is treated as a means of amusement and ironically force readers to be reproducers of gendered violence as well. The enormous success of *2666* in the literary market—a representative review described it as "compulsively readable"—suggests that its aestheticization of horror transforms the femicides into art for the pleasurable consumption of readers.[29] The compulsive desire to read descriptions of horror and gendered violence functions as an excuse, an act of complicity, and a reward for the aestheticization of violence. Describing the novel as "compulsively readable" also connotes a pathological drive in its consumption, further implying that the reader has something in common with the perpetrators of femicide violence.

The policemen's outlandish depiction and display of the female corpse satirizes the violence by transforming the repulsive into the monstrously humorous. Discussing the various orifices through which women can be raped, and even creating new ones, makes the corpse a fantastic spectacle of the grotesque. Textual modifiers of exaggeration enable the continuation of violence that re-creates a grotesque amalgamation of violated women for the reader. Each policeman replicates it through the ears, eyes, and belly button, fabricating more spaces through which to enter and abuse the corpse. Each new orifice exposes women's bodies as empty spaces through which the text can project its own fantasies of horror. A gaping wound, the corpse grotesquely personifies Anzaldúa's "herida abierta," continually pointing to itself as a body, its boundaries as an object, and the ways the object can be ruptured.[30]

As in Anzaldúa's work, the corpse denotes the boundaries and porosities of the landscape in which it is found. Through grotesque descriptions, the text exposes the body not as a closed system but as part of a relational network that includes the outside world. The corpse's various "conductos" (orifices) are textually transformed into spaces through which "the world enters the body or emerges from it, or through which the body itself goes out to meet the world," generating far-reaching networks of horror and pleasure.[31] Whereas Mikhail Bakhtin's definition of the grotesque reads it as a celebration of interconnect-edness even beyond death and defines the body as a significant site for the representation of positive community networks, *2666* establishes an aesthetics of the grotesque that suggests no possibility of forming affective ties via anything other than violence and horror.

What does it mean for women's bodies to be introduced in the text solely through acts of violation and deadly force? *2666* continually returns to the female corpse as the site of spectacle, desire, and horror on the border. Its insistent portrayal of women's tortured bodies paradoxically gestures to a textual avoidance that leaves rape and murder off the page. Omitting the brutality of rape and murder, the text displaces its violence onto the displayed tortured body, which compels readers to imagine and individually create the violence the text elides. The constant return to descriptions of violated bodies, with few variations that make them almost indistinguishable, "immure[s] us to pain" while paradoxically creating an overwhelming repetition of violence.[32] The excessive discursive creations used to stage the violated corpse euphemize the violence performed on it and displace it. Formally, the text exposes its inability to reach the source of violence and resorts instead to excessive depictions of its aftereffects. These corpses have no textual purpose outside their violation and death. This section of the novel, which is organized around a decontextualized finding of each corpse, stages each woman as nonexistent before her death. The women materialize solely as objects of sexual desire, orifices to be violated, and recipients of the deadly violence that defines women on the borderland as always already dead. Their rape, moreover, turns them into sites of sexual desire that are simultaneously the expression of disgust.

Women's genitalia are a meaning-making space on the border where readers can access the imagined landscape and its violence. The violence performed on their bodies happens primarily through the vagina, which the text clearly points to throughout this section. The novel, therefore, defines women's bodies as monstrous because of the extreme violence performed on them, and the repeated acts of penetration reify the conception of the vagina as "sexually insatiable and as animated erotically by a desire for annihilation."[33] Women's corpses function textually as tools for destruction and discovery through which readers can encounter the savage horror of the borderlands. The text defines men's sexual desire as wasteful, pathological, and violent, while presenting women's sexual expression, particularly that of poor Mexican women, as haunted by the specter of death.

The Part about Disposable Women and the
Export Processing System

Set against the industrial backdrop of a fictionalized Ciudad Juárez, the novel presents the city as a deathscape mired within the time of the maquiladora, a factory run by US companies in Mexico to take advantage of cheap labor and lax tax and tariff regulations, as well as the free trade agreement between the two countries. Between 1993 and 2014, more than 1,500 women were violently killed, and over a third of the victims suffered a form of sexual assault.[34] In the context of the export processing system, the novel frames the femicides as "natural" within this geopolitical space and implies that gendered violence is a tool for securing the nation-state.[35] The maquiladoras who employ the majority of femicide victims rely on the movement of global capital and a constant flux of labor. At the time of the novel's publication, Ciudad Juárez was the "leader in low-cost, high-quality, labor-intensive manufacturing processes."[36] The city's proximity to the United States and constant flow of migrants contributed to its popularity on the global market.[37] As Melissa Wright underscores, gender is central to the maquiladora system, in which women's bodies are policed and monitored in a fashion that produces a workforce of "assorted body parts" that, while not resembling the human, are expected to function as a working body on the assembly line.[38] Violence is wreaked on the body through discursive and structural acts, revealing how the free market depends on the "myth of the disposable third world woman."[39] This discursive violence holds a paradoxical logic at its center: whereas the disposable woman is transformed into a "form of industrial waste . . . discarded and replaced," she simultaneously possesses traits that make her labor invaluable for the preservation of global capitalism.[40]

The novel narrates the myth of the disposable third world woman through the tropes of apocalyptic horror and the crime novel. The descriptions of finding corpses in garbage dumps, industrial zones, and the desert circumscribe women's bodies as dirty, surplus, part of the scenery. The monstrous excess assigned to their bodies is reflected in the landscape itself, a situation that creates a quagmire of violence in which body and landscape relentlessly mirror each other. Moreover, the corpses, and all the women who will inevitably become corpses, are exposed as dismembered and monstrous. For example, Margarita López Santos is found forty days after her disappearance after leaving a maquiladora. She "worked at the K&T maquiladora, in the El Progreso industrial park near the Nogales highway. . . . The day of her disappearance she was working the third shift at the maquiladora, from nine at night to five in the morning . . . which meant that her disappearance could be fixed around the time of the shift change and her exit [leaving work]."[41] Margarita's body is legible only through her labor and death, the movements she makes associated solely with her role as worker and corpse. The text is unable to describe anything that happens after she leaves the maquiladora and resorts to assumptions—"Perhaps she saw"; "But she wasn't hungry."[42] It contrasts these conjectures with absolutes reserved for descriptions of the cityscape and the factory: the poor lighting of the streets, the sewer system that ends in colonia Las Rositas, and the van that sells foodstuffs to workers at the WS-Inc. maquiladora.[43]

The company each woman works for is inconsequential: corpses continue to appear, highlighting the insatiability of the global market and the centrality of gendered violence for its survival. As the text reminds us, the "coming and going of workers was unending," and the novel underscores the triviality of company names in relation to the significance and surety of the corpses' appearance and the violence enabled by the global export processing system.[44] Furthermore, the text dismisses the process by which each corpse is transported from one maquiladora to the location of its disposal as an oddity that does not require further investigation. Tethering the women's deadness to industrial labor and occluding the event of their murder and the movement of their bodies, the text presents them instead as simply appearing in the spaces where they are found and therefore defines them as always having been dead or pre-dead. As "waste-in-the-making," women's bodies emerge through the language of excess, horror, and grotesquerie.[45] 2666 presents women as tautological formations: that which defines them as women makes them always already dead, and in their death, they are made women.

The world-building in 2666 reveals the capaciousness of ethno-racial and imperial violence, which it reproduces through the language of approximation, its fragmented narrative structure, and the aesthetics of the grotesque. While the use of the simile throughout the novel exemplifies the impossibility of redressing the violence performed on the racialized and gendered subject, it also underscores how violence is reproduced by the silences of the historical archive and in narration itself. Scholars such as Saidiya Hartman and Guidotti-Hernández, among others, have shown how writing about racialized and gendered violence is based on an impossible task: replete with inscrutable silences, the "numbers, ciphers, and fragments of discourse" produced by ethno-racial violence are as close as the author comes to an intact depiction of the body in pain.[46] Guidotti-Hernández mines the unspeakable nature of violence and its opposite, the utterance, in which one finds "the unspeakable qualities of material and representational violence," and proposes that the "utterance and representational violence echo each other as material and historical cognates."[47] The unspeakability of violence elides specific histories that, paradoxically, must be acknowledged in order to deny them, and therefore, Guidotti-Hernández argues, violence is the foundational force behind their omission from the archive.[48] The excessive depiction of women's corpses, the violence performed on their bodies, and the repeated fragmentation that lends the novel its structure create a dizzying effect that makes the violence of the border unutterable, even though the astute reader can detect the unsayable violences enacted on the racialized and gendered bodies in the silences and gaps of narration.

One of the largest omissions of *2666* is the number in its title, which paratextually connects this work to others in Bolaño's oeuvre. While the number never appears in the novel, it acts as an ominous threat that presides over the plot from the outset. The enigmatic number does appear, however, in Bolaño's previous works *Los detectives salvajes* and *Amuleto* (published in Spanish in 1999, in English in 2006 as *Amulet*), which together portray the US-Mexico border as a future space of apocalyptic horror. In *Los detectives salvajes*, members of an avant-garde poetics group reach Santa Teresa, where they are told a vanished poet they are searching for spent most of her time sketching a cryptic factory that signaled "something about days to come. . . . [She] wrote down a date: sometime around the year 2600. Two thousand six hundred and something."[50] In *Amuleto*, an exiled poet living in Mexico City recounts walking down a street that looked, "above all else, like a cemetery, but not a cemetery in 1974, or a cemetery in 1968, or a cemetery in 1975, but a cemetery in 2666, a forgotten cemetery under the eyelid of a corpse or an unborn child, the dispassionate fluids of an eye that in wanting to forget one thing ended up forgetting it all."[50] Taken together, the three novels point to the apocalyptic threat that pervades Bolaño's work. In this schema, *2666* is the apogee of the otherworldly violence promised in the texts that precede it. *2666* delivers the "cryptic" factory and the "forgotten cemetery" promised in his previous work, where the future industrial cruelty necessitates expression in numerical and written form that can only ever be an approximation. The horror of the borderland is displaced to an estimated date ("Two thousand six hundred and something";

"Dos mil seiscientos y pico"), which is itself a repetition ("2600"), one that is only discernible when written and when read.

The Santa Teresan landscape and its apocalyptic horror enact aggregate ominous effects in all of *2666*'s sections, even those that do not take place in the city. Whereas women's corpses haunt the text before becoming textually legible, the city is the black hole that forces all characters into its dark center. It is through the city that all other geographies (London, Italy, Spain, New York, Germany) must be read. The novel opens with the search for a reclusive, never-before-seen German author, Benno von Archimboldi, by four European academics, Liz Norton (British), Jean-Claude Pelletier (French), Manuel Espinoza (Spanish), and Piero Morini (Italian). Their section, "The Part about the Critics," follows many of the literary tropes of noir and hard-boiled fiction, such as the genre's pared-down prose, its focus on gritty urban spaces and the city's "underbelly," the trope of the antihero (or antiheroes) who crosses ethical lines in search of answers, the moral breakdown of the protagonist, the centrality of violence, and the prevalence of unresolved endings.

The presence of the Archimboldians in the novel is a biting critique of academia, institutional practices, and the entrenched factions within literary studies and the obsession of scholars with mysterious and reclusive authors, such as Bolaño himself. As I have discussed, however, from the outset of *2666* the overflowing horror and the global reach of the US-Mexico border is foregrounded. This section is part of this project. As in hard-boiled fiction and noir, the text presupposes the crimes. Readers enter the text expecting the violence they vividly encounter in "The Part about the Crimes" (three hundred pages after the novel's start), and the plot is haunted by this horror. For example, early in the novel, Norton is drinking tea in her home in England, where she reflects that the sky looks like "the rictus of a robot or a god made in our likeness."[51] This image makes Norton feel overwhelmed and inscribes a sense of impending doom through the most quotidian of British activities—a sense of doom that recurs throughout the novel and culminates in the portrayal of women's corpses. The horror of the border, therefore, extends beyond the geopolitical space of the borderland, as if the novel were anticipating the arrival of the Archimboldians and their psychic undoing in Santa Teresa.

The psychosexual, affective, and physical horrors of the border surpass this geopolitical space to establish a global network woven by carnage and desire. In London, Pelletier and Espinoza physically assault a Pakistani taxi driver as Norton watches, after which "they were sunk for a few seconds in the strangest calm of their lives. It was as if they'd finally had the *ménage à trois* they'd so often fantasized of."[52] The physical violence they inflict on the driver is intimately linked to sexual pleasure—"Pelletier felt as if he'd come. Espinoza, with some nuanced differences, felt the same. Norton, who stared at them without seeing them in the dark, seemed to have experienced multiple orgasms"—foreshadowing the violence that will be inflicted on the postcolonial subject in Santa Teresa in part 4 of the novel through the contemporary archetypal British Other.[53] This scene underscores the communal aspect of taking pleasure in violence and the pleasure generated by turning excessive violence inward in acts of self-harm. The Archimboldians feel "as if they were fucking themselves" while beating the Pakistani, "as if they were digging into themselves."[54] Using the language of approximation, *2666* once again signals a textual anxiety about its desire to describe horror. The sadomasochistic attack that Pelletier and Espinoza perform is not only a vehicle through which they can experience sexual pleasure but a form of enjoyment that destroys the body—"But they . . . dug and dug, tearing fabric and ripping veins and damaging vital organs."[55] The text transforms the symbolic digging and ripping apart experienced by the critics into the literal violence inflicted on the corpse.

Thus, *2666* constructs a world in which violence is ubiquitous, a world that always refers back to the aesthetic production it defines as lacking. For example, Amalfitano's obsession with Rafael Dieste's *Testamento geométrico* (geometric treatise) (1975) becomes another aperture for the novel's consideration of the landscape's extremity and the distortion of the *Testamento* in and beyond the border. This allusion to Dieste's treatise becomes an object through which the novel textualizes the aestheticization of horror. Deciding to imitate Marcel Duchamp's readymade, Amalfitano follows the instructions the Dadaist gave for the object and hangs the book on a clothesline so that it will be affected by the elements. The *Testamento* becomes "coffinlike" and begins reflecting the landscape to which it is exposed.[56] At this point, Amalfitano starts dreaming of a voice that speaks to him about "'history broken down' or 'history broken down and put back together,' although clearly the reassembled history became something else, a comment in the margin, an intelligent footnote . . . the American mirror, said the voice, the sad American mirror of wealth and poverty . . . the mirror that sails and whose sails are pain."[57] In this way, Amalfitano's art experiment foreshadows the "fragmentación constante" of Kessler's simile that readers will encounter hundreds of pages later, which does and undoes, forms and deforms the landscape and its people. Kessler's atomic vision of terrestrial and corporeal violence is repeated by Amalfitano's dream voice. Kessler's vision, however, extends the affected space beyond Santa Teresa and suggests, once again, that the American hemisphere is a postapocalyptic space defined through pain.

The *Testamento* is a reflection of the "American mirror" that, through its oceanic description, returns us to the colonial conquest in the sixteenth century and underscores the long history of horror that ensued after the modern/colonial divide. The change the book goes through because of its exposure to the environment, and its link to the American mirror-as-ship, associates the colonial history of the Americas with the contemporary export processing system on the border and the bodies it produces. The violence of the landscape transforms the book into a dead object, one that is not fulfilling its purpose of being read to acquire knowledge. Instead, it links the landscape back to itself. Like the Duchampian Dadaist project, which explored the chaos of post–World War I society, Amalfitano's art object is an opening through which to examine the collapse of history by considering the export processing system and the industrial waste it creates: the woman on the border who is always already dead. And like Kessler's fragmented landscape and the monstrous walking-dead subjects it imagines, the *Testamento* instigates an apocalyptic textual vision that not only destroys Amalfitano's mental health but also emulates his mental collapse through its narrative structure. Its multiplicity of characters, locations, and subjects propagates the landscape's horror, weaving each description of violence into a fragmented and overwhelming whole. Each description amends the one that comes before it; each is a fragment that magnifies the mystery and horror of the border.

The Part about Blackness on the Border

Quincy Williams, a journalist for *Black Dawn*, a Harlem periodical, is known throughout *2666* as Oscar Fate. His "real" name is seen only once at the start of this section, but his pen name lends Fate's presence in the novel portentous weight. Much like Mark Spitz's moniker in Colson Whitehead's *Zone One* (2011), which I discussed in chapter 2, Fate's pseudonym veils him from readers, while the novel's foregrounding of his Blackness marks him as a signifying body whose race, and the history it connotes, cannot be extricated from the violence on and of the border. In contemplating the femicides, Fate considers his position as a citizen of the United States and what this position means in a hemispheric context. The novel therefore indexes Fate's Blackness through the histories of racialized and gendered violence, presenting it as limited by narration and international kinship. In this section, I show that the continued intrusions of the corpse in Fate's plot force him to imagine the possibilities of exposing the violence enacted on the racialized and gendered body, even as he fails to make this violence legible. The addition of Fate to *2666*'s world reflects the novel's concern with the shortcomings of narratives of violence while also placing this violence within a global network of doom. Fate's section also acts as a reminder of the novel's as-ifness by delving into Black discourse without being Black discourse itself—a narrative involvement that is yet another manifestation of the novel's textual anxiety.

Like the sections that precede it, "The Part about Fate" spends substantial time on other topics before introducing the femicides. Fate's plotline opens with the death of his mother and a series of questions that remain unanswered:

> When did it all begin? he thought. When did I go under? A dark, vaguely familiar Aztec lake. The nightmare. How to control the situation? And then other questions: Did he really want to leave everything behind? And he also thought: pain doesn't matter anymore. And also: maybe everything began with the death of my mother. And also: pain doesn't matter, unless it gets worse and becomes unbearable. And also: fuck, it hurts, fuck, it hurts. It doesn't matter, it doesn't matter. Surrounded by ghosts.[58]

This passage and its unanswered questions create a vertiginous effect that untethers the text from specific temporal demarcations. Fate is introduced through a sense of disorder couched in a language of pain and mourning that directly links him to the border, while Mexico is inscribed within an ancient (and stereotypical) mythical past. More importantly, the "dark, vaguely familiar Aztec lake" is staged with a general concept of horror that returns us to the Black body in pain through a series of overwhelming and rhetorical statements that exceed Fate the character but not fate as a concept. "The nightmare" instigates a mysterious vortex of horror signaled by the unanswerable and atemporal questions Fate asks, which portray the Black body as equally amorphous—a textual construction that aligns Fate with the monstrous formation of the corpse.

The turn to descriptions of the corpse and the aftermath of physical pain in the following section, "The Part about the Crimes," can be read as an attempt to provide answers to Fate's questions. He is told by a Mexican reporter that "the secret of the world is hidden" in the femicides, a statement that appears in the final pages of Fate's narrative and forces us to return to the questions that open it.[59] The enigmatic horror of the lake that makes Fate "go under" is associated with an embodiment of horror, textually marked by the approximation that unbearable pain produces. Statements such as "fuck, it hurts, fuck, it hurts" and "It doesn't matter, it doesn't matter" remind readers once again of the shattering power of violence. These fragmented statements do not describe the pain that produces them. Instead, they signal that language is capable only of approximating the cause of pain. The vision of the ancient lake brings Fate back to his mother's death and leads readers to ask: Who are the ghosts surrounding him? Are the ghosts those of the ancient Aztecs, the Santa Teresan femicide victims, or the Black characters Fate invokes throughout this section? Ultimately, uncertainty underscores the inability to disentangle one ghost from another, and the necessity of reading them together with attention to the ways they affect each other.

The apocalyptic descriptions of the Mexican landscape and intimations of the femicides always lead Fate back to memories of his mother, to thoughts of Black spaces in the United States, and to his knowledge of the history of Blackness in the Americas. Traveling to Santa Teresa, for example, triggers a long flashback of Fate's visit to Detroit to write an article about Barry Seaman, an ex–Black Panther turned cookbook author. In Detroit, Fate attends one of Seaman's lectures, where the latter tells the audience a story about his friend Marius Newell, a fellow Black Panther who sent Seaman postcards from prison.[60] In these postcards, Newell wrote about dreaming of being by the sea with a group of young Black Panthers. Seaman places himself within Newell's narrative: the group leaves their weapons in the car; Seaman can see "the deep dissatisfaction on our faces" even as he feels the danger of the ocean, "even though it's my brother there beside me . . . I think: the danger is the sea."[61]

Seaman's story invokes militant resistance and violence in the face of white supremacy and a deep frustration that is visually marked on the body. The sea is the central force that threatens their bodies, even as it inspires joy in Newell. Seaman's vision frames the sea and the history it calls up as a force of violence that extends beyond the 1960s and 1970s, to the past and future. The sea thus returns the Black body to the history of chattel slavery, while Newell's smile "beyond it all" taps into the longing for homecoming, even while knowing it is impossible. When Fate remembers this lecture in Santa Teresa, he introduces the history of the transatlantic slave trade into the US-Mexico border and depicts the Black body as always under the threat of death. Seaman's statement— "the danger is the sea"—comes after the audience is told of Newell's murder, marking the sea as the constant reminder of the original form of violence, which exceeds the gun. The sea's ominous threat is framed around notions of utterance and legibility. Newell's physical gesture toward the sea in lieu of verbal expression also returns us to the novel's framing of violence as too excessive for narration. This moment is a reminder of the continued "semiotics of the slave ship" and the inexorable signification of the Middle Passage, which, through Fate's presence in Santa Teresa, floods the border with the violence of the history of chattel slavery.[62]

Fate's memories introduce a wide range of historical periods of Black struggle in the United States. Triggered in the text by a mention of or reflection on women's corpses, Fate's return to the history of the slave trade, his mother, and other Black characters creates a network across ethno-racial and national boundaries that extends the violence of the border across the hemisphere and beyond. The femicides cause Fate to reflect on his own racial expendability and the history of violence signaled by his body. For instance, at a restaurant near the border, Fate overhears a conversation about the femicides and is reminded of the elisions in the historical archive of racialized violence and suffering. The conversation he overhears focuses on the possibility of narrating death through language, of filtering death "through the fabric of words" and the violence that exceeds language for those populations that fall outside definitions of the human and are omitted from historical archives.[63] The men having the conversation compare the "merchandise" on a slave ship, who "weren't part of society," to the "plantation owner" killed by his neighbor and the "woman killed in a French provincial capital," who are defined as part of society and whose deaths are therefore legible.[64] This conversation confirms that the femicide victims are industrial waste, disposable byproducts of export processing capitalist markets. No desire is expressed to include them within the national historical archives. Because they are the monstrously excessive products of extreme violence, there is no possibility of translating the brutality inflicted on their bodies into language.

This invocation of French provincial murders, plantation owners' deaths, and the femicides within the same construction extends the network of violence even further: here it appears as a transnational and transhistorical network that surpasses and repeats history, from the seventeenth century to the present. Through this conversation, Fate is reminded that violence against Black and brown bodies is commonly omitted from the historical archive and that it is so commonplace and excessive that it cannot be narrated. In this way, the overheard conversation creates a transracial network of violence and pain in which Fate cannot participate even as he is reminded of his precarious subjectivity. Ironically, this experience points to the futility of Fate's role as a journalist. While his occupation and expertise in language presuppose his ability to translate the world into text, *2666* forecloses this possibility because the violence inflicted on women's bodies surpasses the capacity for narration. Confronted with this violence, Fate wants to write about the femicides but cannot. Instead, this encounter is translated as a series of fragmented memories that bring the past and present together in a far-reaching web of violence.

After the men finish their conversation, Fate watches the sunset. From the natural beauty of the landscape, he turns to thoughts of his mother, her neighbor, the magazine, and the New York City streets, and finally he turns to a random page of Hugh Thomas's *The Slave Trade* (1997). On it he reads about how difficult it was for traffickers of enslaved people to collect the proceeds of their "cargo" and obtain a return shipment of goods.[65] Merchants, the book stipulates, preferred bills of exchange instead of "sugar, indigo, cotton, or ginger in exchange for the slaves."[66] This passage leads Fate into another reverie in which he considers the "pretty names" of objects: "Indigo, sugar, ginger, cotton. The reddish flowers of the indigo bush. The dark blue paste, with copper waves. A woman painted indigo, washing herself in the shower."[67] In this passage, as in many others, *2666* tethers violence (physical, emotional, terrestrial) to beauty. References to historical violence—past and present, national and international—return Fate to his mother and to Black spaces that, through the replication of *The Slave Trade*, place his memories within a larger historical context of Black mourning. Nevertheless, reading about the purchase of enslaved people in return for goods produces a reflection not on the brutality of the system but on the beauty of source materials that produce pleasure and cultures of taste. Reading *The Slave Trade* prompts Fate to consider the "pretty names" and the aesthetic qualities of these materials, expounding on their pleasing details and even speculating about their proximity to the carnal. In this way, *2666* juxtaposes the violence of Atlantic slavery with beauty, both on and off the page. The text also suggests that the pleasure these materials denote cannot be extricated from their use as goods of exchange for Black bodies. "The Part about Fate" exemplifies the novel's investment in exploring the pleasures experienced in depictions of excessive violence.

It is worth pausing to ask why "The Part about Fate" constantly returns readers to racial identifiers and questions about race. Fate continually notices race, and the text presents details that seem inconsequential for the plot but that serve as reminders of racial difference and his own desire to see this difference. On an airplane, Fate notes that the "stewardess was blond, about forty. . . . The man in the seat next to him was Black and was drinking from a bottle of water."[68] After his mother's death, Fate looks "for porn on the TV. He found a movie in which a German woman was making love with a pair of Black men. The German woman was speaking German and the two Black men were as well. He wondered if there were Black people in Germany too."[69] His attention to race underscores his desire to ground himself and others in national and racial specificity, while also attempting to find Blackness visually represented and, more importantly, available in spaces where Blackness seems out of reach, or which the novel seems to textually foreclose, such as in sexual acts and on the US-Mexico border. Fate's surprise at hearing German-speaking Black men is a projection that extends the possibilities of Blackness outside his body, outside the United States and the American hemisphere, and into international terrain. The international Blackness that Fate considers shows a desire to find racial kinships outside those he knows to be possible and expands the definition of Blackness within the text.

In fact, the femicides in Santa Teresa elicit a broader ideological meditation on the bodies that are allowed to participate in national cultural imaginaries. Fate's juxtaposition of "German woman" and "two Black men" exposes the systemic exclusion of Black bodies from national imaginaries of belonging. His reflection is predicated on the threat of death that haunts the text and follows Fate into the border city. The femicides and the haunting by the corpse throughout "The Part about Fate" progressively undo him. Fate's international assignment generates a sense of insecurity and uncertainty, specifically in relation to his race and its symbolic positioning. Waiting for "trucks to pass on their way from Santa Teresa to Arizona," Fate considers his comment to a cashier—"I'm American"—which leads to further reflections on his national affiliation and his position within the nation-state: "Why didn't he say African American? Because I'm in a foreign country? But can I consider myself to be in a foreign country when, if I wanted, I could go walking right now to my own country and it wouldn't take very long? Does that mean that in some places I'm American and in some places I'm African American and in other places, by logical extension, I'm no one?"[70] Here Fate meditates on the permeability of the border and the absurdity of its demarcation, especially considering that Santa Teresa operates within a global capitalist system that relies on the concept of the postnational, and simultaneously illustrates the "undoing" or the "nobodyness" of the Black subject within the hemispheric American imaginary.

The questions that Fate asks as he watches the trucks move from Mexico to the United States remain unanswered. At the end of the series of questions, Fate is (hypothetically) "no one." The break in the text after this question leaves Fate as an excessive body that can be defined only through potentially conflicting forms of being. The following fragment in Fate's narrative opens with "When he woke up."[71] This phrase marks his awakening as an ill-defined subject who is unable to locate the boundaries of his identity or his position within American definitions of citizenship. The text's refusal to provide answers to Fate's questions, moreover, can be read as an example of the novel's dabbling in Black discourse without engaging with it substantively.

The hauntingly beautiful but violent spaces described in the novel generate a growing sense of ambiguity and insecurity, not only in Fate, but also in the novel generally. As Fate makes his way out of Santa Teresa, he is unable to recognize the landmarks he saw only a few days earlier. He assumes that New

York is "where everything would take the consistency of reality again."[72] In this ideologically constructed space of death, logic becomes warped and dangerous, yet we never see him reach his anticipated destination of sanity. Instead, this section of *2666* returns readers to an event before his departure, where he visits the presumed femicidal killer, Archimboldi's nephew, in jail. This moment creates a connection between the seemingly disparate parts of the novel. As the suspect enters the room, the reporter Fate is with "raised her hand to her mouth, as if she were inhaling a toxic gas, and she couldn't think what to ask."[73] The invocation of toxic gas foreshadows the atomic violence that created the city and the genocidal violence of World War II, introduced in the last section of the novel. These concluding lines in "The Part about Fate" bring the violence of the Holocaust into the narrative and suggest that the victims are small pieces in a vast mechanism of systemic violence. Fate's section hints at the possibility of transnational, transracial, or even intra-ethnic alliances. Yet *2666* ultimately treats the borderland's "herida abierta" as a space that impedes translation, a space that requires the language of approximation and horror to attempt its narration of violence.

The Part about *Latinidad*

Trussing the brutal violence of the border's landscape to the decomposition of the body has a long history in Latinx literary and cultural production. It can even be traced to a period before the construction of what we now consider the designation *Latinx*. María Amparo Ruiz de Burton's now-canonical *The Squatter and the Don* (1885) portrays the decay of the Mexican-Californio body as accompanying the destruction of the landscape by Anglo settlers and corporate enterprise. *The Squatter and the Don*'s plot revolves around two families living near San Diego shortly after the annexation of California after the Treaty of Guadalupe Hidalgo in 1848. Tracing the obstacles faced by ill-fated lovers, one from a Californio family and the other from an Anglo one, this social-reform novel builds on the tension in the region as Anglo settlers wrest this new US land away from Californios. Told through the mode of the romance novel, *The Squatter and the Don* focuses on the demise of the aristocratic population of Mexican descent because of the railroad monopoly and its collusion with Congress. This "neo-Marxist critique of capital's spatial appetite" showcases the tradition in Latinx literature of representing and re/producing the US-Mexico border as an apocalyptic wasteland formed by a violent relationship with the United States.[74] A proto-Chicanx text, *The Squatter and the Don* suggests other cataclysmic events that highlight the invasions and annexations that have occurred in the various borderlands of the Americas, and it equates the history of annexation and land grabs after the US intervention in Mexico with the decomposition of the proto-Latinx body.[75] *The Squatter and the Don* concludes with an apocalyptic threat to the new "American" nation. In conjunction with the text's melodramatic sentimentalism, which is a form of affective excess in itself, and the invocation of godly redemption—"pray for a Redeemer who will emancipate the white slaves of California"—the novel hints at the impact of otherworldly vengeance that will transform the nation and leaves readers to contend with the white space that follows a biblical invocation and the textual end the threat enacts.[76]

More than a century later, the graphic novel *Feeding Ground* (2011) showcases a new generation of Latinx fiction that continues the discussions introduced by *The Squatter and the Don*. Unlike Ruiz de Burton's focus on the threat to white, wealthy masculinity, *Feeding Ground* highlights the violence of migration and the corporatization of the border that produces monstrous bodies, particularly that of young women. A famine caused by Blackwell Industries drives Diego Busqueda and his family to cross the Devil's Highway, a deadly stretch of land between Mexico and the United States that migrants use to cross the border. Attacked by a pack of werewolves—of which Blackwell is the leader—Flaca, Diego's daughter, is turned and stalked across the desert in order to return her to Blackwell. The graphic novel ends abruptly. The first of six volumes, *Feeding Ground* leaves readers with an ambiguous ending that personifies the borders as a threat (figures 3.1 and 3.2). Statements like "I have eroded nations" and "My children will always feed" appear amid depictions of werewolves violently killing humans on the border, reiterating the piecemeal foundation of the genre and the violence it draws and writes.[77] *Feeding Ground* ends with Flaca's embodiment of the border and its insatiable hunger for violence and vengeance. The graphic novel renews the biblical warning introduced by Ruiz de Burton and produces an overtly monstrous presence, this time shown not saving white "slaves" but ripping bodies apart. Flaca's werewolf transformation at the hands of Blackwell Industries evinces the damage that modern capitalism inflicts on landscapes and bodies, particularly women's bodies.

2666 echoes this fleshy portrayal of the border's monstrosity and the violence it perpetrates. Florita Almada, a "seer" who appears on TV throughout "The Part about the Crimes," talks about the femicides and the "visions" they create. Florita connects these visions to an overwhelming force: whereas "an ordinary murder" generates a "liquid image, a lake or a well that after being disturbed grows calm again," the "serial murders, like the ones in the border city, projected a *heavy* image, metallic or mineral, an image that burned."[78] These

FIGURE 3.1. Graphic novel cells from *Feeding Ground* (2011). Story by Swifty Lang, illustrations by Michael Lapinski, and lettering by Chris Mangun.

FIGURE 3.2. Graphic novel cells from *Feeding Ground* (2011). Story by Swifty Lang, illustrations by Michael Lapinski, and lettering by Chris Mangun.

visions tether the industrial backdrop to monstrous women's bodies created through repeated violence. The heavy image of Florita's visions repeats itself throughout Bolaño's novel, pathologically drawing all characters to its horrific center. The routinized violence leaves women speechless and peripheral, defining all women's bodies in the novel (dead or alive) as always already murdered or expected to be murdered.

As I have shown throughout this chapter, *2666* narrates the US-Mexico border as a postapocalyptic landscape strewn with the remnants of neo/colonization and imperialism. Yet even as the novel uses the tropes of "border discourse" made famous by Anzaldúa—in particular the trope of the border as an open wound—Bolaño's biography means that the novel does not neatly fit within borderland literature or the Latinx canon. Using the language of approximation, Bolaño's novel attempts to encapsulate the violence of this region, which is always out of reach, while tapping into the Chicanx and Latinx literary traditions. The border discourses it uses expand the definitions of Chicanx and Latinx literature, with their focus on questions of immigration, assimilation, nationhood, citizenship, and bilingualism, among others. As I show throughout *Doom Patterns*, the reading protocols of Latinx speculative fiction bring to light depictions of cyclical violence that foreclose the possibility of political remedy. This is true of *2666*, which—unlike works such as Alicia Gaspar de Alba's *Desert Blood* (2005) and Stella Pope Duarte's *If I Die in Juárez* (2008)—offers no hope of political transformation. Bolaño's novel instead presents an apocalyptic landscape that interminably excretes dead bodies.

This chapter has extended my exploration of the "Latinx" literary canon by showing how the reading protocols of Latinx speculative fiction can reveal the otherworldly in a novel. It has also suggested that Latinx literature can include works that belong to the field because of their subject matter rather than because of their authors' biographies. Like Junot Díaz (chapter 1), Bolaño enjoys a semi-mythological status within the literary market, the academy, and popular culture. One of his major contributions to Latin American and world literature has been to create a space where this literature is not solely assessed against standards and expectations influenced by magical realism. Although Bolaño is considered the "literary heir" of the Latin American Boom generation, *2666*, like his previous fiction, presents a clear aesthetic opposition to Boom literature, which ossified magical realism as the only desirable style coming from Latin America and disseminated this aesthetics within US Latinx literature as well. The world literary market and US readership have produced Bolaño's prominence, which, as I argue in this chapter, is predicated on the replication of horror on the US-Mexico border. The commodification of the novel uses translation as a tool to reinterpret Latin American culture for US readers and confirms the American Global South as a space of horror, chaos, and death. This situation is indicative of institutional practices that manufacture designations such as "Latinx" literature through critique, marketing, teaching, and translation. Yet Bolaño's novel, read through the protocols of Latinx speculative fiction, can open new avenues for exploration in the Latinx literary canon and across literatures. Through the character of Benno von Archimboldi, the sought-after author who bookends the novel, *2666* creates an intricate and mysteriously ungraspable network of enduring violence that yokes European genocides to the violence of the border. The metanarrative that dominates "The Part about Archimboldi" not only critiques the concerning tendency to treat a single authorial figure (such as Díaz and Bolaño) as representative of an entire literary field but also upends the possibility of evaluating the novel through a reparative reading practice.

2666 does not conclude predictably. The book ends abruptly, leaving many unanswered questions that magnify the sense of ominous foreboding that permeates the novel. The final section of *2666* highlights the novel's consistent use of approximation and grotesquerie to create the landscape of transnational and transtemporal horror that sees its apex in Santa Teresa and the femicide. Archimboldi's presence in the text exposes what Walter Benjamin called the "single catastrophe" of history, "which keeps piling wreckage upon wreckage" and which "progress" cannot rectify.[79] As Benjamin's "angel of history" illustrates, the "storm" of progress is itself a perpetrator of history's wreckage, propelling the angel forward and forbidding him to reconstitute that which has been destroyed. *2666* does not equate the violence of the war with that of the borderland, yet it does characterize them as systemically linked through an interminable march through history that ties Nazi Europe to twentieth-century Mexico—a long, global history of violence mediated through extermination and reifying monstrosity, a violence that transforms the mundane into the horrific.

4

REKONKISTA

Brownface, Time Travel, and Cyberfascism in "Greater Mexico"

The murals of the Farmer John slaughterhouse in Vernon, California, are notorious. Covering ten acres, the murals show cartoon pigs enjoying various forms of play and leisure: lying in a pasture alongside dogs and birds, swimming in a creek, eating grass, even flying with small pig wings—or are they bound for pig heaven after being made into sausage inside? These cartoon pigs are creepily humanesque, wearing baseball caps, flying airplanes, and selling lemonade behind a lemonade stand (figures 4.1 and 4.2). The idyllic farm life depicted by the murals is, as Anthony Lovett and Matt Maranian put it in *L.A. Bizarro*, a "jolly" distraction from "the ugly business that goes on just behind it." Indeed, they conclude, rarely do art and industry "collide in such an effective manner."[1]

Farmer John, a provider of meat products purchased by Smithfield Foods in 2017, was the maker of the proprietary Dodger Dog from the 1960s until 2021, when Smithfield and the Dodgers could not agree on a new contract and the name Farmer John was removed from the product. In 2023, Farmer John

FIGURE 4.1. Mural on the side of Farmer John Processing Plant, Vernon, California. Photograph by Citizen of the Planet, 2010.

announced the closure of the slaughterhouse in California, and the Dodger Dog is now being made by the Vernon-based company Papa Cantella. Yet, like the Dodger Dog and baseball as a whole, Farmer John's products have participated in other nation-building projects. According to Farmer John's company website, during World War II, Clougherty Packing LLC, the corporation that owned Farmer John before Smithfield's acquisition, began supplying meat to local military bases and the Pacific Ocean military effort after the attack on Pearl Harbor. Located in the "exquisitely dismal" industrial zone of Vernon—a city five miles south of Los Angeles—the Farmer John murals were started in 1957 by the Hollywood set painter Leslie "Les" Allen Grimes, who fell to his death while completing the work.[2] The murals have been expanded and retouched by various painters, including Arno Jordan, an Austrian-born muralist, who enlarged and restored the mural well into the 1980s before he mysteriously disappeared, prompting the urban legend that Jordan was made into sausage himself.[3]

A little over half a mile away from the Farmer John slaughterhouse is the headquarters of the Hundreds, a streetwear label that describes itself as a

FIGURE 4.2. Mural on the side of Farmer John Processing Plant, Vernon, California. Photograph by Tibrina Hobson, 2012.

"two-part project that houses a Classic Californian Streetwear brand and media platform dedicated to Global Street Culture."[4] After founding the Hundreds in 2013, Bobby Kim and Ben Shenassafar moved their headquarters to Vernon and commissioned a mural that revises the story depicted on the walls of Farmer John. As Kim states in his blog for the Hundreds, "The [Farmer John] mural, as beautiful and historical as it is, is a lie."[5] Completed by the painters who most recently retouched the mural at Farmer John, the painting at the streetwear company revises the narrative of pigs contentedly awaiting their execution inside. In this alternate reality, the pigs are the perpetrators of violence, stringing humans up by the neck to cut off their limbs, impaling them with thick wooden spears, burning them with a blowtorch, and hacking them to pieces with a chainsaw and Jason Voorhees mask (figure 4.3).

The pleasures in violent depictions and the competing, kitschy, and humorous worlds signaled by the dueling pig murals of Vernon are at the center of this chapter. Set partly in a fictionalized Farmer John plant, Sesshu Foster's *Atomik Aztex* (2005) uses experimental aesthetics to highlight violence, pleasure, and

FIGURE 4.3. Mural outside the office of the Hundreds, Vernon, California. Photograph by Bobby "Hundreds" Kim, 2013.

excess while colliding with the expectations of academic and literary industries. The novel uses the speculative tropes of time travel and alternate realities to reimagine the historical cataclysm of Spanish conquest in the Americas. It does this by exhibiting what I call a *Latinxface* performance that both participates in and challenges minstrelsy traditions and the idea of multiethnic literature, especially multiethnic speculative fiction. Instead of opening a space of political remedy, the novel showcases the lingering effects of violence's relation to power regardless of race or culture. I use the term *Latinxface* or *brownface performance* to indicate how a novel by an Asian American author assumes the history, culture, and language of Chicanx populations past and present in both generative and challenging ways.

Unlike the previous works explored in *Doom Patterns*, *Atomik Aztex* is not a canonical text, and Foster is far from a household name.[6] Born to an Anglo-American father and Nisei mother, Foster was raised in East Los Angeles and, although relatively unknown, has an impressive literary pedigree. After attending the Iowa Writers' Workshop for his MFA, Foster returned to LA, where he is a teacher, writer, and community organizer. Known primarily for his poetry,

Foster is the author of *City Terrace Field Manual* (1996), *American Loneliness* (2006), *World Ball Notebook* (2009), and *City of the Future* (2018). The small press that published *Atomik Aztex*, City Lights, also has a noteworthy history. Founded in San Francisco by Lawrence Ferlinghetti in 1953, the press gained national attention during Allen Ginsberg's obscenity trial for publishing *Howl and Other Poems* (1956). Today it is known for its publication of "world literature" and its progressive politics. *Atomik Aztex*, Foster's only novel, has received favorable, albeit few, reviews. His prose has been compared to the postmodern fiction of Thomas Pynchon, Don DeLillo, Ishmael Reed, and Philip K. Dick and has been identified with "punk sci-fi and kitchen-sink realism."[7] Susan Salter Reynolds of the *Los Angeles Times* states that a book like *Atomik Aztex* "require[s] slightly different reading skills from more traditional novels" and equates its difficulty with aesthetic mastery and literary expertise.[8] The comparison to works of "high art" by Pynchon, DeLillo, Reed, and the Beats can be seen in phrases used to describe *Atomik Aztex*, such as "genre-straddling tour de force" and "twisting masterpiece of hybrid vigor."[9] It is significant that in praising the book's literariness, most reviewers compare the novel to works by white, canonical postmodern writers. This type of praise is racially coded and in tension with literary history. As Ursula Heise explains, the common narrative that white male authors of the 1970s and 1980s wrote antirealist fiction whereas minoritized authors returned to realism is far too simplistic.[10] Foster's *Atomik Aztex* turns to the tropes of speculative fiction to show how historical events like the Spanish conquest of Mexico in the sixteenth century are cataclysmic. This excessive violence directs the prose into metafictional references, multilingual prose, sardonic humor, time travel, advertisement lingo, and the use of images—breakages in traditional linear form that signal the text's spilling over and returning us to historical apocalypse.

Set in two worlds, *Atomik Aztex* reimagines how history would have unfolded if the Aztecs had defeated the Spanish in the sixteenth century. The first world of the novel is set in Anahuac, now in Southern California, where Zenzontli, Keeper of the House of Darkness for the Aztek Socialist Imperium, is a leading military dignitary. The Aztek Socialist Imperium, following a common conception of Aztec tradition, generates its economic power through human sacrifice, offering up the human hearts of conquered war prisoners to grow their empire. Zenzontli and his Jaguar Unit are sent to Stalingrad, Russia, to fight against the Nazis in 1942. However, Zenzontli suffers from debilitating headaches and hallucinatory visions, which his superiors recommend fixing with a dangerous brain surgery. These visions are our entry point into the novel's second world, where Zenzón, a worker in the Farmer John slaughterhouse, becomes involved in an effort to unionize its workers. Zenzontli and Zenzón are confronted with similar obstacles, primarily in the form of superiors/elders and bureaucratic power structures. In fact, the two characters act as mirror images of each other, illustrating the long-lasting effects of history and the recursive power of violence.

In *Atomik Aztex*, time travel, multilingual prose, sardonic humor, and experimentations in metatextual form act as doom patterns that return readers to colonial, imperial, fascistic, and contemporary institutional violence as a pleasurable aesthetic practice. In its reimagination of the past, *Atomik Aztex* unsettles key Chicanx concepts such as Indigenous identity, ancestry, and nationhood. The novel also performs a speculative reimagination of Los Angeles as part of what José Limón designates "Greater Mexico." Following the work of Américo Paredes, Limón defines Greater Mexico as the areas inhabited by people of Mexican culture within Mexico and across the border in the United States.[11] The idea that Mexican nations have always continued to exist in US territorial spaces, even after the 1848 Treaty of Guadalupe Hidalgo, is central to Foster's novel, underscoring the significance of the borderlands and borderland literature in the Latinx and American imaginary. Los Angeles, Foster suggests, never stopped being Mexico. In building this claim, *Atomik Aztex* continually reminds its readers of the violence of this geopolitical space.

While the novel offers an alternate history in which the Aztecs defeated the Spanish and the American hemisphere was not affected by European colonialism, it also capsizes any potential for sanguine equity by positing the Aztecs (interchangeably Aztexs or Azteks in the novel) as a cyberfascistic force that emulates the bellicosity of European and American imperialism. *Atomik Aztex* thus presents us with a revenge fantasy that addresses enduring questions in speculative and science fiction studies: What does redemption look like when minoritized and racialized subjects speak for themselves and reclaim power? Does the reimagination of the historical past effect political remedy? Does the new world look like redemption? Most scholarship about this text positions it as a "scathing satire" or a speculative effort to politically educate its readers.[12] The intimate link between history making and world making, for these scholars, is associated with what is usually described as the novel's political imperative and optimistic regenerative drive, implicit in the reimagination of the Chicanx past.[13] In my reading, however, the novel does not hold a hopeful view of resistance movements or uprisings, or imply "that their mere imagination is enough to bring about change."[14] While overturning the trajectory of European colonial history in the Americas, the novel underscores the spectral Mexican presence in contemporary Southern California—indeed, in North

America more generally—and illustrates the intimate relationship between death and the North American national body.[15] *Atomik Aztex*, then, disinters constitutive American voices and histories that have been ignored or omitted from the national archive.

The long history of Latinx presence and influence in the United States has been made invisible in political institutions, literary history, and "the national-pedagogical complex that relies" on this presence and influence "to produce definitions of what is 'American.'"[16] Kirsten Silva Gruesz and others have significantly revised the national tradition that renders Latinx presence as spectral, emphasizing the important role of Latinx and Spanish-language writing in the United States before the twentieth century.[17] Foster's *Atomik Aztex* similarly stresses the foundational role of Mexican and Indigenous peoples and cultures in the United States (and in the northern hemisphere as a whole), yet instead of advancing a revisionist ameliorative project, the novel highlights the loss and violence inflicted by Spanish colonialism, which remain as a haunting presence in the present. In this way, Foster's novel can be read as an often-overlooked text that scholars like Gruesz might add to their catalog of Latinx writing in the United States, an addition that invites them to consider what speculative fiction contributes to the historical archive.

Atomik Aztex epitomizes the central argument throughout this book by drawing attention to issues of canonicity and the instability of ethno-racial designations, and by exemplifying how to implement the protocols of Latinx speculative fiction as a reading praxis. *Atomik Aztex* expands the domain of Latinx literature and underscores the capacious messiness of racialization. The novel's Latinx performance is itself an element of its spillover. More than Chicanx, more than Asian American, more than *x*-fiction—science, speculative, historical—*Atomik Aztex* defies common literary categories. In its description of Chicanx and colonial histories, it directs the reader simultaneously to Chicanx history and to other forms of national and local historical violence, such as the Immigration Act of 1924, the internment of Japanese Americans after the bombing of Pearl Harbor, and the chronicles of the many Indigenous groups across the continent. Alongside its paratextual historical referents, the novel deploys a variety of textual styles (shifting among italicized, bolded, and underlined type), a mix of languages (English, Spanglish, Caló, Nahuatl, Russian), photographs, prose intermixed with brief moments of verse, infomercial-speak, a haphazard replacement of English's hard *c*'s with *k*'s, and references to musicology, communist theory, and canonical journals, all of which are academically mis/cited.[18] *Atomik Aztex* also draws from multiple literary traditions, including fantasy, the muckraking novel (particularly Upton Sinclair's 1906 *The Jungle*), *crónicas de Indias*, Spanish accounts of the "discovery" of the Americas, science fiction, the historical novel, and LA noir. The novel includes a wide variety of self-conscious postmodern references, invoking "high art" and "lowbrow" popular culture, Chicanx history, aesthetics, and Indigeneity while challenging accepted notions of ethno-racial identity, the American literary tradition, and canonization.

In this chapter, I explore these thematic and formal excesses by first showing how *Atomik Aztex* draws on a multiplicity of literary genres and styles in its attempt to retell the trauma of the historical past. Instead of presenting readers with a manageable plot, it stages an excessive and unruly world that reproduces the violence it is trying to narrate. Second, I turn to the novel's engagement with violence and aesthetics, showing how it portrays them as mutually constituted while veering into the affective. Finally, I turn to the novel's performance of brownness to show how *Atomik Aztex* participates in the mythologization of Aztlán, and the erasure of Indigeneity seen in Chicanx studies, while offering new avenues for investigating how literary fields are formed, what constitutes Latinx literature, and how *latinidad* can be defined expansively.

Aztlán Is Where the Heart Is: The Songs
of the Mockingbird

Debate over *Atomik Aztex*'s "plot" and temporal setting points to the erratic inconsistency of the prose that prevents the readers from achieving a concrete grip on the text. Instead, *Atomik Aztex* forces readers to plummet into a novel organized around confusion without an eye toward resolution. The text is not incoherent, as some scholars have suggested, yet the notion of a plot cannot be readily applied to the novel, as it rejects the spatial-temporal linearity and causality of the term.[19] The novel clearly sets the Aztex world of Zenzontli primarily in 1942; Zenzón's world is slightly more uncertain. Scholars place this timeline of the novel variously in 2005, an "undesignated time after 1961," or a "reality modeled on our [unspecified] own."[20] This confusion and discrepancy point to how *Atomik Aztex* establishes its violence as inescapable, unintelligible, and persistently reproduced. The novel's unpredictability, excess, and multiplicity of meaning speak to the tradition of "historiographic metafiction" as defined by Linda Hutcheon in *A Poetics of Postmodernism* (1988). *Atomik Aztex* falls within this genre, self-consciously defining itself as high art yet also as an incomplete source for the portrayal of history. The postmodern, according to Hutcheon, is that which is "contradictory, resolutely historical, and inescapably political."[21] Most importantly, contradictions, while byproducts of late capitalism, are manifest in the postmodern concept of "the presence of the past."[22] Hutcheon's concept of historiographic metafiction illuminates *Atomik Aztex*'s formal investments in its reinvestigation and revision of the historical past and its violence. Historiographic metafiction, Hutcheon states, is a form that is "intensely self-reflexive" while paradoxically laying claim "to historical events and personages."[23] Following this definition, to reinvestigate the past is not an act of nostalgia but an action that critically revises what came before and engages in a dialogue with the past in light of the present.[24] However, the historical past is only accessible via the text, and in the case of *Atomik Aztex* (as is the case generally in postmodernist fiction), this past is presented to us by an unreliable narrator who is limited, provisional, and difficult to locate and who constantly undermines their ostensible omniscience. *Atomik Aztex*'s cyclical, contradictory, and confusing narrative continually calls attention to the question of "*whose* truth gets told" and through its use of pastiche mocks the historical archive while simultaneously reminding us of the violent events within it.[25]

The competing narratives seen on the facades of Farmer John and the headquarters of the Hundreds illustrate the tension between the desire to rewrite the historical past and the impossibility of illustrating violence in language. While scholars have argued about the plausibility of time travel in the novel as well as whether Zenzontli and Zenzón could be the same person, my concern here is with the speculative reimagination of the Chicanx historical past and the excessive formal qualities of the novel that foreclose any possibility of imagining a regenerative future.[26] In these formal qualities, *Atomik Aztex* indexes the violence of colonial conquest, fascistic occupation, and even the slaughterhouse. In other words, much as Farmer John's idyllic mural reminds us of what takes place behind its walls, the tongue-in-cheek premise of *Atomik Aztex* reminds readers of the Spanish conquest in the sixteenth century and the subsequent colonization of the region. The gruesome yet playful depictions of violence throughout the novel point back to the historical archive, while the overwhelming effect of reading *Atomik Aztex* indicates an excess that verges on the pleasurable. As Reynolds asserts, the "parallel realities, the lack of warning about shifts in time and place, the characters with multiple personalities can make you dizzy if you struggle too hard to keep all the details in line. Instead, you have to let go and let the writing wash over you."[27] Our usual reading practices, as Reynolds suggests, require us to "keep all the details in line." This novel, however, demands an immersive experience without particular concern for detail. Her review, despite being somewhat dismissive of the novel because of its speculative elements, lends support to my reading: letting the words "wash over you" is a way of experiencing the unfixed, tenuous, and seemingly erratic prose and the confusing elements of Foster's work.[28] The turn to speculative and science fiction in *Atomik Aztex* signals a surplus of violence in the history it is retelling that forces the novel to spill over itself, drawing on a variety of literary traditions and genres, languages, characters, and textual fragmentations in order to attempt (yet ultimately fail) to capture the horror of colonial violence. These extravagant elements of the text challenge the widespread tendency to use ethnic literature as a tool of political remedy. Through gruesome but humorous depictions of colonial violence and extra- and intratextual references, the novel continually reminds readers of the real violences in "our world" and illustrates the impediments to looking outside or beyond the anathema of colonialization and coloniality.

The novel opens with Zenzontli, whose name is derived from the Nahuatl Zenzontle or Centzontle and is translated into English as "mockingbird." From *centzontleh*, *centzontle* means "possessor of four hundred words" (*centzontli*, "four hundred" + *tlahtolli*, "language, word, statement" + *-eh*, "possessor of").[29] The North American mockingbird is a "virtuoso bird," an "open-ended learner" who can add new vocalizations to its repertoire throughout its life.[30] As its binomial name stipulates (*Mimus polyglottos*), the mockingbird is an imitator of many tongues, known for mimicking the calls of other birds and animal species such as frogs and insects, and even human-made sounds like car alarms.[31] Zenzontli's name, then, not only indicates that multilingualism is essential to the text but also suggests that the shifts in language in the novel are a type of forgery. *Atomik Aztex* thus indicates the impossibility of reaching an authentic original source for the histories relayed within. In place of such an origin, it creates a dissonance of sound that is excessive and engulfing and points readers multidirectionally outside itself, ad infinitum. Like the mockingbird, the voices in *Atomik Aztex* display adaptability and elusiveness, a playful jeering that consistently reminds readers of various forms of violence: historical, lingual, racial, and colonial. The novel illustrates the need to incorporate a multiplicity of vocalizations to describe the extreme nature of this violence.

From the outset, readers are forewarned of the profusion of voices and literary traditions they will encounter. Yet before the novel begins, we come across a preliminary "Note" that, like the exposition of fukú in Junot Díaz's *The Brief Wondrous Life of Oscar Wao* (2007), instructs us how to read the pages that follow it:

NOTE

This is a work of fiction. Readers looking for accurate information on Nahua and Mexica peoples or the Farmer John meat packing plant in the City of Vernon need to *read nonfiction*. (See Michael Coe and Miguel

Leon-Portilla.) Persons attempting to find a plot in this book should read Huck Finn. Also, in this book a number of dialects are used, including the extreme form of the South-Western pocho dialect, caló, ordinary inner-city slang, and modified varieties of speech from the Vietnam era. This is no accident.[32]

With this opening note, the text lays claim to a literary tradition ("work of fiction"), while simultaneously refusing a central element of this tradition: the plot. The note playfully directs readers to Mark Twain's *Adventures of Huckleberry Finn* (1884), whose formal qualities it emulates even as it taunts the canonical novel's attachment to a storyline. Unlike the "Notice" and "Explanatory" that open Twain's text, the "Note" in Foster's novel remains unsigned, leaving its origin and author unknown. The citation of *Huck Finn* might seem to be "pointing from the high ground of experimental fiction of doubtful ontologies to the solid ground of a classic text," yet, as Sascha Pöhlmann points out, *Atomik Aztex* actually "situates both itself and *Huck Finn* within a textual multiverse in which no world is the real one and every world is an alternative world."[33] Opening the novel with this extratextual reference to canonical American fiction allows Foster to lay claim to being conversant in high art while signaling that his novel is contesting this labeling practice.

The novel's engagement with (and push against) the high/low division, the literary canon, the postmodern, and speculative aesthetics is further clarified by Antonio Viego's Lacanian framework of the ethno-racialized subject. In *Dead Subjects* (2007), Viego explores ego psychology, wholeness, and transparency to argue that the ethno-racial subject is pathologized in ego psychology and, furthermore, is divided and split in language. This framework offers an opening for considering the fragmentary and excessive in *Atomik Aztex* as well as the novel's narrator/s and its formal opaqueness and impenetrability. Viego proposes a parallel between the border-queer subject in Latinx studies and the hysteric and barred subject in Lacanian psychoanalysis. As he explains, the hysteric or barred subject disrupts the notion of a universal subject in ego psychoanalysis, while the border-queer threatens master narratives and the notion that archives of knowledge can be complete. In this way, both the border-queer and the hysteric redefine the parameters of the normal, displaying their assemblages and producing new symptoms in need of interpretation. The border-queer and hysteric thus affirm their symbolic elusiveness and resistance at the level of language and classification, inviting us to cultivate their piecemeal nature and the multiplicity they inspire.[34] The hysteric, like the border-queer, undermines the "master's discourse" by producing new symptoms and requiring the formation of new and more knowledges because the hysteric "gets off on knowledge."[35] To get off on knowledge is precisely what *Atomik Aztex* and its alternate realities propose—with all the implications of pleasure, sex, pain, and power the phrase *getting off* connotes. The many knowledges introduced by the text create a cacophonous and overwhelming effect that causes several forms of fragmentation and breakage.

In this way, the "Note" indicates the novel's excessiveness from the outset, referencing elements outside the American historical archive such as the history of the Nahua and Mexica peoples and various non-English dialects. Placing these histories side by side with "ordinary inner-city slang" and "speech from the Vietnam era" creates a hemispheric network of colonial, imperial, and contemporary military violence. The text writes a new history in which these elements coexist and congeal in Vernon, driving local Southern California history and the cruelty of the industrial meat complex. Unlike Twain's prefaces, which call forth various nonstandard forms of English—"Missouri negro dialect; the extremest form of the backwoods Southwestern dialect; the ordinary 'Pike County' dialect"—the dialects and languages invoked by *Atomik Aztex* introduce a network of communication that is acquired through warfare or lost because of colonial and imperial histories.[36] The text also invokes the work of Michael Coe and Miguel León-Portilla, an American and a Mexican anthropologist, respectively, by placing itself in opposition to their work on pre-Columbian Mesoamerica.[37] Yet, as with the various dialects, locations, and peoples introduced in the "Note," the citation of two prominent anthropologists points readers to the centrality of anthropological research in the novel. Refusing a linear plot, identifying itself as fiction (versus nonfiction), and making multiple extratextual references, *Atomik Aztex* invites readers to act as archivists, sending us on a seemingly unending and impossible quest to unearth the many violences and problematic national, lingual, cultural, and regional histories that have been erased from the accepted American historical archive.

The choice to end the "Note" with "This is no accident" ties the novel to the literary canon by invoking Twain's preface—"The shadings have not been done in a haphazard fashion, or by guesswork; but painstakingly"—while pointing to the text as a constructed object that expands common theories of postmodernist fiction: unreliable narrators, dark humor, metafictional self-referentiality, blurring of the lines between high and low.[38] The mention of unexpected languages, traditions, and histories elucidates the indispensable role that Latinx and hemispheric oral and literary traditions have played in the nation's writing. And like Twain, the novel's "Note" uses humor and irony, paradoxically incorporating and challenging that which it parodies, forcing "a reconsideration of the idea of origin or originality" and traditional narrative perspectives.[39]

The humor in *Atomik Aztex*'s "Note," however, is quickly undercut, as it is followed on the same page by an excerpt from Charlotte Delbo's *Auschwitz, et après (Auschwitz and After)* (1965):

> Step out of history
> to enter life
> try that all of you
> you'll get it then.[40]

Delbo's poem is an added explanation, similar to the one from *Huck Finn*. Delbo's work here acts as another extratextual lesson that instructs readers on how to approach the text that follows while also drawing them away from it, to Delbo's work and the violence of World War II. Much like Nazism and World War II in Roberto Bolaño's *2666* (chapter 3), this history of genocide creates a transatlantic and transtemporal network established through violence that points back and forth among colonial, midcentury fascist, and contemporary violence. Delbo's verse affirms the fracturing capacities of war and the necessity of atemporal and atypical forms of narration when addressing the experience of trauma and violence. However, as her memoir demonstrates, her project is impossible. *Atomik Aztex*, then, creates an inescapable system of extratextual references that organize the novel before it truly begins, and with Delbo's work, readers are informed of the limitations of seeing, the limitations of using language to convey meaning. Known for her mantra "il faut donner à voir" (They must be made to see), in *Auschwitz and After* Delbo repeatedly asks readers to "Essayez de regarder. Essayez pour voir" (Try to look. Just try and see).[41] Her repeated requests, however, become, as Michaela Hulstyn argues, "confrontations in the place of invocations," words that "call for imagining while at the same time suggesting the reader's inability to fully visualize the scenes."[42] The formal qualities of *Auschwitz and After* indicate as much: composed of postmodern vignettes, titled and untitled poems, and narrative prose fragments that hold the voices of survivors other than Delbo, the book illustrates that linear narrative and typical forms of storytelling cannot fully convey the horror and violence of the experience of Auschwitz.

Accordingly, *Atomik Aztex* is constructed through repeated moments of uncertainty and recursive violence. From the opening of the text, readers are confronted with a reimagined form of colonial violence that is simultaneously shaped by indecision and ambiguity. The novel opens as follows: "I am Zenzontli,

Keeper of the House of Darkness of the Aztex and I am getting fucked in the head and I think I like it. Okay sometimes I'm not sure. But my so-called visions are better than aspirin and cheaper."[43] With these sentences, the narrative introduces an unreliable narrator who at first asserts an identity that modifies colonial history through the creation of a fictionalized Aztex figure, yet quickly amends the claim to "I am" with vacillation. The ambiguous "Okay sometimes I'm not sure" sets the tone for the rest of the novel, calling into question not only his "so-called visions" (which lead us to the Farmer John world) but also the novel's premise. The novel thus establishes "getting fucked in the head" as its modus operandi, and much like *Oscar Wao* with its humorous-sounding "fukú," *Atomik Aztex* vows to fuck with the reader's head in the pages that follow.

Beginning with this self-conscious contention is jarring for many reasons: readers are presented with a protagonist—who quickly becomes two—bearing an "exotic" name that is difficult to pronounce for English-speaking readers and/or those with little familiarity with Mesoamerican languages; with an alternate reality with uncertain yet official-sounding ranks; and with an action being performed on the protagonist's head that wavers between violence and pleasure. *Atomik Aztex*, then, reimagines and reproduces colonial and ethno-racial violence through highly manicured prose that vacillates between high literary fiction and the lowbrow tongue-in-cheek.

Atomik Aztex's world-building, in fact, continually returns readers in form and content to moments of colonial, imperial, fascistic, and contemporary institutional violence. Recognizing that this return is a pleasurable aesthetic practice makes it difficult to see the novel simply as a progressive vision of a just future free of colonial-imperial inheritances. The dual worlds of 1942 Tenochtitlán and modern-day Vernon, California, indicate the inescapable and recurring nature of colonial violence. When this violence is portrayed in a self-referential and tongue-in-cheek fashion, reading about cataclysms becomes a pleasurable act. For example, to establish the novel's alternate reality, Zenzontli addresses the reader directly: "Perhaps you are familiar with some worlds, stupider realities amongst alternate universes offered by the ever expanding-omniverse, in which the Aztek civilization was 'destroyed.'"[44] Zenzontli catalogs the "planned genocide" Europeans *"thot"* they would perpetrate, invites the reader to act as a historian, and asks them, much like the sardonic footnotes in Díaz's *Oscar Wao* with their reference to the reader's lack of knowledge about Dominican history, to consider how much we actually know about the Aztec conquest or hemispheric colonial history more generally. In explaining the Aztex victory, *Atomik Aztex* enumerates a long list of colonial violence and its victims:

They planned genocide, wipe out our civilization, build cathedrals on TOP of our pyramidz, bah, hump our women, not just our women but the Tlaxkalans, the Mixteks, the Zapoteks, the Chichimeks, the Utes, the Triki, the Kahuilla, the Shoshone, the Maidu, the Klickitat, the Mandan, the Chumash, the Yaqui, the Huicholes, the Meskwaki, the Guarani, Seminoles, endless peoples, decimate 'em with smallpox, measles, and shit fits, welfare lines, workaholism, imbecility, enslave 'em in the silver mines of Potosí, the gold mines of El Dorado & Disneylandia, on golf courses & country clubs, *chingados*, all our brothers, you get the picture.[45]

The collection of Indigenous peoples exterminated by European colonialism, as John Alba Cutler states, "resists dominant Mexican and North American conceptions of what it means to be Indian," as the list is missing its "usual suspects" like the Inca, Cherokee, and Iroquois.[46] Thus, the novel upends the recognizable story of the conquest of the Americas and shows a more historically and geographically expansive scope.[47] The novel once again introduces unfamiliar (sometimes misspelled) proper nouns into the text, this time in a long list that leans toward the excessive, which produces an overwhelming effect that can create a pause in reading or even force readers to skip over the text. As in the novel's opening "Note," the incorporation of these Indigenous peoples into the world-making of destruction points readers outside the text and encourages them to act as historians and archivists themselves. This catalog of genocide also leads to an inventory of colonialism's repercussions that continue into the present, from smallpox to the golf course. Asserting that the "planned genocide" was prevented, the novel effectively also narrates the events recorded in our historical archive: invoking a thwarted genocide actuates it in the text, creating an inexorable world system in which the genocide of (unfamiliar) Indigenous populations continues into our present through modern forms of violence.

While the text creates a network of hemispheric genocide that elicits the mythical (El Dorado) in conjunction with the real (Potosí), the novel treats its violence as specifically Mexican and Mexican American. Using the word *chingado*, for example, launches the history of Spanish conquest in Mexico into the text. Most famously used by Octavio Paz in *El laberinto de la soledad* (*The Labyrinth of Solitude*) (1950), the verb *chingar* is translated as "to bother," to "practice coitus," or to "drink alcohol with frequency."[48] In "Los hijos de la Malinche" ("The Sons of La Malinche"), Paz illustrates how the verb "denotes violence," especially that done to another: "The verb is masculine: active, cruel: it stings, injures, gashes, stains."[49] In this way, *chingar* denotes an excess of feeling that gestures back to Hernán Cortés's conquest of Mexico (1519–21) and his "relationship" with La Malinche (Malinalli, Malintzin, or Doña Marina), which defines the Mexican nation as having been instituted through rape.[50] Cataloging Indigenous populations exterminated through contact with Europeans and, indeed, by the byproducts of colonialism into our present, *Atomik Aztex* creates a speculative universe that defines the American hemisphere as constructed through recurring and inescapable violence.

This form of repetition is central to the novel's plot. As anthropologists and historians of Mesoamerican cultures have established, Aztec culture was characterized by a belief in cyclical time. *Atomik Aztex*'s world-building draws on this belief system to depict and reproduce cyclical colonial and ethno-racial violence. Zenzontli describes the Aztex belief in circular time and "cyklikal konceptions of the universe where reality infinitely kurves back upon itself endlessly so all that has existed does exist and will always exist and so forth into infinity. . . . It's the only POV that makes sense in the end. Which is the beginning."[51] Much like Yunior's statement that opened chapter 1—"As soon as you start thinking about the beginning, it's the end"—Zenzontli's depiction of beginnings and endings narrates simultaneous creation and destruction that are inextricably associated with colonial domination and Indigenous genocide. Correspondingly, the novel yokes the cyclical repetition of violence with literary depictions by using the terminology of the MFA workshop or the English classroom while mocking Western conceptions of linear time and the writing of history.

At the heart of Aztec belief lies not only cyclical time but cyclical apocalypse. The Aztec calendar stipulated that the world had been created and destroyed four previous times over the span of 2,028 years and that our current world would similarly be destroyed. In this system, past events structured the present and the patterns for the future.[52] Similarly, *Atomik Aztex* presents all notions of the future through an expectation of its destruction, reconceiving the historical archive through the foundational impact the Spanish conquest had on the Americas. In the novel, a cyclical understanding of time is linked to contemporary Southern California highway culture: "The world is some shifty joint where universes intersekt & spin away into new directions like car crashes on the Golden State Freeway at the intersektion with the 101."[53] This transtemporal presentation of time as chaotically intersecting and "spin[ning] away" is analogized to the car crash and the game of Russian roulette, both unpredictable but unquestionably violent occurrences. "Somebody played Russian roulette with reality," Zenzón states at the end of the novel, "everything turned out kinda funny, nobody told us this (One Reed) wuz happening— now it's time to start again."[54] The insertion of "One Reed" into the passage's conception of time exposes the foundational importance of apocalyptic thinking and colonial violence in the text (and in the Aztec concept of cyclical time). The common explanation for Cortés's success in conquering Mexico with a small number of Spaniards is that the Aztecs thought he was Quetzalcoatl, their returning god. Because of this, they did not resist the Spanish effectively. This interpretation is based on the fact that Cortés reached Mexico in 1519, year 1 Acatl (Reed 1) in the Aztec calendar, which is associated with Quetzalcoatl. However, as Ross Hassig notes, this is "a conflation of the god with a historical Toltec ruler and priest of his cult, Ce Acatl Topltzin Queztalcoatl (I Reed, Our Lord Quetzalcoatl)."[55] His birth year was the same named year in the fifty-two-year Aztec cycle as Cortés's arrival (1 Acatl), and therefore the Aztecs surrendered to him.[56] Invoking this date inscribes the destruction of worlds in the text and reproduces the violence of colonialism within it. Spoken at the culmination of the novel, the protagonists' declaration that they are "start[ing] again" introduces a history of violence and destruction—a beginning that once again is a simultaneous evocation of the world's end.

Swastikas and Pigs: Meditations on Beauty

Atomik Aztex provocatively stresses how aesthetics and violence are mutually constituted, meditating on the aesthetic power of violence and the violence in the production of aesthetics. As I explored in the introduction of *Doom Patterns*, the development of the aesthetic as a distinct and valuable category in culture during the Enlightenment imbues it with the histories of white supremacy and hierarchization that maintain specific modes of representation as universal, beautiful, and true. As such, the aesthetic is marked by violence. Foster's novel simultaneously describes how even the most violent objects, ideas, and histories are also constructed by the aesthetic and conjure aesthetic responses.

Highlighting the visual appeal of Nazism, for example, Zenzontli emphasizes the use value of its aesthetic practices, which, however, exceed its principal utility by veering into the affective. His evaluation of German aesthetics consistently returns the reader to portrayals of violence, genocide, and colonial domination, overturning the sentimental view of the Indigenous past in the Latinx imaginary. Similarly, it is through meditations on aesthetics that the novel introduces labor politics and a concern with neoliberalism. Zenzontli's consistent return to questions of beauty and pleasure in relation to war, fascism, and human sacrifice underscores how aesthetic depictions of violence always in some fashion re-create violence.

Specifically, *Atomik Aztex* challenges the idea that aesthetic beauty leads to a greater concern for justice—as posited by theorists like Immanuel Kant, Elaine Scarry, and Iris Murdoch—even while the novel itself participates in aesthetic practices currently upheld as high art. Zenzontli calls the swastika a "cute Nazi insignia" and notes that Nazism produces "interesting color coordinations and design graphiks based on German Expressionism or the muted or flat matte color schemes of **Modernism**."[57] Fascism's morality and genocidal practice are not highlighted as threats in the text; instead, it is the "hard-edged aesthetik concept & color scheme to their ideology that was a definite real threat to the entire globe, that's why their regime had to be destroyed."[58] Zenzontli's description defines ideology as an aesthetic endeavor, created and reproduced through writing, visual art, and music, classifying itself—the novel—as a producer of belief systems.

Zenzontli also taunts Western conceptions of high art and challenges what is considered beautiful by introducing revered forms of representation such as modernism and expressionism as being inextricably linked to victory in warfare and historical conquest. *Atomik Aztex* therefore positions readers at the center of this paradox, implicating them in the system that confers value on certain aesthetic forms and not others, disseminating and reproducing them. In a jeering tone, the novel mocks established aesthetic choices that the reader can laugh at as well, while their knowing laugh establishes their erudite knowledge and self-awareness. The novel, then, suggests that aesthetic pleasure and violence are mutually composed, demonstrating the long-lasting effects of colonialism as seen in language. Slipping outside a diner as he runs from an armed person inside, Zenzón describes the fall as "br[eaking] my glottal stop on a slippery dipthong derived from middle English."[59] The novel depicts the acquisition of language and its use in writing as the byproduct of violence, yoking aesthetic practices and the spread of languages such as English to conquest, colonialism, immigration, and warfare. As Zenzontli ponders the early success of the Nazis in Europe, he again ties genocidal violence and territorial occupation to aesthetic choices:

> The Germans, it must be said, did have a highly developed aesthetik sensibility about how to conduct their war—which accounted for their early success—becuz they chose the koolest immaculate uniforms of gray wool, Sam Brown belts with snap-on attachments or accoutrements and flared helmets like industrial samurais and stylistik master strokes like zippy emblems such as swastikas (we assume they took them from the Navajos, cuz Navajos swear they invented the swastikas first by staring

at the sun for a long time without sunglasses), which did a lot for their cause, having all those great authentik items and perks of office, and they had kool designs like the iron cross, Death's Head insignia, double lightning bolts for the SS, etc., all that good stuff, *plus the proper attitude (a certain pride in business undertakings, giving it 100%),* which led to enormous successes penetrating new markets all across the world from North Afrika to Paris, Amsterdam, Kiev, Smolensk, Prague, etc. *But they were about to meet their match with the Azteks on the scene!*[60]

The use of "aesthetik" as a synonym for the success of Nazism positions the relationship between aesthetics and Nazism as decorative and superficial, similar to the effect produced by the novel's replacement of hard *c*'s with *k*'s, random italicization, bolding, slang, and online-speak.[61]

These formal elements present aesthetics and Nazism as successful only because of marketing strategies, cool accessories, and branding.[62] Yet the replacement of hard *c*'s with *k*'s and the text's seemingly haphazard stylistics exceed the decorative by revealing the weight of aesthetics in creating, reproducing, and disseminating violence. This letter replacement also playfully exemplifies the difficulty, if not the impossibility, of portraying colonial, imperial, and genocidal violence through a linear narrative and the need to incorporate satiric elements and the dislocation of style that points to itself as a constructed object in order to tell these stories. As Zenzontli states, the swastika is a symbol of cultural appropriation that has been emptied of its Indigenous origin and transformed into a marker of genocide. By highlighting the swastika's lineage, the narrator attempts to evacuate the horrific Nazi symbology—and by extension Western aesthetics—with terms such as "zippy emblems." However, the long list of accouterments once again signals a recourse to the excessive and inscribes into the text images of violence that cannot be erased even if they are described as "kool." Zenzontli describes a map of violence that moves from Africa and across Europe, which will be occupied by the Azteks. Azteks, it is clear, do not have political remedy on their minds. Instead, Zenzontli concludes that there is beauty in killing: in *"human rites,* especially in human sakrifices, *aesthetiks* are of prime importance. . . . It's got to *look good* or otherwise Huizilopochtli, Tezkatlipoka, Coyoxaukee, Tlazayotl, or whoever won't even notice; the whole bloody affair won't *accrue* the same economik benefit as you would get from a *fine, graceful, beautiful* sakrifice."[63] Kristy Ulibarri notes that through the use of the word *accrue,* the text demonstrates that its concern is with the optics of killing for capitalistic gain and not the ethos of ritual sacrifice. In this sense, *Atomik Aztex* mocks neoliberal economics but also "plays right into the hand of neoliberal desire: maximizing (abstract) profit at the expense of human bodies."[64] This formulation expands our understanding of the novel's concern with labor, capitalism, and the traditional rendition of an Indigenous past as previous to or opposed to these endeavors. In all this, *Atomik Aztex* foregrounds the pleasure in violence and economic exploitation through its combination of narrative styles and tongue-in-cheek narration, illustrating the pleasure, confusion, and aesthetic value in descriptions of violence.

Much as the novel presents Nazism and human sacrifice through an analysis of aesthetic properties, *Atomik Aztex* portrays the slaughtering of pigs through a turn to the emotive. The first-person descriptions of slaughtering pigs throughout the novel are fleshy, sensual, and intimate, a portrayal that disrupts the boundary between animal and human and, notably, is staged as analogous to the use of human hearts for the propagation of the Aztex Imperium. Zenzón describes killing each pig as a private moment of closeness with the hog but also as the medium through which to reminisce on familial ties. "I reach my left arm around the hog's shoulders as I lean into its girth, the warm, grizzly skin prickling worse than your old man's two-day stubble," he says.[65] Giving the pig "the last firm goodbye hug," Zenzón presses the knife "into its throat at the same time, drawing it diagonally down, slicing the carotid with one motion, then on out the other side."[66] Like the spaces of memory and mourning that the dismembered corpse elicits for Oscar Fate in *2666*—short-lived affective bonds between himself and the victims of femicide—the slaughtering of pigs in *Atomik Aztex* generates ephemeral moments of emotion that transcend the act of butchering. When the labor of slaughtering elicits Zenzón's memory of his father's "two-day stubble," the animal flesh enables an exploration of his familial past and reestablishes a physical and emotional closeness with his father. The language used to describe the act of killing a pig unexpectedly veers into affection, redefining not only animal-human relationships but also the act of killing itself. The pig's body is "warm" as Zenzón gives the hog a firm "goodbye hug" and finally describes what should be routine procedure as a "dance step." In these references to pleasure and play, what should be a gruesome and bloody action—inserting the knife into the pig's carotid—is depicted in the inviting language of nourishment; the knife is soft, quiet; the act of killing (and reading about killing) is satisfying and pleasurable, albeit estranging. Affective ties are suggested but, in the end, prove to be still more reminders of violence. In *Atomik Aztex*, killing and eating pigs is a medium for introspection, short-lived moments of human-animal and human-human kinship, meditations on loss and failure, and the opportunity for Zenzón to show care: he attempts to establish a connection with his children through butchering. Yet his efforts fall short of communicating his encoded message, much as the novel itself falls short of conveying the scope of colonial violence and so reverts to the excessive.

Atomik Aztlán, Atomik Latinx

Atomik Aztex uses the doom pattern of excessive narration—description, textual breakages, polyglottal form, multilingual prose—to return readers in form and content to textual catastrophe and the haunting remainders of history. *Doom Patterns* opened with an examination of Junot Díaz's oeuvre to highlight the work of an author who until recently was considered the apex of Latinx literature. This first chapter offered new ways of reading his work and raised questions about canonicity and definitions of "high art" versus the "lowbrow." In the chapters that followed, the same questions reappeared, showing how reading through the protocols of Latinx speculative fiction can uncover otherworldly dimensions of literature usually read as realist and highlight thematic networks across ethno-racial and national boundaries that open new avenues for defining not only Latinx literature but also fields in literary studies writ large. If Bolaño calls into question the redemptive politics of Chicanx border studies through a "world novel" that participates in discussions of the US-Mexico border without belonging to the border itself, then *Atomik Aztex* draws attention to unexplored literary and thematic networks that show how it participates in depictions of Chicanx and Mexican American history and culture without fitting neatly into any of these ethno-racial and national categories.

Foster has stated that he wrote *Atomik Aztex* because he "wanted to get away from the barely veiled autobiography of his poems, 'to do something that leaned on the imagination, that made it bear the burden of storytelling.'"[67] Many, including Foster himself, have pointed to his proximity to and involvement in Chicanx communities as a reason for the novel's subject matter, citing his upbringing in East LA as the novel's raison d'être: "Growing up in East L.A., Foster is no stranger to the history of Chicano cultural nationalism or East L.A.'s continual working class plights, which makes his satiric narrative on these cultural and labor politics a significant contribution to thinking about Chicana/o and Latina/o representations of indigeneity."[68] Foster frames this "significant contribution" in challenging terms: "This is what I'm going to do because who else is going to do it? . . . Even Chicanos who want to do it don't do it. [Representing the community] 'is one of my principal tasks.'"[69] In fact, Foster's own race and ethnicity haunt the novel and criticism about it. His revisionist savior fantasy notwithstanding, the Latinx performance in *Atomik Aztex* points not only to the messiness of racial and ethnic constructions but also to the histories of colonial, imperial, and militaristic violence that bring together Asians, Asian Americans, Latinx, and Chicanx peoples in California.

As Stephen Hong Sohn asserts, Asian American literature tends to be read and marketed as autobiographic and autoethnographic, a characteristic shared with Latinx literature.[70] In taking on the voice of another ethnic group, Sohn argues, Foster "undermines the assumption that only one racial or ethnic group can claim ownership over the representation of the minority experience."[71] This approach dovetails with Foster's negotiation of racial identity in which Asian American and Chicanx writing blur in form and content, and within the represented timelines that blend into each other in the novel.[72] *Atomik Aztex*, therefore, articulates why the Chicanx experience is relevant to Asian American studies, exposing the inequities manufactured by global capitalism, especially for racialized minorities, and "takes inspiration from an activist model" that foments relationships between ethno-national groups to uncover interrelated histories.[73]

The relationships across ethno-national groups and the interrelated histories *Atomik Aztex* exposes also emphasize the permeable and unsteady terrain on which things like Latinx literature and *latinidad* are determined, authenticated, and reproduced. These questions have arisen in the field before, as in the notable case of Danny Santiago's *Famous All Over Town* (1983), a novel initially considered an important contribution to Chicanx literature and praised for its authentic depiction of life in East LA but later revealed to have been written by a white septuagenarian originally from Kansas City, Missouri, named Daniel James. Ulibarri notes that *Famous All Over Town* challenges the practice of categorizing Latinx literature by an author's descent from a Latin American nation and/or former Spanish colony, pointing to its racial performance and issues surrounding "authenticity" and the depiction of an ethno-racial experience. Ralph Rodriguez similarly argues that *Famous All Over Town* "brings into sharp relief the definitional complexities of identifying a proper Latinx subject, and that, then, must bring along with it the complexities of defining the body of literature known as Latinx because, as matters currently stand, the identity of the author is one of the necessary and most heavily leaned-upon criteria for defining Latinx literature."[74] He goes on to state that the case of Santiago/James also raises the complex question of what constitutes recognizable Latinx themes if we take into consideration the vast array of subject positions under what might be considered Latinx.[75]

Atomik Aztex does not attempt to answer the question of what comprises an authentic Latinx subject, suggesting instead that worrying over questions of authenticity is senseless and can in fact reproduce dangerous white supremacist logics of racial classification. What the novel offers is an expanded definition of both Latinx literature and Asian American literature. The work of Rodriguez, Ricardo Ortiz, and José Esteban Muñoz, among others, illustrates how categorizing a heterogeneous group of people with terms such as *Hispanic*, *Latina/o*, *Latin@*, *Latinx*, and *Latine* is insufficient, though politically useful. Rodriguez, for example, highlights the difficulties of defining a literary canon based on an author's identity, which could "harken back to dangerous nineteenth-century, pseudoscientific racial understandings based in blood, for it would seem to lead one into debates over the author's heritage and blood-line."[76] If the identity of an author is a necessary criterion for defining Latinx literature, then the contextual background of a text should also be considered, such as Foster's proximity to and knowledge of Chicanx history and culture and life in East LA. This is not to say that *Atomik Aztex* is a Chicanx text but rather that it participates in "Chicanesque" writing. In doing so, it stages a brownface performance that accents the complexity of defining Latinx subjectivity and its adjoining body of literature.[77] I agree with Rodriguez that race and ethnicity are invented categories that are imposed on texts and that Latinx literary studies has subscribed to a taxonomic practice through a Foucauldian "author-function" (and authorship protocol). *Atomik Aztex*, however, brings us into recognizably Latinx worlds without a recognizably Latinx surname, a "pairing that unsettles the semiotics of books we recognize as Latinx."[78]

By claiming that *Atomik Aztex* is participating in a Latinxface and brownface performance, I do not intend to dismiss Foster's work or associate it with the white supremacist logics of exploitation in films like *The Birth of a Nation* (1915) or *The Jazz Singer* (1930), which rely heavily on blackface and minstrelsy. Nor do I intend to claim that Foster is a Latinx author. Effectively, Foster disrupts the minstrel tradition while negotiating his own ethno-racial identity by subscribing to the surplus elements of the genre, including humor and over-the-topness. *Brownface* has been defined as the practice among non-Latinx, Anglo white people of adopting a category of Latinx identity that "has animated both Latino resistance practices . . . and their containment."[79] This practice, as Frances Negrón-Muntaner explains, is "a way to get outside of 'white' skin—although not too far—and into the skin of another without risk."[80] Because Foster is an Asian American author, however, his performance of *Chicanidad* is not easy to classify as traditional minstrelsy.

Ethnic impersonations are not anomalous in the United States. Laura Browder's investigation of ethnic autobiographical impersonations, for example, leads her to ask what it is about American discourse "that makes us accept these impersonators so readily."[81] We can extend this question to consider the role of racial and ethnic performance, asking what makes these specific instances easily digestible and even commercially successful. What insight emerges when we read Foster's novel, for example, alongside more recent controversial cases such as that of H. G. Carrillo/Herman Glenn Carroll's *Loosing My Espanish* (2004) or Jeanine Cummins's *American Dirt* (2019) as examples of Latinx literature?[82] Before his death in April 2020, Carrillo was thought to be an Afro-Cuban novelist, and his first book, presumed to be autobiographical, was celebrated by notable Latinx authors.[83] After his death, however, it was revealed he had fabricated his Afro-Cuban identity and was in fact a Black man from Detroit, Michigan. Cummins's *American Dirt* generated a great deal of controversy following its seven-figure advance and promotion by Oprah Winfrey's Book Club. Many Latinx writers and scholars decried its stereotypical rendition of Mexican culture and peoples, the glamorization of cartel violence, the distortion of immigration, and, above all, the plagiarizing of Latinx authors on the same topic. During this media storm, Cummins stubbornly justified the writing of a story about undocumented Mexican immigrants making their way to the United States by using her husband's undocumented status (he is Irish) and her descent from a Puerto Rican grandparent. As various Latinx literature scholars have argued, the Latinx writer is typically put in the fraught position of being a "native informant" and cultural spokesperson to mainstream audiences, a position that shapes and limits the narrative.[84] Indeed, Kirsten Silva Gruesz and Rodrigo Lazo's work on *Loosing My Espanish* shows that Spanish has become a powerful marker of Latinx identity to the point that it has created the "loophole of linguistic posing" into which various authors, including Carrillo and Cummins, can slip. For Gruesz and Lazo, linguistic posing "requires intricate acts of performance that are staged for specific audiences."[85] These temporary performances are enacted in the text, and as Gruesz and Lazo argue, they emphasize how strongly Latinx identity is projected onto these linguistic signals: Cummins and Carrillo constructed their "authentic" texts by relying on a mainstream audience's uninformed assumptions about *latinidad*.

As generous readers, we might consider how these works productively unsettle conceptions of race and ethnicity, or our assumptions about who has the "right" to certain stories. Instead of policing race and ethnicity or stipulating who can or cannot write these narratives, we might ask how identity formations, racialization, and writing intersect, and how *latinidad* becomes legible, marketable, and critiqued. This chapter has been an exercise in how we might approach a text like Foster's through its formal conventions, with attention to the ways a text betrays and writes against itself. These conversations are, of course, mired within institutional power structures, gatekeeping, the literary market, visibility and access, and the legible forms of *latinidad* in fiction. In

Racial Immanence (2019), Marissa López, for example, argues that "reading for representation" not only forecasts and confirms a reader's knowledge but also forecloses a meaningful engagement with a text.[86] While overtly signaling *Chicanidad, Atomik Aztex* exceeds this history and identity through Foster himself.

But even as we debate these weighty questions, *Atomik Aztex* mocks the fetishization of Chicanx history and culture in which it participates. The "real thing" that the public expects from a book like Santiago/James's, which trades on the readers' expectations of Latinx life and positions them as voyeuristic consumers, is upended in Foster's novel.[87] It similarly mocks expectations for Asian American depictions in literature by rerouting militaristic violence through Chicanx history and culture. The novel underscores the limitations for Asian American representation, which in the United States is usually established through tropes of the model minority, internment, or victimization. We can see this friction in the language used by City Lights to market the novel: "A fantastical gonzo Aztlán mythology, where modern Aztecs and immigrant ghosts uncover blood sacrifice in Los Angeles."[88] Using Chicanx and Latinx literary tropes to describe it, the press has categorized *Atomik Aztex* as "Asian American Writing" and promotes it for Hispanic Heritage Month, highlighting the difficulty of cataloging a work such as this. The tension between embodied ethnic identities and depictions of Chicanx violence is addressed with metafictional humor in the novel itself: "You are a Party member, full-fledged Aztek warrior (tho there's some rumor about Japanese infiltration of your bloodlines someplace)."[89] The tongue-in-cheek nod to the author's Japanese heritage takes readers outside the narrative and draws attention to the limits of empathy, the possibility of inhabiting the Other, and the obstacles of identification in reading fiction. All this is done while expanding ethno-racial boundaries and the possibility of representing other racial minorities in fiction, as Sohn suggests. Foster's "appropriation" of Latinxness concurrently challenges this expansion, even while the novel's excessive qualities redeem its brownface performance. By this I mean that his defensive justification for tapping into Chicanx history is offset by the novel's form: *Atomik Aztex*'s attempt at Chicanx history fuses onto other histories as well, such as Asian American identities that contradict the trope of the model minority in an effort to become that which is commonly understood as a less-than ethnic minoritized subject, the Latinx. It is also possible that *Atomik Aztex*'s use of the mythology of Aztlán and the warrior Aztec/x is a way to invoke the hypermasculinity of the Chicano Movement and La Raza of the 1960s in an attempt to eschew the stereotype of Asian and Asian American men as feminized.

Muñoz's conceptions of brownness and the "brown commons" throw into relief the reimagination of Chicanx history staged in *Atomik Aztex*. Muñoz argues that "brown" is a dissenting stance against the conventions of a majoritarian public sphere and a state that exceeds those who live under the sign of *latinidad*. As a "way of being in the world," brownness is the state of a "majority of those who exist, strive, and flourish within the vast trajectory of multiple and intersecting regimes of colonial violence."[90] This brown commons includes a complex network of racial and ethnic formations that are not stringently demarcated. In this respect, brownness is a medium for "being with" others who have been racialized; a practice of living in relation to forms of difference that "touch and contact but do not meld"; a togetherness that is part of the here and now rather than a utopian vision.[91] A sense of brownness and the brown commons then are constructed through a "situational commonness" and, in my estimation, emerge as a result of the violent histories of colonization, enslavement, imperialism, and exile. Latinxness is one vector for the understanding of brownness, and a case like Foster's illustrates how *Atomik Aztex* and its author participate in the brown commons and how we can read for elements of *latinidad*. To consider the brownness of *Atomik Aztex* is to recognize how, as Joshua Javier Guzmán establishes, brown cannot be reduced to a singular identity because it does not participate in an "identity-knowledge project."[92] Significantly, brown depresses what is "notably and nobly understood as White America, thereby staining it and dragging it to its limits."[93]

The expansive Muñozian sense of brown that allows us to read the brownface performance of *Atomik Aztex* as contributing to Chicanesque writing is paradoxically complicated by the novel's own depiction of Indigeneity. Even designations such as Chicanesque, as Juan Bruce-Novoa explains, do not solve the problem of ethno-racial authenticity but rather "focus our attention more acutely on the unsolved nature of Chicano identity."[94] The formation of a collective Chicanx identity privileged ancestral Indigeneity and brown/bronze pride, a mobilization of *mestizaje* that scholars like María Josefina Saldaña-Portillo have forcefully condemned for its erasure of present-day Indigenous populations. Saldaña-Portillo rebukes Mexican state policy and Chicanx cultural production for their reliance on the tropes of *mestizaje* and the "logic of representation to which these tropes belong" instead of creating political ties with contemporary U.S. Native Americans or Mexican Indians.[95]

The erasure of contemporary Indigenous populations and dependance on ancestral notions of Indigeneity for the construction of Aztlán are evident in *Atomik Aztex* as well. Aztlán, the mythic homeland mobilized by El Movimiento (the Chicano Movement) in the 1960s and 1970s, harkens back to an ancient

Aztec utopian space that has been used by activists as a political tool of community building and resistance. As Richard Griswold del Castillo and Arnoldo De León explain, the Aztecs believed that their ancestral homeland was located in the North, a spatial fantasy of nostalgia that was turned into a political symbol by Chicano leaders in the 1960s and 1970s, who disregarded the fact that the Aztecs had not lived in the American Southwest.[96] Most famously introduced by Rodolfo "Corky" Gonzales in 1969 during the First National Chicano Liberation Youth Conference, "El Plan Espiritual de Aztlán" (Spiritual Plan of Aztlán) was a pro-Indigenist manifesto that emphasized moral and historical ties between Chicanos and Mexicans with a particular focus on Indigeneity and *mestizaje*.

The search for Aztlán, however, was a failed endeavor for the Aztecs. Moctezuma I, who ruled Tenochtitlán from 1440 to 1469, for example, sent yearly expeditions to search for the homeland. As the empire expanded, Aztec rulers became actively concerned with strengthening a collective sense of identity, and "the notion of finding a place of origin appears to have assumed a special significance."[97] Indeed, Aztlán has always held a utopian position within the Aztec and Chicanx imaginary. As such, Aztlán is an "empty signifier" used by writers, artists, historians, and social scientists, an imaginary space that foments the connection among land, identity, and (Indigenous) experience.[98] In "Refiguring Aztlán," Rafael Pérez-Torres lays the foundation for thinking of Aztlán as a contested space that is at once the signifier of home and dispossession, a metaphor for connectivity and unity, a site for contesting national identity as defined by hegemonic cultural discourses, and part of exclusionary nationalist projects. In short, as a continually modified space, Aztlán remains relevant in Chicanismo. The centrality of Aztlán in the Chicanx imaginary also contests colonial and neocolonial presences in the Americas by asserting the significance of the Indigenous and affirming the importance of Native civilizations.[99] Yet, as Saldaña-Portillo points out, the ancestry of the Chicanx nation "does not derive from the Aztecs, but from the 'history of its losses,'" a racial melancholia that Anne Anlin Cheng shows is supported by a system of rejection and internalization and is constitutive of racial formations in the United States.[100] In other words, Chicanx identity is formed through the incorporation of a lost Indigenous heritage that includes the Aztec but also a variety of others, such as the Apache, Comanche, Pueblo, Caddo, and Navajo. In this way, *Atomik Aztex* pushes against Saldaña-Portillo's critique of Chicanx cultural production and presents a more expansive history of Indigenous genocide that extends across the Americas. For her part, Ulibarri argues that the novel draws on the notion of a pre-Columbian Indigenous identity to challenge typical representations of

Latinx Indigeneity as precapitalist.[101] I follow Ulibarri in arguing that *Atomik Aztex* illustrates that Indigeneity is itself a style, commodity, and spectacle that shows how Aztlán and pre-Columbian imagery have been used to create a sense of community and resistance by El Movimiento.

"El Plan Espiritual de Aztlán" activates a speculative imaginary that looks to a mythical past in order to galvanize the "spirit of a new people." That is, El Movimiento implemented Aztlán as a speculative project that looks to the Indigenous past to imagine a future for Chicanx peoples: "Conscious not only of its proud historical heritage, but also of the brutal 'gringo' invasion of our territories, we, the Chicano inhabitants and civilizers of the northern land of Aztlán, from when came our forefathers, reclaiming the land of their birth and consecrating the determination of our people of the sun, declare that the call of our blood is our power, our responsibility, and our inevitable destiny."[102] Latinx studies is similarly in a moment of tension between looking to the future and expressing the need to reassess the archive which, as I discussed in the introduction to this book, can also be seen in contemporary discussions surrounding the use of the *x* in *Latinx*. What does the *x* in "Aztex" designate? While *Atomik Aztex* precedes the prevalent use of *Latinx*, the novel's title and the term act in similar ways. The novel never includes discussions of atoms, atomic energy, or the atom bomb. Yet the novel explodes all expectations of form and narrative, while demonstrating the constitutive importance of Indigenous history in the Americas. The *x* was originally used in the terms *Xicano* and *Xicana* to indicate a reemerging political deportment that highlighted the importance of the Aztec past, Nahuatl, and Indigeneity in Chicanx and feminist projects.[103] More recent debates surrounding the use of the *x* to replace *Latina/o* or *Latin@* illustrate the destabilizing power of the *x*. The *x* in "Aztex" generates a disruption that points readers to the history of Indigeneity in the Americas and the ancestry of Mexican, Mexican American, and Chicanx peoples. Yet the *x* also portrays the Azteks in the novel and the Aztecs of history as strange, more than, otherworldly. In effect, the use of the *x* makes the novel and its Indigenous people inaccessible.

But what makes the Azteks of the novel *Atomik*? Like the *x*, the use of *atomik* destabilizes the narrative's alternate history of the Spanish conquest. The substitution of the *k* for the word's hard *c* not only alerts readers to the spelling system in the novel but also emphasizes the harsh sound of the word. The atom is the smallest constituent unit of ordinary matter. From the Middle English *attomos*, *athmus*, from the Latin *atomus*, and the Greek *átomos*, meaning "undivided" and "indivisible," atoms compose all solids, liquids, gases, and plasmas. The novel's title thus indicates the foundational importance of Indigenous cultures in the histories of the Americas, while sending a signal not only about the violence—atomic energy, the atom bomb—that the readers will encounter within the text but also about the violence perpetrated through colonialism and European conquest. These destabilizing modes are central to all the texts examined in *Doom Patterns*, which rewrite the historical past and many forms of trauma by reimagining them through the conventions of genre fiction. The disruptions occur particularly through the speculative reimagination of history, the excessive narrative style that asks us to reconceive our reading practices and definitions of literature, and the aesthetic pleasure derived from reading about violence. If *2666* taps into border rhetorics, Foster's novel expands ethno-racial literary categories through its Latinx performance, while using postmodern aesthetics, a multiplicity of languages and references, and science fiction time travel to reimagine the Chicanx historical past in ways that are overwhelming and pleasurable.

5

HER BODY, OUR HORROR

Self-Abnegation; or, On Silence,
Refusal, and Becoming the Un/Self

What would happen if one woman told the truth about her life?
The world would split open
—Muriel Rukeyser, "Käthe Kollwitz"

Food, eating, the body: what should be sources of nourishment and pleasure engender discomfort, pain, denial. Forbidding yourself food so the numbers on the scale decrease as your body does; watching your hip bones, your clavicle, jaggedly display themselves; taking pride in their accomplishment. Delight in seeing how far you can push your body, delight in its pain. How far can I go? How small can I make myself? Seeing the least amount of space you can take—do I want to become invisible? How much pain can it endure? *It*, not *I*—a separation of body from self. How much pleasure can I achieve from its pain? To separate yourself from your body gives you control; it allows you to dissociate yourself from the pain, the hunger, the uncomfortableness you put yourself through.

I was a fat child and a fat teenager, a form of embodiment maligned by my family. My fatness was a source of worry, reproach, and secret debates. What diet can we put her on? Why won't she exercise? When will she change? The questions and criticism that circumscribed my body turned it—and therefore me—into a future-oriented project of improvement, which also defined present me as both incomplete and already malformed. This type of rhetoric is intent on disciplining, policing, and controlling girls' and women's bodies. The objections to my aesthetic presentation did not make me look to a future in which I would be thin, beautiful, and accepted. Instead, they made me double down. I ate; I refused. This revolt was not a loud one: large sweatshirts that attempted to hide me away; jeans and black T-shirts that in their nondescriptness gave me the illusion that I, too, could be out of sight; food deemed unacceptable for my already unacceptable body. I did not know then, as I am starting to understand now, the power of fatness. I did not recognize the fatphobic questions that transform eating into overindulgence and propose the fat body as too expansive, too layered, too fleshy, taking up too much space.

I place myself as a narrative "I" at the outset of this chapter as a gesture to the subjective nature of reading, literary criticism, and aesthetics. This mode of analysis also loosens the generic margins of literary criticism and in this way mirrors the texts examined in *Doom Patterns*. Throughout this book, the texts in my archive expand our understanding of the speculative, of minoritized literature, and even of where and how pleasure can be found in a text. It is usually assumed that all viewpoints are subjective, yet these individual perspectives exceed the particular because of the broad historical structures that assemble them.[1] The convergence of the personal and critical echoes the saying in feminist and student movements that "the personal is political." Writers like Audre Lorde and Gloria Anzaldúa integrated themselves into rounded articulations and debates about queer Black identity or mestiza consciousness and border subjectivity. Following in this tradition, I turn to the individual and personal as a way to enter the text and embark on narrative explorations of complicated historical and thematic networks. I analyze the text through my subject position: as a woman, a Venezuelan immigrant, a white person, someone of Jewish heritage, someone with creative writing training in an MFA program, someone from a privileged background. My attention to and interpretation of aestheticized forms of violence come from the intersection of these identities.

The relationship I have with my body is also an assemblage of violence and pleasure. As a young woman, I caved and un-became fat, showing not only how I internalized the world's fatphobic language that always surrounds women's bodies but also how I continue to police and discipline my own appearance and maintain a difficult relationship to food. Every day I contend with the body in which I reside. The fat body in many ways is also a demand for space, an assertion that you matter and will not reduce yourself according to societal expectations. As I argue in chapter 1 in relation to Junot Díaz's *The Brief Wondrous Life of Oscar Wao* (2007), fat is a disruption of entrenched categories and normativizing imperatives. Fat as excess disobeys corrective narratives, legibility, and notions of progress.

Women's bodies are constantly pathologized, haunted by the extremes of what could or should be, what is not and can become. It is here—in the too much or too little—that the women of Carmen Maria Machado's fiction reside, underscoring the possibilities and limits of the choices and demands made by women. *Her Body and Other Parties* (2017) foregrounds women's bodies, using the tropes of speculative fiction to imagine them as the arena in which self-abnegation, refusal, hunger, and desire are explored. In particular, women in this collection respond to violence from others by turning the violence inward toward themselves, as manifested in silences, refusals, and a desire to undo the self. Women's bodies act as the space in which ethno-racial and gendered violences are surveyed and through which women enact their resistance and defiance in the face of systemic domination. This resistance is enacted not through expected methods of dissent but through refusal that hurts the self. As I show in this chapter, and as *Doom Patterns* generally attempts to illustrate, the haunting traces of violence in the text arrive as otherworldly. The short-story collection represents misogynistic and gendered violence through the tropes of speculative fiction: losing one's head, being haunted by a fat-ghost, dissipating into stitchwork. While the characters resist this violence by undoing themselves, the text is simultaneously narrating Latinx identity and embodiment in covert fashion. Using the conventions of genre fiction to portray ethno-racial forms of embodiment, *Her Body and Other Parties* illustrates how *latinidad* is imbued with strange and excessive violence.

The textual performances of silence, unanswered questions, ellipses, decapitation, invisibility, and fat-ghosting in *Her Body and Other Parties* act as narrative doom patterns that portray "woman" as an otherworldly form of embodiment and that, keeping in line with the formal blueprints seen throughout *Doom Patterns*, remind readers of violent destruction as an implacable and cyclical force. Silence, elisions, and obfuscations are doom patterns that perform as the consummation of an excess that causes the text to break, pushing women to become solid, to become viscous, and to dissipate. As I argue in relation to both *Oscar Wao* and in chapter 3 with Roberto Bolaño's *2666* (Spanish 2004, English 2008), silence marks the page with language's inability to encapsulate violence, from the sweeping scope of global imperialism to the close intimacy of the domestic. The encounter with the otherworldly—be it in the unweaving of a head, the desire to be a mollusk, the confrontation with a fat-ghost, or the experience of becoming immaterial and being sewn into a dress—and the multiplicity of silences and unknowns resist and challenge transparent subjectivity as construed by phenomenology and ego mastery. In Machado, silence enacts a refusal of and challenge to heteropatriarchal violence, while the desire to embody post-/supra-/ab-human forms elicits a masochistic repudiation that undoes the self.

My own relentless return to questions of food, eating, and the body indicates a continuation of trauma that I see emulated throughout Machado's eight short stories. It is a line of inquiry I try to (must) actively prohibit, yet ultimately fail to keep at bay. Allowing myself this indulgence would force me to recognize the satisfaction and arrogance I feel when I am hungry, the difference I perceive in the mirror that makes me like what I see more. It is not that I envy the mindlessness of an oyster, the immaterial silence of women sewn into colorful dresses, or the feeling of becoming headless (as the characters in Machado's collection experience) but that I find comfort in thinking of my body as separate from myself, something I can control and extricate myself from—if I am an object and not a subject, I can mold *it* accordingly.

Her Body and Other Parties uses the tropes of horror and the speculative to investigate women's bodies and the violences enacted on them, as well as the emotional and psychological trauma women experience. The collection was released by Graywolf Press, an independent, nonprofit publisher that has issued the work of authors like Denis Johnson, Percival Everett, Elizabeth Alexander, Maggie Nelson, and Anna Burns. Machado, a graduate of the Iowa Writers' Workshop MFA program, writes the kind of polished literary fiction that many associate with the influence of what Mark McGurl calls the "Program Era."[2] Lyrical, lush, and precise, her writing is enthralling. Writing for the *New York Times*, for example, Parul Sehgal calls Machado's prose "both matter-of-factly and gorgeously queer," and in the *Los Angeles Times*, Ellie Robins describes her collection as "that hallowed thing: an example of almost preposterous talent that also encapsulates something vital but previously diffuse about the moment."[3] The combination of gorgeously queer prose with strangely seductive settings has earned Machado numerous nominations, such as for the National Book Award and Nebula Award; fellowships from institutions such as the John Simon Guggenheim Memorial Foundation and the Wallace Foundation; and awards, such as the National Book Critics Circle's John Leonard Prize and the Shirley Jackson Award.

The women in *Her Body and Other Parties* contend with the horror of being queer, fat, and woman within the confines of a violently patriarchal culture, ultimately becoming ab-, post-, suprahuman. The collection makes this horror visible in a self-abnegation that destroys the self and in an imagination of the self outside the life/death binary. And yet, through this self-destruction, the women of *Her Body and Other Parties* propose a radical posthumanism that illuminates the significance of centralizing race and ethnicity within explorations of the posthuman, and the possibilities beyond configurations of the human as we know it. *Her Body and Other Parties* not only foregrounds pain but also paradoxically interlaces depictions of violence and hurt with the pleasures of the body: eating, writing, having sex. This interplay between violence and pleasure is experienced by the reader as well, in the sense that stories that should be put down because of their difficult subject matter are rendered in aesthetically beautiful prose that introduces the possibility of enjoyment. Although so far little scholarship has been published about *Her Body and Other Parties*, that which is in print draws mostly on queer theory and women and gender studies.[4] I extend these lines of inquiry in two ways: first, I challenge the common claim that minoritized literature and speculative fiction provide political remedy by underscoring how these short stories foreground repeated forms of violence; and, second, I show that despite the collection's obfuscation of overt ethno-racial markers, it exposes *latinidad* through its use of speculative tropes and narrative form.

The questions that organize this chapter are deeply personal, and I have been asking them since I was a teenager. They at once have to do with my body, its shape and size, its perception and relation to culture, and my position in my field of study, or, to put it another way, my relationship to femaleness and *latinidad*. These questions also imbricate conceptions of the aesthetic, how we read, and how we evaluate literary beauty, as well as the paradox inherent in narrating extreme violence that consequently transforms it into an art object, with all the questions of taste and the marketplace that accompany artistic production. While seemingly mundane, this line of inquiry has important implications for Machado's text and for how we think of women's bodies, their portrayal, and minoritized literature and speculative fiction more generally: How do I consider my body? Where do I find its beauty and pleasure? How does the world demand I consider it, and how do I make space for it within the world? The lines of poetry that serve as this chapter's epigraph provide a theoretical framework for considering how depictions of women's bodies, sexuality, and desire rip apart not only the world but the body and the text itself. I begin from the individual to think about the effects of violence on the body, as well as the unstable formation of *latinidad*—or a *latinidad* in the making—and the changing composition of the field of Latinx literature and culture. This chapter began with the personal and turns to *Her Body and Other Parties* to think not only about how speculative tropes launch new and unexpected ways to think about Latinx representation in literature but also about how history affects the body and becomes circumscribed in it and by it. In this chapter, my argument is presented in a form of accretion that emulates the monstrous embodiment that is forbidden to the women of these texts, thereby pushing against phallic and logocentric thinking. I begin by using personal experience to meditate on a radical posthumanism that decenters subjectivity and finds pleasure in self-harm.

Focusing on women's bodies and the violence performed on them underscores a major thread in this book: the idea that while doom patterns expose the widespread remnants of historical trauma, it is women and their bodies that continually experience violence in exorbitant ways. In keeping with the rest of *Doom Patterns*, the doom pattern examined in this chapter—the many instances of undoing and desubjectivizing the self in *Her Body and Other Parties*—paradoxically reveals paratextual, textual, and metatextual pleasures in centering women's bodies as receptacles of trauma with which to speculatively imagine many forms of violence. These pleasures can be seen in the high-literary style of Machado's prose, the inventive worlds constructed in each story, and the play with genres such as horror, gothic fiction, and fairy tales. They can also be experienced by readers voyeuristically participating in psychosexual violence or the titillation of sexual descriptions and enjoying the intertextual references to fairy tales, urban legends, or canonical horror, and by the characters as they eat, fuck, and injure themselves.

Pleasure can also be found in considering *Her Body and Other Parties* as an art object that skirts classificatory practices for minoritized literature. The collection resists organizational systems that would designate it "ethnic fiction" and creates pleasurable frustrations and forms of unknowability for its readers. To use Latinx speculative fiction as a protocol for reading means recognizing the elements of *Her Body and Other Parties* that are overtly fantastical while seeing how they also unveil *latinidad*. As Ralph Rodriguez posits, genre "allows us to make more regular and compelling connections to literatures that fall outside of the Latinx parameters."[5] In this way, *Doom Patterns* turns in this final chapter to a text that uses the tropes of speculative fiction overtly while withholding *latinidad* from its surface. Yet, in its depictions of gendered violence, *Her Body and Other Parties* demonstrates how speculative tropes can illuminate the Latinx elements in the text. In this chapter, I focus on three forms of embodiment—the solid, the viscous, and the dissipating—to examine the opacity of *latinidad*. These forms of embodiment reveal practices of negation and resistance in the face of heteropatriarchal domination and reading practices without the end goal of political remedy.

Solid: Losing the I, Becoming an It

Her Body and Other Parties opens with the story "The Husband Stitch," a rei-magination of the classic fairy tale "The Green Ribbon."[6] This fairy tale tells the story of a young girl with a green ribbon tied around her neck who refuses to tell her boyfriend-and-then-husband why she wears it. In their old age, how-ever, her husband unties the ribbon, causing her head to fall off. Machado's retelling expands this plotline to focus on psychosexual desire, men's control and power over women, and a refusal that pleasurably undoes the self. "The Husband Stitch" ultimately asks readers to consider who has the power to undo and unbecome. Upending conventional depictions of male-female power dynamics and generic expectations, the nameless narrator states in the story's first line, "In the beginning, I know I want him before he does. This isn't how things are done, but this is how I am going to do them."[7] "In the beginning" marks not only the beginning of the story but also the creation of the world the reader is about to enter, putting godlike power in the narrator's hands. This is a world eerily like our own, filled with routine minutiae: the narrator and her husband marry and then honeymoon in Europe; they have a son; when the boy is old enough to go to school, the narrator enrolls in art classes and helps make costumes for his school plays. Yet this world is also uncanny. Lacking distinct spatial or temporal markers, the story could take place in 1954, 2024, or 5024 in New York or Dallas or Boise. Everywhere there are women like the narrator with a red ribbon around an ankle, a yellow one around a finger, os-tensibly holding these body parts in place just as the green ribbon fastens the narrator's head to the rest of her body.

The narrator's opening statement is not, however, the world-building device she thinks it is. Readers have already received a first opening and a set of stage directions about how to read the text:

(If you read this story out loud, please use the following voices:

ME: as a child, high-pitched, forgettable; as a woman, the same.
THE BOY WHO WILL GROW INTO A MAN, AND BE MY SPOUSE: robust with serendipity.
MY FATHER: kind, booming; like your father, or the man you wish was your father.
MY SON: as a small child, gentle, sounding with the faintest of lisps; as a man, like my husband.
ALL OTHER WOMEN: interchangeable with my own.)[8]

Before the readers meet the story's protagonist, she attempts to set the rules of the world they are about to inhabit. Already readers are confronted with generic flail: is this a play, a realist story, a speculative alternate universe? The stage directions create an unmooring effect while also asking readers to consider not only the text as an artistic fabrication but gender as a construct and performance. The characters in the story are archetypes, and the narrator and her stage directions conscript the readers into following a set of instructions. The authority the narrator wishes to exhibit, however, is undercut by the description of her own voice (and all other women's) as unremarkable and by the omission of her mother, which means that the narrator is defined only in relation to men. The repeated parenthetical directives that point to the text-as-text also gesture to the book-as-object. Another form of unsettling takes place in these stage directions through the word "If," which calls these commands into question and insinuates that the narrator's influence over the story's world and the reader is conditional.

From the outset, then, the narrator is intent on voicing her ability to make her own choices and exerting her power to decide—staking a claim to humanhood and subjectivity—even as these choices are undercut by the text. "I have always wanted to choose my moment, and this is the moment I choose," she states, selecting a young man at a party to date, have sex with, and ultimately marry.[9] The ribbon tied around her neck, however, marks the narrator as an object. The power she seems to seize is counterposed by her boyfriend-husband's desire to know why she has it and then his anger at her refusal to disclose the reason for the ribbon. Her husband cannot accept the narrator's secret knowledge or, more ominously, his lack of access to it. His curiosity and anger about the ribbon are mirrored in their son, who at first playfully touches her throat and then more hungrily demands its discovery. The story makes clear that her son's demands are a learned behavior. Seeing his mother and father argue over the ribbon transforms the child's innocent fingering, "hou[sing] no wanting," into a gendered form of violence.[10]

The narrator's ribbon is crucially linked to her body's unity and stability, which are ultimately undone. When first asked about the ribbon by her husband, the narrator calls it "just my ribbon," a dismissive characterization that as the narrative progresses takes on portentous weight.[11] The ribbon goes from being "just my ribbon" to "my ribbon" as the narrator struggles to establish physical and psychic autonomy. The narrator continually asserts that the ribbon is not a secret, yet it is also an object that demarcates the boundaries between herself and the world. The ribbon indicates the limitations of her husband's world as well, as much as it designates his knowledge or lack of knowing. Accordingly, the narrator's husband insists on her transparency and through this insistence objectifies her. The narrator stops being a woman and wife and is metonymically turned into the ribbon. But while the narrator is pushed by the male insistence and demands of her husband, the ribbon is untied only after the protagonist verbally allows him to do so. In their middle age, after their son has left for university, the narrator resigns herself to her husband's desires. After having sex throughout the house, her husband once again reaches for the ribbon, "gaily" and "greedily."[12] Her body, and her self, cannot be separated from the ribbon as her husband "runs his hand up [her] breast and to [her] bow."[13] Realizing that there will never be a space or time in which she will not be called to expose herself fully, the narrator chooses to undo herself: "'Then,' I say, 'do what you want.'"[14] When he unties her ribbon, the narrator's "lopped head tips backwards" and rolls off the bed, making her "feel as lonely as [she has] ever been."[15]

The decision to unmake herself, literally unstitching her own head to appease her husband, is intimately tied to her affective position—she is separated not only from herself but from her husband, her son, and the world. This untying appears as a contrast to the other stitchwork in the story (the "husband stitch"), which fastens her other head (her vagina) and objectifies her. Also known as the *daddy stitch*, the term refers to an extra stitch made when the perineum is repaired after childbirth. The purpose of this extra stitch is to tighten the vagina to enhance male pleasure during sex, and the narrator intimates it is performed on her while she is slipping into unconsciousness during the birth of their son. By titling the story after this procedure, Machado displaces any agency the narrator ostensibly holds through her first-person narrator status onto the doctor and her husband, who intimate their control by joking about the stitch. The procedure that preserves her physical wholeness is done with needle and thread, objects of domesticity and frivolity, and unlike the impenetrable object the narrator will become, the body is penetrated by the stitch, exposing the constant presence of violence against women.

Alongside its many silences, "The Husband Stitch" returns readers to moments of violence and destruction. For example, meditating on her husband's relentless pawing at her ribbon, the narrator states that to "describe him as evil or wicked or corrupted would do a deep disservice to him. And yet—."[16] The em dash marks the space of violence that exceeds language, grammatically directing readers to systemic harm, and, because of its haunting on the page, implicates readers in its replication.

By the end of the text, the parenthetical directives from the story's opening—"(If you are)"—become fully integrated into its narrative world:

"If you are reading this story out loud, you may be wondering if that place my ribbon protected was wet with blood and openings, or smooth and neutered like the nexus between the legs of a doll."[17] Yet the narrator refuses to answer our questions. Like her husband, we want to know what is behind the ribbon and what its unraveling will do, but our curiosity will not be satisfied. The ribbon is "not a secret; it's just [hers]," and the results of its untying will remain in her sole possession. Yes, readers and her husband see the head severed from her body, but questions about the appearance of her severed neck, the other women with ribbons in this world, and the purpose of the ribbon continue to haunt the text. Her husband's reaction, in fact, is omitted, and the relational system foregrounded is between the narrator and her reader: "For these questions and others, and their lack of resolution, I am sorry."[18] An apology is not disclosure, and we are left in the dark. Another displacement is enacted in this final moment, as the narrator's address moves from her husband to the reader, finally settling on objects: her husband's face "falls away," and the narrator focuses on the "ceiling, and the wall behind" her.

> The ribbon falls away. It floats down and curls on the bed, or so I imagine, because I cannot look down to follow its descent.
> My husband frowns, and then his face begins to open with some other expression—sorrow, or maybe preemptive loss. My hand flies up in front of me—an involuntary motion, for balance or some other futility—and beyond it his image is gone.[19]

The ribbon delineates the limits of the narrative as much as her liveness: it obstructs her husband's attempts to know and possess her; it erects her head, prevents her from becoming an object; and it prevents the reader from knowing as much as her husband while keeping us titillated and interested in the outcome. The irony of her husband's desire is that once the ribbon is untied, the protagonist will transform into the object of psychosexual desire he has longed for without being able to give either of them sexual pleasure. The narrator's beheading at the end of "The Husband Stitch" alludes to what Jack Halberstam calls "shadow feminism," a praxis that is not subjected to the frameworks that imagine "Woman" within definitions of Western philosophy but that recognizes the possibilities within the political project of refusal and unmaking. In this unmaking, we see "subjects who cannot speak, who refuse to speak; subjects who unravel, who refuse to cohere; subjects who refuse 'being' where being has already been defined in terms of a self-activating, self-knowing, liberal subject."[20] Within Halberstam's framework, we see subjects who refuse to become "woman"—or, in the case of Machado, who undo their womanhood through violence to the self. The women of *Her Body and Other Parties* enact a shadow feminism that manifests itself through self-destruction, masochism, and a rejection of the typical bonds that define us as women. In many ways, the women of her texts refuse to reproduce their relationship to patriarchal power, yet in doing so hurt themselves and at times self-destruct. In a world that continually performs violence on the body of the female subject, why not assume control over your own destruction? Why not untie your ribbon and let your head drop to your husband's feet?

The narrator's final act of acquiescence is also an act of resistance to her husband, the world she inhabits, and the reader. The story's culmination and the unanswered questions surrounding her ribbon make the protagonist unknowable. The story's ending, in which the narrator's head falls off, transforms her from subject to object, closed off from interpretation. In "The Husband Stitch," the ribbon is more than a piece of cloth: it sits at the edge of the narrator's head, marking the threshold of her subject position as well as the contours and limitations of her agency. It also symbolizes her genitalia (her other head), and the story imbues the ribbon with sexual desire, which makes its final untying an undoing of the narrator as both a desiring woman-subject and a source of pleasure. In this way, the story creates a network of pain and pleasure that fastens together sexual desire, physical pleasure, undoing, and becoming a solid. Her husband "presses the silky length with his thumb . . . touches the bow delicately, as if he is massaging [her] sex."[21] Desire and pleasure are saturated with the dangers of being undone. The thumbing of her ribbon makes the narrator plead with her husband to stop, fearful that it will be untied, and she realizes how close her body is at all times to being unfastened: "He could have done it then, untied the bow, if he'd chosen to."[22] The power to choose the world she is narrating is undermined here once again.

Sexual pleasure and subjugation coalesce with death in the story's final moments. As the narrator's ribbon is untied, she reassures her husband by saying, "I love you . . . more than you can possibly know."[23] To this, her husband answers, "No." Although the protagonist asserts that she does not know "to what he's responding"—the proclamation of love or her claim that she has more knowledge than him—her husband negates both simultaneously, emptying her of thought and feeling. In fact, this response makes the protagonist fully an object, a head that falls lonely on the floor without the possibility of communicating with her husband or her readers.

Whereas at the outset of "The Husband Stitch" the narrator wishes to assert interiority through her subject position, by the end of the story she has no inwardness; she has become a solid object whose interior neither the husband nor the reader can see. The story, therefore, rejects Cartesian dualism, wherein mind and body are considered separate, by placing all thought and feeling within the impenetrable object. If the narrator is speaking to us after the ribbon has been untied and is expressing unprecedented loneliness, where is she speaking from? Is the emotion she is expressing emanating from her body or from her severed head? The narrator and the text itself refuse to answer these questions, presenting only silence. Instead of exhibiting knowledge about the narrator's condition, both the narrator and her husband illustrate "epistemologies of ignorance" surrounding women and their bodies, which Nancy Tuana defines as gaps in knowledge actively produced for the purposes of oppression and domination. These epistemological oversights, Tuana further explains, can also demarcate those things that transcend our knowledge capacities and even tools used for survival.[24] The narrator of "The Husband Stitch" ironically uses this survival tactic while undoing herself, pushing ignorance to its limit and withholding all forms of knowledge from the reader by becoming a solid object. By desubjectivizing her and making her an impenetrable object, the narrative illustrates the constancy of violence against women and their bodies, and the pleasure in coming undone.

Viscous: A Fat Body, a Fat-Ghost

If "The Husband Stitch" illustrates the desubjectification of the self and the rejection of interiority to the point of becoming a solid form, "Eight Bites" asks readers to consider viscosity as a hermeneutic that reveals refusals that hurt the self and the pleasures that happen alongside them. Viscosity links the body to self-abnegation through eating, the rejection of food, and the ultimate rejection of the self. The narrator's self-inflicted violence finds its most poignant expression through the supernatural being that haunts her: a fat-ghost, fat that she has attempted to get rid of through surgery but that now resides in her home.

"Eight Bites" tells a seemingly mundane story that, through the tropes of speculative fiction, upends the readers' expectations. Like in "The Husband Stitch," this protagonist narrates the encounter with her body and her body-as-object through a first-person account that circulates between pleasure and pain and ultimately relishes self-harm. The protagonist of "Eight Bites" loses not a head but rather undesired fat, which haunts her until her death. She undergoes gastric bypass surgery like her sisters before her; fatness, surgical intervention, and a desire for thinness are part of a female family tradition and kinship formation. Having haunting remnants after the procedure is commonplace in the world of the story: her sisters hear joy dancing through the house, inner beauty curling up in the sunlight like a cat, or shame silently slinking away in the shadows. The narrator, however, finds her fat-ghost threatening, as she is haunted by viscous materiality, taking the shape of externalized hatred and anger toward the self.

"Eight Bites" touches not only on the toxic messages women internalize about body image but also on the pleasures of self-harm and abnegation. The fat-ghost offers an enticing, albeit unforgiving, evocation of what it could mean to be postwoman. Before the surgery, the narrator wishes she could "relinquish control," making everything "right again"—a desire to be unthinking and perhaps uncritical of her own body.[25] Enjoying one last indulgent meal before her surgery, the narrator orders a "cavalcade of oysters" and savors the possibility of thinking outside the limits of her body and toward that of viscosity:

> Most of [the oysters] had been cut the way they were supposed to be, and they slipped down as easily as water, like the ocean, like nothing at all, but one fought me: anchored to its shell, a stubborn hinge of flesh. It resisted. It was resistance incarnate. Oysters are alive, I realized. They are nothing but muscle; they have no brains or insides, strictly speaking, but they are alive nonetheless. If there were any justice in the world, this oyster would grab hold of my tongue and choke me dead.[26]

In a letter to William Cavendish, René Descartes repeats a sentiment previously expressed in *Discourse on Method* (1637), wherein he uses the oyster to illustrate the limits of animal life as well as to show how humans uniquely possess souls.[27] As Karl Steel illustrates, premodern and classical writing is fascinated with the oyster: the mollusk enacts borderness and is a potential classifier without being classifiable itself. To "catch a touch of oystermorphism," Steel suggests, will enable us to consider how fields of agency are established and how they operate.[28] Indeed, the oyster's anatomy, texture, and stubborn attachment to its shell in "Eight Bites" foreshadow the hinge of flesh that will haunt the narrator after surgery. The oyster also embodies the resistance, mindless viscosity, and undoing of the self she wishes to inhabit: "I was jealous of the oysters. They never had to think about themselves," she muses.[29] The freedom to be nothing but muscle offers a fantasy outside her subject position and beyond the limitations of the body, even as it lets her exhibit a desire for self-harm. The pleasure of eating, giving oneself over to the body's wanting, is also affixed to a craving to be punished from the inside out. Effectively, this punishment takes place. The narrator of "Eight Bites" homes in on the exacting position women are put in when they become "beautiful"—they enter a constant state of repair and improvement that defines women's bodies as deficient, inadequate, and always in need of more. Yet the oyster, and later the narrator's fat-ghost, illustrates the enticing and dangerous possibilities of being viscous. The viscous is thick and sticky, like fat; it exists as an in-between state, neither solid nor liquid. As such, the viscous extends outside binary systems and suggests the potentiality of being slippery, inconclusive, and therefore unending, while also suggesting an intimate adherence to the body unburdened by thought and feeling.

The surgery the narrator undergoes is the beginning of a transformation that will always be in process. "Will I ever be done, transformed in the past tense, or will I always be transforming, better and better until I die?" she asks.[30] Managing never being good enough is unrelenting and exhausting work. I have been fat and have also undone myself; both were and continue to be sorrowful practices of hurting the self. For the narrator of "Eight Bites," as for me, the notion of transformation should have an end point, a moment when alteration will no longer be necessary, and we can be the thing we were always supposed to have been. Yet the text illustrates that becoming—becoming woman, becoming imperceptible, becoming a head, a mollusk, a fat-ghost—can break the rigid lines of segmentary thinking and serve as a "line of flight" that moves toward excess and exteriority, and away from fixed subjectivity.[31] As Gilles Deleuze and Félix Guattari argue, a line of flight connotes escape, deterritorialization, and becoming. In *A Thousand Plateaus* (1987), they explore how lines of flight refer to movements or trajectories that break free from the constraints of established structures and norms, presenting a creative and transformative force that operates outside fixed boundaries while opening up new possibilities of existence. A line of flight offers individual and communal modes of transformation and liberation with no fixed path or destination; it is a fluid process of becoming that allows connections, intensities, and forms of life to emerge. As Deleuze and Guattari further suggest, "becoming-other" is a means of escaping rigid and violent norms. It is a process of osmosis involving de-identitized entities that resist dominant modes of representation.[32] The most significant term in "becoming-," as Jerry Aline Flieger emphasizes, is the verbal gerund, making "other," "woman," "mollusk" not an end goal "but a potential, a valence."[33] This "escape (or flight)" primarily, and significantly, happens in *Her Body and Other Parties* through acts of (self-)harm that undo the self, acts that cause the text to break—a narrative strategy that returns us to the violence inflicted on women's bodies. These acts of (self-)harm and textual undoing are interspersed with pleasure and exhibit elements of masochism, which illustrate the desire to relinquish control in exchange for sensation.[34] Amber Jamilla Musser, for example, reformulates masochism as an analytic where difference is revealed, showing it as a lens through which to examine structures of power, coloniality, and racism.[35] Machado's protagonists engage in masochistic (self-)harm as a method of surrendering control that enables them to dislocate themselves as subjects and lay down their claims to agency "by replacing it with temporal suspension, sensation, objectification, and passivity."[36] The oyster in "Eight Bites" is a vehicle for the narrator's physical pleasure and a medium for fantasies about what it would mean to suspend the self, to become a "pre-me body."[37]

Her Body and Other Parties shows that masochism is an arena for social critique and a path out of subjectivity. It offers freedom through the manipulation of the body as the body enacts power and submission in relation to pleasure and pain. This process of unbecoming can be clarified by Jacques Lacan and Leo Bersani's notion of *jouissance*, which defines a state beyond pleasure and pain but also a state beyond identity, a "self-shattering" that "disrupts the ego's coherence and dissolves its boundaries."[38] While queer psychoanalytic theorists focus on how sexuality is tied to masochism and self-annihilation, my reading of Machado shows that the anti-identitarian desubjectification and undoing-of-the-self need not take place only through sexual acts. The women of these stories do not center subjectivity without identity; instead, they go a step further by fully undoing both concepts. In *Her Body and Other Parties*, women wish to escape their ugly feelings—their participation in violence and deadly harm, psychosexual objectification, shame around fatness, confusion, and dissipation. Unable to do so, they resort—willingly in some cases and unwillingly in others—to an anti-identitarian and desubjectivized state of thingness. What Sianne Ngai would call their minor or ugly feelings, however, highlight the major sources of pain and violence that engender silence and refusal, while their passive resistance makes them inaccessible to the reader. The "suspended agency" Ngai theorizes in *Ugly Feelings* (2004) is interrupted and foreclosed with each short story. The subjectivity turned to anti-identitarian thingness in these texts illustrates the continued violence inflicted on women's bodies.[39]

Through the tropes of speculative fiction, "Eight Bites" performs the narrator's fantasies and terrors: the fat-ghost embodies the desire to be postwoman and the potentialities of viscosity, such as being in between, amorphous, and slippery, that objects like the oyster illuminate. Yet it also enacts a haunting reminder of her self-hatred that forecloses this becoming-. In fact, the fat-ghost, like the narrator of "The Husband Stitch," becomes all solid surface, an unreadable mass of resistance. Following the oyster, the fat-ghost "is a body with nothing it needs: no stomach or bones or mouth. Just soft indents."[40] The pliancy that both the oyster and the fat-ghost exhibit is craved by the narrator, who turns to them as easily accessible sources of masochistic pleasure. Finding the fat-ghost in the basement of her home, the narrator tells her she is unwanted, sending a rippling tremor through her "mass." The narrator proceeds to kick the ghost, an act of violence that momentarily allows her to inhabit the mindlessness she desires: "I do not know I am kicking her until I am kicking her. She has nothing and I feel nothing."[41] The opportunity to become desubjected happens through affective excess and hatred of the self. Yet the fat-ghost frustrates the narrator's viscous-becoming by meeting her foot with the density of a solid mass. Each time the narrator kicks the fat-ghost, "she seems to solidify" before the foot meets her body, a solidity that is pleasurable as well—"so every kick is more satisfying than the last."[42] The act of kicking seems to give the ghost materiality, giving the narrator pleasure in the certainty of her violence's result. As she inflicts violence on an externalized formation of the self, the narrator is unsatisfied until the ghost is fully ripped apart. After kicking the fat-ghost, the narrator swings a broom into her, breaking its handle inside her body and finally pulling "soft handfuls of her body out of herself" and throwing them against the wall.[43] And again like the oyster, the fat-ghost also refuses to satisfy the narrator's desire to be punished—the oyster does not choke her to death, and the fat-ghost frustrates her wish that "she would fight back."[44] Common forms of resistance are stymied in "Eight Bites," and the story offers no possibility of readerly comfort in a happy ending for its protagonist. The fat-ghost's inactive and quiet withholding resists dominance: it paradoxically models an intractable affect that is present in absence and through which the performance of incomprehension resists the demand for transparency. This demand, as I explore in the final section of this chapter, is closely linked to the demands imposed on minoritized subjects and their aesthetic production.[45]

The viscosity of the fat-ghost is a form of withholding that "withdraws from radical exposure and vulnerability."[46] The fat-ghost remains an impenetrable substance, exemplifying what Vivian Huang calls aesthetic modes of inscrutability, performances that reconfigure and disturb social conventions.[47] In fact, the narrator's self-harm that produced the fat-ghost becomes eternal and impenetrable: "She will outlive me by a hundred million years; more, even . . . and the earth will teem with her and her kind, their inscrutable forms and unknowable destinies."[48] In this way, "Eight Bites," like the other stories in *Her Body and Other Parties*, provides no easy answers. The fat-ghost and the severed head impede the reader's ability to see and know. The demand for legibility imposed on minoritized subjects, or the demand for what Antonio Viego calls "transparency signifiers," is answered by the narrative's resistance to completeness, transparency, and disclosure.[49] This ethico-political response is a form of withholding that is physical, affective, and temporal. Withholding is an aesthetic mode of inscrutability that signals a relational project ("with/

holding") and underscores that the social mission to "understand" minoritized subjects is based in colonialist and imperialist projects.[50]

Dissipation: Becoming a Dress

After moving from the solidity of the severed head through the viscosity of fat and the oyster, we reach the dissipating body as another evocation of post-/ab-/ suprahuman desire and the silent resistance that hurts the self. If masochism throws the self off-kilter by providing a glimpse of the self beyond identity, then posthuman critique destabilizes concepts such as "human." As posthumanist scholars have shown, with the deconstruction of the boundaries between human and inhuman comes the distortion of distinctions between fiction and reality. It is here that the margins between speculative fiction and "social reality [become] an optical illusion."[51] Mel Chen, for instance, proposes the notion of animacy (as opposed to liveness) to activate new theoretical models that unsettle binary systems and have the potential to revise intimacy and communalism.[52] Facing the contradictions of humanism, most posthumanist scholars have explored the posthuman—the Anthropocene, cyborgs, object-oriented ontology, technoculture—but have often overlooked questions of race and ethnicity. Attending to these constructions through a posthumanist lens, however, can illuminate the organizing systems and hierarchies that are intrinsic to them.[53] Classificatory principles that categorize organisms are at the center of posthumanist investigations, where embodied difference does not have to be "mired in the residual effects of white liberal subjectivity."[54] In this sense, posthumanism does not indicate being "beyond" the human but marks its structural legacies.[55]

The story "Real Women Have Bodies" draws on the tropes of speculative fiction to examine the materiality of women's bodies, their relation to labor in late-stage capitalism, and the self-destructive opportunities that the posthuman, dissipating body engenders. The story's guiding speculative principle introduces a world very much like our own, except that an unexplained epidemic is causing women to slowly fade and become immaterial. At the center of "Real Women Have Bodies" is yet another nameless narrator, this time an employee at Glam, a dress store in a shopping mall. In the course of this seemingly menial labor, the narrator begins dating the store's delivery woman, Petra, who is the daughter of the store's dressmaker. She unveils for the narrator an important secret about the dissipating women: some of them are being sewn into the dresses sold at Glam. Like the corpses at the center of 2666, the immaterial-becoming women are the impetus for the text, and as the story progresses, the mystery of their dissipation slowly unfurls. This development, however, does not lead to a resolution or clarification. The women remain opaque. The counterpart of the inscrutable solidity of the head in "The Husband Stitch" and the quiet viscosity of the fat-ghost in "Eight Bites" is the mysterious dissipation of the women of "Real Women Have Bodies." Like the fat-ghost, the women adhere to the solidity of fabric without relinquishing their immateriality, and like the head and the ghost, they quietly produce an eerie mystery that the story preserves.

As the narrative unfolds, the dissipation of the women is slowly exposed to the readers. At first the narrator sees their condition as worse than death and describes them as "victims." The readers come to understand that the women's immateriality is not an absence like death but rather a diaphanous presence that cannot make itself (or does not want to make itself?) known. One of the first women the narrator sees appears in a viral video at the outset of the epidemic: "She was naked, and trying to conceal it. You could see her breasts through her arm, the wall through her torso. She was crying. The sound was so soft that the inane chatter of the landlord had covered it until then. But then you could hear it—miserable, terrified."[56] It is crucial that the woman's crying is almost imperceptible, that a man is talking over her, and that the fear she exhibits is related to both her dissipation and her nudity. This scene is a speculative reimagination of the fear women routinely experience because of their vulnerability to physical harm, and simultaneously it alludes to the demand that minoritized subjects be transparent.

The wordless and almost imperceptible dissipation of women in the story draws readers' attention to the violence enacted on women and their bodies. Yet their dissipation is also a site of refusal that illustrates a desire to extend beyond the reach of the human into the post-, ab-, suprahuman instead. The cause of the disappearance of hundreds of women is never explained, leading people to imbue them with unearthly capacities that have radical transformative potential in late-stage capitalism. The dissipating women are rumored to be terrorists, "getting into electrical systems and fucking up servers and ATMs and voting machines. Protesting."[57] These rumors bespeak anxieties about modern consumerism, neoliberal ideology, and the voyeuristic treatment of women's bodies as consumable goods in the media and market. It comes as no surprise, then, when we learn that the women are bound to the fabric in a factory-cum-workshop in a motel. The choice of this site alludes to capital and the commodification of women's bodies in sex and sex work.

Through her relationship with Petra, the story's narrator discovers that she has been selling dresses inhabited by disembodied women that are sewn into the material and occupy the space in dress form. Working out of a motel that is also their home, Petra shows the narrator her mother's studio, where the narrator observes one of the ghost-women go into a dress: she "presses herself into it, and there is no resistance, only a sense of an ice cube melting in the summer air. The needle—trailed by thread of guileless gold—winks as [the seamstress] plunges it through the girl's skin. The fabric takes the needle, too."[58] As in "The Husband Stitch," the image of the needle and thread brings together bondage and domesticity, themselves associated with sexuality and womanhood. Bondage in this sense means both a woman's containment within social norms and a sexual practice. Although the ghost-woman appears willing to be sewn into the dress, the image of the needle piercing her skin is weighted with violence, while the humanness that should be associated with the dissipated woman is displaced onto the needle and thread. "Real Women Have Bodies" toys with the lines that separate kink, pleasure, pain, the sexual debasement from which pleasure is derived, and the role of labor in late-stage capitalism. The relationship between class struggle and capitalist modes of production that Karl Marx and Friedrich Engels describe in *The Communist Manifesto* (1848) is speculatively reimagined in Machado's story, wherein human labor is made immaterial, and women disappear only to become sewn into commodities. The narrator explains that the dissipation of women begins at the height of an economic recession, bringing the world of the story close to that of the early twenty-first-century reader, while illustrating the otherworldly nature of capitalism. The world-building of "Real Women Have Bodies" makes literal the Marxist adage that in modernity and bourgeois rule, "All that is solid melts into air."[59] Women inexplicably flock to the seamstress's workshop, and the dresses holding them inside are Glam's bestsellers. "It's like people want them like that, even if they don't realize it," Petra explains.[60] "Women" in "Real Women Have Bodies," therefore, are defined outside corporeality and their ability to communicate and instead are disintegrated into the incorporeal commodity.

The story also considers how the dissipation of "woman" represents a threat, even in women's immateriality and silence. The fear women inspire in the story comes not from overtly aggressive or violent acts but from silence and passivity, from their unmaking of themselves as embodied subjects, and from the possibility that they are extricating themselves from capitalist labor. This removal from the workforce points to the violence inflicted on women's bodies. The narrator describes the dissipating women not as enacting defiance but as passively and quietly relinquishing their bodies. The women in the workshop glow "faintly, like afterthoughts," and fold themselves into the needlework, "like it was what they wanted."[61] And they remain, like the fallen head and the fat-ghost, fully unreadable. Seeing a faded woman in the woods, the narrator cannot tell if she is smiling or grimacing, and similarly she cannot tell whether the women in the workshop are "holding on for dear life or if they are trapped. The rustling and trembling of the fabric could be weeping or laughter."[62] She also understands that all women—including herself—are destined to disappear and recognizes that the world for them is an uninhabitable place. Yet paradoxically, their unbecoming—their quiet immateriality—enacts a form of passive resistance against these forms of violence.

With each new dress, "Real Women Have Bodies" showcases pleasure in violence: the sartorial beauty of each garment also holds violence, pain, and self-abnegation at its center. The dissipating women inter themselves within the fabric and so participate in an act of refusal or resistance that neither the text nor the women can name. The women seem to refuse to escape their sartorial prison, a form of resistance that confuses the narrator (and the reader). The narrator tries to comprehend their choice to be sewn into the dresses—as well as the speculative world she inhabits—by cutting "where one thing is stitched to another" and beckoning for them to "get out."[63] Yet the women remain impassive. They reveal that what the narrator sees as a prison could in fact be a new home, a new skin, and a posthuman relation. The narrator, previously so disturbed by the sight of the women being sewn into the dresses, becomes the agent of violence instead.

In "Real Women Have Bodies," as throughout *Her Body and Other Parties*, we see a version of woman that is messy, porous, violent, self-loathing; one who refuses to remake and rebuild. The women of Machado's narratives seek "instead to be out of time altogether, a body suspended in time, space, and desire."[64] In fact, women in *Her Body and Other Parties* enact a mystery that can never be solved. The substance of being (human, woman, head, mollusk, immaterial) resides within a system where the coordinates of "ethnic" femininity are predetermined and violently exposed. This bind is explored as a protagonist loses her head, another vanishes into nothingness and stitchwork, and yet another loses pounds around her waistline while carrying around the weight of a fat-ghost. It is also made visible on the level of form: the repeated punctuation marks, intertextual references and rewrites, and specific tactics and forms of characterization. These trace a life/text overlap where the end of the text coincides with the end of the protagonists—their refusal, defiance, and self-abnegation are taken to the extreme: unbecoming. Yet Machado's stories move us outside the realm of live subject/dead subject to a place beyond subjectivity to a set of subject-object relations that engages a framework of life/nonlife. This spectrum of existence organizes things by degree, not kind:

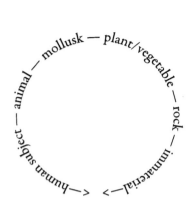

Machado's protagonists move from (agential) subjects to consumable things. These women become "it," not "I," and the real onset of cataclysm is the decentering of the human subject. This decentering moves us beyond the reach of language and produces pleasure in the novelty, the undoing, the recalibrating of pleasure. It is here that narrative doom patterns establish themselves: women's bodies not only display the advance of destruction but also, in their many silent resistances and inconclusive positions within the text, signal a return to violence that marks the ethno-racial.

Mujeres Fugazes, Opaquing *Latinidad*

The speculative tropes of *Her Body and Other Parties*, which illuminate the violence inflicted on women's bodies and the refusals that hurt the self, also reveal unexpected elements of *latinidad*. The text interweaves violence that requires the language of the speculative and a *latinidad* that is excessive and otherworldly, eluding the written word and refusing the performativity of the ethnographic imperative. This refusal, like that of "womanhood," displaces *latinidad* onto the tropes of speculative fiction and demands an interpretive practice that is attuned to this formal exchange.[65] The collection thus asks literary scholars to think carefully about *latinidad* and other minoritized identities and their portrayals in literature: as historical constructions, as representatives of epistemological structures in Western modernity, and as practices within academic and literary institutions. The collection also offers an opportunity to consider generic expectations, assumptions within the field about what Latinx identity looks like in literature, and the burden sometimes imposed on "ethnic" literature to be politically salient and recognizable as both socially conscious and "ethnic."

While most of the texts in *Doom Patterns* mention race and ethnicity explicitly while unveiling the speculative through their depictions of violence and historical trauma, *Her Body and Other Parties* exhibits *latinidad* through the otherworldly. That is, Machado's short stories do not overtly display Latinx identity, but they are undisputedly speculative, which makes it possible to read them as texts that treat *latinidad* as an element of genre fiction. Historical violence is veiled from the reader in Machado's collection, and while race and ethnicity are not easily seen, the tropes of speculative fiction lay them bare.

Like the potentially world-destroying Blackness I read in chapter 2, the minoritarian position of "woman" here carries dangerous and enticing possibilities of refusal and destruction. In centering the experiences and desires of women, Machado breaks with the expectation that fiction will provide linearity, wholeness, resolution, and legibility. At the same time, she inflicts pain on the self. Rejecting the burden placed on "ethnic" literature to provide recognizable depictions of ethno-racial communities and, in some cases, progressive political meanings, Machado's work announces a moment of generative crisis within the field of Latinx literature and culture, one whose impact cannot be fully gauged yet amid what some are calling a cancellation of *latinidad* or its reimagination.[66] Many of the scholars who address Machado's work engage questions of gender, queerness, and sex and sexuality, and some examine how Machado uses the tropes of genre fiction. A few scholars, like me, address the significance of race and ethnicity in her work and are invested in claiming Machado as a Latinx author. While the following statement might sound dramatic, the resistance to transparency, knowability, and circumscription that *Her Body and Other Parties* exhibits marks an end point, an apocalypse of sorts for Latinx literary studies: the field in generic flail. The term *generic flail*, taken from Lauren Berlant, implies that *latinidad*, its modes of representation, and the disciplines that study it are in catastrophe. Genre flailing, Berlant argues, is a mode of crisis management used when an object, or "object world," is disrupted and interferes with our confidence about how to move in it.[67] The objects here are Latinx literature, modes and forms of depicting Latinxness, canon formations, and conceptions of genre. If Latinx literature as a genre provided an "affective expectation of the experience of watching something unfold," it also offered a glimpse of "potential openings within and beyond the impasse of adjustment that constant crisis creates."[68] This sense of order is crucial, even as it holds breakage—the fear that the expectation will not be met—at its center. But what if breakage is the only thing available now? What if the text and its field of study are flailing? This is not to say that flailing is failing, to return to Berlant, but instead that flailing is a mode of resistance to and refusal of taxonomies, genealogies, and narrative modes as they have been.[69]

Recent work in Latinx studies uses a relational framework to show, as Lisa Lowe does, the importance of reading "*across* the separate repositories organized by office, task, and function, and by period and area, precisely implicating one set of preoccupations in and with another."[70] This relational framework allows us to expand our reading practice beyond the representational. Ralph Rodriguez, for example, implements a neo-formalist approach to think about how literary form (genre) offers "more satisfying taxonomies and heuristics for grouping and analyzing literature" than identity signifiers or the usual groupings that fall under "Latinx literature." Rodriguez urges scholars to "unbind" themselves from the racial and ethnic parameters that dominate the field.[71] Like Rodriguez, I am interested in complicating and augmenting the construction of racialized and ethnic identities, and I expand this practice to consider how examining a text that eschews conventional depictions of *latinidad* allows us to see the speculative within Latinx literature. What do we learn about race and ethnicity from such a text that we could not have known otherwise? How do we read *latinidad* in a text that excludes or avoids racial and ethnic markers? What does this avoidance accomplish? Should we affix an ethno-racial reading to a text or author who circumvents it? This is another way of asking how we can envision *latinidad* without Latinxs or what Latinx literature is now that generic expectations have been upended.[72] Ramón Saldívar's work on "speculative realism" and postrace aesthetics identifies a trend among minoritized writers who have turned to the tropes of genre fiction to create an aesthetic for thinking about race in the twenty-first century and its relation to a "just society."[73] Similarly, Paul Allatson argues that contemporary Latinx writers challenge essentialist understandings of *latinidad*, ways of interpreting ethno-racial markers in a text, or notions of authenticity, generating postidentitarian narratives "that reflect the constant flux of transculturation and their potential to modulate the United States' twenty-first-century future."[74] These postidentitarian narratives speak to the elasticity of *latinidad*, to follow Marta Caminero-Santangelo's investigation of the term, and, as Allatson suggests, make it possible to disidentify with and dissolve the term in literary production.[75] Others, like Aarón Aguilar-Ramírez, present *latinidad* as a "narrative terrain" that can enable "pan-ethnic modes of recognition under specific reading attention and within particular social, political, and cultural contexts."[76] *Latinidad*, then, is not a set of identitarian logics that are depicted in narrative but a mode of reading, a protocol much like speculative fiction.

Texts like Machado's *Her Body and Other Parties* propose that thinking about Latinx subjectivity and *latinidad* requires the language of the speculative. From the position of prescriptive frameworks that interpolate Latinx literature via filiative backgrounds and direct engagement with Latinx content, Machado's fiction is Latinx only insofar as Machado is biologically Latinx.

Yet *Her Body and Other Parties* indexes the ethno-racial through excessive affect and violence, displacing it onto form and the tropes of speculative fiction. Stories like "Especially Heinous"—a speculative reimagination of the television series *Law & Order: SVU*—narrate violence against women as banal horror that is illuminated as spectacular and otherworldly. As Saidiya Hartman, who in *Scenes of Subjection* (1997) contests the notion of the "exemplary violence" of slavery as that which is seen in "the most heinous and grotesque," points out, serial and routinized sexual and gendered violence occurs not only in the most brutally evident ways but also in the quotidian.[77] The myriad ghosts that haunt Detective Benson in "Especially Heinous" are compared to the produce she continually buys and discards. These ghosts showcase the mundanity and excess of gendered violence while implicating the text's consumer in the pleasure derived from reading and watching stories of women's bodies being destroyed. The story metafictionally depicts New York City's "dum-dums," echoing *SVU*'s musical theme refrain, marking itself as participating in the voyeuristic consumption of police procedurals—the audience "watches our suffering like it's a game. Can't stop. Can't tear themselves away. If they could stop, we could stop, but they won't, so we can't."[78] The story indicates its participation in discussions surrounding global femicide epidemics, most notably that of Ciudad Juárez. As I argue in chapter 3, the excessive narration of dead women's bodies showcases, among other things, the readerly pleasure in repetition and the formulaic expectation that women will be destroyed.

The rendition of *latinidad* in *Her Body and Other Parties'* grammar is obliquely evident from the collection's outset. In fact, the book's dedication to Machado's grandfather—"Reinaldo Pilar Machado Gorrin, *quien me contó mis primeros cuentos, y sigue siendo mi favorito*"(who told me my first stories, and is still my favorite)—frames the text through a form of "linguistic posing": a performative structure and set of acts that linguistically emphasize how Latinx identity is projected formally rather than through visible identitarian logics.[79] The Spanish italics here follow a tradition in print culture that marks the language as foreign to the text that surrounds it. The italicization that occurs in Spanish in the book's dedication permeates the rest of the text, such that when a thinly veiled version of Machado attends a writers' residency and etches her initials into the desk she has been using during her stay, the text latinizes her as well. The inscription reads, "*C__ M__ . . . Resident colonist & colonizing resident & madwoman in her own attic*."[80] The phrase "madwoman in her own attic" evokes Bertha Mason, the original dark-other who serves as the exotic racial foil to the Anglo Jane Eyre. This use of form that betrays the ethno-racial is evident in other minute details throughout the collection as well.

In "Mothers," for example, two women procreate through sex with each other, an unexpected impossibility that opens the narrative. The nameless narrator's ex-partner, Bad, leaves the baby in her care, which sets the stage for a surreal meditation on being in and surviving an abusive relationship. The narrator of "Mothers" navigates through fantasy, ending up in a fairy-tale-like home in the woods that is turned askew and dangerous. Here she considers the baby's appearance and that of a second child who crops up later in the story: "Mara and Tristan, brown-haired children. Brown like—someone's grandmother. Maybe mine."[81] The narrator is referring to the children's hair, yet the em dash and period that separate "brown-haired children" and "Brown" extend brownness to invoke *latinidad*. The brown-haired children of the story, and by extension the narrator and her grandmother, obfuscate the visual and social perceptions of what is considered ethno-racial, and as Claudia Milian points out, they produce the type of ambiguity that the term *Latinx* itself does by operating in the absence of a "single referent of an ontological grammar of race and sociocultural existence."[82] Ambiguity is displaced onto the grammar through which the *latinidad* the story withholds from its readers can be read.

The advent of the *x* has made it plain that *latinidad* is far from a stable or fully articulated identity. As José Esteban Muñoz argues, *latinidad* is a form of affect, a "structure of feeling," that is both singular and plural and will always remain incomplete.[83] So, what happens when we apply brownness as a structure of feeling to a text? If, as Muñoz posits, ethnicity is less an identity than a structure of feeling, then it is "a way of being in the world, a path that does not conform to the conventions of a majoritarian public sphere and the national affect it sponsors."[84] The challenge the term *Latinx* poses for pronunciation and identity articulation is a driving force throughout this book, which I end by blurring the lines between fields while highlighting illegibility.

When asked how her identity as queer and Latina affects her writing, Machado states, "I think writing is inextricable from the body; there's no such thing as pure reason, pure intellect. My body, my identity, is a lens through which I can view the world and reflect it back in my work."[85] Machado is a white-presenting Latina, and her collection emulates her subject position. The phrase "white-presenting" mirrors how readers interpret for race in a text. As I argue in relation to Colson Whitehead's *Zone One* (2011), Machado's "studiously deracinated" characters, to use Michelle Huang's term, "ironiz[e] assumptions of white universalism and uncritical postracialism."[86] For Whitehead's protagonist, Mark Spitz, the withholding of his Blackness until the end of the novel is a deliberate narratorial choice that challenges this prejudice, and the ultimate disclosure of his race occurs as a world-destroying element of the text. In Machado, a similar evasion is seen: the overt tropes of Latinx literature and *latinidad* escape us, while those of speculative fiction are foregrounded. *Latinidad* is obfuscated and displaced onto the otherworldly portrayal of women's bodies. In a sense, the refusal to mark characters ethnically or racially in *Her Body and Other Parties* can be read as an intentional indication of the text's *latinidad*.[87] The collection calls attention to the need for alternative modes of articulation and aesthetic theorization that, as scholars like Joshua Javier Guzmán and Christina León, Leticia Alvarado, and Muñoz have argued, signal the excessive nature of *latinidad*.[88]

Fugitive, opaque, quiet, withholding: intermediaries between the text and reader, these notions reveal that language is not a vehicle for fully understanding the minoritized subject or for encapsulating violence. Using the tropes of horror, the women in Machado embody that which is desired and feared. Their refusals not only resist narrative closure but take us to the limit of reason, showing that there is no place outside violence for women's bodies in this world, and the only alternative is to extricate oneself from it. Their unraveling from the self, the human, and the world paradoxically uses methods that emulate the violence inflicted on their body by others. This unraveling ultimately destroys the self. Pain and refusal in *Her Body and Other Parties* is, following the trend explored throughout *Doom Patterns*, also a source of aesthetic pleasure that mirrors the position of women in society: desired and reviled, enthralling and feared, the women in these texts exemplify what Carol Clover calls the "female victim-hero":[89] they are suprahuman in their revolt against the patriarchal forces of monstrosity, yet in this resistance they become monstrous.

Physical, sensual, temporal, and affective modes like fugitivity, quiet, opacity, and withholding explain how the women in Machado's collection operate within each story and together, as well as the text's relationship to *latinidad* and the field of Latinx studies writ large. Although these concepts develop from distinctive socio-historical-material localities and should not be conflated, they all address the expectation that racialized subjects be transparent and subject to domination. By evading the demand for transparent depictions of racial and ethnic identities in fiction, these stories show us a new way to read and find *latinidad* in a text: by looking to the tropes of speculative fiction that illustrate the otherworldliness of minoritized subjectivity as well as intractability. The frequent use of nameless narrators in the collection, for example, challenges the reader's desire for transparent, knowable characters. As Kandice Chuh argues, impersonality can be an aesthetic strategy that "de-narrativizes virtuous personhood," a strategy that, in the case of *Her Body and Other Parties*, is also marked with the elements of *latinidad* that surpass the capacity of language and cause the text to resort to the speculative.[90] In "The Husband Stitch," the nameless narrator illustrates what Muñoz and others have described as the burden of ethnic excess, which her husband constantly attempts to mediate, apprehend, unravel, and unveil.[91] The excessiveness of *latinidad* is displaced onto the form of the narrative and onto the ribbon the narrator wears around her neck. Yet this excessiveness is also a marker of mystery.

The women in Machado are *fugaz, se fugan* (elusive, they flee) from our grasp. From the Latin *fugāx, fugitive* and *fugaz* signal that which is swift, arriving and departing instantaneously, and therefore fleeting and transitory. This elusive condition also makes the *fugaz* powerfully avoidant. In *Her Body and Other Parties*, women's *fugazivity* happens textually and metatextually, marking the pages with a doom pattern that returns us to various forms of violence, as well as challenging the conventions of the field of Latinx studies. As León suggests, opacity—and, for our purposes, quiet, withholding, and fugitivity—cites the visual to "play with it, to change the rules of the game, and to provide a textured resistance to transparent elucidation."[92] These discursive modes frustrate readers who demand completeness or ethno-racial legibility, while simultaneously underlining the central role of the tropes of speculative fiction in telling stories of extreme violence.

Much as the ribbon causes confusion and anger because of the unanswerable questions it raises, women's bodies are sources of mystery and fear in "Real Women Have Bodies." As Renee Hudson argues, the story is an allusion to *Real Women Have Curves*, the stage play (1990) and its film adaptation (2002).[93] In both "Especially Heinous" and "Real Women Have Bodies," speculative tropes upend common depictions of race and ethnicity. Machado expands our imagination by refusing to depict race and ethnicity in a way that would classify her work as Latinx. In "Especially Heinous," the disappearance of women evokes the borderland's history of femicides while "signaling a crisis of representation."[94] Going incorporeal, with no scientific or supernatural explanation, enacts the text's deidentitarian and desubjectivizing project.

The women of Machado's fiction offer an opportunity to consider what it would mean to think outside the confines of my body, the desire and hunger it feels, the abstention and restraint I force it to undergo. Their turn to the headless body, the mollusk, the dress—solid, viscous, dissipating—poses an invitation to think beyond the confines of our bodies and the exigencies of the world. The women of *Her Body and Other Parties* refuse these constrictions by becoming less and less and extricating themselves from the world. They inflict pain on their bodies until they are desubjected; they subject themselves to hurt and echo what has always been done to their bodies. To a large extent, these refusals are also about pleasure—debasement through sex, hunger, unbecoming human, hurting the fat self, lush and beautiful language. The boundaries between the executer of violence and the recipient of violence are made hazy, and the women provide no easy solutions—only the enticing invitation to think beyond the self.

This chapter is part of a body of scholarship that considers the relational framework of constructions of race and ethnicity. These analyses emerge from a long history of women-of-color feminism and queer-of-color critique that centers relational understandings. Through the transnational and diasporic turn in academia, scholars have made power structures visible and spelled out the logics that underpin violence and dispossession.[95] As the editors of *Relational Formations of Race* (2019) make clear, colonialism and white supremacy are relational practices that "rely on logics of sorting, ranking, and comparison that produce and naturalize categories of racial difference necessary for the legitimation of slavery, settler colonialism, and imperial expansion."[96] They argue that relational analyses compel scholars to go beyond their comfort zones into the unfamiliar. As a scholar trained in Latinx literary studies, I have attempted to do just that: I am engaging in new and unfamiliar territory and putting texts in strange positions to scrutinize the ways we read, talk about, and construct fields of knowledge. A relational treatment of race, ethnicity, and gender formations contextualizes them within the debates about the meanings, boundaries, and hierarchies of race, ethnicity, and gender that occur across time and space. A relational analysis enables an understanding of how power operates within a wider framework, while cautioning against simplistic analogies or comparisons between forms of racialization and gendering in the United States and forms of colonization and misogyny in other parts of the globe.

The forms of embodiment that I examine here show that to be Latinx and to be woman is such an excessive endeavor, so weighted with various violent histories, that this experience must be narrated as speculative fiction. The readings throughout *Doom Patterns* expose the boundaries and overlaps of forms of racialization, gender formations, ethno-national constructions, and class structures. Yet *Her Body and Other Parties* foregrounds this study's overarching argument that putting works in uncomfortable alignment reveals things previously unseen. Placing works in conversation according to thematic similarities and reading by the protocols of Latinx speculative fiction enable new perspectives not only about what it means to be "woman" but also about interethnic possibilities of analysis. Machado's stories illustrate how to be woman is a horrific endeavor imbued with danger and violence, and that to think about the ethnic is a speculative venture that calls for the language of the otherworldly to articulate its hazy and equivocal borderlines.

CODA

Thinking from the Hole:
Latinidad on the Edge

At the beginning of this book, I asked readers to imagine how the protocols of Latinx speculative fiction can illuminate the ways violence is depicted in a text and how we read this violence. I also asked readers to envision how this reading practice can elucidate and clarify previously unseen thematic networks across hemispheric American texts, and how these arrangements offer nuanced understandings of the formation of race, ethnicity, and nationhood across the continent. This reading practice involves identifying the textual forms and narrative strategies that consistently return readers to instances of destruction—what I call *doom patterns* throughout this book. As my primary hermeneutic, doom patterns establish how texts attempt to encapsulate the violence of the historical past, yet ultimately fail to do so.

Doom Patterns: Latinx Speculations and the Aesthetics of Violence engages Latinx speculative fiction as a reading praxis that reveals how depictions of violence in hemispheric American literature are frequently both mundane and excessive. The texts in my archive and my methodological approach to them paradoxically illustrate that historical violence and its narrative portrayal elicit many forms of pleasure. At the heart of my study is the irresolvable contradiction of consuming literary works saturated with horrific violence that are aesthetically pleasing and continue to be praised and successful in the literary market, academy, and prize circuit. By reading such works through the protocols of Latinx speculative fiction, we can establish a new orientation in the field, one predicated on moving beyond strict boundaries within literary studies. Examining the literary depictions of violence and aesthetic pleasure that emerge in the work of contemporary Latinx and what I am reading as Latinx-adjacent texts, as well as texts that are readily identifiable as speculative fiction and those that are not, *Doom Patterns* addresses the imbrication of race, class, gender, and ethnicity across the Americas. The concepts in each chapter open discursive spaces through which to imagine and reimagine how we read for identity in "minority" literature, how violence is represented and discussed within this literature, and how narratives of violence map archives of excess that simultaneously elicit pleasure.

Following Seo-Young Chu's statement that the "objects of science-fictional representation, while impossible to represent in a straightforward manner, are absolutely real," I argue that while it is impossible to encapsulate the horror of history in narrative form, the tropes of speculative fiction illuminate this past and allow us to see its excess, otherworldliness, and cyclical haunting.[1] In *Do Metaphors Dream of Literal Sleep?* (2010), Chu contends that science fiction is a "mode rather than a genre" that through its literary qualities becomes a mimetic discourse whose objects of representation are cognitively estranging.[2] What differentiates speculative fiction from realism is its "capacity to generate mimetic accounts of aspects of reality that defy straightforward representation."[3] My archive shows how the attempt to capture the violence of the historical past not only causes breaks in the text—textual "failures"—but also forces the narrative to turn to elements such as fragmentation, multivocal and multilingual prose, unresolved plots, and metafictionality that concomitantly point back to violence's excess, the inability to portray it in language, and the replication of violence in the text.

Using the protocols of Latinx speculative fiction is a practice that moves beyond reading for representation or for the reparative, two trends that usually dominate the field. Reading for representation, Marissa López argues, is an interpretative approach that not only indicates a division between reader and text but can impede a reader's consequential engagement with the text. Representational reading "anticipates learning what we already think we know."[4] In addition to López's argument, I find that representational reading obfuscates underlying historical-material conditions in the construction of ethno-racial subjectivity, and I opt instead for a reading process that gestures to more complicated and elastic formations. As Juana María Rodríguez reminds us, to gesture underscores "intentions, process, and practices over objectives and certainty."[5] The texts in *Doom Patterns* gesture rather than arrive, defy expectations, and illuminate new ways of reading that are messy while revealing unfinished connections in-the-making that require more nuanced and expansive definitions and understandings of what *latinidad* and the speculative make possible.

Reparative reading, for its part, has dominated the field of literary studies, especially in relation to multiethnic literature and speculative fiction by people of color. *Doom Patterns* introduces a set of tools for reading that moves away from repair and instead recognizes the enmeshment of violence and pleasure in literature, or, more precisely, the pleasure that can be derived from the aestheticization of violence. Latinx studies, itself in a cadre of race and ethnicity fields, foregrounds political activism and social transformation, which are rooted in the sociopolitical movements that inaugurated the field within the university. There is an imperative within Latinx studies to articulate scholarship in the language of social transformation and community building, which, as Kandice Chuh illustrates for Asian American studies, stems from the struggle to establish ethnic studies generally within the academy, wherein giving back to the community serves as a controlling ideology.[6] Rafael Pérez-Torres's introduction to the *Aztlán* dossier, "Latinx Temporality as a Time of Crisis," was organized around a reflection on the "temporality of Latinx and Chicanx studies" and similarly questions the institutionalization of the field and the ability of scholars to serve as "agents of transformation" or "defuse any potential for significant dissent."[7] Robyn Wiegman's study of academic identity-based fields, *Object Lessons* (2012), describes social justice as the "self-defining critical obligation" of these disciplines.[8] Indeed, in her discussion of academic identity knowledges, Wiegman foregrounds the centrality of social change as their raison d'être and modus operandi, defining social justice as a generic "political destination of identity knowledges."[9] Latinx studies, one of the fields in her analysis, is animated by political intentions and structures its methods and modes of critical engagement around political amelioration. This commitment to the reparative tends to lead scholars to assume that Latinx literature and speculative fiction by people of color are invested in reimagining the historical past in order to illustrate and model resistance to current forms of violence and oppression. These reimaginations cannot make the violence of the past disappear, however, and reading reparatively becomes a form of solidarity that focuses on survival strategies and coping mechanisms "as beautiful seeds of that which might one day, in the future, save the world," instead of attempting to break from the world of the present.[10]

Ultimately, *Doom Patterns* offers the protocols of Latinx speculative fiction as a theory of representation and a reading method that illuminates the excessive nature of historical violence and the overlapping networks it creates across the Americas. I also suggest a speculative fictional theory of representing *latinidad*. By this I mean not only a temporal hypothesis for an identity in-the-making but also an understanding of *latinidad* through the otherworldly. This means that *latinidad* and Latinx subjectivity have been imagined throughout these pages as a speculative endeavor. It is an identity formation that is at once in process—a conjecture projected over time—and also otherworldly, in that it invokes the fantastical and supernatural. *Doom Patterns* opened with Junot Díaz, exploring the storytelling habits of his primary narrator, Yunior, to highlight how he authors a new Caribbean mythology that defines the Caribbean as postapocalyptic and Afro-Dominican people as monstrous. Chapter 1 began with a reading of Díaz's short story "The Sun, the Moon, the Stars" and Yunior's experience in the Cave of Jagua, which the story calls the "birthplace of the nation." I use his experience in the birthplace to illustrate how Yunior's narrative tendencies are circumscribed by the apocalyptic, a condition attributable to his postcolonial subjectivity that he continually replicates in the histories he attempts to narrate throughout Díaz's oeuvre. His replication of cataclysmic violence is manifested at its apex in the concept of "fukú," what *The Brief Wondrous Life of Oscar Wao* (2007) calls the curse of the New World and which Yunior mobilizes to illustrate how the Caribbean is a science-fictional space. If Díaz offers a straightforward way of both seeing Latinx representation in literature and toeing the line of the speculative, as *Doom Patterns* progresses *latinidad* is unraveled, ending with texts that ask us to scrutinize how we understand depictions of Latinx identity in fiction and how the tropes of speculative fiction lay them bare. This book's last chapter, in which I explore Carmen Maria Machado's short stories, shows how identity markers are displaced onto narrative form and how racialization takes on different material valences: the solid, the viscous, and the dissipating. The obfuscation of race and ethnicity that takes place in Machado's work leads me in this conclusion to an exploration of *latinidad* in a text that even more thoroughly eschews Latinx ethno-racial representation. I therefore turn to Hernan Diaz's *In the Distance* (2017) to show how the speculative elements of this novel reveal the ethno-racial, even as the novel defies the ethnographic imperative in the most provocative ways.

Doom Patterns has another organizing principle: I begin and end by thinking from a hole and by thinking with Díaz/Diaz. The Cave of Jagua, which opened my first chapter, is revealed to be a hole in the ground, one that, in combination with the spatial-temporal markers of the Dominican Republic, exposes the speculative dimension of overt ethno-racial and national elements in the text. This hole elicits the apocalyptic thinking, writing, and narration typical in Yunior's narrative practices. Yet the repetition of apocalyptic violence that the hole reveals is also mired in the narrator's heterosexist and misogynistic behavior that polices and curtails queerness. Hernan Díaz's *In the Distance* presents us with another hole, one that also asks us to consider how the historical past violently persists and evinces itself on the level of form. This second hole is in a space at a seeming remove from the markers of *latinidad*. But these markers can be glimpsed, I argue, in the novel's language and form. In fact, I offer *In the Distance* as a Latinx novel in disguise as well as a novel that incorporates elements of the speculative in what appears to be a hyperrealist depiction of the violence of the American frontier. This hole, in many ways, sits in direct contradistinction to Yunior's, in that the possibilities of queer kinship are embraced without necessarily being named as such, and where the markers of *latinidad* and the speculative emerge. Beginning and ending with Díaz and Diaz suggests a new way to think about the formation of the Latinx literary canon and how we might begin examining texts that elude easy categorization: a future for the field of Latinx studies that we might not have the language for yet, a speculative endeavor in itself.

"A Western without Cowboys": *Latinidad* without Latinxs

Imagine a hole in ice. You don't know where this ice is or its expanse, only that the hole interrupts it: "The hole, a broken star on the ice, was the only interruption on the white plain merging into white sky. No wind, no life, no sound."[11] These are the opening lines of *In the Distance*. This opening is followed by a stark break on the page that mirrors the whiteness of the ice and the hole in it (figure C.1).

The text has already lied to us, however. There *is* life: an enormous, almost monstrously large Swede emerges from the hole. We have not seen him yet—only his hands appear at the hole's edge—but we have seen the rift on the page. Intriguingly, the text interrupts itself again, not with another formal break but linguistically: "It took the searching fingers some time to climb up the thick inner walls of the opening, which resembled the cliffs of a miniature cañon, and find their way to the surface."[12] The white space that mirrors the ice is itself mirrored with the use of "cañon," which creates another rift in the text. *Cañon* is an alternative spelling of *canyon*, from the French and Spanish. What is it

The hole, a broken star on the ice, was the only interruption on the white plain merging into the white sky. No wind, no life, no sound.

A pair of hands came out of the water and groped for the edges of the angular hole. It took the searching fingers some time to climb up the thick inner walls of the opening, which resembled the cliffs of a miniature cañon, and find their way to the surface. Having reached over the edge, they hooked into the snow and pulled. A head emerged. The swimmer opened his eyes and looked ahead at the even, horizonless expanse. His long white hair and beard were threaded with straw-tinted strands. Nothing in him revealed agitation. If he was out of breath, the vapor of his exhalations was invisible in the uncolored background. He rested his elbows and chest on the shallow snow and turned around.

I

FIGURE C.I. First page of Hernan Diaz's *In the Distance.*

doing littering the pages of *In the Distance*? How can we consider Diaz's novel a Latinx text? Does the simple belonging because of ancestry (with the one-drop rule dangerously close) make a text Latinx? Or can Latinx literature be designated through genre, as Ralph Rodriguez argues in *Latinx Literature Unbound* (2018)? Born in Argentina, Diaz emigrated with his family to Sweden when he was two years old because of his parents' left-leaning politics, which put them in danger during the 1970s military coup. Diaz and his family returned to Argentina when he was a boy, and he later received a PhD from New York University. He currently serves as the managing editor of the Spanish-language journal *Revista Hispánica Moderna*, housed in the Hispanic Institute at Columbia University. *In the Distance* was a finalist for the Pulitzer Prize, and his second novel, *Trust* (2022), was named one of the ten best books of 2022 by the *Washington Post* and the *New York Times*, was shortlisted for the Booker Prize, and won the 2023 Pulitzer Prize in fiction. Diaz's talent and his success in the literary market and prize circuit are quickly cementing him within the canon, although it is difficult to declare him a "Latinx writer" in a similar vein to authors like Junot Díaz and Cristina García, both of whom occupy principal positions within Latinx letters, have accumulated prestigious awards, and produce works that are easily identifiable as Latinx.

I have intentionally ended *Doom Patterns* with texts that trouble conventional notions of Latinx representation in literature. Authors like Colson Whitehead, Roberto Bolaño, and Sesshu Foster, I argue, participate in Latinx discourses and show us the importance of reading intra-ethnically and across national and generic borders. However, removed from ascriptions to brownness or traditional markers of *latinidad*, texts like Machado's *Her Body and Other Parties* and Diaz's *In the Distance* challenge our definitions of Latinx literature, and the situation they invoke invites us to re/define our canon.

Canon, (n.): the body of ecclesiastical law; body of rules and principles accepted as axiomatic and universally binding in a field of study; a standard.[13] Throughout *Doom Patterns*, I have argued for an expansion and redefinition of the Latinx literary canon, showing how reading intra-ethnically, transnationally, and inter- and transgenerically illustrates important networks that can lead to a deeper understanding of the formation of race, ethnicity, and depictions of violence. The literary canon as axiomatic—obvious, clear, manifest—is productively destabilized by many of the texts included in my study. *Cannon, cañon, (n.): a gun, mortar; (v.): to discharge said gun.*[14] Sound the alarms—barriers to entry are being dismantled! Part of the reason I am interested in *In the Distance* is that in its quiet starkness, the novel explodes what is deemed obvious by taking us to a time before labels such as Latino/a/x, *latinidad*, and homosexual were salient. *Canyon, (n.): a deep valley, steep sides, a stream flowing through it; gorge or ravine.*[15] The formation of canyons happens slowly, over time, by the down-cutting of water in a dry area where there is insufficient rainfall to erode the sides of the valley. How can this gorge and its homophones serve as a space through which to explore the formation of what we now call Latinx identity or the literary canon that would seem to represent it, or representations of race and ethnicity in literature, or speculative fiction and depictions of violence? A gorge in which to explore the depth of language and its possibilities and limitations?

In the Distance tells the story of Håkan Söderström as he emigrates from Sweden to the United States with his brother Linus in the mid-nineteenth century. While attempting to reach "Nujårk" (New York), the brothers are separated. As Håkan lands in California at the beginning of the state's incorporation into the republic after the Mexican-American War (1846–48) and moves to the Great Plains and back again, he encounters Gold Rush miners, a toothless female mercenary, a naturalist attempting to discover the origin of life, Native Americans, murderous Christians calling themselves "the brethren," and a Finish vintner. What, if anything, makes this novel Latinx? Is there a name more removed from *latinidad* than Håkan? What makes this novel speculative fiction? *In the Distance*, in fact, teeters between hyperrealism and the prototypical Western novel, a historical fantasy that veers into the strange and uncanny: a young Swedish immigrant grows to inhuman proportions and gains a mythical, godlike status based on his killing powers and healing abilities, all while living for what appear to be hundreds of years in a labyrinthian underground dwelling of his own creation. In my view, much like discovery narratives of the fifteenth and sixteenth centuries, Håkan's discovery of the "New World" presents the American landscape as otherworldly and fantastical. It is as if the West is being created as Håkan sees it and steps on it, with the land being formed through each step and each word on the page. The white space of the novel's opening reinforces the lifeless, desolate, cold landscape from which the protagonist emerges, almost as if he is birthing himself even as he forms the landscape by touching the edges of the hole.

In the Distance circulates in the reimagination of the past, especially in relation to American notions of expansionism and Manifest Destiny. But the novel also destabilizes temporal demarcations: placed squarely in the nineteenth century, *In the Distance* screams of the apocalyptic, presenting the American landscape as the remnant of a place recently destroyed. This elliptical narrative mode attends to current scales of catastrophe, from the global climate crisis to local ecological conservation and to large-scale immigration and the effects of foreign policy on individual emigrants/immigrants/migrants. Diaz has stated that in writing the novel, he wanted to "convey a sense of the past without fetishizing the past," a move that veers away from the idyllic romanticization of the American West.[16] This fetishization, with Manifest Destiny at its center, upholds a picture of the West as a rough, masculine space in which individualist identities and Americanness are forged. The image of the West, famously cemented in the United States' imaginary by Frederick Jackson Turner, was invoked to advocate a colonialist mission and lament the closing of the frontier.[17] Håkan arrives in the United States in the aftermath of this enterprise, and as Gary Okihiro states, Turner views the American West as the site that "sired and fostered the American spirit—rugged individualism, initiative and self-reliance, and democratic values."[18] Yet *In the Distance* subverts the genre of the Western by underscoring the illusions involved in the myth of the birth of the nation, starkly showcasing the greed, racism, and violence this birth elicited and required. Effectively, as Diaz states, *In the Distance* is a "Western without cowboys" that presents not only a portrait of radical foreignness but also a landscape with no heroes or hope.[19] Diaz's subversion of the genre cannot help but remind readers of the pervasive violence executed in the name of American expansionism, Manifest Destiny, and the settling of the West. As a Western that upends the genre's conventions, the novel continues to foreground the manliness associated with Westerns, presenting a world with few women but extending this logic to its conclusion by implicitly centering queer love.

The novel teeters between unnaming or obfuscating identity formations and calling them forth through spectral hauntings. The incongruous use of "cañon" in the opening and again with much more frequency as Håkan returns to California pushes the word conspicuously to the forefront and lends the landscape a foreignness that cannot help but remind its reader that this space was and still is Mexico. *In the Distance* is an anti-Western that does not glamorize westward expansion with all its imperialist implications. In fact, Håkan wishes to go east in search of his brother, and his journey is a labyrinthian trajectory of reverse Manifest Destiny that critiques the romanticization and mythmaking that went into the creation of the American nation. All of this makes the novel a powerful meditation on what it means to be an immigrant. What is more Latinx than this? For example, at the outset of the novel, as Håkan sails unknowingly to California from Sweden, through England and then Cape Horn, the journey looks as though he is going "to the end of the world" and underscores the unmooring experience of hearing a new language and arriving in a foreign land, an experience akin to science-fictional space travel and alien encounters: "To him, English was still a mudslide of runny, slushy sounds that did not exist in his mother tongue—r, th, sh, and some particularly gelatinous vowels. Frawder thur prueless rare shur per thurst. Mither freckling thow. Gold freys yawder far cration. Crewl fry rackler friend thur. No shemling keal rearand for fear under shall an frick."[20]

Yet, although *In the Distance* centers immigration, foreignness, and nationhood, *latinidad* in the novel must be read by, as Rodriguez proposes, "unbinding Latinx literature" from the parameters that govern the field—race, ethnicity, identity—and the questions of ethnic expectations, political agendas, and authenticity.[21] Ricardo Ortiz similarly asks scholars to consider the "seductive nature of at least one (meta)narrative of identity that still enjoys a powerful pull in contemporary U.S.-based Ethnic and Cultural Studies. As such, [preexisting identitarian hermeneutics] already show the impress of a field that too often mistakes the *content* of the narrative of historical cause, event, and consequence to the detriment of its deeper relational, even grammatological structures—that is, of its *form*."[22] *In the Distance* offers other avenues for reading *latinidad* as a speculative mode. In other words, *latinidad* is a temporal speculation and a generic convention that proposes to think about being Latinx as a speculative endeavor that necessitates the language of genre fiction.

Speculation takes on many valances in the novel, from the financial speculation of the prospectors on the boat headed to Alaska and Gold Rush miners in California to the myth and rumors surrounding Håkan himself, as well as his relationship with Asa, a man he meets while being returned to the brethren. Even his body teeters on the edge of the suprahuman, much like the nation-in-the-making does on the edge of the otherworldly. Throughout his travels in the United States, Håkan becomes an amalgam, his clothing taking on an impossible-to-determine provenance that mirrors his own unfixed self: "the European peasant, the Californian trapper, and the itinerant Indian had come together on an equal footing."[23] While his experience in the United States could have promised the fantasy of the multicultural melting pot, the novel undercuts this naive vision. In effect, Håkan's experience is evocative of many immigrant stories in that he feels displaced and never at home. Although the West is immense and expansive, the

> territories had never held him or embraced him—not even when he dug into the ground and found shelter in the earth's bosom. Anyone he met, including children, had, in his eyes, more right to be in that land than he did. Nothing was his; nothing claimed him. He had gone into the wilderness with the intention of coming out on the other end. That he had stopped trying did not mean that this was now his place.[24]

The inhospitable nation-in-the-making illustrates the violence of colonialism into which he unforgivingly writes himself: "Håkan realized now that he had always thought that these vast territories were empty—that he had believed they were inhabited only during the short period of time during which travelers were passing through them, and that, like the ocean in the wake of a ship, solitude closed up after the riders. He further understood that all those travelers, himself included, were, in fact, intruders."[25] The novel interpolates the reparative reading scholars like Patricia Stuelke write against.[26] Meditating on his role of tending to the wounded, for example, Håkan concludes that the correct approach is one of detachment, because anything else, including compassion, degrades the sufferers' pain: "Pity was insatiable—a false virtue that always craved more suffering to show how limitless and magnificent it could be."[27] As Lauren Berlant argues, sentimentality transforms what could or should be "acts of publicness" into a "world of private thoughts, leanings, and gestures," a "passive and vaguely civic-minded ideal of compassion."[28]

This "feeling of ethical action" that Håkan refuses illustrates the reading practice I outline in this book. If the opening page of In the Distance depicts a textual rift that emulates the hole in the ice from which Håkan emerges, it also signals a Mexicanidad that the use of "cañon" projects back into the landscape of Alaska in the novel's conclusion. California, and San Francisco specifically, is the space in which Håkan not only is cut off from his only familial connection but also becomes an American subject-in-formation, a designation he ultimately refuses. Another break occurs at the novel's culmination, which echoes and extends the one on the first page, this time illustrating a way to surpass the nation-state as much as that of the citizen subject. By the end of In the Distance, Håkan has given up any hope of finding his brother or finding peace within the American landscape, and his wandering takes on the unearthly valence of time travel in speculative fiction: "Years vanished under a weightless present. . . . Through countless frosts and thaws, he walked in circles wider than nations."[29] The gap of white space, which births Håkan's monstrous figure and surprises readers at the novel's outset, here assumes a destabilizing quality that destroys time and space, making concepts such as the nation or the West obsolete (figure C.2).

Returning to California after his failed journey in search of his brother, Håkan boards a ship to Alaska, which becomes stuck in the ice. In the novel's final pages, Håkan decides to disembark and walk to Sweden, a choice that signals his rejection of any form of incorporation into the American nation. "Now, I may walk over the sea. Otherwise, next winter. Then, a straight line west. To Sweden," he states.[30] Unable to forge meaningful and long-lasting con-

be settlements along the coastline. Whenever he stopped, it was at an inhospitable location—never in a meadow, by a water source, or in a plentiful spot—barely pitching camp and seldom making fires. It was dead quiet in his mind. He rarely thought of anything that was not at hand. Years vanished under a weightless present.

Through countless frosts and thaws, he walked in circles wider than nations.

And then he stopped.

Years of marching almost barefoot had turned his feet into dark knotty things. Blisters, splinters, and wounds had affected his gait, and now he walked by resting mostly on the outer edges of his soles. This bowlegged stance had damaged his knees, as a result of which, his legs were not as agile as they used to be. Even if, in time, he had learned to get by with almost nothing, he had always packed a few essentials on his

FIGURE C.2. Page 206 of Hernan Diaz's *In the Distance*.

nections or to imagine a space for himself in the United States, Håkan undoes himself and the novel. Just as when Mark Spitz walks into the zombie horde, which I examine in chapter 2, we do not see Håkan's death or his survival but are left to contend with the white space in his wake. Will he make it to Sweden? One can only hope. But it is the white space of the page—almost as if he is returning us to the hole that opened the novel—that is so enticing. If we are truly thinking beyond binaries and borders, what does this white space offer?

Is the *X* in *Latinx* a Grave?

If *In the Distance* is a Western without cowboys, it is also a gay novel without gay people and, to use William Orchard's phrase, it illustrates a "latinidad without Latinos."[31] Another entry point for this conclusion is Leo Bersani's 1987 essay "Is the Rectum a Grave?" I use *entry point* deliberately here as an invitation to think with and in the ass but also with the implications of thinking from the bottom, the rear, and, of course, the hole, with all the dirty and messy associations that these words connote. I want to think from the bottom as a way to reflect on what concepts such as *jouissance* and the undoing of the self offer for this book's methodology and the unfastening of ethno-racial identitarian subjectivity it proposes. To think from the bottom is also about challenging canon formations and expected depictions of *latinidad* in literature; it is to think from the hole we have dug for ourselves in the field.

As Bersani illustrates, the rectum is a space of pleasure and desire, as well as violence and death, in which this interplay opens up spaces through which to consider new and important ways to undo the self. Writing at the height of the HIV/AIDS crisis and in light of state-sponsored erasures of and violence toward the gay community, Bersani argues that conventional notions of sex and sexuality limit the potential for intimacy and pleasure. He further suggests that the rectum is the place where the "masculine ideal . . . of proud subjectivity is buried," where a self-annihilation can be observed and where "the opposition between pleasure and pain becomes irrelevant, in which the sexual emerges as the *jouissance* of exploded limits, as the ecstatic suffering into which the human organism momentarily plunges when it is 'pressed' beyond a certain threshold of endurance."[32] My reading of *In the Distance* and Bersani's question about the rectum focus on how the rectum dismantles the self in the same way that the *x* in *Latinx* proposes not only a way to destabilize male-female gender binaries and heterosexist language practices but also a way to think at the limits of *latinidad* and consider what might take its place.

The cañons of the novel, the tunnels and holes where Håkan dwells for years, invite us to reexamine the Latinx literary canon as well as the formation of various identities, from the ethno-racial to the gendered and sexual. While on his journey, Håkan meets a man named Asa who rescues him from being returned to the brethren for a ransom. After fleeing to the cañons, the two live together for what seem to be many years, although narratively this time is never specified. The cañons are, significantly, outside the official borders of the United States, which enables the characters to evade the law and gives them a space through which open-ended and fluid identities can begin to take shape while never being finite. Their time together in the cañons elicits a new set of affective possibilities for Håkan and Asa, as well as for the reader's understanding of identity formations.[33] Helping Håkan escape, Asa says that the cañons are their "only hope," a place they can get lost in, a "land like no other. Like a bad dream. Red tunnels carved by long-gone rivers. Like old scars in the ground. Very deep. For leagues and leagues. Few go in. Fewer get out."[34] Their method of escaping the brethren assumes the language of the strange and otherworldly while offering a space to investigate new desires. Although it is never stated outright, the two are what we, as modern readers, would think of as being in love. In the cañons, Håkan learns to smile for the first time, and Asa even changes the landscape for our protagonist. The topography is no longer "the oppressive immensity whose existence, for such a long time, had somehow been entrusted to Håkan's lonely gaze."[35] As Bersani's text does, Diaz's novel shatters identificatory practices out of the body while signaling the body linguistically: gay sex or its intimation does not reproduce the social order. While living in the cañons, Asa lies down next to Håkan one night:

> At first, the proximity of Asa's body frightened him. Not daring to move, he looked up at the stars, wondering if Asa, who held him from behind, perfectly still, was also awake. Not knowing why, Håkan matched his breathing with Asa's. They breathed together. . . . From that night on, always around the darkest hour and after the embers had paled under the ashes, Asa would come over to Håkan and lie by his side.[36]

The two never speak of this new routine, but readers can identify it as homosocial or even gay. Håkan finally asks him, albeit indirectly, "Why did you do this?" He clarifies that "this" means "help me," but we can also interpose other meanings: "love me," perhaps, or be "gay" with me. To this Asa simply responds, "Because I saw you and I knew."[37] Asa's statement is the end of this chapter, and the silence that follows is at the heart of my argument. What does "I knew" mean? I knew you would lie with me; I knew you were gay too; I knew you were a good person?

Within this shattering, *In the Distance* presents readers with a context for illegibility: the novel offers a historical construction of the concept of *latinidad* through its setting in the mid-nineteenth century while also speculating about a future construction for this identity that cannot yet be seen and simultaneously predates the concept of a gay identity while indicating its presence and composition in the past that cannot name it yet. The confluence among proto-gayness, proto-Americanness, and Latinx-in-disguise suggests that *In the Distance* offers other avenues for reading *latinidad* as a speculative mode. Following Bersani, I wonder if the *x* in *Latinx* is a grave that delimits where the field has been, where it is now, and to what unknown places it is going. This *x*, like *x* in a mathematical equation, is the symbol that must be solved. In "Burning X's," Ortiz reads the *x* as announcing itself "not merely as a gesture toward both a past it desires to connect and outgrow and a future it hails but refuses to name, but also a deep, critical dig into the complicated now."[38] Ortiz also reads the *x* as a deferral—in time space—that positions this ending not as an alternative but as a refusal to conclude at all. Foremost for my reading of *In the Distance*, this "suspension in time's unfolding" does not just include queerness and transness more visibly within the construction of *latinidad* but "saturates *latinidad* with queerness, with transness, insisting instead on an alternative construal of a *latinidad* that itself now becomes unthinkable and unsayable without queerness, without transness."[39] Seen in this way, the *x* can help us read *In the Distance* as proposing a *latinidad* that is a temporal speculation and a generic convention, and can invite us to think about being Latinx as a speculative endeavor that requires the language of genre fiction. Thinking from the hole, the *x* elaborates itself as an absence as well, an erasure of the histories of Indigeneity, Blackness, queerness, and transness from *latinidad* that scholars have criticized.[40] The calls for the cancellation of *latinidad* nevertheless open up other holes and possibilities. As Ortiz argues, the *x* refuses Latin_ an ending at all, and I follow him in this line of thinking by proposing the *x* as a grave that not only undoes expected identitarian representations but also generates new openings that we cannot yet name or define.

Díaz's novel offers a field on the edge: will we collapse through texts that move away from representations as they have been? To suggest that *latinidad* is on the edge is to tease the threads of sexual innuendo and push the boundaries of ethno-racial depictions in fiction. Among the claims that *latinidad* is cancelled, can we imagine what will become of the field as it reckons with its erasure of Indigeneity and Blackness in the Americas or as more authors circumvent what until now have been considered authentic portrayals of Latinx identity in fiction? Is *latinidad* like porn, in that we know it when we see it?

Throughout *Doom Patterns*, I examine how these novels use the forms of genre fiction to imagine identity categories as fluid and capable of maneuvering nimbly from nation-based to pan-Latinx networks and beyond. These texts re-scale from the national to the global, signaling specific historical moments and the *longue durée* and exposing vast systems that oppress minoritized people. This book offers scholars invested in the study of race, ethnicity, form, and speculative fiction a set of tools with which to build a reading practice that uses the speculative to erode boundaries, signaling the interethnic transnational alliances that drove ethnic studies in the era of its formation. Debates about the use of *Latinx* similarly show a field contending with itself. Perhaps Håkan's journey offers a speculation about where the field is heading without being able to fully name it yet: "traveling away from the past but not into the future. He had remained in a constant present, leaving landscapes and people behind but never heading toward a more or less certain destination that he could not foresee."[41] Texts like *In the Distance* return us to *Latinx* and its own speculative signification, expanding this theorization of *latinidad* to underscore how being Latinx in all its diverse ethno-national and racial forms is an otherworldly and fantastical mode of existence that entails thinking beyond the analogical. This speculative theorization of *latinidad* is concretized in the protocols of Latinx speculative fiction, which remind us that the histories that have shaped Latinx subjectivity are so excessive and outrageous that they seem taken from the plots of speculative fiction.

Notes

INTRODUCTION

1. Caitlin Roper, "Preface," in *New York Times Magazine*, "Decameron Project," ix.

2. Rivka Galchen, "Introduction," in *New York Times Magazine*, "Decameron Project," xv.

3. Boccaccio, *Decameron*.

4. I say "lost" here because the manuscript that Adana destroys is retold by Maxwell to Saul's grandfather when they meet as teenagers in Chicago. Saul's grandfather in turn transcribes the book and ostensibly rewrites (and therefore "re-finds") the novel.

5. Zapata, *Lost Book*, 48. This is also how the Dominican Republic is framed in Junot Díaz's *The Brief Wondrous Life of Oscar Wao* (2007), which establishes the island as the catalyst for the modern/colonial divide and which I explore in chapter 1.

6. Zapata, *Lost Book*, 48.

7. Throughout this book, I use the term *realist* to refer to traditional narrative forms that are distinct from genre fiction and the fantastic, not necessarily to realism as a literary movement.

8. Zapata, *Lost Book*, 167 (emphasis in original).

9. Zapata, *Lost Book*, 167.

10. Zapata, *Lost Book*, 169.

11. My definition of *elsewheres* differs from that of Paula Moya and Lesley Larkin, who define them as "alternative worlds . . . that facilitate the development of more racially just and life-affirming selves and ways of living." "Decolonial Virtues," 228. Yomaira Figueroa-Vásquez similarly presents "worlds/otherwise" to consider ruptures across modernity and coloniality that contain possibilities for the future and are "part and parcel of a reparation of the imagination." *Decolonizing Diasporas*, 148. As I explain in this introduction and throughout *Doom Patterns*, *elsewheres* designates alternative worlds that are created by narrative strategies that return readers again and again to historical violence and destruction.

12. In *Race and Upward Mobility*, Elda María Román shows the various strategies Mexican Americans and African Americans use to negotiate US power relations and the constraints of neoliberal capitalism that compel them to align with white middle-classness.

13. *Rasquachismo* is a theory developed by Tomás Ybarra-Frausto to describe "an underdog perspective," a view from "*los de abajo*" (from below) and which uses elements of "hybridization, juxtaposition, and integration" as a means of resistance. Ybarra-Frausto, "Rasquachismo," 85–90.

14. Renee Hudson's *Latinx Revolutionary Horizons* also destabilizes *latinidad* by proposing a historicized sense of the term to argue for its political abilities in-the-making.

15. I have been greatly inspired in particular by Machado Sáez, *Market Aesthetics*; Rohrleitner, *Transnational Latinidades*; Lamas, *Latino Continuum*; Harford Vargas, *Forms of Dictatorship*; and Hudson, *Latinx Revolutionary Horizons*.

16. Delany, "Generic Protocols," 176.

17. Delany, "Generic Protocols," 177.

18. Delany, "Generic Protocols," 177.

19. Sperling, "How to Read."

20. Rosen, *Minor Characters*, 22.

21. Berlant, *Cruel Optimism*, 6 (emphasis in original); and Berlant, *Female Complaint*, 19.

22. Hartman, "Venus in Two Acts," 14.

23. Hartman, "Venus in Two Acts," 11. Nicole Guidotti-Hernández similarly takes up the silencing of racialized and sexualized subjects from the archives of the American borderlands. *Unspeakable Violence*, 4–6. Dixa Ramírez proposes the concept of "ghosting" for thinking about how colonial, imperial, and nationalist forms of power are enacted. See D. Ramírez, *Colonial Phantoms*. Anne McClintock turns to "imperial ghosting" to speak of the erasure that takes place through US imperialism. See McClintock, "Imperial Ghosting." See also Trouillot, *Silencing the Past*; Taylor, *Archive and the Repertoire*; and Bergland, *National Uncanny*.

24. Hartman, *Wayward Lives, Beautiful Experiments*, xiii.

25. Muñoz, *Cruising Utopia*, 65–81.

26. Muñoz, *Cruising Utopia*, 3. Guidotti-Hernández examines the meaning found in the "unspeakable" and "the utterance" as a reminder of violence's foundational role in the formation of national histories and subjectivities that are usually elided. *Unspeakable Violence*, 5–7.

27. Chuh, *Difference Aesthetics Makes*, 20. Wai Chee Dimock similarly uses the concept of "deep time" to thread previously unimagined kinship networks, routes of transit, and attachment relations. See Dimock, *Through Other Continents*, 3–4.

28. See Benjamin, *Illuminations*, 257–58.

29. Gordon, *Ghostly Matters*, xvi.

30. Gordon, *Ghostly Matters*, 7.

31. Gordon, *Ghostly Matters*, 25.

32. Del Pilar Blanco, *Ghost-Watching American Modernity*, 8. Mary Pat Brady's *Extinct Lands/Temporal Geographies* similarly turns to literature to explore the changing and haunted spaces of the US borderlands.

33. Adorno and Horkheimer, *Dialectic of Enlightenment*, 215.

34. Gordon, *Ghostly Matters*, xvi. See also Holland, *Raising the Dead*.

35. Gordon, *Ghostly Matters*, 25.

36. Dictionary.com, s.v. "doom (*n.*)," accessed April 1, 2024, https://www.dictionary.com/browse/doom.

37. Postmodern aesthetics have been most importantly theorized by Linda Hutcheon, Fredric Jameson, and Jean-François Lyotard. The work of Robert Elliot Fox, Henry Louis Gates Jr., and Madhu Dubey has greatly informed my thinking about the specificity and difference in postmodern aesthetics in works by people of color. See Fox, *Conscientious Sorcerers*; Gates, *Signifying Monkey*; Dubey, "Contemporary African American Fiction"; and Dubey, *Signs and Cities*.

38. *Oxford English Dictionary*, s.v. "doom (n.)," accessed April, 11, 2024, https://www.oed.com/dictionary/doom_n?tab=meaning_and_use#6132789.

39. See Kermode, *Sense of an Ending*.

40. Saldívar has presented this argument in "Imagining Cultures," "The Second Elevation of the Novel," and "The Other Side of History, the Other Side of Fiction."

41. R. Saldívar, "Other Side of History," 158.

42. R. Saldívar, "Speculative Realism," 519.

43. Jameson, *Postmodernism*. His exploration of Vincent van Gogh's and Andy Warhol's paintings of shoes (6–16) is particularly demonstrative of this point. Terry Eagleton also takes this view of postmodernism in "Capitalism, Modernism and Postmodernism."

44. Marcus, Love, and Best, "Building a Better Description"; Cheng, *Second Skin*; McMillan, "Introduction"; Muñoz, "From Surface to Depth"; and Musser, *Sensual Excess*.

45. McMillan, "Introduction," 5. Kadji Amin, Amber Jamilla Musser, and Roy Pérez show how form operates beneath the surface of the visual, to account for the affective and sensuous. See Amin, Musser, and Pérez, "Queer Form." To the affective and sensuous, I would also add the historical as it makes itself manifest in form.

46. Musser, *Sensual Excess*, 49; Hutcheon, *Poetics of Postmodernism*, 50; Cheng, *Second Skin*, 9-10.

47. Hutcheon, *Poetics of Postmodernism*, 4.

48. In my analysis of excessive forms and aesthetics, I draw on the work of Jack Halberstam's *Skin Shows*, Eve Kosofsky Sedgwick's *The Coherence of Gothic Conventions*, Jillian Hernandez's *Aesthetics of Excess*, Deborah Vargas's "Ruminations on *Lo Sucio*," and Leticia Alvarado's *Abject Performances*.

49. Berlant, "Genre Flailing," 157.

50. Scarry, *Body in Pain*.

51. *Oxford English Dictionary*, s.v., "pattern (n.)," accessed April 11, 2024, https://www.oed.com/dictionary/pattern_n?tab=meaning_and_use#31803324.

52. *Oxford English Dictionary*, s.v., "pattern (v.)," accessed April 11, 2024, https://www.oed.com/dictionary/pattern_v?tab=meaning_and_use#31807458.

53. Scholars have turned to the literary for its particular use for exploring the world. Gordon argues that literary fiction illuminates, through imaginative design, what cannot be accessed with the rules and methods of professionalized social sciences. *Ghostly Matters*, 25. See also Levine, *Forms*.

54. Trouillot, *Silencing the Past*, 24. See also Anderson, *Imagined Communities*.

55. Goyal, *Runaway Genres*, 31, 30. The politics of artistic practice has been debated by theorists and artists, who interrogate the relationship among cultural production, society,

history, and politics. The debates among Ernst Bloch, George Lukács, Bertolt Brecht, Walter Benjamin, and Theodor Adorno in the 1930s illustrate differing views of what they considered the committed artist's responsibility and function in creating works of art for the transformation of society, and the importance of artistic form—expressionism, abstraction, naturalism, and so on—and modes of production in this endeavor. See Adorno et al., *Aesthetics and Politics*.

56. Harford Vargas, *Forms of Dictatorship*.

57. Scholars have shown the importance of formal analysis and the relation of the literary to the sociohistorical. See Harford Vargas, *Forms of Dictatorship*; Woloch, *One vs. the Many*; Moya, *Social Imperative*; and Levine, "Strategic Formalism."

58. See Chuh, *Difference Aesthetics Makes*, 3–4, 21. See also Eagleton, *Ideology of the Aesthetic*, 8–9.

59. Chuh, *Difference Aesthetics Makes*, 18–21; and Welsch, *Undoing Aesthetics*, 8.

60. Chuh investigates how aesthetics have been formed through subjugated ways of knowing and offers new avenues for examining what she calls "illiberal" humanism. *Difference Aesthetics Makes*, 6–7. See also Felski, *Hooked*.

61. Nixon, *Slow Violence*, 3.

62. Sedgwick, *Touching Feeling*, 1–37; and Ricœur, *Freud and Philosophy*. Rita Felski similarly decenters "critique" as a leading practice in literary studies. See Felski, *Limits of Critique*.

63. Robyn Wiegman's *Object Lessons* investigates identity-based fields in the academy as organized around questions of social justice. In Latinx literary and cultural studies, Raphael Dalleo and Elena Machado Sáez's *The Latino/a Canon and Post-Sixties Literature* argues that contemporary Latinx writers continue to formulate political projects that renew the tradition of the 1960s and 1970s, and Rafael Pérez-Torres's introduction to the "Latinx Temporality as a Time of Crisis" dossier for *Aztlán* questioned the institutionalization of Latinx and Chicanx studies and these fields' ability to serve as "agents of transformation." Pérez-Torres, "Introduction," 154. See also Olguín, *Violentologies*, 11; Rivero, "Hispanic Literature"; and J. Flores, *From Bomba to Hip-Hop*, 199–200. Marta Caminero-Santangelo notes that Latinx literary texts are assumed to advance a progressive ideology and that when they do not fit this mold, they are excluded from the field. Caminero-Santangelo, *On Latinidad*, 12.

64. Anzaldúa, *Borderlands/La Frontera*, 25.

65. Torres, *We the Animals*, 116.

66. Torres, *We the Animals*, 125.

67. Appelbaum, *Aesthetics of Violence*, 13.

68. Olguín, *Violentologies*, 37.

69. Olguín, *Violentologies*, 12.

70. Jerng, *Racial Worldmaking*, 8.

71. Maldonado Torres, *Against War*; O'Gorman, *La invención de América*; Mignolo, *Idea of Latin America*; and Quijano and Wallerstein, "Americanity as a Concept."

72. Others who have focused on violence as fundamentally inscribed in Latinx subjectivity include Anzaldúa, Roberto Hernández (in *Coloniality of the US/Mexico Border*), and Guidotti-Hernández (in *Unspeakable Violence*). Violence is also central to many minoritized literatures and fields of study; see Fanon, *Wretched of the Earth*.

73. Guidotti-Hernández, *Unspeakable Violence*. Monica Muñoz Martinez's *The Injustice Never Leaves You* similarly underscores the horror of anti-Mexican violence in the borderlands that undermines official narratives that would whitewash these stories of violence.

74. Guidotti-Hernández, *Unspeakable Violence*, 2.

75. See Pinto, *Infamous Bodies*, 7, 19; Goyal, *Runaway Genres*, 32–33; Keen, *Empathy and the Novel*; Guidotti-Hernández, *Unspeakable Violence*, 23–24; and Vogler, "Moral of the Story." In *Migrant Aesthetics*, Glenda Carpio makes the distinction between art that creates empathy and that which seeks "truthfulness," the latter being that which works toward political justice (9).

76. Pinto, *Infamous Bodies*, 22; and Guidotti-Hernández, *Unspeakable Violence*, 24.

77. Muñoz, *Sense of Brown*, 119.

78. *Merriam-Webster.com*, s.v., "speculate," accessed April 12, 2024, https://www.merriam-webster.com/dictionary/speculate.

79. *Merriam-Webster.com*, s.v., "speculate," accessed April 12, 2024, https://www.merriam-webster.com/dictionary/speculate.

80. Žižek, *Living in the End Times*, xii. See also Derrida, "Of an Apocalyptic Tone"; and Benjamin, "Theses."

81. Berger, *After the End*, 5.

82. Said, *Beginnings*, 41–42. Kyle Powys Whyte and Kim TallBear have shown how the apocalypse has already occurred for Indigenous peoples. See Whyte, "Our Ancestors' Dystopia Now"; and TallBear, "Indigenous Genocide and Reanimation."

83. Berger, *After the End*, 14.

84. Fish, "Literature in the Reader."

85. Fish, "Literature in the Reader," 125.

86. I am, of course, invoking Stanley Fish's renowned formulation of literature here.

87. Jameson, *Archaeologies of the Future*, xv–xvi; and Maguire, "Science Fiction."

88. carrington, *Speculative Blackness*; Jerng, *Racial Worldmaking*; Lavender, *Race*; C. Ramírez, "Cyborg Feminism"; Rivera, "Future Histories"; Schalk, *Bodyminds Reimagined*; and Darieck Scott, *Keeping It Unreal*.

89. Emily Maguire's survey of Latinx science fiction opens with the question, "Is there a Latino/a science fiction?" Maguire, "Science Fiction," 351. Christopher González begins his chapter for *Latinos and Narrative Media* (2013) with a similarly inclined question, "Why are there so few such works created by Latinos in the United States?" González, "Latino Sci-Fi," 211.

90. Goodwin, *Latinx Files*, 6.

91. Goodwin, *Latinx Files*, 6.

92. Latinx speculative fiction is in dialogue with Alejo Carpentier's notion of "lo real maravilloso" (the marvelous real). See Carpentier, *El reino de este mundo*. Gabriel García Márquez also presented Latin America's "outsized reality" in his Nobel acceptance speech, "The Solitude of Latin America." Other useful sources that consider the effects of history on genre are Jameson, *Archaeologies of the Future*; Gil'Adí and Mann, "New Suns"; and R. Saldívar, "Imagining Cultures."

93. C. Ramírez, "Cyborg Feminism," 396.

94. Hogan, "Chicanonautica Manifesto"; and Merla-Watson, "Latinofuturism." Linda Heidenreich, Luz María Gordillo, Amalia Ortíz, and Cynthia Saldívar Hull all propose that horror, the gothic, and the postapocalyptic are enduring truths of Latinx subjectivity. See Heidenreich, "Colonial Pasts, Utopian Futures"; Gordillo, "Contesting Monstrosity"; A. Ortiz, "Canción Cannibal Cabaret"; and C. Saldívar, "#rapetreesarereal."

95. Bahng, *Migrant Futures*; Jerng, *Racial Worldmaking*; Merla-Watson and Olguín, *Altermundos*; Sanchez Taylor, *Diverse Futures*; Kondo, *Worldmaking*; Dubey, "Octavia Butler's Novels"; Keeling, *Queer Times, Black Futures*; Gil'Adí, "Sugar Apocalypse"; Mann, "Pessimistic Futurism"; C. Ramírez, "Cyborg Feminism"; Schalk, *Bodyminds Reimagined*; and Michelle Wright, *Physics of Blackness*.

96. R. Saldívar, "Imagining Cultures," 1.

97. Merla-Watson and Olguín, *Altermundos*; Merla-Watson and Olguín, "Dossier: Latin@ Speculative Literature, Film, and Popular Culture"; and Merla-Watson and Olguín, "Dossier: From the Horrific to the Utopic."

98. In "The Law of Genre," Jacques Derrida shows how "genre" is always already announcing its "limit" and "contamination," and therefore exceeds classification and policing. Also see Goyal, *Runaway Genres*; and Goddu, *Gothic America*. Antecedents of contemporary Latinx speculative fiction can be seen in Anzaldúa's *Borderlands/La Frontera*, Oscar "Zeta" Acosta's *The Revolt of the Cockroach People* (1973), and Ron Arias's *The Road to Tamazunchale* (1975).

99. Hogan, "Chicanonautica Manifesto," 131.

100. C. Ramírez, "Cyborg Feminism," 389.

101. On the usefulness of *latinidad*, see Milian, "Extremely Latin, xoxo"; Viego, "LatinX"; Aparicio, "Latinidad/es"; J. Rodríguez, "Latino/a/x"; R. Ortiz, *Latinx Literature Now*; Orchard, "Bruja Theory"; and Guzmán and León, "Cuts and Impressions." On the term's cancellation, see T. Flores, "'Latinidad Is Cancelled.'"

102. Lamas, *Latino Continuum*, 5. In *Cotton Mather's Spanish Lessons*, Kirsten Silva Gruesz illustrates how the entangled histories of the Americas in the seventeenth and eighteenth centuries inform and develop contemporary understandings of literary history, space, the nation, race, racialization and its relationship to language, and *latinidad*. In this way, Gruesz, as Lamas does, exemplifies how what we now understand as Latinx and *latinidad* have a longer and more complicated history than imagined. Also see Cutler, "Latinx Historicisms."

103. Mary Pat Brady's *Scales of Captivity* describes how scalar ideologies order the world into social and nested hierarchies, producing a singular world order at the service of containment under colonial and capitalist structures of power.

104. Harford Vargas, *Forms of Dictatorship*, 25. On how the term whitewashes difference, see Gruesz, "Once and Future Latino," 117; Beltrán, *Trouble with Unity*, 6; R. Ortiz, *Latinx Literature Now*, xiii.

105. H. González, "Why I Chose"; Morales, "Why I Embrace"; and Staff, "What's the Right Way to Pronounce Latinx?"

106. Hudson, "Latinidad."

107. Milian, *LatinX*, 12.

108. Viego, "LatinX," 162. Alan Pelaez Lopez similarly argues that the *x* functions as a wound that marks the histories of settler colonialism, anti-Blackness, femicide, and inarticulation. See Pelaez Lopez, "X in Latinx."

109. Hartman, "Venus in Two Acts," 14.

110. Gómez-Barris and Fiol-Matta, "Introduction," 504.

111. Ellen McCracken investigates the important effect Latina writers had on American fiction in the past two decades of the twentieth century in *New Latina Narrative*. Dalleo and Machado Sáez's *The Latino/a Canon and the Emergence of Post-Sixties Literature* also considers the 1990s as instrumental for the construction of a Latinx canon and the incorporation of Latinx authors within the literary market.

112. Mignolo, *The Idea of Latin America*, xii–xiii; Mignolo, *Local Histories/Global Designs*, xxv, 3.

113. This phrase comes from Ralph Rodriguez's *Latinx Literature Unbound*.

CHAPTER 1. DOOM PATTERNING THE POSTCOLONY AND THE NEW CARIBBEAN MYTHOLOGY

A section of chapter 1 appeared as "'I Think about You, X—': Re-reading Junot Díaz after 'The Silence,'" *Latino Studies* 18, no. 4 (2020): 507–30.

1. Díaz, *This Is How You Lose Her*, 22.

2. Díaz, *This Is How*, 24.

3. Díaz, *This Is How*, 24.

4. My use of *repeatedly* is a reference to Antonio Benítez-Rojo's influential text *The Repeating Island*, in which he reorients Caribbean identity through a postmodern theorization of the "geographic accident" of the Antilles as a "historico-economic" geography of repeating histories and, in my estimation, repeating violences. See Benítez-Rojo, *Repeating Island*, 2, 9.

5. Hall, "Cultural Identity and Diaspora," 234.

6. Hall, "Cultural Identity and Diaspora," 236.

7. Hall, "Cultural Identity and Diaspora," 235.

8. Díaz's writing, and *Oscar Wao* in particular, has generated a large volume of scholarship. Most centers fukú as a metaphorical framework for thinking about the remainder of coloniality within the Americas, and specifically as embodied by Rafael Trujillo. It would be impossible to provide a comprehensive list of scholarship on Díaz's fiction, but the following thinkers have influenced and pushed my analysis of his work: Figueroa-Vásquez, *Decolonizing Diasporas*; Hanna, "Reassembling the Fragments"; Harford Vargas, *Forms of Dictatorship*; Irrizary, "This Is How You Lose It"; Lethabo King, *The Black Shoals*; Machado Sáez, *Market Aesthetics*; D. Ramírez, *Colonial Phantoms*; and R. Saldívar, "Imagining Cultures."

9. Yomaira Figueroa-Vásquez argues that *Oscar Wao* is narrated with a decolonial imperative in which legacies of violence (coloniality of power, gender, knowledge) are "countered and confronted." See Figueroa-Vásquez, *Decolonizing Diasporas*, 85-86.

10. Díaz, *This Is How*, 25.

11. Yunior is a creative writer who constantly reflects on his writerly process. The narrative act in Díaz's work is significant not only for its telling (in its aural and oral

qualities)—and in the case of sections of *Oscar Wao*, its retelling—but also for the act of creating a tangible written record.

12. Díaz, *Oscar Wao*, 22.

13. I refer here to Hannah Arendt's "banality of evil," from *Eichmann in Jerusalem* (1963), in which she delineates how the "terrifying normal" (Eichmann) participated in the horrifying events of the Holocaust. B. V. Olguín's *Violentologies* examines a pan-Latinx archive that demonstrates how violence is embedded in Latinx subjectivities.

14. Ramón Saldívar argues that *Oscar Wao* carries a "recurrent motif of doom which structures the fantasy about this intersection of history, fantasy, and racial otherness." See R. Saldívar, "Imagining Cultures," 6. I, too, argue that *Oscar Wao* is organized around this principle but emphasize how fukú enacts an inescapable violence that never allows for the possibility of decolonial political remedy and that, moreover, enables Yunior and the reader to find pleasure in recreations of violence.

15. Cognitive estrangement is developed from the work of Viktor Shklovsky's "ostranenie" and Bertolt Brecht's "Verfremdungseffekt." See Suvin, *Metamorphoses of Science Fiction*, 18-19.

16. Darko Suvin's notion of the "novum" derives from Ernst Bloch's *The Principle of Hope* (1954), which describes the novum as the unexpectedly new that pushes us out of the present to imagine the not yet realized in the future. This notion is most beautifully taken up by José Esteban Muñoz in *Cruising Utopia*.

17. In "'I Think about You, X—,'" I offer a close reading of Díaz's nonfiction account and show how representations of women's bodies in "The Silence" complicate his public apology and essay about his experience of sexual abuse. See Gil'Adí, "'I Think about You, X—.'"

18. It has been assumed that *Oscar Wao* has multiple narrators, and that Lola, Oscar's sister, narrates two sections. See Figueroa-Vásquez, *Decolonizing Diasporas*, 81. Elena Machado Sáez also argues that there are many and oftentimes differing Yuniors, as does Glenda Carpio in *Migrant Aesthetics*, 160. Yunior, however, is the writer of this "fukú story" and, as a result, all information is mediated through his pen.

19. Díaz, *Oscar Wao*, 1.

20. Omise'eke Natasha Tinsley examines the gendered language in Benítez-Rojo's work. See Tinsley, "Black Atlantic, Queer Atlantic"; and Benítez-Rojo, *Repeating Island*, 2.

21. Benítez-Rojo, "Three Words toward Creolization," 54.

22. Although Benítez-Rojo argues that the Caribbean is "anti-apocalyptic" (*Repeating Island*, 10), Martin Munro illustrates how the region's history has been shaped by apocalyptic events with no apparent end. See Munro, *Tropical Apocalypse*, 11. The *Small Axe* project "The Visual Life of Catastrophic History" similarly illustrates how the Caribbean was inaugurated by catastrophe and continues in a perpetual state of emergency.

23. Díaz, *Oscar Wao*, 1.

24. The text also grounds itself in the tradition of the post-9/11 novel, presenting its scope of analysis as one that underscores fukú's remaining presence by equating the Columbian encounter and colonialism with contemporary terrorism, and the Caribbean as analogous to the deep crevasses that remain in the wake of the World Trade Center's destruction. José David Saldívar sees Oscar's murder in 1995 as part of the novel's "nuclear

sublime Cold War fantasies" and not within a post-9/11 imaginary. While I agree that the novel is clearly invested in the sociopolitical impact of Cold War–era global politics, I also think it would be facetious to dismiss *Oscar Wao*'s clear participation in and contribution to the post-9/11 novel by writers of color published in the early and mid-2000s. See J. D. Saldívar, *Trans-Americanity*, 209.

25. I am indebted to Walter Mignolo and José Buscaglia-Salgado, who have explored the "Atlantic imaginary" and "European Ideal," respectively. See Mignolo, *Local Histories/ Global Designs*; and Buscaglia-Salgado, *Undoing Empire*. They are by no means the only ones who have discussed this issue, and my thinking is also indebted to Edward Said, José Rabasa, Enrique Dussel, Susan Gillman, and Kirsten Silva Gruesz.

26. Quijano, "Coloniality of Power," 218.

27. Quijano, "Coloniality of Power," 218.

28. Mignolo, *Local Histories/Global Designs*, 13.

29. Lincoln, *Discourse and the Construction of Society*, 24–25, quoted in Wald, *Contagious*, 10.

30. I do not mean this list to be exhaustive, as that would reaffirm the erasure of specificity by mythic speech. My brief list is intended to highlight a few of the violences performed in the Columbian Encounter and in its aftermath, and moreover is mentioned here as a way to elicit other instances in the reader's mind.

31. See Buscaglia-Salgado, *Undoing Empire*; and DeGuzmán, *Spain's Long Shadow*. Dixa Ramírez explores the intersection of European colonialism, US empire, and Dominican patriarchal nationalism, arguing that working-class and diasporic Dominican men resist the imperialist and nationalist violence seen in the celebration of figures like Columbus. See D. Ramírez, *Colonial Phantoms*, 111–52.

32. See Horsman, *Race and Manifest Destiny*; and Gómez, *Manifest Destinies*.

33. Díaz, *Oscar Wao*, 6.

34. Díaz, *Oscar Wao*, 6.

35. The "Watcher" is a reference to the *Fantastic Four*'s Uatu the Watcher. It is easy for readers (myself included) to be seduced by Yunior's voice, but we should always remember that he is an effect of *Oscar Wao*'s narration and is being narrated, even as his story appears to be told by an unmediated voice. Anna Rodríguez Navas and Ruth McHugh-Dillon also investigate Yunior's conspiratorial storytelling. See Navas, "Words as Weapons,"; and McHugh-Dillon, "'Let Me Confess.'"

36. I'm being playful here in referencing Yunior's turn to the reader when referencing his goal of not cheating on Lola: "Don't laugh. My intentions were pure." Díaz, *Oscar Wao*, 199.

37. For more on Yunior's narrative strategies, see Machado Sáez, *Market Aesthetics*; Harford Vargas, *Forms of Dictatorship*; and Hanna, "Reassembling the Fragments."

38. Díaz, *Oscar Wao*, 3 (emphasis in original).

39. See Machado Sáez, *Market Aesthetics*, 175. Lyn Di Iorio also touches on humor in the novel and the curse's phonetic similarity to "fuck you" in "Laughing through a Broken Mouth."

40. For the etymology of "fucu," see Deive, *Diccionario de Dominicanismos*, 95; and Derby, *Dictator's Seduction*. Díaz did not invent the concept of *fukú* but uses it as a

foundational framework for his novel and the history of the Americas. See Díaz, "Junot Díaz by Edwidge Danticat."

41. Machado Sáez argues that Yunior disciplines Oscar's nonconformity to erase the homosocial romance between them. This requires Yunior, as the "more authentic" Dominican, to "de-Other" Oscar, and the novel's conclusion, she argues, fulfills heterosexual desire while simultaneously hinting at a homosocial romance that cannot be transparently written. Machado Sáez, *Market Aesthetics*, 162–75.

42. Díaz, *Oscar Wao*, 5.

43. Díaz, *Oscar Wao*, 5.

44. Díaz, *Oscar Wao*, 11.

45. Díaz, *Oscar Wao*, 5. Many scholars have explored how Yunior's writing/narration imitates the violence enacted by the Trujillato and is a consequence of dictatorial violence. See Hanna, "Reassembling the Fragments," 56; and Harford Vargas, *Forms of Dictatorship*, 34–59.

46. Díaz, *Oscar Wao*, 29.

47. Freeman, *Time Binds*, 3.

48. For more on "queer time" as an opposition to heteronormative systems and practices and a formation with alternative logics, locations, and movements, see Halberstam, *In a Queer Time and Place*.

49. White, "Fat, Queer, Dead," 5.

50. Freccero, "Queer Spectrality," 196; and Levy-Navarro, "Fattening Queer History," 18.

51. Strings, *Fearing the Black Body*.

52. Díaz, *Oscar Wao*, 20.

53. *Bachatero* is literally translated as someone who performs bachata, but in Dominican slang it refers to a reveler or carouser.

54. Díaz, *Oscar Wao*, 253. *Criada* can be translated as *maid* or *servant*. The term *restavek* comes from the French *rester avec* (to stay with) and in Haiti refers to a child who is given away by their parents to work as a domestic servant in another household.

55. Díaz, *Oscar Wao*, 257.

56. Díaz, *Oscar Wao*, 257.

57. Díaz, *Oscar Wao*, 248.

58. I take my inspiration from Michelle Wright, who argues that the only way to create a viable definition of Blackness is to understand it as the intersection of constructs in history. See Wright, *Physics of Blackness*, 14. Stuart Hall illustrates the difficulties of defining Blackness, understanding the construction of a collective identity through a shared history that nonetheless considers this history and its ancestry realities that, as Wright notes, give "Blackness its 'weight'" (5). See also Hall, "Cultural Identity and Diaspora."

59. In "The Silence," Díaz explains that much of his fiction and its characters emerged as a way to hide his own experience of abuse.

60. The production of sugar in the Caribbean was essential in the construction and development of Western empires. Through the staging of violence in the sugarcane fields, Yunior reasserts the centrality of sugar production in the propagation of colonial and dictatorial violence, calls forth the literary history of the Latinx canon, and demonstrates the connection of fukú to colonial violence and the Trujillato.

61. Díaz, *Oscar Wao*, 146.

62. Scarry, *Body in Pain*, 4–5.

63. Hartman, *Scenes of Subjection*, 3.

64. Hartman, *Scenes of Subjection*, 3.

65. Moten, *In the Break*, 4, 5.

66. Hartman, *Scenes of Subjection*, 3.

67. Moten, *Black and Blur*, 4.

68. Moten, *Black and Blur*, x.

69. Laura Mulvey refers to scopophilia as the pleasure in looking at other people's bodies that facilitates both the voyeuristic objectification of the female body and a narcissistic process of identification with the image seen. Particularly salient to Yunior's description is his seeming absence from the page that allows us to forget his authorial hand. See Mulvey, "Visual Pleasure and Narrative Cinema."

70. Díaz, *Oscar Wao*, 146.

71. Díaz, *Oscar Wao*, 146.

72. Díaz, *Oscar Wao*, 147.

73. Scarry, *Body in Pain*, 14.

74. Scarry, *Body in Pain*, 4.

75. Díaz, *Oscar Wao*, 331; Moore and Gibbons, *Watchmen*, vol. 12, p. 27.

76. Díaz, *Oscar Wao*, 229.

77. Díaz, *Oscar Wao*, 333.

78. Díaz, *Oscar Wao*, 335.

79. Michel-Rolph Trouillot, *Silencing the Past*, 27.

80. Hartman, "Venus in Two Acts," 11.

81. Díaz, *Oscar Wao*, 243.

82. Monica Hanna also examines how "They say" injects doubt from the novel's first sentence and presents an alternative Dominican archive compiled by Yunior. See Hanna, "Reassembling the Fragments," 502. Yet, as Elena Machado Saéz points out, Yunior's "guise of objectivity" exposes the pitfalls of recording history. See Machado Sáez, *Market Aesthetics*, 166–67.

83. *Diccionario de la lengua Española*, s.v. "dizque," https://dle.rae.es/dizque?m=form.

84. Díaz, *Oscar Wao*, 330.

85. Díaz, *Oscar Wao*, 298.

86. Díaz, *Oscar Wao*, 304.

87. Díaz, *Oscar Wao*, 321.

88. Díaz, *Oscar Wao*, 322.

89. For praise of the book, see Kakutani, "Travails of an Outcast"; Scott, "Dreaming in Spanglish"; Glock, "We're All Fuku'd"; and Villalon, "In 'The Brief Wondrous Life of Oscar Wao,' a New America Emerges."

90. Torres-Saillant, "Artistry, Ancestry, and Americanness in the Works of Junot Díaz," 121.

91. Hannah, Harford Vargas, and Saldívar, "Introduction. Junot Díaz and the Decolonial Imagination," 5. It would be impossible to provide a comprehensive list of the scholarship on Díaz. There are thousands of articles, reviews, dissertations, and book chapters

written on the author and his work. Outside of the references in note 8, these references have been useful in thinking about Díaz's oeuvre: Bautista, "Comic Book Realism"; Miller, "Preternatural Narration"; J. D. Saldívar, "Conjectures of 'Americanity'"; and J. D. Saldívar's idolization in *Junot Díaz: On the Half-Life of Love*.

92. See Díaz, "The Search for Decolonial Love: An Interview with Junot Díaz"; and Fassler, "How Junot Diaz Wrote a Sexist Character, but Not a Sexist Book."

93. Díaz, "The Silence."

94. Clemmons, (@zinziclemmons). "As a Grad Student," *Twitter*, May 4, 2018, 3:05 a.m.

95. King, *Black Shoals*, 48.

96. Díaz, "The Silence."

97. A good resource that explores sexual abuse and abjection in relation to the Blackened body is Darieck Scott's *Extravagant Abjection*, especially chap. 3. Scott's work participates in a longer tradition of abject and trauma theory, which is useful for thinking of how the racialized body and, in particular for this case, the male subject, experiences and reacts to pain and trauma.

98. Ana Rodríguez Navas also argues that Yunior blurs the boundaries of private and public through the use of gossip, drawing the reader into the story in a way that establishes a sense of intimacy and complicity. Mieke Bal explains how the second-person point of view is "simply an 'I' in disguise," the narrator "talking to himself." Instead of creating dialogue with the reader, Yunior centralizes his authority and experience. See Bal, *Narratology*, 29.

99. Elena Machado Sáez argues that these demands shape and limit Yunior's narrative. See Machado Sáez, *Market Aesthetics*, 163; and Dalleo and Machado Sáez, *Latino/a Canon*, 77.

100. McHugh-Dillon, "'Let Me Confess,'" 25.

101. Subramanian, "In the Wake of His Damage."

102. Díaz, "The Silence."

103. Reactions to "The Silence" acclaimed it not only for the story it was telling but also for its rendition, calling it "powerful" and "wrenching," descriptions that speak to affective responses to the writing's aesthetic qualities.

104. Scholars (and Díaz himself) have described this trend in his work as a symptom of colonial and dictatorial violence and, more importantly, as evidence of Díaz's anti-misogynist project. In fact, the editors of *Junot Díaz and the Decolonial Imagination* present this as their primary raison d'être. It is difficult to find scholarship that engages with Díaz's work as misogynist or as replicating gendered violence. Writing for *Avidly*, Dixa Ramírez reasserts not only the irresolution at the heart of Díaz's work but also the seduction that Yunior's consistent failure presents for readers. See D. Ramírez, "Violence, Literature, and Seduction."

105. Loofbourow, "Junot Díaz and the Problem of the Male Self-Pardon."

106. Machado makes this comment in relation to an infamous recording at the Iowa Writers' Workshop and a series of tweets. The audio of the encounter between Machado and Díaz was released via Soundcloud, but I will not provide a link here for the dubious ethical grounds through which it was distributed.

A portion of chapter 2 appeared as "Sugar Apocalypse: Sweetness and Monstrosity in Cristina García's *Dreaming in Cuban*," *Studies in American Fiction* 47, no. 1 (2020): 97–116.

1. Nato Thompson, chief curator of Creative Time, which commissioned and presented the installation, describes the figures as "black boys" or blackamoors. Thompson, "Curatorial Statement." There have been many wonderful analyses of Walker's *A Subtlety*, including Peabody, *Consuming Stories*; Nyong'o, *Afro-Fabulations*; Musser, *Sensual Excess*; Lindsey and Johnson, "Searching for Climax"; and Anker, *Ugly Freedoms*.

2. This era was known as the "special period" of economic crisis in Cuba. Ironically, as Esther Whitfield observes, while food scarcity, decreased production, rationing, and austerity measures on the island defined the special period, at this time Cuba was also participating in the capitalist world by exporting its culture, particularly literature. See Whitfield, *Cuban Currency*.

3. Roberts and Stephens, *Archipelagic American Studies*, 17.

4. Stratford et al., "Envisioning the Archipelago," 125.

5. Figueroa-Vásquez, *Decolonizing Diasporas*; Glissant, *Treatise on the Whole-World*; Hey-Colón, "Transformative Currents"; McKittrick, *Demonic Grounds*; and Moreno, *Crossing Waters*. Kamau Braithwaide's theory of "tidalectics" also emphasizes an interplay between the individual and collective while illustrating how history is a haunting remnant that laps onto the shores of the present. Braithwaite is cited in DeLoughrey and Flores, "Submerged Bodies," 134.

6. Hey-Colón, "Transformative Currents," 10. See also Pérez-Rosario, "On the Hispanophone Caribbean Question."

7. See García-Peña, *Borders of Dominicanidad*; and Fumagalli, *On the Edge*.

8. The historical and cultural role of sugar has been the focus of various scholars who provide invaluable context for this chapter, including Fernando Ortiz, whose classic work *Cuban Counterpoint* examines the impact of the commodity in Cuba. Other studies include Kutzinski, *Sugar's Secrets*; Sandiford, *Cultural Politics of Sugar*; Woloson, *Refined Tastes*; and Follett, *Sugar Masters*.

9. Mintz, *Sweetness and Power*, 6.

10. Scholars like Elisabeth Anker and Kyla Wazana Tompkins take on Mintz's important study and explore the centrality of sugar in the construction of empire, notions of democracy and freedom, and modern forms of racialization. See Anker, *Ugly Freedoms*; and Tompkins, "Sweetness, Capacity, Energy." Sugar has held a central place within proto/capitalist systems and is always inextricably linked to racialized (slave) labor. For a more detailed account of how Europe was transformed by the consumption of sugar, see Plasa, *Slaves to Sweetness*; Sheller, *Consuming the Caribbean*; and Sandiford, *Cultural Politics of Sugar*.

11. For more on the cultural and political hegemony of sugar, see Benítez-Rojo, *Repeating Island*, particularly "Azúcar/Poder/Literature and Nicolás Guillén and Sugar"; and Merleaux, *Sugar and Civilization*. Simon Gikandi addresses the centrality of sugar for the construction of cultures of taste in Europe and the violence of the slave trade in *Slavery and the Culture of Taste* (109–11).

12. Although not directly addressed in this chapter, notions of the fantastic in Latin American literature are in dialogue with and indebted to Alejo Carpentier's concept of "lo real maravilloso"(the marvelous real), in which he presents Latin American history and geography as so extreme as to appear magical. See Carpentier, *El reino de este mundo*.

13. Duncan, "Urban Undead."

14. *Genre* in this instance, of course, means plot-driven, mass-market novels (understood as "lowbrow") that contrast with "high art" literature, a definition in tension with more conventional uses of the term in literary studies that address the history and characteristics of the novel, poetry, and drama. For other reviews, see Chiarealla, "How It Ends"; and Sky, "Colson Whitehead's Brain." These views are changing with the advent of what is typically called "elevated" or "heightened" genre.

15. See Marshall, "What Are the Novels"; R. Saldívar, "Second Elevation"; Sorensen, "Against the Post-apocalyptic"; and Hurley, "History Is What Bites."

16. Whitehead, *Zone One*, 58.

17. Barbara L. Solow's *Slavery and the Rise of the Atlantic System* and Mimi Sheller's *Consuming the Caribbean* are helpful in their investigation of how consumer culture emerged alongside the transatlantic slave trade and the consumption of sugar.

18. Anker, *Ugly Freedoms*, 44–47; and Williams, *Capitalism and Slavery*, 45.

19. The origin of the zombie is tied to the cannibal as conceived by Europeans in the sixteenth century. The term *cannibal* has its origins in the 1500s and derives from *Caníbales*, the Spanish name for the Caribs of the West Indies (which further derives from *caribal*, the Spanish word for "a savage"). In the accounts of his four voyages, Christopher Columbus mentions the presence of native peoples who eat human flesh. See Columbus, *Log*, 68, 83, 87, 163. Bartolmé de las Casas confirms this in *A Short Account of the Destruction of the Indies*, 66, 79. In the eighteenth century, authors such as Edward Long (*The History of Jamaica*, 1774) and Bryan Edwards (*The History, Civil and Commercial, of the British Colonies in the West Indies*, 1793) spoke of cannibals as being African in origin. In these ways, the notions of savagery, monstrosity, and the bestial are intimately tied to the Caribbean.

20. Boon, "Zombie as Other," 5–6; Dayan, *Haiti, History*; Hurston, *Tell My Horse*; and Kee, "'They Are Not Men.'"

21. See Lauro, *Transatlantic Zombie*, 43; Rhodes, *White Zombie*, 70–72; and Dayan, *Haiti, History*, 37–38.

22. In *Hayti, or the Black Republic*, Spencer St. John describes cannibalism, human sacrifice, and grave robbing as a part of voodoo, and as a widely read author during the nineteenth century, he influenced many writers and readers. Moreover, St. John claims that cannibalism did not occur under French colonial rule. Inherent in this presentation is the notion that cannibalism appears in voodoo because of Haitian independence. Through this lens, cannibalism is used to critique the Haitian government, and voodoo is seen as a threat not only to civilization but to Haiti's future. See Kee, "'They Are Not Men,'" 13.

23. See Dayan, *Haiti, History*; and Trefzer, "Possessing the Self," 300.

24. Recent scholarship on the zombie theorizes the monster as a manifestation of general contemporary anxieties that divest it of its Haitian roots and ignore the important histories of transnational exchange that are always cited on its body. See Cohen, "Undead"; and Newitz, *Pretend We're Dead*. Both argue that the zombie reflects con-

temporary anxieties surrounding globalization and capitalism. However, this type of argument often overlooks the zombie's Caribbean origins. For scholars who centralize race and the importance of Haiti for the zombie, see Lauro, *Transatlantic Zombie*; and Swanson, *Zombie*.

25. See Wallace, *Greater Gotham*. See also Klein, *Empire State*.

26. Wallace, *Greater Gotham*, 72, 120.

27. We see this same type of argument in abolitionist discussions that presented eating sugar as a form of cannibalism, painting a gruesome picture of sugar tainted with the blood of enslaved people. See Plasa, *Slaves to Sweetness*; and Sandiford, *Cultural Politics of Sugar*.

28. Tompkins, *Racial Indigestion*, 5.

29. Whitehead, *Zone One*, 280.

30. Whitehead, *Zone One*, 26.

31. Whitehead, *Zone One*, 4.

32. Whitehead, *Zone One*, 73.

33. Whitehead, *Zone One*, 42.

34. Whitehead, *Zone One*, 81.

35. Justin Mann explores the centrality of securitization in the novel in "Black Insecurity at the End of the World."

36. Sorensen, "Against the Post-apocalypse," 570.

37. Whitehead, *Zone One*, 128.

38. Del Pilar Blanco, *Ghost-Watching American Modernity*, 7.

39. Del Pilar Blanco, *Ghost-Watching American Modernity*, 1, 8.

40. In "History Is What Bites," Jessica Hurley argues that Spitz "passes" in the text, and through the revelation of his race the novel unravels. While I also read Spitz's Blackness as the vehicle through which the novel unravels toward the world's redestruction, I resist Hurley's designation of this novel as a passing narrative and propose instead that Spitz is strategically camouflaged: the lack of overt racial markers in combination with a nickname that signals a white cultural figure hides Spitz's race, purposefully surprising readers and highlighting established reading practices, prejudices, and assumptions about racial markers. The historical Spitz was also the son of Russian Jewish people, which designates him as ambiguously white in the racial imagery of the 1970s United States.

41. Whitehead, *Zone One*, 230.

42. See Glissant, *Poetics of Relation*, 189–94.

43. Whitehead, *Zone One*, 43.

44. Gilroy, *Black Atlantic*, 17.

45. King, *Black Shoals*, 5. Hortense Spillers's "oceanic," in "Mama's Baby, Papa's Maybe" (72); Gilroy's "Black Atlantic"; Glissant's "abyss"; Benítez-Rojo's "rhythms"; Christina Sharpe's "wake work"; and King's "shoals" are some of the many examples of aquatic language that surfaces in Black studies as a reminder of the dehumanization of Black and Indigenous populations that persists to this day.

46. Whitehead, *Zone One*, 307.

47. JanMohamed, *Death-Bound-Subject*, 2. Others who have taken up this line of inquiry are Sexton, "Social Life of Social Death"; and Warren, "Black Nihilism." Other

useful sources in this discussion include Wilderson, *Red, White and Black*; Moten, "Blackness and Nothingness"; and Holland, *Raising the Dead*.

48. See Warren, "Black Nihilism," 217.

49. Anker, *Ugly Freedoms*, 42, 56.

50. Sharpe, *In the Wake*, 16.

51. Sharpe, *In the Wake*, 28–29.

52. Many theorists have taken up the unremitting violence experienced by people of color in the Americas. Specifically addressing racial violence as the legacy of chattel slavery, Saidiya Hartman speaks of the "afterlife of slavery" as the imprint of slavery and the enduring presence of racialized violence in contemporary society. See Hartman, *Scenes of Subjection*. In line with Hartman's work, Sharpe delineates the "orthography of the wake," illustrating how Black life is animated by the afterlives of slavery while also showing how survival is accomplished in spite of insistent violence. See Sharpe, *In the Wake*. Fred Moten and Stefano Harney theorize the hold of the ship as a productive space for the "not yet" experience of freedom, an experience that cannot be articulated because it has not been archived. Moten and Harney, *Undercommons*, 94. King uses the shoal as an entry point to theorize the legacy of conquest, slavery, and anti-Black and anti-Indigenous violence. King, *Black Shoals*.

53. Whitehead, *Zone One*, 322.

54. Sharpe, *In the Wake*, 16.

55. Hartman and Wilderson, "Position of the Unthought," 187.

56. Moten, "Blackness and Nothingness," 738.

57. The novel also touches on Felicia's children—the twins, Luz and Milagro, and her son Ivanito—and her friend Herminia Delgado. The plot, however, is primarily focused, in terms of story and narrative space, on del Pino, her daughters, and her granddaughter.

58. The scholarship on *Dreaming in Cuban* and García's other works is extensive. See Machado Sáez, "Global Baggage of Nostalgia"; del Carmen Gómez-Vega, "Journey Home"; and Payant, "From Alienation to Reconciliation," for more recent and nuanced discussions of this novel.

59. Pérez Firmat, *Life on the Hyphen*, 3.

60. García, *Dreaming in Cuban*, 220.

61. García, *Dreaming in Cuban*, 219.

62. García, *Dreaming in Cuban*, 17.

63. García, *Dreaming in Cuban*, 20.

64. García, *Dreaming in Cuban*, 170.

65. A. López, *Unbecoming Blackness*, 191.

66. A. López, *Unbecoming Blackness*, 12.

67. María DeGuzmán explores the notion of "off-whiteness" as a fiction of Spanish racial purity that in the eighteenth- and nineteenth-century United States becomes "not-right-white." See DeGuzmán, *Spain's Long Shadow*. For 1990s Cuban Americans, conceptions of whiteness were linked to racial superiority but also shaped in tension with ideologies of Anglo-American whiteness, which cast Latinx whiteness as "off-white." A. López, *Unbecoming Blackness*, 186.

68. García, *Dreaming in Cuban*, 170–71.

69. García, *Dreaming in Cuban*, 136.

70. R. Ortiz, *Cultural Erotics*, 144, 155.

71. R. Ortiz, *Cultural Erotics*, 155.

72. García, *Dreaming in Cuban*, 4.

73. *Dreaming in Cuban* gestures to the Zafra del los Diez Millones (the ten-million-ton harvest) in 1970 through Celia's volunteer work in the sugarcane field. Fidel Castro, like Celia, was fully convinced that sugar would save the island's economy, while the subsequent drop in the price of sugar, and the failure of the harvest despite the dedicated work of almost the entirety of the island's population, illustrates how Cuba was still caught in the capitalist monocrop boom-and-bust cycle. For more on the Zafra, see Guerra, *Visions of Power*, 290–316.

74. García, *Dreaming in Cuban*, 4.

75. García, *Dreaming in Cuban*, 44. On her return to Cuba at the end of the novel, Lourdes is described as "chew[ing] cane until she tastes the guarapo, the sticky syrup inside" (219). While her consumption of Cuban sugarcane could be seen as symbolizing the connection between her Cuban past and American present—a means of finding a balance between Celia's trenchant revolutionary ideals and Lourdes's capitalist American ideology—she also notes that "it's not as sweet as I remember," even as she asks Pilar to try some, indicating Lourdes's renunciation of Cuba and the impossibility of return and familial reconciliation in the novel (219).

76. García, *Dreaming in Cuban*, 44.

77. García, *Dreaming in Cuban*, 45.

78. García, *Dreaming in Cuban*, 45.

79. For more on how the relationship between the United States and Cuba shaped the latter's identity, nationality, and sense of modernity, see Pérez, *On Becoming Cuban*.

80. García, *Dreaming in Cuban*, 117.

81. García, *Dreaming in Cuban*, 245.

82. Machado Sáez, "Global Baggage."

83. García, *Dreaming in Cuban*, 197–98.

84. Machado Sáez, "Global Baggage," 134.

85. García, *Dreaming in Cuban*, 236.

86. Aparicio, "Blackness of Sugar," 226.

87. This same type of zombification of Cruz can be seen in Jennine Capó Crucet's story "Resurrection," in *How to Leave Hialeah*, 1–10.

88. García, *Dreaming in Cuban*, 31.

89. García, *Dreaming in Cuban*, 31.

90. García, *Dreaming in Cuban*, 30–31.

91. García, *Dreaming in Cuban*, 140.

92. García, *Dreaming in Cuban*, 141.

93. Musser, *Sensual Excess*, 42.

94. One observer stated of Walker's sculpture that it is an object that encourages "us to look at things that are so visible in our society we wish were invisible." See Jay Buim's short film *Creative Time Presents Kara Walker's "A Subtlety."*

95. Cruz, "Azúcar Negra," in *Azúcar Negra* (1993): "I am sweet as molasses / Happy like the drum / I carry the rhythmic swagger" (my translation).

96. Cruz, "Azucar Negra." "My blood is black sugar / It is love and music / Black sugar / Oh, how much I like it and enjoy it" (my translation).

97. Tompkins, *Racial Indigestion*, 8.

98. Walker, "Sweet Talk."

99. Lindsey and Johnson, "Searching for Climax," 185.

100. Musser, *Sensual Excess*, 36. Examinations of *A Subtlety* by Anker and Sharpe have also been instrumental to my own interpretation. See Anker, *Ugly Freedoms*, 67–76; and Sharpe, *Monstrous Intimacies*, 98–99.

101. Musser, *Sensual Excess*, 43.

102. Musser, *Sensual Excess*, 43.

CHAPTER 3. APPROXIMATION, HORROR, AND THE GROTESQUE ON THE US-MEXICO BORDER

Epigraph: "History, which is a simple whore, has no decisive moments but is a proliferation of instants, brief interludes that vie with one another in monstrosity" (Bolaño, *2666*, 794).

1. Bolaño, "Roberto Bolaño."

2. I adhere to Rosa-Linda Fregoso and Cynthia Bejarano's definition of *femicide* as murders of women and girls based on a "gender power structure." Fregoso and Bejarano, "Introduction," 5.

3. García Márquez's "realidad desaforada" is itself a reworking of Alejo Carpentier's "real maravilloso" (marvelous real). See Carpentier, *El reino de este mundo*. Bolaño's relationship to García Márquez and other Boom writers was overtly contentious. See Zalewski, "Vagabonds."

4. Sánchez Prado, "Persistence of the Transcultural," 357; and Hoyos Ayala, *Beyond Bolaño*, 7.

5. Pollack, "Latin America Translated (Again)," 355.

6. Pollack, "Latin America Translated (Again)," 347.

7. Molloy, "Postcolonial Latin America," 373–75; and Echevarría, "Bolaño extraterritorial," 341.

8. See Bassnett and Lefevere, *Constructing Cultures*.

9. For approaches to world literature, see Apter, *Against World Literature*; Damrosch, *What Is World Literature?*; Moretti, "Conjectures on World Literature"; and Spivak, *Aesthetic Education*. For more on Bolaño in relation to the world literature market, see Villalobos-Ruminott, "Kind of Hell"; and Sánchez Prado, "Persistence of the Transcultural."

10. Zavala, "Repolitization," 82.

11. See Grandin, *Empire's Workshop*.

12. Guidotti-Hernández, *Unspeakable Violence*, 27.

13. Clover, *Men, Women, and Chain Saws*, 18–19.

14. For more on the grotesque, see Bakhtin, *Rabelais and His World*; Bloom, *Grotesque*; Carroll, *Minerva's Night Out*; and Foucault, *Abnormal*.

15. Peláez, "Counting Violence"; and Villalobos-Ruminott, "Kind of Hell."

16. Bolaño, *2666*, 752. Unless otherwise noted, all citations are from the Spanish edition, and all translations are my own.

17. Bolaño, *2666*, 752–53.

18. In *The Open Veins of Latin America*, Eduardo Galeano echoes this representation by equating poverty with atomic annihilation: "Every year, without making a sound, three Hiroshima bombs explode over communities that have become accustomed to suffering with clenched teeth" (5).

19. Brady, *Extinct Lands, Temporal Geographies*, 17. She also underscores how language and translation play an essential role in the construction of a landscape.

20. Anzaldúa, *Borderlands/La Frontera*, n.p.

21. Anzaldúa, *Borderlands/La Frontera*, 24.

22. To list the vast amount of scholarship that employs or responds to Anzaldúa's work is beyond the remit of this project, but these thinkers have influenced my work: C. Ramírez, "Cyborg Feminism"; Saldívar-Hull, "Feminism on the Border"; Muñoz, *Cruising Utopia*; Hernández-Ávila and Cantú, *Entre Guadalupe y Malinche*; and Anzaldúa, *Gloria Anzaldúa Reader*.

23. Bolaño, *2666*, 443.

24. In the 2008 English version of the novel, Natasha Wimmer translates this opening as "The girl's body turned up" (353). However, it is important to note the implications of the Spanish. While "girl" gives the dead body a specific age range and infantilizes her, Bolaño uses "muerta," which inscribes her as nothing more than a dead body, consistent with the clinical tone used throughout the rest of this section of the novel. "Turned up" can also be interpreted in many ways, carrying the connotation that the woman's body was being looked for and found. "Apareció" (appeared), on the other hand, while an awkward Latinate in English, signals to readers the almost-magical presence of the woman's body in the landscape.

25. Bolaño, *2666*, 444.

26. Ngai, *Ugly Feelings*, 248–97.

27. Bolaño, *2666*, 530, 565, 576.

28. Bolaño, *2666*, 576–77.

29. Kurnick, "Bolaño to Come."

30. For more about the grotesque and the limits of the body, see Bakhtin, *Rabelais and His World*; and Stott, *Comedy*, 67–69.

31. Bakhtin, *Rabelais and His World*, 26.

32. Hartman, *Scenes of Subjection*, 4.

33. Halley, *Split Decisions*, 151.

34. Cave, "Wave of Violence."

35. Melissa Wright, "Necropolitics, Narcopolitics, and Femicide," 708. Other scholars have discussed the relationship of precarious bodies to the fortification of the state. See Giorgio Agamben's notion of "state of exception," Achille Mbembe's "necropolitics," and Michel Foucault's "biopolitics" in Agamben, *States of Exception* (2005), 1–31; Mbembe, *Necropolitics* (2009), 66–92; and Foucault, *Society Must Be Defended*, 239–64. For more on femicides and their relation to Mexican culture, neoliberalism, and export processing, see Staudt, *Violence and Activism*; Washington Valdez, *Killing Fields*; Gaspar de Alba and Guzmán, *Making a Killing*; and Melissa Wright, *Disposable Women*.

36. Melissa Wright, *Disposable Women*, 7.

37. Melissa Wright, *Disposable Women*, 72; and Grandin, *Empire's Workshop*, 199–200.

38. Melissa Wright, *Disposable Women*, 17.

39. Melissa Wright, *Disposable Women*, 2.

40. Melissa Wright, *Disposable Women*. Teresa Brennan, in *Globalization and Its Terrors*, also addresses the disposability of the human body in relation to the market.

41. Bolaño, *2666*, 469.

42. Bolaño, *2666*, 469, 470.

43. Bolaño, *2666*, 469, 470.

44. Bolaño, *2666*, 518.

45. Melissa Wright, *Disposable Women*, 73.

46. Hartman, "Venus in Two Acts," 12.

47. Guidotti-Hernández, *Unspeakable Violence*, 5.

48. Guidotti-Hernández, *Unspeakable Violence*, 5.

49. Bolaño, *Los detectives salvajes*, 546.

50. Bolaño, *Amuleto*, 76–77.

51. Bolaño, *2666*, 23.

52. Bolaño, *2666*, 103.

53. Bolaño, *2666*, 103.

54. Bolaño, *2666*, 105.

55. Bolaño, *2666*, 105.

56. Bolaño, *2666*, 266.

57. Bolaño, *2666*, 264.

58. Bolaño, *2666*, 295.

59. Bolaño, *2666*, 348.

60. Seaman and the other Black Panther characters are modeled on real-life members like Bobby Seale and Huey Newton.

61. Bolaño, *2666*, 316.

62. Bolaño, *2666*, 21.

63. Bolaño, *2666*, 337.

64. Bolaño, *2666*, 338.

65. Bolaño, *2666*, 340.

66. Bolaño, *2666*, 340.

67. Bolaño, *2666*, 340.

68. Bolaño, *2666*, 305.

69. Bolaño, *2666*, 236.

70. Bolaño, *2666*, 359.

71. Bolaño, *2666*, 359.

72. Bolaño, *2666*, 396.

73. Bolaño, *2666*, 440.

74. Brady, *Extinct Lands, Temporal Geographies*, 10.

75. Ruiz de Burton, *Squatter*, 325.

76. Ruiz de Burton, *Squatter*, 344.

77. Lang, Lapinski, and Mangun, *Feeding Ground*, 171, 174.

78. Bolaño, *2666*, 714.

79. Benjamin, *Illuminations*, 260.

1. Lovett and Maranian, *L.A. Bizarro*, 286.

2. Lovett and Maranian, *L.A. Bizarro*, 286.

3. The murals have activated a lot of press, at both the local and national levels. See Ferrel, "As Far as Murals Go"; Martin, "Sharpening Vision of Pig Paradise"; and Pear, "This Slaughterhouse Mural."

4. "About the Hundreds," LA Original, accessed April 22, 2024, https://laoriginal.com /makers/the-hundreds/.

5. B. Kim, "Hogtied"; see also Zamora, "Streetwear Brand 'The Hundreds.'"

6. Foster has received various awards such as the 2010 American Book Award for *World Ball Notebook*, the 2009 Asian American Literary Award for Poetry for *World Ball Notebook*, and the 2005 Believer Book Award for *Atomik Aztex*. His work has mostly been published by small presses, yet he also holds a semi-cult following within academia and the literary market. A search in the Modern Language Association's International Bibliography database provides five results, and *Atomik Aztex* holds position no. 811,765 in the Amazon Best Seller Rank in "Books," no. 985 in "Hispanic American Literature and Fiction," no. 2,582 in "Fiction Urban Life," and no. 4,431 in "Dystopian Fiction" as of December 2023.

7. *Publishers Weekly*, review of *Atomik Aztex*.

8. Reynolds, "Monster in the Man."

9. *Publishers Weekly*, review of *Atomik Aztek*; *The Believer*, review of *Atomik Aztek*, 3. See also Cutler, "Borders and Borderland Literature."

10. Heise, "Postmodern Novels," 978.

11. Limón, *American Encounters*; and Paredes, *Texas-Mexican Cancionero*, xiv.

12. Yun et al., "Signifying 'Asian,'" 211.

13. R. Saldívar, "Other Side of History"; and R. Saldívar, "Second Elevation."

14. Pöhlmann, "Cosmographic Metafiction," 239.

15. Holland, *Raising the Dead*.

16. Gruesz, *Ambassadors of Culture*, xi.

17. Gruesz, *Ambassadors of Culture*; Lamas, *Latino Continuum*; and Coronado, *World Not to Come*.

18. A few of the extratextual references cited in *Atomik Aztex* include Donald Megill and Richard Demory's *Introduction to Jazz History* (1984), Isaac Babel's *1920 Diary* (1995), Karl Marx's *Capital* (1867), and Vladimir Lenin's *Materialism and Empirio-criticism* (1909).

19. On the "incoherence" of the novel, see Pöhlmann, "Cosmographic Metafiction," 234; and for further investigations of plot structures, see Forster, *Aspects of the Novel*, 86.

20. Esposito, "Swimming through the Omniverse"; Ulibarri, "Consuming Aztecs," 215; and Sohn, *Racial Asymmetries*, 74.

21. Hutcheon, *Poetics of Postmodernism*, 4.

22. Hutcheon, *Poetics of Postmodernism*, 4.

23. Hutcheon, *Poetics of Postmodernism*, 5.

24. Hutcheon, *Poetics of Postmodernism*, 19.

25. Hutcheon, *Poetics of Postmodernism*, 123. On pastiche as an imprisonment of the text within the past, see Jameson, "Postmodernism and Consumer Culture." While Fredric Jameson is addressing the ability of postmodernist artists to make something "new," I am taking his claim literally: in its implementation of pastiche and postmodern aesthetics generally, *Atomik Aztex* formally returns readers to moments of violence within the content of the text that metafictionally return us to the historical archive.

26. See Sohn, *Racial Asymmetries*, 74; D. Lee, "Postquantum"; Pöhlmann, "Cosmographic Metafiction"; and Ulibarri, "Consuming Aztecs."

27. Reynolds, "Monster in the Man."

28. I see Reynolds's review as standing in stark opposition to those of "genius" postmodern works like Don DeLillo's *White Noise* (1985), David Foster Wallace's *Infinite Jest* (1996), and Thomas Pynchon's *Mason & Dixon* (1997), which praise the difficulty of their prose, their wealth of knowledge, and the quiddity of their language. See Phillips, "Crowding Out Death"; Moss, "*Infinite Jest* at 20"; and Kakutani, "Pynchon Hits the Road."

29. See the *Online Nahuatl Dictionary*, edited by Stephanie Wood and housed at the University of Oregon, accessed April 23, 2024, https://nahuatl.wired-humanities.org/content/centzontlatole.

30. Gill, *Ornithology*, 230.

31. Gill, *Ornithology*, 237; Joblin, *Helm Dictionary* ; and Levey et al., "Urban Mockingbirds."

32. Foster, *Atomik Aztex*, n.p. Unless otherwise noted, all variation in formatting, spelling, and the like in my quotations from *Atomik Aztex* is original to the text.

33. Pöhlmann, "Cosmographic Metafiction," 227.

34. Viego, *Dead Subjects*, 113. See also Cutler, *Ends of Assimilation*, 2.

35. Viego, *Dead Subjects*, 113.

36. Twain, *Adventures of Huckleberry Finn* (2015), n.p.

37. Coe is best known for his work *The Maya* (1966) and *Breaking the Maya Code* (1992). León-Portilla is known for his research on Nahua history and culture such as *Aztec Thought and Culture* (1967), *The Broken Spears* (1959), and *Pre-Columbian Literatures of Mexico* (1986).

38. Twain, *Adventures of Huckleberry Finn* (2015), n.p.

39. Hutcheon, *Poetics of Postmodernism*, 11.

40. Delbo, *Auschwitz and After*, 278, quoted in Foster, *Atomik Aztex*, n.p.

41. Delbo, *Auschwitz and After*, 84.

42. Hulstyn, "Charlotte Delbo à l'écoute," 75.

43. Foster, *Atomik Aztex*, 1.

44. Foster, *Atomik Aztex*, 1.

45. Foster, *Atomik Aztex*, 1.

46. Cutler, "Borders and Borderland Literature," 169.

47. Cutler, "Borders and Borderland Literature," 169.

48. *Diccionario de la lengua Española*, s.v. "chingar," Real Academia Española, accessed April 23, 2024, http://dle.rae.es/?id=8pLhBqB.

49. Paz, *Labyrinth of Solitude*, 77.

50. Paz, *Labyrinth of Solitude*, 99, 105. The first Indigenous group the text mentions is the Tlaxcalans, famously known as the group that allied themselves with Cortés. For reformulations of Paz's sexist and problematic readings of Malinche, see Esquivel, *Malinche*; Moraga, *Loving in the War Years*; Romero and Harris, *Feminism, Nation and Myth*; and Pratt, "'Yo Soy La Malinche.'"

51. Foster, *Atomik Aztex*, 3.

52. Hassig, *Time, History, and Belief*, 3–7.

53. Foster, *Atomik Aztex*, 200.

54. Foster, *Atomik Aztex*, 200.

55. Hassig, *Time, History, and Belief*, 58.

56. Hassig questions this common interpretation of the conquest, citing previous encounters with the Spanish. *Time, History, and Belief*, 58–60.

57. Foster, *Atomik Aztex*, 81, 108.

58. Foster, *Atomik Aztex*, 108.

59. Foster, *Atomik Aztex*, 130.

60. Foster, *Atomik Aztex*, 125.

61. Ulibarri, "Consuming Aztecs," 222.

62. Ulibarri, "Consuming Aztecs," 220.

63. Foster, *Atomik Aztex*, 141.

64. Ulibarri, "Consuming Aztecs," 222.

65. Foster, *Atomik Aztex*, 7.

66. Foster, *Atomik Aztex*, 7.

67. Ehrenreich, "Naked Lunch."

68. Tabios, "Sesshu Foster's Coming of Age." See also Ulibarri, "Consuming Aztecs"; and T. Kim, "Los Angeles Poet's Revolution."

69. T. Kim, "Los Angeles Poet's Revolution" (bracketed insertion in original).

70. See R. Rodriguez, *Latinx Literature Unbound*, 36; L. Lee, "Racial Invisibility and Erasure"; and Machado Sáez, "Generation MFA," 362.

71. Sohn, *Racial Asymmetries*, 64–65.

72. Sohn, *Racial Asymmetries*, 75.

73. Sohn, *Racial Asymmetries*, 65.

74. R. Rodriguez, *Latinx Literature Unbound*, 31.

75. R. Rodriguez, *Latinx Literature Unbound*, 31.

76. R. Rodriguez, *Latinx Literature Unbound*, 33. Rodriguez addresses this in relation to Santiago's *Famous All Over Town*; his discussion has been important for my analysis of *Atomik Aztex*.

77. For more on "Chicanesque," see Lomelí and Urioste, *Chicano Perspectives in Literature*; and R. Rodriguez, *Latinx Literature Unbound*.

78. R. Rodriguez, *Latinx Literature Unbound*, 36.

79. A. López, *Unbecoming Blackness*, 174.

80. Quoted in A. López, *Unbecoming Blackness*, 174.

81. Browder, *Slippery Characters*, 6.

82. Myriam Gurba's review in *Tropics of Meta*, for example, called the novel "trauma-porn melodrama," and other Latinx writers commented on how the publishing industry promotes and distributes work by white authors at a disproportionate rate, while Latinx writers telling these stories more authentically are dismissed and omitted from the field. See Gurba, "Pendeja, You Ain't Steinbeck"; Olivas, "Yes, Latinx Writers Are Angry"; and Vázquez, Barrera, and Machado Sáez, "What the *New York Times* Gets Wrong." For discussions about Carrillo/Carroll, see Max, "Novelist Whose Inventions Went Too Far"; Mejía, "The Secret Life of H. G. Carrillo"; and Page, "When the Writer Hache Carrillo Died."

83. See Helena María Viramontes's book blurb, in *"Loosing My Espanish*, by H. G. Carrillo,"* Penguin Random House, accessed April 23, 2024, https://www.penguinrandomhouse.com/books/24429/loosing-my-espanish-by-hg-carrillo/.

84. See Dalleo and Machado Sáez, *Latino/a Canon*; Machado Sáez, *Market Aesthetics*; López-Calvo, *God and Trujillo*; and Irizarry, *Chicana/o and Latina/o Fiction*.

85. Gruesz and Lazo, "Linguistic Posing," 5.

86. M. López, *Racial Immanence*, 4–5.

87. See R. Rodriguez, *Latinx Literature Unbound*, 28; Machado Sáez, *Market Aesthetics*; and Irizarry, *Chicana/o and Latina/o Fiction*.

88. See "Publisher Comments," https://www.powells.com/book/-9780872864405.

89. Foster, *Atomik Aztex*, 8.

90. Muñoz, *Sense of Brown*, 122.

91. Muñoz, *Sense of Brown*, 138. See also Joshua Chambers Letson and Tavia Nyong'o's introduction to Muñoz's *Sense of Brown*, "Editors' Introduction: The Aesthetic Resonance of Brown," xxxi.

92. Guzmán, "Brown," 28.

93. Guzmán, "Brown," 28.

94. Bruce-Novoa, *Retrospace*, 140.

95. Saldaña-Portillo, "Who's the Indian in Aztlán?," 413, 415. Tatiana Flores similarly problematizes the construction of *latinidad* by foregrounding how it reproduces the erasure of Blackness and Indigeneity. T. Flores, "'Latinidad Is Cancelled.'"

96. Griswold del Castillo and De León, *North to Aztlán*, 127.

97. Townsend, *Aztecs*, 55.

98. Pérez-Torres, "Refiguring Aztlán," 104. Aztlán is a place and idea that has been discussed by numerous scholars within Latinx studies. This is by no means a comprehensive list but one that is indicative of argument trends that I find both useful and interesting for thinking about Aztlán: Brady, *Extinct Lands, Temporal Geographies*; Saldaña-Portillo, *Revolutionary Imagination*; Saldaña-Portillo, *Indian Given*; Ontiveros, *In the Spirit*; and Cutler, *Ends of Assimilation*.

99. Pérez-Torres, "Refiguring Aztlán," 104.

100. Saldaña-Portillo, *Indian Given*, 226–27; and Cheng, *Melancholy of Race*.

101. Ulibarri, "Consuming Aztecs," 215.

102. Gonzales, "El Plan Espiritual de Aztlán," 27.

103. Milian, "Extremely Latin, XOXO," 127; and Guidotti-Hernández, "Affective Communities," 142.

1. I take inspiration from Monica Huerta's criticism-through-storytelling in *Magical Habits* in my use of the personal as an entry point to an analysis of Carmen Maria Machado's fiction.

2. In *The Program Era*, Mark McGurl argues that postwar fiction in the United States has been transformed by the rise of the creative writing program, which has influenced and shaped aesthetic production and interest in literature. Authors like Elif Batuman reject the basic notion in McGurl's argument that there is such a thing as "program fiction." See Batuman, "Get a Real Degree."

3. Sehgal, "Fairy Tales"; and Robins, "Carmen Maria Machado's 'Her Body.'"

4. Few peer-reviewed articles about *Her Body and Other Parties* have been published to date, but some of these works include Campbell, "Real Women Have Skins"; Hood, "Desire and Knowledge"; and Więckowska, "Silence and Fecundity."

5. R. Rodriguez, *Latinx Literature Unbound*, 3.

6. "The Green Ribbon" is the third story in *In a Dark, Dark Room, and Other Scary Stories* (1984), a collection of horror stories, poems, and urban legends written for children by Alvin Schwartz.

7. Machado, *Her Body* , 3.

8. Machado, *Her Body*, 3.

9. Machado, *Her Body*, 4.

10. Machado, *Her Body*, 18.

11. Machado, *Her Body*, 4.

12. Machado, *Her Body*, 30.

13. Machado, *Her Body*, 30.

14. Machado, *Her Body*, 30.

15. Machado, *Her Body*, 31.

16. Machado, *Her Body*, 30.

17. Machado, *Her Body*, 31.

18. Machado, *Her Body*, 31.

19. Machado, *Her Body*, 30–31.

20. Halberstam, *Queer Art of Failure*, 126. See also Ahmed, *Living a Feminist Life*, 264.

21. Machado, *Her Body*, 12.

22. Machado, *Her Body*, 13.

23. Machado, *Her Body*, 31.

24. Tuana, "Speculum of Ignorance," 15.

25. Machado, *Her Body*, 158.

26. Machado, *Her Body*, 155–56.

27. Quoted in Steel, *How Not to Make a Human*, 136–37.

28. Steel, *How Not to Make a Human*, 164.

29. Machado, *Her Body*, 157.

30. Machado, *Her Body*, 160.

31. Deleuze and Guattari, *Thousand Plateaus*, 9, 88–89, 277.

32. Deleuze and Guattari, *Thousand Plateaus*, 232–309. See also Jardine, "Woman in Limbo," 52.

33. Flieger, "Becoming-Woman," 47.

34. Musser, *Sensational Flesh*. Musser offers a detailed overview of masochism in psychoanalytic theory through the work of Sigmund Freud, Michel Foucault, Jacques Lacan, and Leo Bersani, among others, in the introduction to their book.

35. Musser, *Sensational Flesh*, 10.

36. Musser, *Sensational Flesh*, 17.

37. Machado, *Her Body*, 161.

38. Musser, *Sensational Flesh*, 15.

39. Ngai argues that in late modernity it is significant to examine noncathartic states of feelings and politically ambiguous affects in cultural production.

40. Machado, *Her Body*, 165.

41. Machado, *Her Body*, 165.

42. Machado, *Her Body*, 165.

43. Machado, *Her Body*, 165.

44. Machado, *Her Body*, 165.

45. For more on quiet, see Campt, *Image Matters*, 4–6.

46. León, "Forms of Opacity," 382.

47. V. Huang, *Surface Relations*. Huang focuses on aesthetic and affective modes of inscrutability in Asian American production (invisibility, silence, flatness, etc.) to challenge assimilation narratives that erase Asianness as a source of sociopolitical critique.

48. Machado, *Her Body*, 167.

49. See León, "Forms of Opacity." Édouard Glissant discusses the "right to opacity" in *Poetics of Relation* (1990), and Viego's examination of transparency and its demands for Latinx subjects is the focus of his book *Dead Subjects*.

50. See V. Huang, *Surface Relations*.

51. Haraway, "Manifesto for Cyborgs," 66; also see Haraway, *Staying with the Trouble*, 2–3.

52. Chen, *Animacies*, 3. Other scholars similarly articulate how in its attempt to decenter the human, posthumanist work like Haraway's whitewashes and obfuscates the centrality of race and ethnicity. See M. Huang, "Posthuman Subject"; Shih, "Is the Post in Postsocialism," 30; Weheliye, "'Feenin'"; M. López, *Racial Immanence*; and Jackson, "Animal."

53. See V. Huang, *Surface Relations*; and Cardozo-Kane and Subramaniam, "Assembling Asian/American Naturecultures," 4.

54. Weheliye, "'Feenin,'" 22.

55. V. Huang, *Surface Relations*.

56. Machado, *Her Body*, 128.

57. Machado, *Her Body*, 144.

58. Machado, *Her Body*, 134.

59. Marx and Engels, *Communist Manifesto*, 54.

60. Machado, *Her Body*, 135.

61. Machado, *Her Body*, 134, 135.

62. Machado, *Her Body*, 145, 136–37.

63. Machado, *Her Body*, 147.

64. Halberstam, *Queer Art of Failure*, 145.

65. This section is informed by M. Huang, "Racial Disintegration"; Fan, "Melancholy Transcendence"; Chuh, "It's Not about Anything"; Cheng, *Ornamentalism*; R. Ortiz, "Carmen Maria Machado's Body"; and Conners, "New Latinx Feelings."

66. For discussions on the "cancellation" of *latinidad* as well as the challenges of mapping *latinidad* and scholars who are destabilizing the term, see T. Flores, "'Latinidad Is Cancelled'"; Alan Pelaez Lopez (@migrantscribble), "Latinidad Is Cancelled," Twitter, November 8, 2018, https://twitter.com/MigrantScribble/status /1060580972138 123264; R. Ortiz, "Burning X's"; J. Rodríguez, *Queer Latinidad*, 13–23; Guzmán and León, "Cuts and Impressions"; Orchard, "Bruja Theory"; and Caminero-Santangelo, *On Latinidad*.

67. Berlant, "Genre Flailing," 157.

68. Berlant, *Cruel Optimism*, 6–7.

69. Berlant, "Big Man."

70. Lowe, *Intimacies of Four Continents*, 5.

71. R. Rodriguez, *Latinx Literature Unbound*, 14.

72. Orchard invites us to think of Latinx literature beyond *latinidad* or as a remaking of *latinidad* in "Bruja Theory." I take the question of what Latinx literature is now from Gruesz, "What Was Latino Literature?"; and R. Ortiz, *Latinx Literature Now*.

73. R. Saldívar, "Historical Fantasy"; and R. Saldívar, "Second Elevation."

74. Allatson, "From 'Latinidad' to 'Latinid@des,'" 129.

75. Caminero-Santangelo, *On Latinidad*, 27–30; Allatson, "From 'Latinidad' to 'Latinid@des,'" 130.

76. Aguilar-Ramírez, "Postmemories of Migration," 50.

77. Hartman, *Scenes of Subjection*, 21.

78. Machado, *Her Body*, 108.

79. I take the notion of linguistic posing and its role in marking Latinx identity in Latinx literature from Gruesz and Lazo, "Linguistic Posing."

80. Machado, *Her Body*, 216. Ricardo Ortiz makes this argument in his paper "Carmen Maria Machado's Body," given at the 2020 NeMLA conference, to which I am indebted.

81. Machado, *Her Body*, 62.

82. Milian, *Latining America*, 1–2.

83. Muñoz, *Sense of Brown*.

84. Muñoz, *Sense of Brown*, 79.

85. Machado, "'Being a Woman.'"

86. M. Huang, "Racial Disintegration," 506.

87. Ortiz makes this argument as well in "Carmen Maria Machado's Body."

88. Alvarado investigates abjection in relation to *latinidad* and the ways it exceeds categorization in *Abject Performances*. In *The Sense of Brown*, Muñoz locates *latinidad* as an affective excess that pushes against dichotomies and the "norms" of whiteness; and in "Cuts and Impressions," Guzmán and León illustrate how the category of *latinidad* requires what they call "lingering."

89. Clover, *Men, Women, and Chain Saws*, 4.

90. Chuh, "On (Not) Mentoring," quoted in V. Huang, *Surface Relations*, 501.

91. Muñoz discusses this in relation to what he calls the "burden of liveness" in *Disidentifications* (182), and Viego explores this through what he calls "deadening" in *Dead Subjects* (59, 93).

92. León, "Forms of Opacity," 378–79.

93. Hudson, "'Real Women Have Bodies,'" 3.

94. Hudson, "'Real Women Have Bodies,'" 3.

95. See HoSang and Gutiérrez, "Introduction: Toward a Relational Consciousness of Race," 3.

96. HoSang and Gutiérrez, "Introduction: Toward a Relational Consciousness of Race," 3.

CODA

1. Chu, *Do Metaphors Dream*, 3.

2. Chu, *Do Metaphors Dream*, 73.

3. Chu, *Do Metaphors Dream*, 10.

4. M. López, *Racial Immanence*, 4.

5. J. Rodríguez, *Sexual Futures*, 5.

6. Chuh, *Imagine Otherwise*, 23.

7. Pérez-Torres, "Introduction," 154.

8. Wiegman, *Object Lessons*, 3.

9. Wiegman, *Object Lessons*, 3n4.

10. Stuelke, *Ruse of Repair*, 17. Also see Namwali Serpell's essay "The Banality of Empathy."

11. H. Diaz, *In the Distance*, 1.

12. H. Diaz, *In the Distance*, 1.

13. *Oxford English Dictionary*, s.v. "canon," accessed April 26, 2024, https://www.oed.com/dictionary/canon_n1?tab=meaning_and_use#10096712.

14. Dictionary.com, s.v. "cannon," accessed April 26, 2024, https://www.dictionary.com/browse/cannon.

15. *Merriam-Webster*, s.v. "canyon," accessed April 26, 2024, https://www.merriam-webster.com/dictionary/canyon.

16. H. Diaz, "Feeling Foreign."

17. Turner's 1893 "frontier thesis" proposed that settler colonial exceptionalism was formed by claiming the rugged American frontier. Stressing the importance of "winning the wilderness," Turner's thesis emphasizes how the frontier shaped American democracy and character, finally proclaiming the closing of the frontier, which scholars argue was partly responsible for redirecting American imperialist aspirations overseas. See Turner, "Significance of the Frontier," 31–60. For scholars who engage with Turner's work and its influence, see Black, *Global Interior*; Horsman, *Race and Manifest Destiny*; Limerick, *Legacy of Conquest*; Okihiro, *American History Unbound*; and Saldaña-Portillo, *Indian Given*.

18. Okihiro, *American History Unbound*, 91.

19. Habash, "Western without Cowboys."

20. H. Diaz, *In the Distance*, 15, 19.

21. R. Rodriguez, *Latinx Literature Unbound*, 20, 127–28.

22. Ortiz, "Edwidge Danticat's *Latinidad*," 167–68.

23. H. Diaz, *In the Distance*, 94.

24. H. Diaz, *In the Distance*, 228.

25. H. Diaz, *In the Distance*, 82.

26. Stuelke, *Ruse of Repair*, 1–30.

27. H. Diaz, *In the Distance*, 84.

28. Berlant, *Female Complaint*, 41.

29. H. Diaz, *In the Distance*, 206.

30. H. Diaz, *In the Distance*, 256.

31. Orchard, "Bruja Theory."

32. Bersani, *Is the Rectum a Grave?*, 29, 24.

33. Jennifer Harford Vargas uses the concept of "el hueco" (the hole) to think about the openings created when larger systems of power disallow or foreclose points of entry. In her case, "el hueco" relates to undocumented migration to the United States and its representation in South American literatures. In my case, I use the hole to think about the field of Latinx literary studies and its expansion. See Harford Vargas, "On Huecos and Desaparecidos."

34. H. Diaz, *In the Distance*, 195.

35. H. Diaz, *In the Distance*, 182.

36. H. Diaz, *In the Distance*, 184.

37. H. Diaz, *In the Distance*, 189.

38. R. Ortiz, "Burning X's," 201.

39. R. Ortiz, "Burning X's," 203.

40. For scholarship on *latinidad*'s cancellation, see note 66 in chapter 5.

41. H. Diaz, *In the Distance*, 185.

Bibliography

Acosta, Oscar Zeta. *The Revolt of the Cockroach People*. San Francisco: Straight Arrow Books, 1973.

Adorno, Theodor, Walter Benjamin, Ernst Bloch, Bertolt Brecht, and Georg Lukács. *Aesthetics and Politics*. New York: Verso, 2007.

Adorno, Theodor, and Max Horkheimer. *Dialectic of Enlightenment*. Translated by John Cumming. London: Blackwell Verso, 1997.

Agamben, Giorgio. *State of Exception*. Translated by Kevin Atell. Chicago: University of Chicago Press, 2005.

Aguilar-Ramírez, Aarón. "Postmemories of Migration: Cuban Exile and Poetics of *Latinidad* in Jennine Capó-Cruet's *Make Your Home among Strangers*." *Journal of Latino-Latin American Studies* 11, no.1 (2021): 42–55.

Ahmed, Sara. *Living a Feminist Life*. Durham, NC: Duke University Press, 2017.

Allatson, Paul. "From 'Latinidad' to 'Latinid@des': Imagining the Twenty-First Century." In *The Cambridge Companion to Latina/o American Literature*, edited by John Morán González, 128–44. Cambridge: Cambridge University Press, 2016.

Alvarado, Leticia. *Abject Performances: Aesthetic Strategies in Latino Cultural Production*. Durham, NC: Duke University Press, 2018.

Alvarez, Julia. *How the García Girls Lost Their Accents*. Chapel Hill, NC: Algonquin Books of Chapel Hill, 1991.

Alvarez, Julia. *In the Time of the Butterflies*. Chapel Hill, NC: Algonquin Books of Chapel Hill, 1994.

Amin, Kadji, Amber Jamilla Musser, and Roy Pérez. "Queer Form: Aesthetics, Race, and the Violences of the Social." *ASAP/Journal* 2, no. 2 (2017): 227–39.

Anderson, Benedict. *Imagined Communities: Reflections on the Origin and Spread of Nationalism*. London: Verso, 1983.

Anker, Elisabeth R. *Ugly Freedoms*. Durham, NC: Duke University Press, 2022.

Anzaldúa, Gloria. *Borderlands/La Frontera: The New Mestiza*. San Francisco: Aunt Lute Books, 2012.

Anzaldúa, Gloria. *The Gloria Anzaldúa Reader*. Edited by AnaLouise Keating. Durham, NC: Duke University Press, 2009.

Aparicio, Frances. "The Blackness of Sugar: Celia Cruz and the Performance of (Trans) Nationalism." *Cultural Studies* 13, no. 2 (1999): 223–36.

Aparicio, Frances. "Latinidad/es." In *Keywords for Latina/o Studies*, edited by Deborah R. Vargas, Lawrence La Fountain-Stokes, and Nancy Raquel Mirabal, 113–17. New York: New York University Press, 2017.

Appelbaum, Robert. *The Aesthetics of Violence: Art, Fiction, Drama and Film*. Lanham, MD: Rowman and Littlefield, 2017.

Apter, Emily S. *Against World Literature: On the Politics of Untranslatability*. London: Verso, 2013.

Arendt, Hannah. *Eichmann in Jerusalem: A Report on the Banality of Evil*. New York: Viking, 1963.

Arias, Ron. *The Road to Tamazunchale*. Albuquerque, NM: Pajarito, 1975.

Babel, Isaac. *1920 Diary*. Translated by H. T. Willetts. Edited by Carol Avins. New Haven, CT: Yale University Press, 1995.

Bahng, Aimee. *Migrant Futures: Decolonizing Speculation in Financial Times*. Durham, NC: Duke University Press, 2018.

Bakhtin, M. M. *Rabelais and His World*. Bloomington: Indiana University Press, 1984.

Bal, Mieke. *Narratology: Introduction to the Theory of Narrative*. Translated by Christine van Boheemen. Toronto: University of Toronto Press, 2009.

Bassnett, Susan, and André Lefevere. *Constructing Cultures: Essays on Literary Translation*. Topics in Translation. Philadelphia: Multilingual Matters, 1998.

Batuman, Elif. "Get a Real Degree." *London Review of Books*, September 23, 2010. https://www.lrb.co.uk/the-paper/v32/n18/elif-batuman/get-a-real-degree.

Bautista, Daniel. "Comic Book Realism: Form and Genre in Junot Díaz's *The Brief Wondrous Life of Oscar Wao*." *Journal of the Fantastic in the Arts* 21, no. 1 (2011): 41–53.

The Believer. Review of *Atomik Aztex*, by Sesshu Foster. *McSweeney's* 4, nos. 1–5 (2006): 3.

Beltrán, Cristina. *The Trouble with Unity: Latino Politics and the Creation of Identity*. New York: Oxford University Press, 2010.

Benítez-Rojo, Antonio. *The Repeating Island: The Caribbean and the Postmodern Perspective, Second Edition*. Translated by James E. Maraniss. Durham, NC: Duke University Press, 1996.

Benítez-Rojo, Antonio. "Three Words toward Creolization." In *Caribbean Creolization: Reflections on the Cultural Dynamics of Language, Literature, and Identity*, edited by Kathleen M. Balutansky and Marie-Agnès Sourieau, 53–61. Gainesville: University Press of Florida, 1998.

Benjamin, Walter. *Illuminations*. Translated by Harry Zohn. Edited by Hannah Arendt. New York: Mariner Books, 2019.

Benjamin, Walter. "Theses on the Philosophy of History." In *Illuminations*, translated by Harry Zohn and edited by Hannah Arendt, 196–209. New York: Mariner Books, 2019.

Berger, James. *After the End: Representations of Post-Apocalypse*. Minneapolis: University of Minnesota Press, 1999.

Bergland, Renée L. *The National Uncanny: Indian Ghosts and American Subjects*. Hanover, NH: University Press of New England, 2000.

Berlant, Lauren. "Big Man." *Social Text Online*, January 19, 2017. https://socialtextjournal
.org/big-man/.

Berlant, Lauren. *Cruel Optimism*. Durham, NC: Duke University Press, 2011.

Berlant, Lauren. *The Female Complaint: The Unfinished Business of Sentimentality in
American Culture*. Durham, NC: Duke University Press, 2008.

Berlant, Lauren. "Genre Flailing." *Capacious: Journal for Emerging Affect Inquiry* 1, no. 2
(2018): 156–62.

Bersani, Leo. *Is the Rectum a Grave? And Other Essays*. Chicago: University of Chicago
Press, 2010.

Black, Megan. *The Global Interior: Mineral Frontiers and American Power*. Cambridge,
MA: Harvard University Press, 2018.

Bloch, Ernst. *The Principle of Hope*. Studies in Contemporary German Social Thought.
Cambridge, MA: MIT Press, 1986.

Bloom, Harold. *The Grotesque*. Bloom's Literary Themes. New York: Bloom's Literary
Criticism/Infobase, 2009.

Boccaccio, Giovanni. *The Decameron: A New Translation, Contexts, Criticism*. Edited and
translated by Wayne A. Rebhorn. New York: W. W. Norton, 2016.

Bolaño, Roberto. *2666*. Edited by Ignacio Echevarría. 2nd ed. New York: Vintage Español, 2017.

Bolaño, Roberto. *2666*. Translated by Natasha Wimmer. New York: Farrar, Straus and
Giroux, 2008.

Bolaño, Roberto. *Amuleto*. New York: Vintage Español, 2017.

Bolaño, Roberto. *Las Sinsabores Del Verdadero Policía*. Narrativas Hispánicas. 1st. ed.
Barcelona: Editorial Anagrama, 2011.

Bolaño, Roberto. *Los detectives salvajes*. 1st ed. New York: Vintage Español, 2010.

Bolaño, Roberto. "Roberto Bolaño by Carmen Boullosa." *BOMB Magazine*, January 1,
2002. https://bombmagazine.org/articles/roberto-bolaño/.

Boon, Kevin. "The Zombie as Other: Mortality and the Monstrous in the Post-Nuclear
Age." In *Better Off Dead: The Evolution of the Zombie as Post-Human*, edited by Deborah Christie and Sarah Juliet Lauro, 50–60. New York: Fordham University Press, 2011.

Brady, Mary Pat. *Extinct Lands, Temporal Geographies: Chicana Literature and the Urgency of Space*. Durham, NC: Duke University Press, 2002.

Brady, Mary Pat. *Scales of Captivity: Racial Capitalism and the Latinx Child*. Durham,
NC: Duke University Press, 2022.

Brennan, Teresa. *Globalization and Its Terrors: Daily Life in the West*. New York: Routledge, 2003.

Browder, Laura. *Slippery Characters: Ethnic Impersonators and American Identities*.
Chapel Hill: University of North Carolina Press, 2000.

Bruce-Novoa, Juan. *Retrospace: Collected Essays on Chicano Literature, Theory, and History*. Houston, TX: Arte Público, 1990.

Buim, Jay. *Creative Time Presents Kara Walker's "A Subtlety."* Creative Time, 2014.
Accessed April 16, 2024. https://www.youtube.com/watch?v=W2sedoeOiB8.

Buscaglia-Salgado, José F. *Undoing Empire: Race and Nation in the Mulatto Caribbean*.
Minneapolis: University of Minnesota Press, 2003.

Caminero-Santangelo, Marta. *On Latinidad: U.S. Latino Literature and the Construction of Ethnicity*. Gainesville: University Press of Florida, 2007.

Campbell, Jessica. "Real Women Have Skins: The Enchanted Bride Tale in *Her Body and Other Parties*." *Marvels and Tales* 33, no. 2 (2019): 302–18.

Campt, Tina. *Image Matters: Archive, Photography, and the African Diaspora in Europe*. Durham, NC: Duke University Press, 2012.

Cardozo-Kane, Karen M., and Banu Subramaniam. "Assembling Asian/American Nature-cultures: Orientalism and Invited Invasions." *Journal of Asian American Studies* 16, no. 1 (2013): 1–23.

Carpentier, Alejo. *El reino de este mundo*. Santiago de Chile: Editorial Universitaria, 2006.

Carpio, Glenda. *Migrant Aesthetics: Contemporary Fiction, Global Migration, and the Limits of Empathy*. New York: Columbia University Press, 2023.

Carrillo, H. G. [Herman Glenn Carroll]. *Loosing My Espanish*. New York: Pantheon, 2004.

carrington, andré. *Speculative Blackness: The Future of Race in Science Fiction*. Minneapolis: University of Minnesota Press, 2016.

Carroll, Noël. *Minerva's Night Out: Philosophy, Pop Culture, and Moving Pictures*. Malden, MA: Wiley-Blackwell, 2013.

Castillo, Ana. *So Far from God: A Novel*. New York: W. W. Norton, 1993.

Cave, Damien. "Wave of Violence Swallows More Women in Juárez, Mexico." *New York Times*, June 23, 2012.

Chambers-Letson, Joshua, and Tavia Nyong'o. "Editors' Introduction: The Aesthetic Resonance of Brown." In *The Sense of Brown*, by José Esteban Muñoz, ix–xxxiv. Durham, NC: Duke University Press, 2020.

Chen, Mel Y. *Animacies: Biopolitics, Racial Mattering, and Queer Affect*. Durham, NC: Duke University Press, 2012.

Cheng, Anne Anlin. *The Melancholy of Race*. New York: Oxford University Press, 2001.

Cheng, Anne Anlin. *Ornamentalism*. New York: Oxford University Press, 2019.

Cheng, Anne Anlin. *Second Skin: Josephine Baker and the Modern Surface*. New York: Oxford University Press, 2011.

Chiarealla, Tom. "How It Ends." *Esquire*, October 1, 2011. https://classic.esquire.com /article/2011/10/1/how-it-ends.

Chu, Seo-Young. *Do Metaphors Dream of Literal Sleep? A Science-Fictional Theory of Representation*. Cambridge, MA: Harvard University Press, 2010.

Chuh, Kandice. *The Difference Aesthetics Makes: On the Humanities "After Man."* Durham, NC: Duke University Press, 2019.

Chuh, Kandice. *Imagine Otherwise: On Asian Americanist Critique*. Durham, NC: Duke University Press, 2003.

Chuh, Kandice. "It's Not about Anything." *Social Text* 32, no. 4 (121) (2014): 125–34.

Chuh, Kandice. "On (Not) Mentoring." *Social Text Online*, January 13, 2013. https:// socialtextjournal.org/periscope_article/on-not-mentoring/.

Cisneros, Sandra. *Woman Hollering Creek, and Other Stories*. New York: Random House, 1991.

Clemmons, Zinzi (@zinziclemmons). "As a Grad Student, I Invited Junot Diaz to Speak to a Workshop on Issues of Representation in Literature. I Was an Unknown Wide-Eyed 26 Yo, and He Used It as an Opportunity to Corner and Forcibly Kiss Me. I'm Far from the Only One He's Done This 2, I Refuse to Be Silent Anymore." *Twitter*, May 4, 2018, 3:05 am. https://twitter.com/zinziclemmons/status /992299032562229248?ref_src=twsrc%5Etfw.

Clover, Carol J. *Men, Women, and Chain Saws: Gender in the Modern Horror Film.* Princeton, NJ: Princeton University Press, 2015.

Cohen, Jeffrey Jerome. "Undead (A Zombie Oriented Ontology)." *Journal of the Fantastic in the Arts* 23, no. 3 (2012): 397–412.

Coe, Michael D. *Breaking the Maya Code.* 3rd ed. London: Thames and Hudson, 2012.

Coe, Michael D., and Stephen D. Houston. *The Maya.* Ancient Peoples and Places. 9th ed. New York: Thames and Hudson, 2015.

Columbus, Christopher. *The Journal of Christopher Columbus (during His First Voyage, 1492–93) and Documents Relating the Voyages of John Cabot and Gaspar Corte Real.* Edited and translated by Clements R. Markham. London: Hakluyt Society, 1893.

Conners, Thomas. "New Latinx Feelings: Race, Affect, and Form in Queer Latinx Literature." PhD diss., University of Pennsylvania, 2020.

Conrad, Joseph. *Heart of Darkness and Other Tales.* Edited by Cedric Watts. New York: Oxford University Press, 1998.

Coronado, Raúl. *A World Not to Come: A History of Latino Writing and Print Culture.* Cambridge, MA: Harvard University Press, 2013.

Crucet, Jennine Capó. *How to Leave Hialeah.* The John Simmons Short Fiction Award. Iowa City: University of Iowa Press, 2009.

Cummins, Jeanine. *American Dirt.* New York: Flatiron Books, 2020.

Cutler, John Alba. "Borders and Borderland Literature." In *The Cambridge Companion to Transnational American Literature*, edited by Yogita Goyal, 157–73. Cambridge: Cambridge University Press, 2017.

Cutler, John Alba. *Ends of Assimilation: The Formation of Chicano Literature.* New York: Oxford University Press, 2015.

Cutler, John Alba. "Latinx Historicisms in the Present." *American Literary History* 34, no. 1 (2022): 102–12.

Dalleo, Raphael, and Elena Machado Sáez. *The Latino/a Canon and the Emergence of Post-Sixties Literature.* New York: Palgrave Macmillan, 2007.

Damrosch, David. *What Is World Literature?* Princeton, NJ: Princeton University Press, 2003.

Dayan, Joan. *Haiti, History, and the Gods.* Berkeley: University of California Press, 2005.

DeGuzmán, María. *Spain's Long Shadow: The Black Legend, Off-Whiteness, and Anglo-American Empire.* Minneapolis: University of Minnesota Press, 2005.

Deive, Carlos Esteban. *Diccionario de Dominicanismos.* 2nd ed. Santo Domingo, Dominican Republic: Ediciones Librería la Trinitaria: Editora Manatí, 2002.

Delany, Samuel R. "Generic Protocols: Science Fiction and Mundane." In *The Technological Imagination: Theories and Fictions*, edited by Teresa de Lauretis, Andreas Huyssen, and Kathleen M. Woodward, 175–93. Madison, WI: Coda, 1980.

Delbo, Charlotte. *Auschwitz and After*. Translated by Rosette C. Lamont. 2nd ed. New Haven, CT: Yale University Press, 2014.

de las Casas, Bartolomé. *A Short Account of the Destruction of the Indies*. Overland Park, KS: Digireads.com Publishing, 2019.

del Carmen Gómez-Vega, Ibis. "The Journey Home: Defining Identity in Cristina García's *Dreaming in Cuban*." *Voces: A Journal of Chicana/Latina Studies* 1, no. 2 (1997): 71–100.

Deleuze, Gilles, and Félix Guattari. *A Thousand Plateaus: Capitalism and Schizophrenia*. Minneapolis: University of Minnesota Press, 1987.

DeLoughrey, Elizabeth, and Tatiana Flores. "Submerged Bodies: The Tidalectics of Representability and the Sea in Caribbean Art." *Environmental Humanities* 12, no. 1 (2020): 132–66.

del Pilar Blanco, María. *Ghost-Watching American Modernity: Haunting, Landscape, and the Hemispheric Imagination*. New York: Fordham University Press, 2012.

Derby, Lauren. *The Dictator's Seduction: Politics and the Popular Imagination in the Era of Trujillo*. American Encounters/Global Interactions. Durham, NC: Duke University Press, 2009.

Derrida, Jacques. "The Law of Genre." *Critical Inquiry* 7, no. 1 (1980): 55–81.

Derrida, Jacques. "Of an Apocalyptic Tone Recently Adopted in Philosophy." *Oxford Literary Review* 6, no. 2 (1984): 3–37.

Descartes, René. *Discourse on Method; and, Meditations on First Philosophy*. Translated by Donald A. Cress. 4th ed. Indianapolis: Hackett Publishing, 1998.

Diaz, Hernan. "Feeling Foreign: An Interview with Hernan Diaz." By Joel Pinckney. *Paris Review*, October 10, 2017. https://www.theparisreview.org/blog/2017/10/10/feeling-foreign-an-interview-with-hernan-diaz/.

Diaz, Hernan. *In the Distance*. Minneapolis: Coffee House Press, 2017.

Diaz, Hernan. *Trust*. New York: Riverhead Books, 2022.

Diaz, Hernan. "A Western without Cowboys: PW Talks with Hernán Diaz." By Gabe Habash. *Publishers Weekly*, October 5, 2018. https://www.publishersweekly.com/pw/by-topic/authors/interviews/article/78261-a-western-without-cowboys-pw-talks-with-hern-n-diaz.html.

Díaz, Junot. *Drown*. New York: Riverhead Books, 1996.

Díaz, Junot. "Drown." In *Drown*, 91–107. New York: Riverhead Books, 1996.

Díaz, Junot. *The Brief Wondrous Life of Oscar Wao*. New York: Riverhead Books, 2007.

Díaz, Junot. "Junot Díaz by Edwidge Danticat." *BOMB Magazine*, October 1, 2007. https://bombmagazine.org/articles/junot-díaz/.

Díaz, Junot. "The Search for Decolonial Love: An Interview with Junot Díaz." By Paula M. L. Moya. *Boston Review*, June 26, 2012. http://bostonreview.net/books-ideas/paula-ml-moya-decolonial-love-interview-junot-d%C3%ADaz.

Díaz, Junot. "The Silence: The Legacy of Childhood Trauma." *New Yorker*, April 16, 2018, 24–28.

Díaz, Junot. *This Is How You Lose Her*. New York: Riverhead Books, 2012.

Dieste, Rafael. *Testamento geométrico*. La Coruña: Del Castro, 1975.

Di Iorio, Lyn. "Laughing through a Broken Mouth in *The Brief Wondrous Life of Oscar Wao*." In *Junot Díaz and the Decolonial Imagination*, edited by Monica Hanna, Jennifer

Harford Vargas, and José David Saldívar, 69–87. Durham, NC: Duke University Press, 2016.

Dimock, Wai Chee. *Through Other Continents: American Literature across Deep Time.* Princeton, NJ: Princeton University Press, 2006.

Duarte, Stella Pope. *If I Die in Juárez.* Camino Del Sol. Tucson: University of Arizona Press, 2008.

Dubey, Madhu. "Contemporary African American Fiction and the Politics of Postmodernism." *NOVEL: A Forum on Fiction* 35, no. 2/3 (2002): 151–68.

Dubey, Madhu. "Octavia Butler's Novels of Enslavement." *NOVEL: A Forum on Fiction* 46, no. 3 (2013): 345–63.

Dubey, Madhu. *Signs and Cities: Black Literary Postmodernism.* Chicago: University of Chicago Press, 2003.

Duncan, Glen. "Urban Undead." *New York Times Book Review*, October 30, 2011, 21.

Eagleton, Terry. "Capitalism, Modernism and Postmodernism." *New Left Review* 152 (July/August 1985): 60–73.

Eagleton, Terry. *The Ideology of the Aesthetic.* Cambridge, MA: Blackwell, 1990.

Echevarría, Ignacio. "Bolaño extraterritorial." In *Bolaño salvaje*, edited by Edmundo Paz Soldán and Gustavo Faverón Patriau, 431–45. Barcelona: Editorial Candaya, 2008.

Edwards, Bryan. *The History, Civil and Commercial, of the British Colonies in the West Indies: In Two Volumes. By Bryan Edwards, Esq., of the Island of Jamaica; F.R.S. S.A. and Member of the American Philosophical Society at Philadelphia.* Second edition, illustrated with maps. London: Printed for John Stockdale, Piccadilly, 1794.

Ehrenreich, Ben. "Naked Lunch." *Village Voice*, November 15, 2005. https://www .villagevoice.com/2005/11/15/naked-lunch-3/.

Esposito, Scott. "Swimming through the Omniverse." SF Station, April 13, 2006. https:// www.sfstation.com/2006/04/13/atomik-aztex-by-sesshu-foster/.

Esquivel, Laura. *Malinche.* Translated by Ernesto Mestre-Reed. Illustrated by Jordi Castells. New York: Atria Books, 2006.

Fan, Christopher. "Melancholy Transcendence: Ted Chiang and Asian American Postracial Form." *Post45*, November 5, 2014. https://post45.org/2014/11/melancholy -transcendence-ted-chiang-and-asian-american-postracial-form/.

Fanon, Frantz. *The Wretched of the Earth.* Translated by Richard Philcox. New York: Grove, 2004.

Fassler, Joe. "How Junot Diaz Wrote a Sexist Character, but Not a Sexist Book." *Atlantic*, September 11, 2012.

Felski, Rita. *Hooked: Art and Attachment.* Chicago: University of Chicago Press, 2020.

Felski, Rita. *The Limits of Critique.* Chicago: University of Chicago Press, 2015.

Ferrel, David. "As Far as Murals Go, This One Really Hams It Up." *Los Angeles Times*, October 27, 1987. https://www.latimes.com/archives/la-xpm-1987-10-27-me-16946 -story.html.

Figueroa-Vásquez, Yomaira C. *Decolonizing Diasporas: Radical Mappings of Afro-Atlantic Literatures.* Evanston, IL: Northwestern University Press, 2021.

Fish, Stanley. "Literature in the Reader: Affective Stylistics." *New Literary History* 2, no. 1 (1970): 123–62.

Flieger, Jerry Aline. "Becoming-Woman: Deleuze, Schreber and Molecular Identification." In *Deleuze and Feminist Theory*, edited by I. A. N. Buchanan and Claire Colebrook, 38–63. Edinburgh: Edinburgh University Press, 2000.

Flores, Juan. *From Bomba to Hip-Hop: Puerto Rican Culture and Latino Identity*. Popular Cultures, Everyday Lives. New York: Columbia University Press, 2000.

Flores, Tatiana. "'Latinidad Is Cancelled': Confronting an Anti-Black Construct." *Latin American and Latinx Visual Culture* 3, no. 3 (2021): 58–79.

Follett, Richard J. *The Sugar Masters: Planters and Slaves in Louisiana's Cane World, 1820–1860*. Baton Rouge: Louisiana State University Press, 2005.

Forster, E. M. *Aspects of the Novel*. New York: Harcourt, 1927.

Foster, Sesshu. *American Loneliness: Selected Poems*. Venice, CA: Beyond Baroque, 2006.

Foster, Sesshu. *Atomik Aztex*. San Francisco: City Lights, 2005.

Foster, Sesshu. *City of the Future*. Los Angeles: Kaya Press, 2018.

Foster, Sesshu. *City Terrace: Field Manual*. New York: Kaya Press, 1996.

Foster, Sesshu. *World Ball Notebook*. San Francisco: City Lights, 2009.

Foucault, Michel. *Society Must Be Defended: Lectures at the Collège de France, 1975–76*. Translated by David Macey. Edited by Mauro Bertani and Alessandro Fontana. New York: Picador, 2003.

Fox, Robert Elliot. *Conscientious Sorcerers: The Black Postmodernist Fiction of Leroi Jones/Amiri Baraka, Ishmael Reed, and Samuel R. Delany*. Contributions in Afro-American and African Studies. New York: Greenwood, 1987.

Freccero, Carla. "Queer Spectrality: Haunting the Past." In *A Companion to Lesbian, Gay, Bisexual, Transgender, and Queer Studies*, edited by George E. Haggerty and Molly McGarry, 194–213. Malden, MA: Blackwell, 2007.

Freeman, Elizabeth. *Time Binds: Queer Temporalities, Queer Histories*. Perverse Modernities. Durham, NC: Duke University Press, 2010.

Fregoso, Rosa-Linda, and Cynthia L. Bejarano. "Introduction: A Cartography of Feminicide in the Américas." In *Terrorizing Women: Feminicide in the Américas*, edited by Rosa-Linda Fregoso and Cynthia Bejarano, 1–42. Durham, NC: Duke University Press, 2010.

Fumagalli, Maria Cristina. *On the Edge: Writing the Border between Haiti and the Dominican Republic*. Liverpool: Liverpool University Press, 2015.

Galeano, Eduardo. *Open Veins of Latin America: Five Centuries of the Pillage of a Continent*. 25th anniversary ed. New York: Monthly Review Press, 1997.

García, Cristina. *Dreaming in Cuban*. 1st ed. New York: Knopf, 1992.

García Márquez, Gabriel. "The Solitude of Latin America." Nobel Lecture, December 8, 1982. https://www.nobelprize.org/prizes/literature/1982/marquez/lecture/.

García-Peña, Lorgia. *The Borders of Dominicanidad: Race, Nation, and Archives of Contradiction*. Durham, NC: Duke University Press, 2016.

Gaspar de Alba, Alicia. *Desert Blood: The Juárez Murders*. Houston, TX: Arte Público, 2005.

Gaspar de Alba, Alicia, and Georgina Guzmán, eds. *Making a Killing: Femicide, Free Trade, and la Frontera*. Austin: University of Texas Press, 2010.

Gates, Henry Louis, Jr. *The Signifying Monkey: A Theory of African-American Literary Criticism*. New York: Oxford University Press, 1988.

Gikandi, Simon. *Slavery and the Culture of Taste*. Princeton, NJ: Princeton University Press, 2011.

Gil'Adí, Maia. "'I Think about You, X—': Re-reading Junot Díaz after 'The Silence.'" *Latino Studies* 18, no. 4 (2020): 507–30.

Gil'Adí, Maia. "Sugar Apocalypse: Sweetness and Monstrosity in Cristina García's *Dreaming in Cuban*." *Studies in American Fiction* 47, no. 1 (2020): 97–116.

Gil'Adí, Maia, and Justin Louis Mann. "New Suns." *ASAP/Journal* 6, no. 2 (2021): 241–55.

Gill, Frank B. *Ornithology*. 3rd ed. New York: W. H. Freeman, 2007.

Gilroy, Paul. *The Black Atlantic: Modernity and Double Consciousness*. Cambridge, MA: Harvard University Press, 1993.

Ginsberg, Allen. *Howl, and Other Poems*. The Pocket Poets Series. San Francisco: City Lights, 1996.

Glissant, Édouard. *Poetics of Relation*. Translated by Betsy Wing. Ann Arbor: University of Michigan Press, 1997.

Glissant, Édouard. *Treatise on the Whole-World*. Translated by Celia Britton. Edited by Celia Britton. Liverpool: Liverpool University Press, 2020.

Glock, Allison. "We're All Fuku'd." *Esquire*, August 21, 2007. https://www.esquire.com /entertainment/books/reviews/a3272/junotdiaz0907/.

Goddu, Teresa A. *Gothic America: Narrative, History, and Nation*. New York: Columbia University Press, 1997.

Gómez, Laura E. *Manifest Destinies: The Making of the Mexican American Race*. 2nd ed. New York: New York University Press, 2018.

Gómez-Barris, Macarena, and Licia Fiol-Matta. "Introduction: Las Américas Quarterly." *American Quarterly* 66, no. 3 (2014): 493–504.

Gonzales, Rodolfo. "El Plan Espiritual De Aztlán." In *Aztlán: Essays on the Chicano Homeland*, edited by Rudolfo A. Anaya, Francisco A. Lomelí, and Enrique R. Lamadrid, 27–30. Albuquerque: University of New Mexico Press, 2017.

González, Christopher. "Latino Sci-Fi: Cognition and Narrative Design in Alex Rivera's *Sleep Dealer*." In *Latinos and Narrative Media: Participation and Portrayal*, edited by Frederick Luis Aldama, 211–23. New York: Palgrave Macmillan, 2013.

González, Hugo Marín. "Why I Chose Not to Be Latinx." *Latino Rebels*, July 20, 2017. https://www.latinorebels.com/2017/07/20/why-i-chose-to-not-be-latinx/.

Goodwin, Matthew David. *The Latinx Files: Race, Migration, and Space Aliens*. New Brunswick, NJ: Rutgers University Press, 2021.

Gordillo, Luz María. "Contesting Monstrosity in Horror Genres: Chicana Feminist Mappings of De La Peña's 'Refugio' and Hamilton's Anita Blake, Vampire Hunter Series." In *Altermundos: Latin@ Speculative Literature, Film, and Popular Culture*, edited by Cathryn Josefina Merla-Watson and B. V. Olguín, 199–212. Los Angeles: UCLA Chicano Studies Research Center Press, 2017.

Gordon, Avery. *Ghostly Matters: Haunting and the Sociological Imagination*. Minneapolis: University of Minnesota Press, 2008.

Goyal, Yogita. *Runaway Genres: The Global Afterlives of Slavery*. New York: New York University Press, 2019.

Grandin, Greg. *Empire's Workshop: Latin America, the United States, and the Rise of the New Imperialism*. New York: Owl Books, 2007.

Griswold del Castillo, Richard, and Arnoldo De León. *North to Aztlán: A History of Mexican Americans in the United States*. Twayne's Immigrant Heritage of America Series. New York: Prentice Hall International, 1996.

Gruesz, Kirsten Silva. *Ambassadors of Culture: The Transamerican Origins of Latino Writing*. Princeton, NJ: Princeton University Press, 2002.

Gruesz, Kirsten Silva. *Cotton Mather's Spanish Lessons: A Story of Language, Race, and Belonging in the Early Americas*. Cambridge, MA: Harvard University Press, 2022.

Gruesz, Kirsten Silva. "The Once and Future Latino: Notes toward a Literary History *Todavía para Llegar*." In *Contemporary Latino/a Literary Criticism*, edited by Lyn Di Iorio Sandín and Richard Perez, 115–42. New York: Oxford University Press, 2007.

Gruesz, Kirsten Silva. "What Was Latino Literature?" *PMLA* 127, no. 2 (2012): 335–41.

Gruesz, Kirsten Silva, and Rodrigo Lazo. "Linguistic Posing: Hache Carrillo and the Problem of LatinX Spanish-Signaling." Work in progress presented at Local Americanists lecture series, University of Maryland, College Park, October 19, 2020.

Guerra, Lillian. *Visions of Power in Cuba: Revolution, Redemption, and Resistance, 1959–1971*. Chapel Hill: University of North Carolina Press, 2012.

Guidotti-Hernández, Nicole M. "Affective Communities and Millennial Desires: Latinx, or Why My Computer Won't Recognize Latina/o." *Cultural Dynamics* 29, no. 3 (2017): 141–59.

Guidotti-Hernández, Nicole M. *Unspeakable Violence: Remapping U.S. and Mexican National Imaginaries*. Durham, NC: Duke University Press, 2011.

Gurba, Myriam. "Pendeja, You Ain't Steinbeck." *Tropics of Meta*, December 12, 2019. https://tropicsofmeta.com/2019/12/12/pendeja-you-aint-steinbeck-my-bronca-with-fake-ass-social-justice-literature/.

Guzmán, Joshua Javier. "Brown." In *Keywords in Latina/o Studies*, edited by Deborah R. Vargas, Lawrence La Fountain-Stokes, and Nancy Raquel Mirabal, 25–28. New York: New York University Press, 2017.

Guzmán, Joshua Javier, and Christina A. León. "Cuts and Impressions: The Aesthetic Work of Lingering in *Latinidad*." *Women and Performance: A Journal of Feminist Theory* 25, no. 3 (2015): 261–76.

Halberstam, Jack. *In a Queer Time and Place: Transgender Bodies, Subcultural Lives*. Sexual Cultures. New York: New York University Press, 2005.

Halberstam, Jack. *The Queer Art of Failure*. Durham, NC: Duke University Press, 2011.

Halberstam, Jack. *Skin Shows: Gothic Horror and the Technology of Monsters*. Durham, NC: Duke University Press, 1995.

Hall, Stuart. "Cultural Identity and Diaspora." In *Identity: Community, Culture, Difference*, edited by Jonathan Rutherford, 222–37. London: Lawrence and Wishart, 1990.

Halley, Janet E. *Split Decisions: How and Why to Take a Break from Feminism*. Princeton, NJ: Princeton University Press, 2006.

Hanna, Monica. "Reassembling the Fragments: Battling Historiographies, Caribbean Discourse, and Nerd Genres in Junot Díaz's *The Brief Wondrous Life of Oscar Wao*." *Callaloo* 32, no. 2 (2010): 498–520.

Hanna, Monica, Jennifer Harford Vargas, and José David Saldívar. "Introduction. Junot Díaz and the Decolonial Imagination: From Island to Empire." In *Junot Díaz and the Decolonial Imagination*, edited by Monica Hanna, Jennifer Harford Vargas, and José David Saldívar, 1–29. Durham, NC: Duke University Press, 2016.

Hanna, Monica, Jennifer Harford Vargas, and José David Saldívar, eds. *Junot Díaz and the Decolonial Imagination*. Durham, NC: Duke University Press, 2016.

Haraway, Donna. "A Manifesto for Cyborgs: Science, Technology, and Socialist Feminism in the 1980s." *Socialist Review*, no. 80 (1985): 65–108.

Haraway, Donna. *Staying with the Trouble: Making Kin in the Chthulucene*. Durham, NC: Duke University Press, 2016.

Harford Vargas, Jennifer. *Forms of Dictatorship: Power, Narrative, and Authoritarianism in the Latina/o Novel*. Oxford Studies in American Literary History. New York: Oxford University Press, 2018.

Harford Vargas, Jennifer. "On Huecos and Desaparecidos: State-Sanctioned Violence and Undocumented Migration in Latinx South American Literary Imaginaries." In *Latinx Literature and Critical Futurities, 1992–2020*, edited by William Orchard. Cambridge: Cambridge University Press, forthcoming.

Hartman, Saidiya. *Scenes of Subjection: Terror, Slavery, and Self-Making in Nineteenth-Century America*. Race and American Culture. New York: Oxford University Press, 1997.

Hartman, Saidiya. "Venus in Two Acts." *Small Axe* 12, no. 2 (2008): 1–14.

Hartman, Saidiya. *Wayward Lives, Beautiful Experiments: Intimate Histories of Social Upheaval*. 1st ed. New York: W. W. Norton, 2019.

Hartman, Saidiya V., and Frank B. Wilderson III. "The Position of the Unthought." *Qui Parle* 13, no. 2 (2003): 183–201.

Hassig, Ross. *Time, History, and Belief in Aztec and Colonial Mexico*. 1st ed. Austin: University of Texas Press, 2001.

Heidenreich, Linda. "Colonial Pasts, Utopian Futures: Creative and Critical Reflections on the Monstrous as Salvific." In *Altermundos: Latin@ Speculative Literature, Film, and Popular Culture*, edited by Cathryn Merla-Watson and B. V. Olguín, 213–34. Los Angeles: UCLA Chicano Studies Research Center Press, 2017.

Heise, Ursula. "Postmodern Novels." In *The Cambridge History of the American Novel*, edited by Leonard Cassuto, 964–85. Cambridge: Cambridge University Press, 2011.

Hernandez, Jillian. *Aesthetics of Excess: The Art and Politics of Black and Latina Embodiment*. Durham, NC: Duke University Press, 2020.

Hernández, Roberto D. *Coloniality of the US/Mexico Border: Power, Violence, and the Decolonial Imperative*. Tucson: University of Arizona Press, 2018.

Hernández-Avila, Inés, and Norma Elia Cantú, eds. *Entre Guadalupe y Malinche: Tejanas in Literature and Art*. Austin: University of Texas Press, 2016.

Hey-Colón, Rebeca. "Transformative Currents: An Exploration of the Sea and Identity in the Works of Angie Cruz and Nelly Rosario." In *Negotiating Latinidades, Understanding Identities within Space*, edited by Kathryn Quinn-Sánchez, 9–29. Newcastle upon Tyne: Cambridge Scholars, 2015.

Hogan, Ernest. "Chicanonautica Manifesto." *Aztlán: A Journal of Chicano Studies* 40, no. 2 (2015): 131–34.

Holland, Sharon Patricia. *Raising the Dead: Readings of Death and (Black) Subjectivity*. Durham, NC: Duke University Press, 2000.

Hood, Mary Angeline. "Desire and Knowledge: Feminist Epistemology in Carmen María Machado's 'The Husband Stitch.'" *Journal of Popular Culture* 53, no. 5 (2020): 989–1003.

Horsman, Reginald. *Race and Manifest Destiny: The Origins of American Racial Anglo-Saxonism*. Cambridge, MA: Harvard University Press, 1981.

HoSang, Daniel Martinez, and Natalia Molina. "Introduction: Toward a Relational Consciousness of Race." In *Relational Formations of Race: Theory, Method, and Practice*, edited by Natalia Molina, Daniel Martinez HoSang, and Ramón A. Gutiérrez, 1–18. Berkeley: University of California Press, 2019.

Hoyos Ayala, Héctor. *Beyond Bolaño: The Global Latin American Novel*. New York: Columbia University Press, 2015.

Huang, Michelle N. "The Posthuman Subject in/of Asian American Literature." *Oxford Research Encyclopedia of Literature*, February 25, 2019. https://doi.org/10.1093/acrefore /9780190201098.013.921.

Huang, Michelle N. "Racial Disintegration: Biomedical Futurity at the Environmental Limit." *American Literature* 93, no. 3 (2021): 497–523.

Huang, Vivian L. *Surface Relations: Queer Forms of Asian American Inscrutability*. Durham, NC: Duke University Press, 2022.

Hudson, Renee. "Latinidad in the Age of Trump: On Ricardo Ortiz's *Latinx Literature Now*." *Los Angeles Review of Books*, March 24, 2020. https://lareviewofbooks.org /article/latinidad-in-the-age-of-trump-on-ricardo-ortizs-latinx-literature-now/.

Hudson, Renee. *Latinx Revolutionary Horizons: Form and Futurity in the Americas*. New York: Fordham University Press, 2024.

Hudson, Renee. "'Real Women Have Bodies' and Carmen María Machado's *Latinidad*." Paper presented at the Northeast Modern Language Association conference, Boston, March 8, 2020.

Huerta, Monica. *Magical Habits*. Durham, NC: Duke University Press, 2021.

Hulstyn, Michaela. "Charlotte Delbo à l'écoute: Auditory Imagery in *Auschwitz et Après*." *Women in French Studies* 2016, no. 1 (2016): 70–82.

Hurley, Jessica. "History Is What Bites: Zombies, Race, and the Limits of Biopower in Colson Whitehead's *Zone One*." *Extrapolation* 56, no. 3 (2015): 311–33.

Hurston, Zora Neale. *Tell My Horse: Voodoo and Life in Haiti and Jamaica*. New York: Perennial Library, 1990.

Hutcheon, Linda. *A Poetics of Postmodernism: History, Theory, Fiction*. New York: Routledge, 1988.

Irizarry, Ylce. *Chicana/o and Latina/o Fiction: The New Memory of Latinidad*. Urbana: University of Illinois Press, 2016.

Irizarry, Ylce. "This Is How You Lose It: Navigating Dominicanidad in Junot Díaz's *Drown.*" In *Junot Díaz and the Decolonial Imagination*, edited by Monica Hanna, Jennifer Harford Vargas, and José David Saldívar, 189–225. Durham, NC: Duke University Press, 2016.

Jackson, Zakiyyah Iman. "Animal: New Directions in the Theorization of Race and Posthumanism." *Feminist Studies* 39, no. 3 (2013): 669–85.

Jameson, Fredric. *Archaeologies of the Future: The Desire Called Utopia and Other Science Fictions.* New York: Verso, 2005.

Jameson, Fredric. *Postmodernism, or, The Cultural Logic of Late Capitalism.* Post-Contemporary Interventions. Durham, NC: Duke University Press, 1991.

Jameson, Fredric. "Postmodernism and Consumer Culture." In *The Cultural Turn: Selected Writings on the Postmodern, 1983–1998*, 1–20. London: Verso, 1998.

JanMohamed, Abdul R. *The Death-Bound-Subject: Richard Wright's Archaeology of Death.* Post-Contemporary Interventions. Durham, NC: Duke University Press, 2005.

Jardine, Alice. "Woman in Limbo: Deleuze and His Br(Others)." *SubStance* 13, no. 3/4 (1984): 46–60.

Jerng, Mark C. *Racial Worldmaking: The Power of Popular Fiction.* New York: Fordham University Press, 2018.

Joblin, James. *Helm Dictionary of Scientific Bird Names.* London: Christopher Helm, 2009.

Kakutani, Michiko. "Pynchon Hits the Road with Mason and Dixon." Review of *Mason & Dixon*, by Thomas Pynchon. *New York Times*, August 29, 1997. https://www.nytimes.com/1997/04/29/books/pynchon-hits-the-road-with-mason-and-dixon.html.

Kakutani, Michiko. "Travails of an Outcast." Review of *The Brief Wondrous Life of Oscar Wao*, by Junot Díaz. *New York Times*, September 4, 2007. https://www.nytimes.com/2007/09/04/books/04diaz.html.

Kee, Chera. "'They Are Not Men . . . They Are Dead Bodies': From Cannibal to Zombie and Back Again." In *Better Off Dead: The Evolution of the Zombie as Post-Human*, edited by Deborah Christie and Sarah Juliet Lauro, 9–23. New York: Fordham University Press, 2011.

Keeling, Kara. *Queer Times, Black Futures.* Sexual Cultures. New York: New York University Press, 2019.

Keen, Suzanne. *Empathy and the Novel.* New York: Oxford University Press, 2007.

Kermode, Frank. *The Sense of an Ending: Studies in the Theory of Fiction.* New York: Oxford University Press, 2000.

Kim, Bobby ("Bobby Hundreds"). "Hogtied" (blog). The Hundreds, February 24, 2013. https://thehundreds.com/blogs/content/hogtied.

Kim, Tammy. "A Los Angeles Poet's Revolution of Every Day Life." *Al Jazeera*, September 6, 2015. http://america.aljazeera.com/multimedia/2015/9/sesshu-foster-los-angeles-street-poet.html.

King, Tiffany Lethabo. *The Black Shoals: Offshore Formations of Black and Native Studies.* Durham, NC: Duke University Press, 2019.

Klein, Milton M. *The Empire State: A History of New York.* Ithaca, NY: Cornell University Press, 2001.

Kondo, Dorinne. *Worldmaking: Race, Performance, and the Work of Creativity*. Durham, NC: Duke University Press, 2018.

Kurnick, David. "Bolaño to Come." *Public Books*, September 5, 2012. http://www .publicbooks.org/bolano-to-come/.

Kutzinski, Vera M. *Sugar's Secrets: Race and the Erotics of Cuban Nationalism*. New World Studies. Charlottesville: University Press of Virginia, 1993.

Lamas, Carmen E. *The Latino Continuum and the Nineteenth-Century Americas: Literature, Translation, and Historiography*. Oxford: Oxford University Press, 2021.

Lang, Swifty. *Feeding Ground*. Illustrated by Michael Lapinski. Production design and lettering by Chris Mangun. Los Angeles: Archaia, 2011.

Lauro, Sarah Juliet. *The Transatlantic Zombie: Slavery, Rebellion, and Living Death*. American Literatures Initiative. New Brunswick, NJ: Rutgers University Press, 2015.

Lavender, Isiah, III. *Race in American Science Fiction*. Bloomington: Indiana University Press, 2011.

Lee, Derek. "Postquantum: A Tale of the Time Being, *Atomik Aztex*, and Hacking Modern Space-Time." *MELUS: Multi-Ethnic Literature of the U.S.* 45, no. 1 (2020): 1–26.

Lee, Lisa. "Report from the Field: Racial Invisibility and Erasure in the Writing Workshop." Vida: Women in Literary Arts, January 11, 2016. http://www.vidaweb.org /report-from-the-field-racial-invisibility-and-erasure-in-the-writing-workshop/.

Lenin, Vladimir Il'ich. *Materialism and Empirio-Criticism*. New York: International Publishers, 1927.

León, Christina A. "Forms of Opacity: Roaches, Blood, and Being Stuck in Xandra Ibarra's Corpus." *ASAP/Journal* 2, no. 2 (2017): 369–94.

León Portilla, Miguel. *Aztec Thought and Culture: A Study of the Ancient Nahuatl Mind*. Translated by Jack Emory Davis. The Civilization of the American Indian Series. 1st ed. Norman: University of Oklahoma Press, 1963.

León Portilla, Miguel. *The Broken Spears: The Aztec Account of the Conquest of Mexico*. Expanded and updated ed. Boston: Beacon Press, 1992.

León Portilla, Miguel. *Pre-Columbian Literatures of Mexico*. The Civilization of the American Indian Series. Norman: University of Oklahoma Press, 1986.

Levey, Douglas J., Gustavo A. Londoño, Judit Ungvari-Martin, Monique R. Hiersoux, Jill E. Jankowski, John R. Poulsen, Christine M. Stracey, and Scott K. Robinson. "Urban Mockingbirds Quickly Learn to Identify Individual Humans." *Proceedings of the National Academy of Sciences* 106, no. 22 (2009): 8959–62.

Levine, Caroline. *Forms: Whole, Rhythm, Hierarchy, Network*. Princeton, NJ: Princeton University Press, 2015.

Levine, Caroline. "Strategic Formalism: Toward a New Method in Cultural Studies." *Victorian Studies* 48, no. 4 (2006): 625–57.

Levy-Navarro, Elena. "Fattening Queer History: Where Does Fat History Go from Here?" In *The Fat Studies Reader*, edited by Esther D. Rothblum and Sondra Solovay, 15–22. New York: New York University Press, 2009.

Lima, Lázaro. "*Sleep Dealer* and the Promise of Latino Futurity." *Border Narratives and Film* (blog), January 19, 2010. http://bordernarrativesandfilms.blogspot.com/2010/01 /lazaro-lima-sleep-dealer-and-promise-of.html.

Limerick, Patricia Nelson. *The Legacy of Conquest: The Unbroken Past of the American West*. New York: W. W. Norton, 2006.

Limón, José Eduardo. *American Encounters: Greater Mexico, the United States, and the Erotics of Culture*. Boston: Beacon, 1998.

Lincoln, Bruce. *Discourse and the Construction of Society: Comparative Studies of Myth, Ritual, and Classification*. New York: Oxford University Press, 1989.

Lindsey, Treva B., and Jessica Marie Johnson. "Searching for Climax: Black Erotic Lives in Slavery and Freedom." *Meridians* 12, no. 2 (2014): 169–95.

Lomelí, Francisco A., and Donaldo W. Urioste. *Chicano Perspectives in Literature: A Critical and Annotated Bibliography*. Albuquerque: Pajarito, 1976.

Long, Edward. *The History of Jamaica, or, General Survey of the Antient and Modern State of That Island with Reflections on Its Situation, Settlements, Inhabitants, Climate, Products, Commerce, Laws, and Government*. London: Printed for T. Lowndes, 1774.

Loofbourow, Lili. "Junot Díaz and the Problem of the Male Self-Pardon." *Slate*, June 24, 2018, https://slate.com/culture/2018/06/junot-diaz-allegations-and-the-male-self-pardon.html.

López, Antonio M. *Unbecoming Blackness: The Diaspora Cultures of Afro-Cuban America*. New York: New York University Press, 2012.

López, Marissa K. *Racial Immanence: Chicanx Bodies Beyond Representation*. New York: New York University Press, 2019.

López-Calvo, Ignacio. *God and Trujillo: Literary and Cultural Representations of the Dominican Dictator*. Gainesville: University Press of Florida, 2005.

Lovett, Anthony R., and Matt Maranian. *L.A. Bizarro! The Insider's Guide to the Obscure, the Absurd, and the Perverse in Los Angeles*. San Francisco: Chronicle Books, 2009.

Lowe, Lisa. *The Intimacies of Four Continents*. Durham, NC: Duke University Press, 2015.

Machado, Carmen Maria. "'Being a Woman Is Inherently Uncanny': An Interview with Carmen Maria Machado." By Lyra Kuhn. *Hazlitt*, September 19, 2017. https://hazlitt.net/feature/being-woman-inherently-uncanny-interview-carmen-maria-machado.

Machado, Carmen Maria. *Her Body and Other Parties*. Minneapolis: Graywolf, 2017.

Machado Sáez, Elena. "Generation MFA: Neoliberalism and the Shifting Cultural Capital of US Latinx Writers." *Latino Studies* 16, no. 3 (2018): 361–83.

Machado Sáez, Elena. "The Global Baggage of Nostalgia in Cristina Garcia's *Dreaming in Cuban*." *MELUS: Multi-Ethnic Literature of the U.S.* 30, no. 4 (2005): 129–47.

Machado Sáez, Elena. *Market Aesthetics: The Purchase of the Past in Caribbean Diasporic Fiction*. New World Studies. Charlottesville: University of Virginia Press, 2015.

Maguire, Emily. "Science Fiction." In *The Routledge Companion to Latino/a Literature*, edited by Suzanne Bost and Frances R. Aparicio, 350–60. Abingdon, UK: Routledge, 2013.

Maldonado Torres, Nelson. *Against War: Views from the Underside of Modernity*. Durham, NC: Duke University Press, 2008.

Mann, Justin Louis. "Black Insecurity at the End of the World." *MELUS: Multi-Ethnic Literature of the U.S.* 46, no. 3 (2021): 1–21.

Mann, Justin Louis. "Pessimistic Futurism: Survival and Reproduction in Octavia Butler's *Dawn*." *Feminist Theory* 19, no. 1 (2018): 61–76.

Marcus, Sharon, Heather Love, and Stephen Best. "Building a Better Description." *Representations*, no. 135 (2016): 1–21.

Marshall, Kate. "What Are the Novels of the Anthropocene? American Fiction in Geological Time." *American Literary History* 27, no. 3 (2015): 523–38.

Martin, Hugo. "Sharpening Vision of Pig Paradise." *Los Angeles Times*, July 5, 2000. https://www.latimes.com/archives/la-xpm-2000-jul-05-me-47938-story.html.

Martinez, Monica Muñoz. *The Injustice Never Leaves You: Anti-Mexican Violence in Texas*. Cambridge, MA: Harvard University Press, 2018.

Marx, Karl. *Capital: Volume I*. London: Penguin Classics, 2004.

Marx, Karl, and Friedrich Engels. *The Communist Manifesto*. Edited by Jodi Dean. London: Pluto, 2017.

Max, D. T. "The Novelist Whose Inventions Went Too Far." *New Yorker*, March 13, 2023. https://www.newyorker.com/magazine/2023/03/20/h-g-carrillo-the-novelist-whose-inventions-went-too-far.

Mbembe, Achille. *Necropolitics*. Translated by Steven Corcoran. Durham, NC: Duke University Press, 2019.

McClintock, Anne. "Imperial Ghosting and National Tragedy: Revenants from Hiroshima and Indian Country in the War on Terror." *PMLA* 129, no. 4 (2014): 819–29.

McCracken, Ellen. *New Latina Narrative: The Feminine Space of Postmodern Ethnicity*. Tucson: University of Arizona Press, 1999.

McGurl, Mark. *The Program Era: Postwar Fiction and the Rise of Creative Writing*. Cambridge, MA: Harvard University Press, 2009.

McHugh-Dillon, Ruth. "'Let Me Confess': Confession, Complicity, and #MeToo in Junot Díaz's *This Is How You Lose Her* and 'The Silence: The Legacy of Childhood Trauma.'" *MELUS: Multi-Ethnic Literature of the U.S.* 46, no. 1 (2021): 24–50.

McKittrick, Katherine. *Demonic Grounds: Black Women and the Cartographies of Struggle*. Minneapolis: University of Minnesota Press, 2006.

McMillan, Uri. "Introduction: Skin, Surface, Sensorium." *Women and Performance: A Journal of Feminist Theory* 28, no. 1 (2018): 1–15.

Megill, Donald D., and Richard S. Demory. *Introduction to Jazz History*. 6th ed. Upper Saddle River, NJ: Pearson Prentice Hall, 2004.

Mejía, Paula. "The Secret Life of H. G. Carrillo." *Rolling Stone*, February 11, 2021. https://www.rollingstone.com/culture/culture-features/h-g-carrillo-hache-identity-herman-glenn-carroll-afro-cuban-1120491/

Merla-Watson, Cathryn. "Latinofuturism." *Oxford Research Encyclopedia of Literature*. April 26, 2019. https://oxfordre.com/literature/view/10.1093/acrefore/9780190201098.001.0001/acrefore-9780190201098-e-648.

Merla-Watson, Cathryn Josefina, and B. V. Olguín, eds. *Altermundos: Latin@ Speculative Literature, Film, and Popular Culture*. Los Angeles: UCLA Chicano Studies Research Center Press, 2017.

Merla-Watson, Cathryn Josefina, and B. V. Olguín, eds. "Dossier: From the Horrific to the Utopic: Pan-Latin@ Speculative Poetics and Politics." *Aztlan: A Journal of Chicano Studies* 41, no. 1 (Spring 2016).

Merla-Watson, Cathryn Josefina, and B. V. Olguín, eds. "Dossier: Latin@ Speculative Literature, Film, and Popular Culture." *Aztlan: A Journal of Chicano Studies* 40, no. 2 (Fall 2015).

Merleaux, April. *Sugar and Civilization: American Empire and the Cultural Politics of Sweetness*. Chapel Hill: University of North Carolina Press, 2015.

Mignolo, Walter. *The Idea of Latin America*. Malden, MA: Blackwell, 2005.

Mignolo, Walter. *Local Histories/Global Designs: Coloniality, Subaltern Knowledges, and Border Thinking*. Princeton, NJ: Princeton University Press, 2012.

Milian, Claudia. "Extremely Latin, xoxo: Notes on Latinx." *Cultural Dynamics* 29, no. 3 (2017): 121–40.

Milian, Claudia. *Latining America: Black-Brown Passages and the Coloring of Latino/a Studies*. The New Southern Studies. Athens: University of Georgia Press, 2013.

Milian, Claudia. *LatinX*. Minneapolis: University of Minnesota Press, 2019.

Miller, T. S. "Preternatural Narration and the Lens of Genre Fiction in Junot Díaz's *The Brief Wondrous Life of Oscar Wao*." *Science-Fiction Studies* 38, no. 1 (2011): 92–114.

Mintz, Sidney W. *Sweetness and Power: The Place of Sugar in Modern History*. New York: Penguin Books, 1985.

Molina, Natalia, Daniel Martinez HoSang, and Ramón A. Gutiérrez. *Relational Formations of Race: Theory, Method, and Practice*. Oakland: University of California Press, 2019.

Molloy, Sylvia. "Postcolonial Latin America and the Magic Realist Imperative: A Report to an Academy." In *Nation, Language, and the Ethics of Translation*, edited by Sandra Bermann and Michael Wood, 370–79. Princeton, NJ: Princeton University Press, 2005.

Moore, Alan, and Dave Gibbons. *Watchmen*. 12 vols. New York: DC Comics, 2005.

Moraga, Cherríe. *Loving in the War Years: Lo Que Nunca Pasó por Sus Labios*. Cambridge, MA: South End, 2000.

Morales, Ed. "Why I Embrace the Term Latinx." *Guardian*, January 8, 2018. https://www .theguardian.com/commentisfree/2018/jan/08/why-i-embrace-the-term-latinx.

Moreno, Marisel C. *Crossing Waters: Undocumented Migration in Hispanophone Caribbean and Latinx Literature and Art*. Latinx: The Future Is Now. Austin: University of Texas Press, 2022.

Moretti, Franco. "Conjectures on World Literature." *New Left Review* 1 (January/February 2000): 54–68.

Moss, Emma-Lee. "*Infinite Jest* at 20: Still a Challenge, Still Brilliant." *Guardian*, February 15, 2016. https://www.theguardian.com/books/booksblog/2016/feb/15/infinite -jest-at-20-still-a-challenge-still-brilliant-emma-lee-moss.

Moten, Fred. *Black and Blur*. Durham, NC: Duke University Press, 2017.

Moten, Fred. "Blackness and Nothingness (Mysticism in the Flesh)." *South Atlantic Quarterly* 112, no. 4 (2013): 737–80.

Moten, Fred. *In the Break: The Aesthetics of the Black Radical Tradition*. Minneapolis: University of Minnesota Press, 2003.

Moten, Fred, and Stefano Harney. *The Undercommons: Fugitive Planning and Black Study*. Brooklyn, NY: Minor Compositions, 2013.

Moya, Paula. *The Social Imperative: Race, Close Reading, and Contemporary Literary Criticism*. Stanford, CA: Stanford University Press, 2016.

Moya, Paula, and Lesley Larkin. "The Decolonial Virtues of Ethnospeculative Fiction."
In *Cultivating Virtue in the University*, edited by Jonathan Brant, Edward Brooks, and
Michael Lamb, 226–49. New York: Oxford University Press, 2022.

Mulvey, Laura. "Visual Pleasure and Narrative Cinema." In *Visual and Other Pleasures*,
14–26. London: Palgrave Macmillan, 1989.

Muñoz, José Esteban. *Cruising Utopia: The Then and There of Queer Futurity*. Sexual
Cultures. New York: New York University Press, 2009.

Muñoz, José Esteban. *Disidentifications: Queers of Color and the Performance of Politics*.
Cultural Studies of the Americas. Minneapolis: University of Minnesota Press, 1999.

Muñoz, José Esteban. "From Surface to Depth, between Psychoanalysis and Affect."
Women and Performance: A Journal of Feminist Theory 19, no. 2 (2009): 123–29.

Muñoz, José Esteban. *The Sense of Brown*. Durham, NC: Duke University Press, 2020.

Munro, Martin. *Tropical Apocalypse: Haiti and the Caribbean End Times*. New World
Studies. Charlottesville: University of Virginia Press, 2015.

Musser, Amber Jamilla. *Sensational Flesh: Race, Power, and Masochism*. Sexual Cultures.
New York: New York University Press, 2014.

Musser, Amber Jamilla. *Sensual Excess: Queer Femininity and Brown Jouissance*. Sexual
Cultures. New York: New York University, 2018.

Newitz, Annalee. *Pretend We're Dead: Capitalist Monsters in American Pop Culture*.
Durham, NC: Duke University Press, 2006.

New York Times Magazine. "The Decameron Project: 29 New Stories from the Pandemic." July 12, 2020.

Ngai, Sianne. *Ugly Feelings*. Cambridge, MA: Harvard University Press, 2004.

Nixon, Rob. *Slow Violence and the Environmentalism of the Poor*. Cambridge, MA:
Harvard University Press, 2011.

Nyong'o, Tavia. *Afro-Fabulations: The Queer Drama of Black Life*. Sexual Cultures.
New York: New York University Press, 2019.

O'Gorman, Edmundo. *La invención de América: El universalismo de la cultura de
Occidente*. Mexico City: Fondo de Cultura Económica, 1958.

Okihiro, Gary Y. *American History Unbound: Asians and Pacific Islanders*. Oakland:
University of California Press, 2015.

Olguín, B. V. *Violentologies: Violence, Identity, and Ideology in Latina/o Literature*. Oxford Studies in American Literary History. New York: Oxford University Press, 2021.

Olivas, Daniel. "Yes, Latinx Writers Are Angry about *American Dirt*—and We Will Not
Be Silent." *Guardian*, January 30, 2020. https://www.theguardian.com/commentisfree
/2020/jan/30/american-dirt-book-controversy-latinx-writers-angry.

Ontiveros, Randy J. *In the Spirit of a New People: The Cultural Politics of the Chicano
Movement*. New York: New York University Press, 2014.

Orchard, William. "Bruja Theory: Latinidad without Latinos in Popular Narratives of
Brujería." In *Posthumanism and Latin(x) American Science Fiction*, edited by Emily
Maguire and Antonio Córdoba, 201–18. Cham, Switzerland: Palgrave Macmillan,
2022.

Ortíz, Amalia. "The Canción Cannibal Cabaret: A Post-apocalyptic Anarcha-Feminist
Revolutionary Punk Rock Musical." In *Altermundos: Latin@ Speculative Litera-*

ture, Film, and Popular Culture, edited by Cathryn Merla-Watson and B. V. Olguín, 422–49. Los Angeles: UCLA Chicano Studies Research Center Press, 2017.

Ortiz, Fernando. *Cuban Counterpoint, Tobacco and Sugar*. Durham, NC: Duke University Press, 1995.

Ortiz, Ricardo. "Burning X's: Critical Futurities within Latinx Studies' Disidentifying Present." *Aztlán: A Journal of Chicano Studies* 45, no. 2 (2020): 201–12.

Ortiz, Ricardo. "Carmen Maria Machado's Body and the Dis-identifying Event of 'Latinx.'" Paper presented at the Northeast Modern Language Association conference, Boston, March 8, 2020.

Ortiz, Ricardo. *Cultural Erotics in Cuban America*. Minneapolis: University of Minnesota, 2007.

Ortiz, Ricardo. "Edwidge Danticat's *Latinidad*: *The Farming of Bones* and the Cultivation (of Fields) of Knowledge." In *Aftermaths: Exile, Migration, and Diaspora Reconsidered*, edited by Marcus Bullock and Peter Paik, 150–72. New Brunswick, NJ: Rutgers University Press, 2008.

Ortiz, Ricardo. *Latinx Literature Now: Between Evanescence and Event*. Cham, Switzerland: Springer International, 2019.

Page, Lisa. "When Writer Hache Carrillo Died, the World Discovered His True Identity. What Does That Mean for His Legacy?" *Washington Post*, July 6, 2020. https://www .washingtonpost.com/entertainment/books/when-writer-hache-carrillo-died-the -world-discovered-his-true-identity-what-does-that-mean-for-his-legacy/2020/07/06 /4e7b9706-b489-11ea-aca5-ebb63d27e1ff_story.html.

Paredes, Américo. *A Texas-Mexican Cancionero: Folksongs of the Lower Border*. Austin: University of Texas Press, 1995.

Payant, Katherine. "From Alienation to Reconciliation in the Novels of Cristina García." *MELUS: Multi-Ethnic Literature of the U.S.* 26, no. 3 (2001): 163–82.

Paz, Octavio. *The Labyrinth of Solitude: The Other Mexico; Return to the Labyrinth of Solitude; Mexico and the United States; The Philanthropic Ogre*. Translated by Lysander Kemp, Yara Milos, and Rachel Phillips Belash. New York: Grove, 1985.

Peabody, Rebecca. *Consuming Stories: Kara Walker and the Imagining of American Race*. Oakland: University of California Press, 2016.

Pear, Mike. "This Slaughterhouse Mural Is Really, Really Creepy." *VICE*, July 8, 2013. https://www.vice.com/en/article/yv5agx/this-farmer-johns-slaughterhouse-mural-is -really-creepy.

Peláez, Sol. "Counting Violence: Roberto Bolaño and *2666*." *Chasqui* 43, no. 2 (2014): 30–47.

Pelaez Lopez, Alan. "The X in Latinx Is a Wound, Not a Trend." *Color Bloq*, September 2018. https://www.colorbloq.org/article/the-x-in-latinx-is-a-wound-not-a-trend.

Pérez, Louis A. *On Becoming Cuban: Identity, Nationality, and Culture*. Chapel Hill: University of North Carolina Press, 2008.

Pérez Firmat, Gustavo. *Life on the Hyphen: The Cuban-American Way*. Austin: University of Texas Press, 2012.

Pérez-Rosario, Vanessa. "On the Hispanophone Caribbean Question." *Small Axe: A Caribbean Journal of Criticism* 20, no. 3 (51) (2016): 21–31.

Pérez-Torres, Rafael, ed. "Dossier: Latinx Temporality as a Time of Crisis." *Aztlán: A Journal of Chicano Studies* 45, no. 2 (2020): 153–242.

Pérez-Torres, Rafael. "Introduction." *Aztlán: A Journal of Chicano Studies* 45, no. 2 (2020): 153–60.

Pérez-Torres, Rafael. "Refiguring Aztlán." In *Postcolonial Theory and the United States*, edited by Amritjit Singh and Peter Schmidt, 103–21. Race, Ethnicity, and Literature. Oxford: University Press of Mississippi, 2000.

Phillips, Jayne Anne. "Crowding Out Death." Review of *White Noise*, by Don DeLillo. *New York Times*, January 13, 1985.

Pinto, Samantha. *Infamous Bodies: Early Black Women's Celebrity and the Afterlives of Rights*. Durham, NC: Duke University Press, 2020.

Plasa, Carl. *Slaves to Sweetness: British and Caribbean Literatures of Sugar*. Liverpool Studies in International Slavery. Liverpool: Liverpool University Press, 2009.

Pöhlmann, Sascha. "Cosmographic Metafiction in Sesshu Foster's *Atomik Aztex*." *Amerikastudien/American Studies* 55, no. 2 (2010): 223–48.

Pollack, Sarah. "Latin America Translated (Again): Roberto Bolaño's *The Savage Detectives* in the United States." *Comparative Literature* 61, no. 3 (2009): 346–65.

Pratt, Mary Louise. "'Yo Soy La Malinche': Chicana Writers and the Poetics of Ethnonationalism." *Callaloo* 16, no. 4 (1993): 859–73.

Prose, Francine. "More Is More: Roberto Bolaño's Magnum Opus." *Harper's Magazine*, December 2008. https://harpers.org/archive/2008/12/more-is-more/.

Publishers Weekly. Review of *Atomik Aztex*, by Sesshu Foster. October 24, 2005. https://www.publishersweekly.com/978-0-87286-440-5.

Quijano, Aníbal. "Coloniality of Power and Eurocentrism in Latin America." *International Sociology* 15, no. 2 (2000): 215–32.

Quijano, Aníbal, and Immanuel Wallerstein. "Americanity as a Concept, or the Americas in the Modern World-System." *International Social Science Journal* 44, no. 4 (1992): 549–57.

Ramírez, Catherine S. "Cyborg Feminism: The Science Fiction of Octavia E. Butler and Gloria Anzaldúa." In *Reload: Rethinking Women + Cyberculture*, edited by Mary Flanagan and Austin Booth, 374–402. Cambridge, MA: MIT Press, 2002.

Ramírez, Dixa. *Colonial Phantoms: Belonging and Refusal in the Dominican Americas, from the 19th Century to the Present*. New York: New York University Press, 2018.

Ramírez, Dixa. "Violence, Literature, and Seduction." *Avidly*, May 8, 2018. http://avidly.lareviewofbooks.org/2018/05/08/violence-literature-and-seduction/.

Reynolds, Susan Salter. "The Monster in the Man." *Los Angeles Times*, January 8, 2006. https://www.latimes.com/archives/la-xpm-2006-jan-08-bk-reynolds8-story.html.

Rhodes, Gary Don. *White Zombie: Anatomy of a Horror Film*. Jefferson, NC: McFarland, 2001.

Ricœur, Paul. *Freud and Philosophy: An Essay on Interpretation*. The Terry Lectures. New Haven, CT: Yale University Press, 1970.

Rivera, Lysa. "Future Histories and Cyborg Labor: Reading Borderlands Science Fiction after NAFTA." *Science Fiction Studies* 39, no. 3 (2012): 415–36.

Rivero, Eliana. "Hispanic Literature in the United States: Self-Image and Conflict." *Revista Chicano-Riqueña* 13, no. 3–4 (1985): 173–92.

Roberts, Brian Russell, and Michelle Ann Stephens. *Archipelagic American Studies*. Durham, NC: Duke University Press, 2017.

Robins, Ellie. "Carmen Maria Machado's 'Her Body and Other Parties' Reclaims the Female Body in Subversive, Joyful Ways." *Los Angeles Times*, September 29, 2017. https://www.latimes.com/books/jacketcopy/la-ca-jc-carmen-maria-machado-20170929-story.html.

Rodríguez, Juana María. "Latino/a/x." In *Keywords for American Cultural Studies, Third Edition*, edited by Bruce Burgett and Glenn Hendler, 154–57. New York: New York University Press, 2020.

Rodríguez, Juana María. *Queer Latinidad: Identity Practices, Discursive Spaces*. New York: New York University Press, 2003.

Rodríguez, Juana María. *Sexual Futures, Queer Gestures, and Other Latina Longings*. New York: New York University Press, 2014.

Rodriguez, Ralph E. *Latinx Literature Unbound: Undoing Ethnic Expectation*. New York: Fordham University Press, 2018.

Rodríguez Navas, Ana. "Words as Weapons: Gossip in Junot Díaz's *The Brief Wondrous Life of Oscar Wao*." MELUS: *Multi-Ethnic Literature of the U.S.* 42, no. 3 (2017): 55–83.

Rohrleitner, Marion. *Transnational Latinidades*. Columbus: Ohio State University Press, forthcoming.

Román, Elda María. *Race and Upward Mobility: Seeking, Gatekeeping, and Other Class Strategies in Postwar America*. Stanford Studies in Comparative Race and Ethnicity. Stanford, CA: Stanford University Press, 2018.

Romero, Rolando, and Amanda Nolacea Harris. *Feminism, Nation and Myth: La Malinche*. Houston, TX: Arte Público, 2005.

Rosen, Jeremy. *Minor Characters Have Their Day: Genre and the Contemporary Literary Marketplace*. Literature Now. New York: Columbia University Press, 2016.

Ruiz de Burton, María Amparo. *The Squatter and the Don*. New York: Modern Library, 2004.

Rukeyser, Muriel. "Käthe Kollwitz." In *The Collected Poems of Muriel Rukeyser*, edited by Janet E. Kaufman and Anne F. Herzog, with Jan Heller Levi, 460–64. Pittsburgh, PA: University of Pittsburgh Press, 2005.

Said, Edward W. *Beginnings: Intention and Method*. New York: Columbia University Press, 1985.

Saldaña-Portillo, [María] Josefina. "Who's the Indian in Aztlán? Re-Writing Mestizaje, Indianism, and Chicanismo from the Lacandón." In *The Latin American Subaltern Studies Reader*, edited by Iliana Yamileth Rodriguez, 402–23. Durham, NC: Duke University Press, 2001.

Saldaña-Portillo, María Josefina. *Indian Given: Racial Geographies across Mexico and the United States*. Latin America Otherwise. Durham, NC: Duke University Press, 2016.

Saldaña-Portillo, María Josefina. *The Revolutionary Imagination in the Americas and the Age of Development*. Latin America Otherwise. Durham, NC: Duke University Press, 2003.

Saldivar, Cynthia. "#rapetreesarereal: Chican@Futurism and Hybridizing Horror in Christopher Carmona's 'Strange Leaves.'" In *Altermundos: Latin@ Speculative Literature, Film, and Popular Culture*, edited by Cathryn Merla-Watson and B. V. Olguín, 185–98. Los Angeles: UCLA Chicano Studies Research Center Press, 2017.

Saldívar, José David. "Conjectures of 'Americanity' and Junot Díaz's 'Fukú Americanus' in *The Brief Wondrous Life of Oscar Wao*." *Global South* 5, no. 1 (2011): 120–36.

Saldívar, José David. *Junot Díaz: On the Half-Life of Love*. Durham, NC: Duke University Press, 2022.

Saldívar, José David. *Trans-Americanity: Subaltern Modernities, Global Coloniality, and the Cultures of Greater Mexico*. New Americanists. Durham, NC: Duke University Press, 2012.

Saldívar, Ramón. "Historical Fantasy, Speculative Realism, and Postrace Aesthetics in Contemporary American Fiction." *American Literary History* 23, no. 3 (2011): 574–99.

Saldívar, Ramón. "Imagining Cultures: The Transnational Imaginary in Postrace America." *Journal of Transnational American Studies* 4, no. 2 (2012): 1–18.

Saldívar, Ramón. "The Other Side of History, the Other Side of Fiction: Form and Genre in Sesshu Foster's *Atomik Aztex*." In *American Studies as Transnational Practice: Turning toward the Transpacific*, edited by Yuan Shu and Donald E. Pease, 156–66. Hanover, NH: Dartmouth College Press, 2015.

Saldívar, Ramón. "The Second Elevation of the Novel: Race, Form, and the Postrace Aesthetic in Contemporary Narrative." *Narrative* 21, no. 1 (2013): 1–18.

Saldívar, Ramón. "Speculative Realism and the Postrace Aesthetic in Contemporary American Fiction." In *A Companion to American Literary Studies*, edited by Caroline F. Lavander and Robert S. Levine, 517–31. Malden, MA: Wiley-Blackwell, 2011.

Saldívar-Hull, Sonia. "Feminism on the Border: From Gender Politics to Geopolitics." In *Criticism in the Borderlands: Studies in Chicano Literature, Culture, and Ideology*, edited by Héctor Calderón and José David Saldívar, 203–20. Durham, NC: Duke University Press, 1991.

Sánchez Prado, Ignacio. "The Persistence of the Transcultural: A Latin American Theory of the Novel from the National-Popular to the Global." *New Literary History* 51, no. 2 (2020): 347–74.

Sanchez-Taylor, Joy. *Diverse Futures: Science Fiction and Authors of Color*. Columbus: Ohio State University Press, 2021.

Sandiford, Keith Albert. *The Cultural Politics of Sugar: Caribbean Slavery and Narratives of Colonialism*. Cambridge: Cambridge University Press, 2000.

Santiago, Danny [Daniel James]. *Famous All Over Town*. New York: Simon and Schuster, 1983.

Scarry, Elaine. *The Body in Pain: The Making and Unmaking of the World*. New York: Oxford University Press, 1985.

Schalk, Sami. *Bodyminds Reimagined: (Dis)Ability, Race, and Gender in Black Women's Speculative Fiction*. Durham, NC: Duke University Press, 2018.

Schwartz, Alvin. *In a Dark, Dark Room, and Other Scary Stories*. Illustrated by Dirk Zimmer. New York: Harper and Row, 1984.

Scott, A. O. "Dreaming in Spanglish." Review of *The Brief Wondrous Life of Oscar Wao*, by Junot Díaz. *New York Times Book Review*, September 30, 2007. https://www.nytimes.com/2007/09/30/books/review/Scott-t.html.

Scott, Darieck. *Extravagant Abjection: Blackness, Power, and Sexuality in the African American Literary Imagination*. New York: New York University Press, 2010.

Scott, Darieck. *Keeping It Unreal: Black Queer Fantasy and Superhero Comics*. Sexual Cultures. New York: New York University Press, 2021.

Seabrook, William. *The Magic Island*. New York: Dover Publications, 2016.

Sedgwick, Eve Kosofsky. *The Coherence of Gothic Conventions*. New York: Methuen, 1986.

Sedgwick, Eve Kosofsky. *Touching Feeling: Affect, Pedagogy, Performativity*. Durham, NC: Duke University Press, 2003.

Sehgal, Parul. "Fairy Tales about the Fears Within." Review of *Her Body and Other Parties*, by Carmen Maria Machado. *New York Times*, October 4, 2017. https://www.nytimes.com/2017/10/04/books/review-her-body-and-other-parties-carmen-maria-machado.html.

Serpell, Namwali. "The Banality of Empathy." *New York Review of Books*, March 2, 2019. https://www.nybooks.com/online/2019/03/02/the-banality-of-empathy/.

Sexton, Jared Yates. "The Social Life of Social Death: On Afro-Pessimism and Black Optimism." *InTensions* 5 (Fall/Winter 2011): 1–47.

Sharpe, Christina. *In the Wake: On Blackness and Being*. Durham, NC: Duke University Press, 2016.

Sharpe, Christina. *Monstrous Intimacies: Making Post-Slavery Subjects*. Durham, NC: Duke University Press, 2010.

Sheller, Mimi. *Consuming the Caribbean: From Arawaks to Zombies*. New York: Routledge, 2003.

Shih, Shu-mei. "Is the Post in Postsocialism the Post in Posthumanism?" *Social Text* 30, no. 1 (2012): 27–50.

Sinclair, Upton. *The Jungle*. Edited by Kenneth W. Warren. New York: W. W. Norton, 2023.

Sky, Jennifer. "Colson Whitehead's Brain." *Interview*, October 28, 2011. https://www.interviewmagazine.com/culture/colson-whitehead-zone-one.

Sohn, Stephen Hong. *Racial Asymmetries: Asian American Fictional Worlds*. New York: New York University Press, 2014.

Solow, Barbara L. *Slavery and the Rise of the Atlantic System*. Cambridge: Cambridge University Press, 1991.

Sorensen, Leif. "Against the Post-Apocalyptic: Narrative Closure in Colson Whitehead's *Zone One*." *Contemporary Literature* 55, no. 3 (2014): 559–92.

Sperling, Joshua. "How to Read Like a Translator." *Public Books*, September 17, 2021. https://www.publicbooks.org/how-to-read-like-a-translator/.

Spillers, Hortense J. "Mama's Baby, Papa's Maybe: An American Grammar Book." *Diacritics* 17, no. 2 (1987): 65–81.

Spivak, Gayatri Chakravorty. *An Aesthetic Education in the Era of Globalization*. Cambridge, MA: Harvard University Press, 2012.

Staff. "What's the Right Way to Pronounce Latinx?" *Remezcla*, January 31, 2018. https://remezcla.com/culture/right-way-to-pronounce-latinx/.

Staudt, Kathleen A. *Violence and Activism at the Border: Gender, Fear, and Everyday Life in Ciudad Juárez*. Inter-America Series. Austin: University of Texas Press, 2008.

Steel, Karl. *How Not to Make a Human: Pets, Feral Children, Worms, Sky Burial, Oysters*. Minneapolis: University of Minnesota Press, 2019.

St. John, Spenser. *Hayti; or, The Black Republic*. Source Books on Haiti, Vol. 9. London: F. Cass, 1971.

Stott, Andrew McConnell. *Comedy: The New Critical Idiom*. New York: Routledge, 2014.

Stratford, Elaine, Godfrey Baldacchino, Elizabeth McMahon, Carol Farbotko, and Andrew Harwood. "Envisioning the Archipelago." *Island Studies Journal* 6, no. 2 (2011): 113–30.

Strings, Sabrina. *Fearing the Black Body: The Racial Origins of Fat Phobia*. New York: New York University Press, 2019.

Stuelke, Patricia Rachael. *The Ruse of Repair: US Neoliberal Empire and the Turn from Critique*. Durham, NC: Duke University Press, 2021.

Subramanian, Shreerekha. "In the Wake of His Damage." *Rumpus*, May 12, 2018. https://therumpus.net/2018/05/in-the-wake-of-his-damage/.

Suvin, Darko. *Metamorphoses of Science Fiction: On the Poetics and History of a Literary Genre*. Edited by Gerry Canavan. Oxford: Peter Lang, 2016.

Swanson, Lucy. *The Zombie in Contemporary French Caribbean Fiction*. Liverpool: Liverpool University Press, 2023.

Tabios, Eileen. "Sesshu Foster's Coming of Age: City Terrace Field Manual." In *Black Lightning: Poetry-in-Progress*, 228. New York: Asian American Writers Workshop, 1998.

TallBear, Kim. "Indigenous Genocide and Reanimation, Settler Apocalypse and Hope." *Aboriginal Policy Studies* 10, no. 2 (2023): 93–111.

Taylor, Diana. *The Archive and the Repertoire: Performing Cultural Memory in the Americas*. Durham, NC: Duke University Press, 2003.

Thomas, Hugh. *The Slave Trade: The Story of the Atlantic Slave Trade, 1440–1870*. New York: Simon and Schuster, 1997.

Thompson, Nato. "Curatorial Statement." Creative Time. Accessed April 11, 2024. https://creativetime.org/projects/karawalker/curatorial-statement/.

Tinsley, Omise'eke Natasha. "Black Atlantic, Queer Atlantic: Queer Imaginings of the Middle Passage." *GLQ: A Journal of Lesbian and Gay Studies* 14, no. 2–3 (2008): 191–215.

Tompkins, Kyla Wazana. *Racial Indigestion: Eating Bodies in the Nineteenth Century*. America and the Long 19th Century. New York: New York University Press, 2012.

Tompkins, Kyla Wazana. "Sweetness, Capacity, Energy." *American Quarterly* 71, no. 3 (2019): 849–56.

Torres, Justin. *We the Animals*. Boston: Houghton Mifflin Harcourt, 2011.

Torres-Saillant, Silvio. "Artistry, Ancestry, and Americanness in the Works of Junot Díaz." In *Junot Díaz and the Decolonial Imagination*, edited by Monica Hanna, Jennifer Harford Vargas, and José David Saldívar, 115–46. Durham, NC: Duke University Press, 2016.

Torres-Saillant, Silvio. "Dominican Literature and Its Criticism: Anatomy of a Troubled Identity." In *A History of Literature in the Caribbean*, edited by A. James Arnold, Julio Rodríguez-Luis, and J. Michael Dash, 49–64. Philadelphia: J. Benjamins, 1994.

Townsend, Richard F. *The Aztecs. Ancient Peoples and Places*. 3rd ed. London: Thames and Hudson, 2009.

Trefzer, Annette. "Possessing the Self: Caribbean Identities in Zora Neale Hurston's *Tell My Horse*." *African American Review* 34, no. 2 (2000): 299–312.

Trouillot, Michel-Rolph. *Silencing the Past: Power and the Production of History*. Boston: Beacon, 2015.

Tuana, Nancy. "The Speculum of Ignorance: The Women's Health Movement and Epistemologies of Ignorance." *Hypatia* 21, no. 3 (2006): 1–19.

Turner, Frederick Jackson. *Rereading Frederick Jackson Turner: "The Significance of the Frontier in American History" and Other Essays*. New Haven, CT: Yale University Press, 1998.

Twain, Mark. *The Adventures of Huckleberry Finn*. New York: Open Road Media, 2015.

Ulibarri, Kristy L. "Consuming Aztecs, Producing Workers: Economies of Indigeneity and Ambivalence in the Chicana/o and Latina/o Imagination." *Latino Studies* 14, no. 2 (2016): 214–33.

Vargas, Deborah R. "Ruminations on *Lo Sucio* as a Latino Queer Analytic." *American Quarterly* 66, no. 3 (2014): 715–26.

Vázquez, David J., Magdalena L. Barrera, and Elena Machado Sáez. "What the *New York Times* Gets Wrong about 'American Dirt' Controversy." *Salon*, February 11, 2023. https://www.salon.com/2023/02/11/what-the-new-york-times-gets-about-the -american-dirt-controversy/.

Viego, Antonio. *Dead Subjects: Toward a Politics of Loss in Latino Studies*. Durham, NC: Duke University Press, 2007.

Viego, Antonio. "LatinX and the Neurologization of Self." *Cultural Dynamics* 29, no. 3 (2017): 160–76.

Villalobos-Ruminott, Sergio. "A Kind of Hell: Roberto Bolaño and the Return of World Literature." *Journal of Latin American Cultural Studies* 18, no. 2–3 (2009): 193–205.

Villalon, Oscar. "In 'The Brief Wondrous Life of Oscar Wao,' a New America emerges." Review of *The Brief Wondrous Life of Oscar Wao*, by Junot Díaz. *San Francisco Chronicle*, September 20, 2007. https://www.sfgate.com/books/article/In-The-Brief -Wondrous-Life-of-Oscar-Wao-a-new-2501543.php.

Viramontes, Helena María. *Under the Feet of Jesus*. New York: Dutton, 1995.

"The Visual Life of Catastrophic History: A *Small Axe* Project Statement." *Small Axe* 15, no. 1 (2011): 133–36.

Vogler, Candace. "The Moral of the Story." *Critical Inquiry* 34, no. 1 (2007): 5–35.

Wald, Priscilla. *Contagious: Cultures, Carriers, and the Outbreak Narrative*. Durham, NC: Duke University Press, 2008.

Walker, Kara. *A Subtlety, or the Marvelous Sugar Baby*. May 10–July 6, 2014. Sugar, polystyrene foam, plastic, molasses. Creative Time, Domino Sugar Refinery, Brooklyn, NY. https://creativetime.org/projects/karawalker/.

Walker, Kara. "Sweet Talk." Lecture at the Radcliffe Institute, Harvard University, Cambridge, MA, December 18, 2014. https://youtu.be/jiDUo24R7lI?si =Cu9z9GyzSc7lSUyw.

Wallace, Mike. *Greater Gotham: A History of New York City from 1898 to 1919*. New York: Oxford University Press, 2017.

Warren, Calvin L. "Black Nihilism and the Politics of Hope." CR: *The New Centennial Review* 15, no. 1 (2015): 215–48.

Washington Valdez, Diana. *The Killing Fields: Harvest of Women: The Truth about Mexico's Bloody Border Legacy*. Los Angeles: Peace at the Border, 2006.

Weheliye, Alexander G. "'Feenin': Posthuman Voices in Contemporary Black Popular Music." *Social Text* 20, no. 2 (2002): 21–47.

Welsch, Wolfgang. *Undoing Aesthetics*. Theory, Culture and Society. London: Sage, 1997.

White, Francis Ray. "Fat, Queer, Dead: 'Obesity' and the Death Drive." *Somatechnics* 2, no. 1 (2012): 1–17.

Whitehead, Colson. *Zone One*. New York: Doubleday, 2011.

Whitfield, Esther Katheryn. *Cuban Currency: The Dollar and "Special Period" Fiction*. Cultural Studies of the Americas. Minneapolis: University of Minnesota Press, 2008.

Whyte, Kyle Powys. "Our Ancestors' Dystopia Now: Indigenous Conservation and the Anthropocene." In *The Routledge Companion to the Environmental Humanities*, edited by Ursula Heise, Jon Christensen, and Michelle Niemann, 222–31. New York: Routledge, 2017.

Więckowska, Katarzyna. "Silence and Fecundity in Carmen Maria Machado's *Her Body and Other Parties*." *Litteraria Copernicana*, no. 3 (35) (2020): 81–89.

Wiegman, Robyn. *Object Lessons*. Next Wave. Durham, NC: Duke University Press, 2012.

Wilderson, Frank B., III. *Red, White and Black: Cinema and the Structure of U.S. Antagonisms*. Durham, NC: Duke University Press, 2010.

Williams, Eric. *Capitalism and Slavery*. Chapel Hill: University of North Carolina Press, 1994.

Woloch, Alex. *The One vs. the Many: Minor Characters and the Space of the Protagonist in the Novel*. Princeton, NJ: Princeton University Press, 2003.

Woloson, Wendy A. *Refined Tastes: Sugar, Confectionery, and Consumers in Nineteenth-Century America*. Baltimore: Johns Hopkins University Press, 2002.

Wright, Melissa W. *Disposable Women and Other Myths of Global Capitalism*. New York: Routledge, 2006.

Wright, Melissa W. "Necropolitics, Narcopolitics, and Femicide: Gendered Violence on the Mexico-U.S. Border." *Signs: Journal of Women in Culture and Society* 36, no. 3 (2011): 707–31.

Wright, Michelle M. *Physics of Blackness: Beyond the Middle Passage Epistemology*. Minneapolis: University of Minnesota Press, 2015.

Ybarra-Frausto, Tomás. "*Rasquachismo*: A Chicano Sensibility" In *Chicano and Chicana Art: A Critical Anthology*, edited by Jennifer A. González, C. Ondine Chavoya, Chon Noriega, and Terezita Romo, 85–90. Durham, NC: Duke University Press, 2019.

Yun, Lisa, William Luis, Albert Chong, Karen Tei Yamashita, and Alejandro Campos García. "Signifying 'Asian' and Afro-Cultural Poetics: A Conversation with William Luis, Albert Chong, Karen Tei Yamashita, and Alejandro Campos García." *Afro-Hispanic Review* 27, no. 1 (2008): 183–217.

Zalewski, Daniel. "Vagabonds: Roberto Bolaño and His Fractured Masterpiece." *New Yorker*, March 19, 2007. https://www.newyorker.com/magazine/2007/03/26/vagabonds.

Zamora, Dominique. "Streetwear Brand 'The Hundreds' Paints a Grisly Picture of Farmer John Hypocrisy." *Huffington Post*, March 4, 2013. https://www.huffpost.com/entry/the-hundreds-farmer-john_b_2784904.

Zapata, Michael. *The Lost Book of Adana Moreau*. Toronto: Hanover Square, 2020.

Zavala, Oswaldo. "The Repolitization of the Latin American Shore: Roberto Bolaño and the Dispersion of 'World Literature.'" In *Roberto Bolaño as World Literature*, edited by Nicholas Birns and Juan E. De Castro, 79–98. New York: Bloomsbury, 2017.

Žižek, Slavoj. *Living in the End Times*. London: Verso, 2011.

Page locators in italics indicate figures.

atomic violence, 47, 53, 85, 97, 108, 115, 148–49, 213n18

Atomik Aztex (Foster), 5, 21, 123–49, 213n6; Aztlán mythology in, 145–48; butchering of pigs in, 140–41; as "Chicanesque" writing, 143, 146; Chicanx concepts unsettled in, 31, 126, 130; doom patterns in, 126, 141; economic issues in, 139–40; excesses in, 127–32, 140, 145; expansive history of Indigenous genocide in, 147–48; extratextual references in, 131–33, 215n18; Farmer John slaughterhouse in, 123–24, 134; human sacrifice in, 125, 137, 139–40; humor in, 132–33; as immersive experience for reader, 129–30; and Latinx literature, 141–49; meaning of title terms, 148; mockingbird figure in, 130; multilingualism in, 127, 130–31; multiple literary traditions in, 127–28; Nazism in, 137–40; "Note," 128–33, 135; paratextual references in, 127, 131; "plot" and temporal setting, 128–33; racial and ethnic constructions in, 141–42; racially coded reviews of, 125; reimagination of the historical past in, 125–26; Spanish conquest of Mexico in, 31, 124, 125, 129, 148–49; as speculative fiction, 125–26, 129–30; unreliable narrator, 133–34; world-building in, 134, 136, 138. *See also* Foster, Sesshu

Auschwitz, et apres (Delbo), 133

"authenticity" issues, 141–42

"author-function," 143

Aztecs: cyclical time as belief, 136–37; genocide of, 134–36; Moctezuma I, 147; as political tool, 146–47; Quetzalcoatl, 137

Aztlán (journal), 24–25, 180, 198n63

Aztlán (pre-Columbian homeland), 31, 146–48, 218n98; "El Plan Espiritual de Aztlán" (Spiritual Plan of Aztlán), 147, 148

"Azucar Negra" (Black Sugar) (Cruz), 88, 211n95, 212n96

Bakhtin, Mikhail, 103

"becoming-other," 163

Benítez-Rojo, Antonio, 39, 66, 201n4, 202n22

Benjamin, Walter, 9, 120

Berger, James, 20

Berlant, Lauren, 8, 13, 171, 188

Bersani, Leo, 164, 190

"birth-through-conquest" rhetoric, 39

Black literary traditions, 7, 65, 76. *See also* oceanic rhetorics; *Zone One* (Whitehead)

Blackness, 46–47, 66, 75, 204n58; Black memory and mourning, 95, 110, 113; on the border, 109–15; international, 113–14; Latinx disassociation from, 81; repeated depiction of Black suffering, 48–49. *See also* race

Blanco, María del Pilar, 10, 75

body: affected by history, 154–55; haunting of by history, 40; individual, 6, 29, 31, 151; landscape associated with women's, 98, 104–5; Mexican-Californio, decay of, 115–16; monstrous, 37, 44, 62, 65, 67, 89, 92, 116; as part of relational network, 103; perception as experience of, 12; "pre-me," 164; racialized, 46, 62, 110; "rhetoric of birth-through-conquest" analogized, 39; splitting (*rajando*) of by violence, 98–99; and sugar, 88; writing the curse onto, 44–50. *See also* corpse, figure of; embodiment; fatness; self-abnegation

Bolaño, Roberto, 5, 7, 21, 28, 30; on distinction between fantastic and realist fiction, 90–91; literary eminence of, 93, 119; translatability of Latin America for US readers, 93, 119–20; "world literature" paradigm, 30, 93, 119, 141; *Writings: Amuleto,* 106; *Los detectives salvaje,* 93, 106; *Los sinsabores del verdadero policía,* 93. *See also 2666* (Bolaño)

Boom generation, Latin American, 93, 119

border: Blackness on, 109–15; discourses of, 7, 17–18, 119; horror of, 91, 106–8; move away from US-centric model, 64–65; as open wound, 17, 119; personification of, 98–99, 116, 119–20; as psychic space of death, 94; "realidad desaforada" of, 92–93; violence of incarnated in women's bodies, 92, 98. *See also* US-Mexico border

Borderlands/La Frontera (Anzaldúa), 17, 18, 25, 98–99, 102–3, 119, 151

Boullosa, Carmen, 90

Brady, Mary Pat, 98, 200n103

futurity, 22–25, 150–51; "Chicanafuturism," 24; *latinidad* as speculative endeavor for, 26–27, 182; "Latinofuturism," 24

Galchen, Rivka, 12
García, Cristina, 5, 21, 28, 62. See also *Dreaming in Cuban* (García)
García Márquez, Gabriel, 92–93, 199n92, 212n3
Gaspar de Alba, Alicia, 119
"Generic Protocols" (Delany), 8
genocide: cultural appropriation of swastika, 139; expanded history of, 147; of Indigenous peoples, 39, 66, 134–36, 147–48
genre fiction, 5–6, 23–25, 79, 208n14; detective novel, 92, 107; "fukú americanus" stitched to, 41–42; low academic regard for, 68; otherworldly in, 30; tropes of, 5, 64, 149, 152, 171–72, 187, 192–93. *See also* horror
genre flailing, 13, 157, 171
Ghostly Matters (Gordon), 9–10
Gilroy, Paul, 76
Ginsberg, Allen, 125
Glissant, Édouard, 76
Gonzales, Rodolfo "Corky," 147
Goodwin, Matthew David, 23
Gordon, Avery, 9–10, 197n53
Goyal, Yogita, 14
"Great American Doom," 45
"Greater Mexico," 30–31, 126
Grimes, Leslie "Les" Allen, 122
Griswold del Castillo, Richard, 147
grotesque, the, 47, 97–98, 120; aesthetic pleasure in, 17, 30, 92, 95, 105; and corpse figure, 101–5; and sugar, 63, 66–67, 89. *See also* fatness; monstrosity; zombie, figure of
Gruesz, Kirsten Silva, 127, 144, 200n102
Guattari, Félix, 163
Guidotti-Hernandez, Nicole, 18, 19, 94, 105–6, 196n23, 196n26
Guzmán, Joshua Javier, 146

Halberstam, Jack, 159–60
Hall, Stuart, 34, 204n58
Harney, Stefano, 210n52

Hartman, Saidiya, 48–49, 77, 105, 210n52; critical fabulation, 9, 27, 52
Hassig, Ross, 137
haunting, 6–10, 24, 114, 196n23; cyclical, 18, 20, 179; by fat-ghost, 161–62, 164–65, 167; by historical violence, 2, 6, 8, 37, 141, 207n5; in present, 76, 127; and temporality, 45, 75; of women by specter of death, 104, 119, 167. *See also* corpse, figure of; monstrosity; zombie, figure of
Heart of Darkness (Conrad), 51
Heise, Ursula, 125
Her Body and Other Parties (Machado), 5, 28, 31, 75, 152–77; doom patterns in, 152, 155, 170, 175–76; *fugazivity in*, 176; fugitivity, quiet, opacity, and withholding in, 170–77; horror tropes in, 152, 155, 173, 175; *latinidad* in, 155, 170–77; post-/supra-/ab-human forms in, 152–53; resistance in, 152, 153, 155, 160, 162–66, 168–71, 175–76; silences in, 151–52; spectrum of existence in, 169–70; *Stories*: "Eight Bites," 161–66; "Especially Heinous," 173, 176; "The Husband Stitch," 156–61, 164, 176; "Mothers," 174; opening statement, 156–57, 158–59; "Real Women Have Bodies," 166–70, 176
Hey-Colón, Rebeca, 64
historiographic metafiction, 12, 128–29
Hogan, Ernest, 24, 25
hole, concept of, 185, 188, 190–92, 223n33; "birthplace of our nation," 33, 181; Cave of Jagua experience, 33–34, 47, 59, 181–82; and corpse, 103
Holocaust, 115, 120, 133, 202n13
Horkheimer, Max, 10
horror, 24, 68, 179; aestheticization of, 21, 92, 95, 100–102, 108; apocalyptic, 93, 97, 104, 106–7; of border, 91, 119–20; displaced onto approximate dates, 106–7; embodiment of, 110, 152, 155, 173, 175; psychosexual, affective, and physical, 107–8
Huang, Michelle, 174
Hudson, Renee, 26–27, 176, 196n14
Hulstyn, Michaela, 133
Hundreds (streetwear label), 122–23
"The Husband Stitch" (Machado), 156–61, 164, 176
Hutcheon, Linda, 12, 128–29

monstrosity, 30; attributed to Afro-Dominican people, 181; Black people, 70; body as monstrous, 37, 44, 62, 65, 67, 89, 92, 116; of border, 116; of corpse, 94, 103–5; fatness represented as, 45–46; of "female victim-hero," 175; of New York City, 71–72; of sugar, 23, 63, 67, 89. *See also* fatness; grotesque, the; haunting; zombie, figure of

Moore, Alan, 51

Moten, Fred, 49, 78, 210n52

mourning, Black, 95, 110, 113

mouth: broken, symbolism of, 54–55; of ouroboros, 56–57; of zombie, 68, 71–72

Muñoz, José Esteban, 9, 19, 146, 174, 176

Musser, Amber Jamilla, 12, 88, 89, 163–64, 220n34

national identity, 26, 46, 68, 86, 147; zombie as threat to, 71, 75

nation-building projects, 74, 77, 81–84, 122

nation-state, 16, 54, 74, 92, 104, 114, 188

Nazism: in *2666*, 115, 120, 122, 133; in *Atomik Aztex*, 137–40

Negrón-Muntaner, Frances, 143

neoliberalism, 139–40, 167

"New World": "discovery" of, 29, 35, 36–37; Hispaniola as birthplace of, 36. *See also* Caribbean; "fukú americanus"; plantation; United States

New York City, 114–15; gentrification, 87–88; historical violence of, 70–72; as island, 64; Manhattan as symbol of, 72–73; as New Amsterdam, 70; plantation economies tied to, 65, 67, 70, 72, 87

Ngai, Sianne, 100, 164, 220n39

Nixon, Rob, 16

North American Free Trade Agreement (NAFTA), 28, 94, 104

nostalgia, 63–64, 74, 85, 147

"no standpoint," 77–78

Obama, Barack, 28, 75

obfuscation: of Blackness, 68, 76, 174; of ethno-racial categories, 75–76, 170–77, 181; of *latinidad*, 170–77, 181; opacity, right to, 76

Object Lessons (Wiegman), 180, 198n63

oceanic rhetorics, 122, 162, 188, 207n5, 209n45, 210n52; in *2666*, 109, 111; in *Dreaming in Cuban*, 64, 86; in "The Silence," 57; in *Zone One*, 76

Okihiro, Gary, 186

Olguín, B. V., 18, 24–25

On Latinidad (Caminero-Santangelo), 26

Orchard, William, 190

Ortiz, Ricardo, 83, 143, 187, 192

otherworldly, 17, 19, 63, 85; Afro-Caribbean people as, 40, 181; American landscape as, 185, 191; Caribbean as, 29; excess as, 5–6, 30, 35–37; in formation of Latinx subjectivity, 24, 181; in genre fiction, 30; juxtaposed with real, 5–6; *latinidad* as, 26–28, 171, 181; post-/supra-/ab-human forms, 152–53; as unutterable, 80; use of *x* as, 148; violence as, 4–5

ouroboros, 56–57, 59

oyster, figure of, 162, 164, 165

"páginas en blanco" (blank pages). *See also* white pages

paratextuality, 20–21, 36, 42, 127, 155

Paredes, Américo, 126

Paz, Octavio, 135–36, 217n50

Pérez-Torres, Rafael, 147, 180, 198n63

plantation, 39, 82; economies tied to New York, 65, 67, 70, 72, 87; racial slavery established on, 69–70; vestiges of, 60–61. *See also* "New World"; sugar

pleasure: *jouissance*, 164, 190; in sugar consumption, 62, 65, 89

pleasure, aesthetic, 10; in gendered and sexual violence, 21, 30, 102, 155, 173, 175; in grotesque, 29, 30, 95, 105; in horror, 95, 100–102; metatextual, 20–21, 155, 176; within narrative "failures," 35–36; in Nazi practices, 137–39; in onomatopoeia, 43; in *Oscar Wao*, 37; paratextual, 20–21, 155; in reimagination of historical trauma, 4, 92; and relation of production and consumption, 21; in self-abnegation, 162, 176–77; in sexual violence, 21, 30, 155, 173; textual, 20–21, 37, 155; in violence, 3–4, 17, 19–21, 46, 48–50, 74, 107–8, 113, 123–24, 128, 138, 140, 169, 179. *See also* pleasure

"The Sun, the Moon, the Stars" (Díaz), 33–34; Cave of Jagua episode, 33–34, 47, 59, 181–82
Sweetness and Power (Mintz), 66

"terror of the mundane," 49, 202n13
Testamento geométrico (Dieste), 108–9
Thomas, Hugh, 113
A Thousand Plateaus (Deleuze and Guattari), 163
Tompkins, Kyla Wazana, 71
Torres, Justin, 17–18
Torres-Saillant, Silvio, 55
translation, 93, 119–20
"transparency signifiers," 165
Treaty of Guadalupe Hidalgo (1848), 115–16, 126
Trouillot, Michel-Rolph, 14, 52
Trujillo, Rafael, 38, 43, 47, 59, 201n8
Trump, Donald, 28
Tuana, Nancy, 161
Turner, Frederick Jackson, 186, 222n17
Twain, Mark, 131, 132, 133

ugly feelings, 164
Ugly Feelings (Ngai), 164
Ulibarri, Kristy, 139–40, 142, 147–48
United States: as capitalist empire, 72; Chicanx identity formation in, 147; as "civilizing" force, 41; Cuba linked to through sugar, 84; "decontinentalizion" of, 64; foreign policy, 42–43; Greater Mexico within, 30–31, 126; historical periods of Black struggle in, 111–12; Manifest Destiny/"frontier thesis," 185–86, 222n17; race-making linked to Barbados, 77; translatability of Latin America for readers in, 93, 119–20. *See also* immigration; US-Mexico border
unspeakable, the, 49, 89, 106, 196n26. *See also* silences/silencing
US-Mexico border, 25, 91–99; as byproduct of violence, 98–99; export processing system, 94–95, 104–9, 112; gendered violence of, 100; as postapocalyptic space, 94–95; as space of horror, 91, 106–8, 119–20. *See also* border; United States
utterance, 106, 111, 196n26

Vargas, Jennifer Harford, 14, 223n33
Viego, Antonio, 27, 131, 165
violence: aesthetic pleasure in, 3–4, 17, 19–21, 46, 48–50, 74, 107–8, 113, 123–24, 128, 138, 140, 169, 179; aesthetics of, 15, 21–22, 25; apocalyptic, 94, 99, 182; and approximation, 97–98; atomic, 47, 53, 85, 97, 108, 115, 148–49, 213n18; of borderlands, 98–99; as both quotidian and spectacular, 18–19, 173; form of, 14, 111, 157; gendered forms of, 157; heteropatriarchal, 16, 153, 155; impossibility of containing, 72; inadequacy of term, 13; internalized by women, 152; intersecting histories of, 16; as intrinsic to *latinidad*, 10–11, 17, 25, 49–50; mundane as otherworldly, 5, 36; naturalization of, 40–41; otherworldly, 4–6; refusal to reproduce, 49; repetition of as both mundane and spectacular, 18–19, 49, 178–79; repetition of as mundane, 5, 18–19, 36, 49, 95, 202n13; reproduced by literature, 20–21, 37–38, 52, 54–55, 56–57, 175; slow, 16; as spectacular, 48–49; as unspeakable, 49, 89, 106, 196n26; *x* tied to, 27
violence, historical: afterlives of, 11, 14; of American frontier, 182; apocalyptic, 29, 34–35, 37, 44, 53–54, 57, 67–69, 72, 81–82, 89; burning as manifestation of systemic project of, 47; as cyclical, 4–5, 35, 50–53, 56, 59, 79, 119, 135–37; haunting by, 2, 6, 8, 37, 141, 207n5; impossibility of representing, 5, 9, 12–13, 48–49, 97, 105–6, 109–10; limitations of language in representation of, 3–4, 9, 13, 20, 35, 51, 58, 80, 109–10, 175; networks of, 2, 4–6, 10, 41, 42, 92, 112, 132, 181; of New York City, 70–72; nonnormative bodies created by, 63, 75; reimagination of, 4, 92, 133–34. *See also* apocalyptic violence
Violentologies (Olguín), 18
viscosity, hermeneutic of, 161–66

Walker, Kara, 60–63, *61, 62,* 87–89, 211n94
war, 84–85, 96, 120, 133, 138
Watchmen (Moore), 51
We the Animals (Torres), 17–18
Whitehead, Colson, 5, 23, 28, 30, 62–63, 174. See also *Zone One* (Whitehead)
white pages in text, *183, 189,* 190
white space, 77–78, 116

white supremacy, 15, 111, 137, 142–43, 177

Wiegman, Robyn, 180, 198n63

Williams, Eric, 69

women: aesthetic pleasure in violence against, 21, 30, 102–3, 155, 173, 175; as always already dead, 103, 105, 109, 119; bodies of used for male self-exploration, 47–50, 56–59; in constant state of repair and improvement, 162–63; excessive violence inflicted on, 37–38; female body as speculative arena, 31, 48; "female victim-hero," 175; haunted by specter of death and violence, 104, 119, 167; landscape associated with bodies of, 17, 98, 104–5; objectification of, 156–61; policing of bodies, 150–51; subjectivity of, 156–61. *See also* export processing system; femicides

world-building, 13–14, 69, 96, 134, 136, 138

"world literature" paradigm, 30, 93, 119, 141

World War II, 115, 120, 122, 133

Wright, Melissa, 104

x: as deferral and grave, 192; instability of, 174; as otherworldly, 148; tied to violence and trauma, 27. See also *Latinx*, as term

Zapata, Michael, 2–3, 195n4

Zavala, Oswaldo, 93

Žižek, Slavoj, 20

zombie, figure of, 70–72, 208–9n24; cannibal, association with, 70, 75, 208n19, 208n22, 209n27; national identity threatened by, 71, 75; "stragglers," 68, 75; sugar linked with, 30, 62–63, 65, 67–78, 79, 86. *See also* monstrosity

Zone One (Whitehead), 5, 23, 28, 62–63; as Afro-Caribbean, 30, 65; American Phoenix government in, 68, 71, 73, 75; birthday cake episode, 68, 69, 74; as Black American text, 65; Blackness as world-destroying element in, 68, 174–75; Blackness obfuscated in, 68, 76, 174; *Dreaming in Cuban* read alongside, 30, 63–67, 79, 87; Mark Spitz and racial markers, 68–69, 72–78, 109, 174, 209n40; past superimposed onto present, 72–74; plot summary, 67–68; remedy foreclosed in, 71, 77–78; revival and continuation of racism in, 68, 78; sugar and zombie figure linked in, 65, 67–78